*The Diary of*
*BISHOP FREDERIC BARAGA*

# GREAT LAKES BOOKS

PHILIP P. MASON, EDITOR
*Department of History, Wayne State University*

DR. CHARLES K. HYDE, ASSOCIATE EDITOR
*Department of History, Wayne State University*

*A complete listing of the books in this series
can be found at wsupress.wayne.edu*

*Bishop Frederic Baraga at the time of his Episcopal consecration, 1854.*

# The Diary of
# BISHOP FREDERIC BARAGA

## First Bishop of Marquette, Michigan

*Edited and Annotated by*
## Regis M. Walling and Rev. N. Daniel Rupp

*Translated by Joseph Gregorich and Rev. Paul Prud'homme, S.J.*

WAYNE STATE UNIVERSITY PRESS     DETROIT

**Library of Congress Cataloging-in-Publication Data**

Baraga, Frederic, 1797–1868.
  The diary of Bishop Frederic Baraga : first bishop of Marquette,
Michigan / translated by Joseph Gregorich and Paul Prud'homme;
edited and annotated by Regis M. Walling and N. Daniel Rupp.
    p.   cm. — (Great Lakes books)
  Translated from the original diary which was chiefly in German,
with passages in English, French, Slovene, Chippewa, Latin, and
Italian.
  Includes bibliographical references.
  ISBN 0–8143–2295–6
  1. Baraga, Frederic, 1797–1868—Diaries. 2. Catholic Church—
Michigan—Marquette Region—Bishops—Diaries. 3. Marquette Region
(Mich.)—Biography. I. Gregorič, Jože. II. Prud'homme, Paul,
1895–1975. III. Walling, Regis. IV. Rupp, N. Daniel, 1940–
V. Title. VI. Series.
BX4705.B18A3   1990
282'.092—dc20
[B]                                                    89–39805

ISBN-13: 978-0-8143-2999-3 (pbk.)    ISBN-10: 0-8143-2999-3 (pbk.)

# CONTENTS

# FOREWORD

As the tenth successor to Bishop Frederic Baraga in the diocese of Marquette, Michigan, I am pleased that the Diary he kept is now available to the public.

Bishop Frederic Baraga was first and foremost a priest. His entire life, writings, and work are inseparable from his priesthood and his intimate, personal relationship with God. However, the life of Baraga also has much in common with the Christian missionaries of all denominations of his time, with persons who value and work for the human and civil rights of others, and, indeed, for each person who goes about his or her daily work with dedication and compassion.

When Charles Lindbergh died, his wife, Anne, commented that his life could be compared to a mighty tree. Looked at daily it seemed ordinary, comprehensible. However, when it had fallen its gigantic mass and enormous length awed the viewer. This comparison is valid for the life of Bishop Baraga. Whether he was writing a book, compiling his Grammar or Dictionary, or writing one of his many letters, Baraga had to put down one word at a time, one word after another. It is when all of his works are collected and seen in their entirety that we realize how well he used his "in-between" moments for these tasks.

We might look at Baraga's many snowshoe treks through the wilderness, one tired and heavy step after another. To consider the total miles so traveled leaves a modern traveler in awe. So, too, do the miles of canoe and steamship travel, the many sessions of instruction of his beloved Indians, the sermons prepared and given, the hours of sacramental confession and personal counsel. The Diary reveals this non-stop activity. Grace Lee Nute, in *Lake Superior* (p. 95), wrote so well that it is Bishop Baraga's Diary

> which give[s] us in detail the comings and goings of this extraordinarily active man. It makes one breathless to follow him—from the Sault by boat to Mackinac to establish a church, to Point St. Ignace with a new priest to see him settled, from writing the *Kagige Debwewinan* (Eternal Truths) at the Sault to translating the Catechism into English for the use of schools, by sleigh to Isle de Bois Blanc, to Detroit by steamboat, back to Mackinac, thence to Little Traverse, to L'Arbre Croche, to the Sault by propeller, on the steamer *Illinois* to Marquette, to L'Anse, Eagle Harbor and La Pointe by steamer *North Star*, by dog sled to Bellanger, by small boat to Traverse City, to the mines, on the *Manhattan* to Eagle Harbor, and on and on, year after year.

Since most people live their lives in daily repetition there is much to learn from this Diary and much inspiration that the reader can derive. For however holy Bishop Baraga was, his life, like ours, was lived in the valley of every day. He knew the closeness of God in prayer and the dryness of discouragement and loneliness. He experienced joy from faithful co-workers and sadness because of those who were disloyal and/or immoral. Baraga could see the intensity of Christian living in many of his converts and the day-to-day failings of others. He shares our humanity and weaknesses, our great desires and our efforts. In this his life illustrates his motto, "One Thing Only is Necessary," that is, the love of God, and speaks to people of all faiths and even of no faith.

It is my prayer and wish for you that you will find inspiration and encouragement as you read this Diary of Bishop Frederic Baraga.

Most Rev. Mark F. Schmitt
Bishop of Marquette

# HISTORICAL INTRODUCTION

Few readers of this diary will remain unmoved by the simple, direct account of Frederic Baraga's almost heroic responses to the severe physical and pastoral challenges of mission life. At the outset I must admit my sense of awe for his practical zeal in a life that was manifested in building churches, ministering to the faithful, preaching in four languages, and sharing with his people the impoverished conditions of village life. Because the diary includes an abundance of rich annotation derived from research in over fifty archives by the editors, Regis M. Walling and Father N. Daniel Rupp, the threads of Baraga's notation are woven into meaningful patterns to form a fascinating tapestry.

Although he was not a first generation missionary, Baraga's task of planting the church was still in the formative stages among the Ottawa and Chippewa people of Michigan and Wisconsin. The diary begins just before he receives word that he may become the first bishop of Marquette. It had been twenty years since he had departed from his Slovene village to embark on a new life in the United States. His appointment as bishop represented a new phase for the church in the Upper Peninsula of Michigan.

*Frontier* does not adequately convey mission existence in his diocese. Within the context of Catholic life in the United States, Baraga's missions were on the rough edges, in contrast to the core dioceses of Baltimore, Boston, New York, Louisville, Cincinnati, New Orleans,

11

and St. Louis. In 1853, the year Baraga was made Bishop of the Apostolic Vicariate of Upper Michigan (which spanned more than 300 miles by ship from Mackinac Island to Ontonagon), there were six churches, five priests, and five schools in the vicariate. In that same year most of the core dioceses mentioned above had Catholic populations of between 40,000 and 120,000, with a proportionate number of parishes, priests, and religious women and men within rapidly developing institutional infrastructures of parish societies, schools, hospitals, and orphanages.

Baraga imported confraternities and parish organizations from Europe. For example, he introduced societies dedicated to the scapular and to the Holy Heart of Mary for the Conversion of Sinners. These devotions were in the native language of the people, as Baraga had received special permission to have hymns sung in the vernacular. As the core of Catholicity in the United States was becoming identified as "the immigrant church," this Slovene bishop was presiding over "a native American church," one which reflected only a faint glimmer of Europe manifested in the Latin liturgy and in the occasional parish devotion. Baraga was "Chippewaized" rather than the people Europeanized or Americanized.

Educated in Vienna, Baraga absorbed the romantic ethos of the post-Napoleonic period with its focus on the reintegration of religion and culture. Although he was no philosopher or theologian, his religious worldview highlighted the divine presence in the simplicity of nature. The light of faith and natural intuition, rather than enlightened reason, guided him from Slovenia to the Upper Peninsula of Michigan. On his first episcopal visitation to Beaver Island (1855) in the middle of Lake Michigan, he recalled that he had been the first priest to step foot on the island years before in 1831. "All inhabitants of our island, who live very simple and peacefully, are now converted to the Catholic religion," because Baraga's successors visited them frequently. "My visit to the romantic island was joyful and stirring for me and these simple children of nature. . . . They now were pleased to receive the bishop's blessing from their old missioner, from whom they and their parents first learned to pronounce the holy names of Jesus and Mary." He considered his people to be so close to nature that their lives clearly reflected the hand of Providence. He was drawn to "the Indian missions [because they] are truly my element."

As a seminarian and as a young priest, Baraga was influenced by the moral theology of Alphonse Liguori, which represented a positive step away from Augustinian rigorism and toward a sense of compassion for the sinner, with a stress on the accessibility of grace in the sacrament of penance. Referred to as "a man of iron," Baraga was certainly a priest of strong conviction; his sense of compassion was evidenced in the long lines at his confessional in Europe and earned him deep respect among villagers he served.

A romantic tone was infused into his traditional spirituality and devotionalism. He wrote about a Marian sermon that he delivered in German, one "that pierced deep into the hearts of the venerators of the dear Mother of God, and which also came from the innermost part of my heart." Characteristic of all missionaries, Baraga's faith in a sense depended on the manifestation of faith among the people. Hence, there were periods of despondency when physical, emotional, and spiritual challenges temporarily affected his spirit. Not a contemplative, he continued his mission activities to the end. In his early sixties, he trekked forty miles through severe weather to minister to a village community long in need of pastoral care. Considering the severity of these rough climatic conditions, Baraga was rather hard on himself; his eating habits were quite ascetical, and on one occasion he noted that he experienced a "great spiritual misfortune" because he arose at 5 A.M. instead of his normal hour of 3 A.M.: "two hours absolutely lost," lamented Baraga. The challenges of mission life were never more evident than in Baraga's journey to Cincinnati for a seven-day meeting of the Third Provincial Council; it took nearly thirty days to travel by snowshoes, sled, and ship.

Between the time of Baraga's appointment as bishop in 1853 and his death in 1868, the church in the Upper Peninsula had experienced significant development: the number of churches grew from six to thirty-two, and the number of priests increased from five to eighteen. No census was taken in 1853, but in 1868 the Catholic population was nearly 20,000, the size of several ethnic parishes in the urban core.

The missions to the Native Americans are relegated to the periphery of historical consciousness among Catholic historians. With the focus on the urban centers of the church, these tiny mission enclaves receive only a line or two in the standard histories. The significance of this diary in Catholic historiography lies in its solid contribution to the rapidly expanding area of local history. One excellent example in the expansion of research into mission history was published in 1984 by the archives of Marquette University. The 450-page *Guide to Catholic Indian Mission and School Records in Midwest Repositories*, edited by Philip Bantin (with assistance by Mark G. Thiel), lists seventeen pages of archival material on Frederic Baraga.

The diocese of Marquette continued to attract missionaries from both Western and Eastern Europe, particularly several Slovene priests who followed the path cleared by their heroic countryman. Hence, Baraga's legacy remained vital in the continuous interaction of faith and culture on a unique rim of Catholicity in America.

Christopher J. Kauffman
Editor, *U.S. Catholic Historian*

# HISTORY OF THE DIARY

On June 27, 1852, when Father Frederic Baraga heard the first indication of his nomination to be Bishop of Upper Michigan, he began to keep a "journal" or diary.

Baraga intended the Diary exclusively as a private document for his own use and reference. In it Baraga logged his travels, observations about weather, ship movement on the lakes, and various tasks that he accomplished. The Diary is not a journal as we understand *journal* in today's spiritual or psychological usage. Between the lines, however, the reader will find hints of Baraga's zeal, desires and hopes, dedication, sacrifices, and the inner spirituality that motivated him in spite of the distances he traveled and the hardships his times imposed.

By the time Baraga began his Diary, the situation and status of the Ottawa and Chippewa were vastly different than when he began his missionary work in Upper Michigan in May 1831. By 1852 the Indian missionary was primarily concerned with ongoing spiritual formation rather than with conversion to Catholicism. The Upper Peninsula contained new and rapidly developing mining communities with a predominantly Irish, German, Finnish, and French population. The work of the priest was more similar to that of a parish priest than that of a missionary. The one element of continuity between the Indian missions and the new ethnic communities was the need for schools. The Diary clearly shows the changes in both the church and in Baraga's work.

## The Diary

The first three of the original volumes remain. They are small books. Volume I is only ¼ inch thick and measures 5½ by 4 inches; Volumes II and III are approximately 7½ by 6 inches. With pencil Baraga drew the vertical line on the left side of each page to form the date column. Volume I has horizontal lines but the other two volumes do not. However, the writing is perfectly even and the lines consistently spaced, suggesting that he may have used a lined paper behind the page on which he was writing. The writing is extremely fine and in small old-style German script. Very rarely is a word difficult to read and only two or three words are illegible. Occasionally an abbreviation is obscure.

The three volumes cover the time between June 27, 1852, and July 16, 1863. At some time he acquired another notebook and continued to record his activities. In his "Eulogy" at the time of Baraga's death, his friend and administrator, Rev. Edward Jacker, remarked that Baraga wrote "in the journal which he had kept for many years" just before he left for the Second Plenary Council in Baltimore in October 1866. This volume is lost as are any additional volumes.

## Translation of the Diary

The primary language of the Diary is German, although Baraga freely interspersed six other languages (English, French, Slovene, Chippewa, Latin, and Italian). A single entry often included several languages, as the reader will note.

The first translation of parts of the Diary is found in *The Life and Labors of Rt. Rev. Frederic Baraga* by Rev. Chrysostom Verwyst, O.F.M., published in 1900. Fr. Verwyst was born in Uden, Holland, on November 23, 1841. With his family he came to the United States in 1848. He was ordained in Milwaukee on November 5, 1865. In addition to the classical languages, he was conversant in Dutch, German, French, English, and Chippewa, which he began to learn in 1878 in preparation for going to Bayfield. For all but a few years of his career, he worked in the Indian missions of Wisconsin. Fr. Verwyst died on June 23, 1925.

When he wrote his life of Bishop Baraga, Fr. Verwyst had access to Volumes II and III of the Diary. He quoted the Diary directly and used much information from it without providing direct citations. He translated all the languages, except Latin.

The next use of the Diary was by Msgr. Antoine Ivan Rezek, who cited many passages in his two-volume work, *History of the Diocese of*

*Sault Ste. Marie and Marquette* (1906, 1907). Antoine Rezek was born in Krasne, Austria, on February 9, 1867. He was educated in Austria and at St. Jerome's College in Ontario. On July 12, 1890, he was ordained a priest. After serving in several parishes he was appointed pastor at St. Ignatius Parish in Houghton, Michigan, on November 8, 1895, where he served until his death on November 20, 1946, at the age of seventy-nine.

Msgr. Rezek had a great interest in the history of the Catholic Church in the Upper Peninsula. Volume I of his work is a biographical study of the first three bishops of the diocese, Baraga, Mrak, and Vertin, and of the early priests of the diocese. Volume II is a history of the parishes, arranged geographically. In recognition of his scholarship, Marquette University in Milwaukee conferred on him an honorary Doctor of Law degree.

Msgr. Rezek had access to all three volumes of Bishop Baraga's Diary. He quoted entries selectively, maintaining Latin where it occurred but omitting completely the Chippewa notations. Msgr. Rezek's version often differs in style and vocabulary from that of Verwyst, although Rezek does cite Verwyst for some information, indicating that he used Verwyst as a source.

The translation used for this edition of the Diary is primarily the work of Joseph Gregorich. He was born in Chicago, Illinois, on September 12, 1889. He was a mechanical engineer by profession and a historian by avocation. His mother was born in one of the parishes in which Baraga had been a parish priest in Slovenia, and she inspired her son with a love of Baraga. Gregorich was one of the founders of the Bishop Baraga Association in 1930 and gave many full-time years after his retirement to work on the cause of Bishop Baraga's canonization. Gregorich was conversant in all the languages Baraga spoke except Chippewa. He relied on Rev. Paul Prud'homme, S.J., for the Chippewa translations. Gregorich died on February 29, 1984.

Gregorich's translation of the Diary differs from both of the previous works. He prepared a typescript of the original text and translated from that source. It does not appear that he referred to either Verwyst or Rezek for his translation.

Rev. Paul Prud'homme, S.J., was born in France on September 8, 1895, and was ordained there on August 14, 1927. In September 1930 he was assigned to his first Indian mission at Spragge, Ontario. In August 1931 he came to Sault Ste. Marie, Ontario, and in 1937 began to include the Indian missions of Sault Ste. Marie, Michigan, in his work. From August 1939 until his retirement in September 1968, he worked among the Chippewa of Michigan. During his retirement he translated three of Bishop Baraga's Indian books from Chippewa into English and assisted with the Chippewa translation of the Diary. Fr. Prud'homme died in Detroit, Michigan, on May 13, 1975.

## Editorship

Rev. N. Daniel Rupp and Regis M. Walling edited the Diary for publication. Fr. Rupp was born in Detroit on October 26, 1940. While he was very young his family moved to Marquette, where he developed an interest in the life of Bishop Baraga. After his ordination in 1966 Fr. Rupp studied in Rome and began to edit the Diary as his master's thesis. Fr. Rupp prepared the notes that comment on the structure of the Diary, such as notations added at a later date, marginal comments, and language changes. He also correlated the letters of Bishop Baraga with the entries in the Diary.

Fr. Rupp is a priest of the Diocese of Marquette and is pastor of St. Joseph Parish in Rudyard.

Regis Walling completed the annotations, biographical footnotes, and indices, and prepared the Diary for publication. Walling was born in Detroit on May 24, 1933. She is a graduate of Marygrove College, Detroit, and holds Master of Arts degrees in history from Loyola University in Chicago and in theology from St. John's Provincial Seminary in Plymouth, Michigan. After teaching for nineteen years, she worked in several social services programs. She has worked for the Bishop Baraga Association for six years.

## Acknowledgments

The publication of Bishop Baraga's Diary owes much to the encouragement of Marquette Bishops Thomas Noa, Charles Salatka (now Archbishop of Oklahoma City), and Mark Schmitt. Rev. Charles Strelick, president of the Bishop Baraga Association, and the financial support of the many dedicated members of the association have been indispensible. Rudi Prusok, Ph.D. of Northern Michigan University, translated the end-page (the page that Baraga pasted inside the back cover) of Volume I from the original German. The Burton Historical Collection of the Detroit Public Library graciously permitted the use of the notes of Fr. Edward Jacker. Jan Foster of Ishpeming provided the map of Baraga's missionary locations, and Robert Bochy of Newberry allowed the use of an oil painting of Baraga at prayer. Numerous archivists throughout the United States and, indeed, the world have cooperated in providing information and material. Finally, without the assistance of Alice Nigoghosian of Wayne State University Press this volume would still be but a dream.

The editors hope that Bishop Baraga's Diary will prove to be a source of generous service to the poor among us. Baraga's motto, "One Thing Only is Necessary," is a reminder that the love of God and neighbor is a practical priority. We hope that the reader will see in Baraga and the missionaries of the nineteenth century, both Catholic and of other Christian denominations, the sincerity with which they endeavored to serve the Native American population.

Regis M. Walling
Rev. N. Daniel Rupp

Marquette, Michigan
Nov. 1, 1989

# BIOGRAPHICAL INTRODUCTION

Bishop Frederic Baraga was born and baptized on June 29, 1797, at the estate of Kleindorf in house number 16, known as Malavas, in Slovenia, the northwestern part of present-day Yugoslavia. His parents were John Nepomucene Baraga, a minor civil servant and proprietor of the family farmland, and Catherine Jencic Baraga. Their first two children, Maria and Vincent, died in early infancy. Three children survived: Amalia, born in 1795, Frederic, and Antonia, born in 1803. They were still young when their parents died, Catherine in 1808 and John in 1812. The earliest records indicate that, with his sisters and their cousins, Frederic enjoyed games, running and jumping activities, and pranks that marked a very normal boyhood. In a letter from his early days in America, he also wrote about having spent many hours walking a tightrope, an adeptness that enabled him to cross many a log over rushing brooks and streams. His youth also had a serious dimension with sincere prayer and youthful penances. Throughout his school years he often took long hikes during his holidays, again developing another skill that aided him in the American wilderness. He also became an accomplished artist. His miniature paintings reveal great perceptiveness as well as skill and delicacy in execution, traits reflected in his handwriting. When he entered the seminary he discontinued painting.

In 1819 Amalia Baraga married Joseph Gressel; their children were Anna Josepha and Karl, the father of Joseph Frederic Gressel whom

Baraga confirmed in 1854. Frederic and Amalia were very close until her death in 1862. Most of the letters Baraga sent to Europe were addressed to Amalia; in turn she sent them to the mission associations, especially the Leopoldine Society, which published them for the edification of the financial supporters of the missions. Through these letters the activities of Baraga and other missionaries have been preserved and provide much of the currently available information about the religious, political, economic, and social history of the midwestern Indian missions.

Antonia Baraga married Felix von Hoeffern in 1824. The von Hoefferns were childless. After Felix died in 1830 Antonia was restless and somewhat improvident. As early as 1833 she expressed a desire to join her brother, then at Arbre Croche, and to assist him by teaching. In 1837 she accompanied him from Europe and spent some time at La Pointe. However, she could not endure the harsh conditions. From La Pointe Antonia wandered, both physically and spiritually, to Philadelphia and later to Rome where Frederic and Amalia visited her in the spring of 1854. Eventually she returned to Ljubljana where she died in 1871.

The formative period of Frederic's life, 1797–1821, saw great upheavals in Europe such as the French Revolution, the Napoleonic occupation, and the subsequent Congress of Vienna in 1815, which redrew the lines on the map around Slovenia. In the educational world the study of languages was most affected. By the time a youth of Baraga's age left school, he was fluent not only in spoken Slovene but also in German, French, Latin, and Greek. This linguistic background facilitated the remarkable skill with which Baraga and the other Slovene missionaries who followed him, such as Fathers Pierz, Mrak, Lautishar, and Chebul, learned multiple Indian tongues.

Frederic's education had begun at home, but in 1806 he was sent to the home of his uncle, Ignatius Baraga, at Belnek where he studied also with private tutors until 1809. He then moved in with his mother's brother, Bernard Jencic, in Ljubljana where he attended regular classes for seven years. When his uncle had to leave the country after a conflict with the French authorities, young Frederic had to find his own accommodations and support. He endured two years of abject poverty. His circumstances improved when he was able to reside at the home of George Dolinar, a professor of church history and canon law. During his university years Frederic became engaged to the professor's daughter, Anna. After a year of "pre-law" at the University of Vienna, he received his Bachelor of Arts degree and entered law school at that same university. He studied both civil and canon law.

At the time Frederic was in law school in Vienna, he became part of a student group that regularly met with Father Clement Hofbauer of the Congregation of the Most Holy Redeemer. The objective of the congregation is personal sanctification by imitating the life of Jesus, by prayer, and by spreading the Gospel to the poorest and most abandoned souls. Frederic's life as a priest, missionary, and bishop shows that, without a doubt, he made these ideals his own. Unfortunately he left no record of how he decided to become a priest. However, in 1821, he broke his engagement, entered the seminary, and was ordained on September 21, 1823.

Baraga was curate for four years at St. Martin Parish in Smartno and for three years at St. Nicholas Parish in Metlika. During these years he became known as a confessor and for inspiring devotion in the people. In contrast to the harsh rigor of Jansenism, which left people discouraged, Fr. Baraga offered them assurance of their worth before God and of God's love for them. People flocked to his confessional, with the lines forming before dawn, because Fr. Baraga seemed to understand their plight and their desire to live good lives. To assist them he also began to write and edit devotional books for the common person. The most famous of these, *Dushna Pasha* (Pasture for Souls), is still in print. *Dushna Pasha* is primarily an anthology of popular prayers with translations of German prayers and writings. Often criticized for its lack of linguistic sophistication, it nevertheless has touched deeply those who have used it.

About this time, Fr. Frederic Résé, vicar general of the Diocese of Cincinnati, came to Europe to solicit funds and clergy for the impoverished missions of the northern Midwest. During his journey he influenced the founding of two mission societies, the Ludwig Mission Central, located in Bavaria, and the Leopoldine Society in Vienna. This activity and the publicity that it generated came to young Fr. Baraga's attention. Upon receiving permission from his bishop, he applied to Bishop Edward Fenwick of Cincinnati for admission to that diocese with the expressed intention of devoting himself to the Indian missions. When he received the letter of acceptance he gave away most of his meager belongings, and on October 18, 1830, he left Metlika and embarked for the Indian missions in the United States.

Fr. Frederic Baraga arrived in New York on December 31 and on January 18, 1831, reached Cincinnati. At that time Bishop Fenwick was preparing several Indian youths to study for the priesthood. Baraga immediately became a student of the Ottawa language. His teachers were William Makatebinessi and Augustin Hamlin, who, soon afterwards, left for Rome to prepare for ordination. Makatebinessi died in Rome and Hamlin returned to Arbre Croche. He and Baraga often worked together on various ventures.

In May 1831, Bishop Fenwick accompanied Baraga from Cincinnati to Arbre Croche in northern lower Michigan. In Detroit he met Fr. Gabriel Richard for the first time. The two priests became good friends. When Richard died in 1832, one of the two priests in attendance was Baraga. Baraga also delivered a eulogy at Richard's burial. Other missionary giants of the age whom Baraga met as he and Bishop Fenwick journeyed north were Fathers Florimond Bonduel and Samuel Mazzuchelli.

At Arbre Croche Baraga continued his study of the language, writing the first of his many Indian-language books in 1832. That the Ottawa and Chippewa Indians of Michigan have a preserved, written language is the direct result of Baraga's prayerbooks, Grammar, and Dictionary.

The hallmark of Baraga's mission life was his great love for the Indians. Unlike many of the Protestant missionaries, his first goal was to learn the Indians' language and to make teaching and prayer aids available to the Indians. He used the Indian language for every service he could, especially for vespers. Later, as bishop, he insisted that his missionaries do the same. He recognized that Indian education had to begin in the native tongue, and, because of Baraga, many Indians achieved literacy first in Ottawa or Chippewa. The Indians thus taught had a great advantage, then, when it came to learning English, which the government insisted should be taught.

As we look back on the history of the education of Indian children, we see a dilemma that all the missionaries faced. In order to reap the "benefits" of the white man's "generosity" the Indians wanted to be "civilized." Civilization required that the Indians speak English, and the Indians themselves asked for English-speaking teachers. The government refused to pay school expenses if the Indian language was used. Missionaries like Baraga could not continue to use and teach the Indian languages in the schools. Today many white persons and most Indians look back with regret over a lost culture.

From Arbre Croche Baraga also traveled to nearby Beaver Island and to the southern shore of the Upper Peninsula of Michigan, to Indian Lake, two miles northwest from Manistique. Baraga remained at Arbre Croche for twenty-eight months. Although it was his intention eventually to go to the Chippewas on Lake Superior, he first went to the area of Grand River where many of the Ottawas wintered and where a significant settlement existed. During his sojourn at Grand

River he experienced a midnight attack on his hut by a group of drunken Indians. Although he had long abstained from alcoholic beverages, he then made a vow to abstain perpetually, a pledge that he observed for the rest of his life. He became an even more intense advocate of temperance among the Indians, a stance that made him a persona non grata to the white traders, especially to Joseph Campau, who trafficked in the liquor trade to the Indians. Baraga would not leave the area, however, until he was able to arrange for a replacement. Bishop Résé had asked Fr. Andrew Viszosky to leave Cottrellville (Marine City) for Lake Superior. Fr. Viszosky did not wish to go north and Baraga suggested that Bishop Résé should send him to Lake Superior and send Fr. Viszosky to Grand River (now Grand Rapids) in his place, a plan to which the bishop agreed.

After two months at Cottrellville, Baraga began his voyage to La Pointe where he arrived on July 27, 1835, with a mere three dollars and only his summer clothes and supplies. After much hardship during the severe winters of 1835–1836 and 1836–1837, he left La Pointe for a brief journey to Europe to solicit funds and material goods for his destitute mission. Among the religious articles he brought to America were several paintings by Matthew Langus. The famous picture, now at St. Ignatius Church in St. Ignace, Michigan, of St. Ignatius of Loyola dedicating himself to God, dates from this journey. However, all of the pictures that adorned the first St. Joseph Church at La Pointe perished in the fire that destroyed the church.

Using La Pointe, and later L'Anse, as headquarters, Baraga often visited the Indian settlements of Fond du Lac (Duluth), Grand Portage, and Fort William on the western shore of Lake Superior. Baraga, like the other Catholic missionaries, recruited the assistance of many lay people to help accomplish his gigantic task. However, one outstanding lay missionary began to instruct the Indians long before he knew Baraga or that Baraga intended to come to Lake Superior. That man was Pierre Cotté. Cotté had obtained a copy of Baraga's first Indian prayerbook and had used it to teach the Indians at Fond du Lac. Great was Baraga's surprise when he reached that location and found a band of Indians who already knew the prayers, hymns, and most of the teachings of the Catholic Church! The names of Pierre Cotté and his wife, Margaret, appear with great frequency in the La Pointe Baptismal Registry as well as in the L'Anse Registry until their deaths in 1845.

In 1841, when Baraga was forty-four years old, an age when many men undergo a "mid-life crisis," he experienced the desolation of knowing that a solitary life would always be his. He wanted to remain faithful despite whatever failings his bishop might have or lack of support his bishop might give to him. Therefore Baraga made a major modification in his daily schedule. Always deeply prayerful since his early years, he now began to rise at 2:30 or 3:00 A.M. to spend two or three hours in meditative prayer, a practice to which he often referred in the Diary.

In May 1843, upon the urging of the Indians and of Pierre Crebassa who had known Baraga at La Pointe, Baraga came to the village of L'Anse, Michigan. Crebassa and his wife, Nancy (probably the daughter of Margaret Cotté by her first husband, Eustache Roussain), were married at La Pointe by Baraga and brought their first three children to La Pointe so that Baraga could baptize them. They, too, were faithful collaborators with Baraga.

Concern for the Indians led Baraga and some of the Protestant missionaries to overlook their denominational differences on many occasions. For example, in 1838, at La Pointe, Granville Sproat, the Presbyterian school teacher, and his wife suffered the loss of a stillborn baby. Mrs. Sproat wrote to her family that Mr. Baraga, the Catholic priest, had joined the funeral procession with the other mourners. Later, at L'Anse, the Methodist missionary, Rev. John Pitezel, and Baraga cooperated often, especially when the Chippewas had a grievance against the government. In particular, with Baraga acting first and Pitezel following his lead, both purchased the land on which their missions were located and deeded the land to the Indians. This action prevented the removal of the L'Anse Indians to the west and made possible the Keweenaw Bay Reservation in L'Anse today. In the 1883 edition of *Lights and Shades of Missionary Life* (pp. 443–44), Pitezel wrote:

> With our differences, we were men and neighbors, and freely exchanged the amenities of social life. Often, in the rude cabin of the Frenchman, and the ruder wigwam of the Indian, who adhered to Romanism, I shared generous hospitality, and the priest was made no less welcome among our people. . . . Rev. Frederick Baraga was the resident priest. . . . Temperate in his habits, devout and dignified in his private and ministerial bearing, he was universally respected by the Indians and mining community, and affectionately loved by those in closer fellowship.

At L'Anse Baraga named the mission "The Church of the Most Holy Name of Jesus," reflecting his great devotion to the name of the

Savior. He tried to model the Christian community after the Jesuit Reductions of Paraguay. From L'Anse he continued to visit settlements at great distances and with great hardships, earning the title of "The Snowshoe Priest." He remained at L'Anse until his consecration as bishop on November 1, 1853. In L'Anse he completed both the Grammar and Dictionary of the Otchipwe (Chippewa) language, and on June 27, 1852, began to keep this Diary.

## The Diary Years

In the period covered in the Diary, 1852–1863, Baraga detailed his many travels, the joys and tribulations his priests gave to him, and his continued efforts to advance the education and cause of temperance among the Indians. He served the Catholics of the multiplying mining communities, especially in the Keweenaw Bay and Negaunee-Marquette regions. During the summers he visited both the missions, which were his because of their location in the Upper Peninsula, and also the Indian missions of northern lower Michigan, Wisconsin, Minnesota, and Ontario. His winters were spent at Sault Ste. Marie. Except for the Diary and his many letters, his work of writing was finished; his chief hobby became carpentry. He delighted in making missal stands, frames for the pictures of the Stations of the Cross, and even pews for some of the poorer missions. Baraga continued to teach, preach, hear confessions, celebrate Mass, and do all that a pastor usually does. His greatest joy came in ordaining twenty new priests during his episcopacy.

## After the Diary

Volume III ended on July 16, 1863. However, in his eulogy on the occasion of Baraga's death, Fr. Jacker wrote that "in the month of September, of the same year [1866], he [Baraga] made his last entry in the journal which he kept for many years." It seems, then, that at least one additional volume and possibly more are now lost.

In the years between the last entry and his death on January 19, 1868, Baraga continued to visit his missionaries and serve the people. Sometime in May 1866, he moved to the city of Marquette. The following October he attended the Second Provincial Council of Baltimore, where he suffered a disabling fall. Upon his insistence he was brought back to Marquette. His last thoughts and gifts were for his beloved Indians. Fr. Terhorst, missionary at Baraga's beloved L'Anse, was the last of his priests to visit. Verwyst (pp. 354–55) described how Baraga, still intensely devoted to the Indians,

> inquired of the good Father how he was getting on with his school. F. Terhorst told him it was doing well. The bishop then pointed to a tin box on a library shelf and requested him to hand him the box, which was done. Then he asked him to take the key of the box from under his pillow and give it to him. With his weak, trembling hand the bishop opened the box and told Father Terhorst to take the money in it, which was twenty dollars. Upon F. Terhorst's remark that it was all the money he [the bishop] had, and that it was not right to take it, the sick prelate answered: "I don't need any more money— take it!" So to the last he showed his great esteem for Father Terhorst and his Indian school.

After fifteen months of incapacity and suffering, Bishop Baraga died at 1:30 A.M., on Sunday, January 19, 1868. It was the Feast of the Holy Name of Jesus. On the evening of the funeral on January 31, in St. Peter's Cathedral, Fr. Jacker delivered a public eulogy, "The Life and Services of Bishop Frederic Baraga," which concluded:

> Thus ended a man, whose purity of soul and singleness of purpose, whose mortified life and burning zeal, joined to uncommon talents and acquirements, faithfully and successfully employed in the service of God, and of the most abandoned of his creatures; a man whose extraordinary achievements as a pioneer of Christianity, will not allow his memory to pass away, as long as souls capable of appreciating so much virtue and excellency will live in this upper country, which has been the principal field of his labors, and where his body now rests to await the summons for resurrection.

The remains of Bishop Frederic Baraga are interred in the crypt of St. Peter's Cathedral in Marquette, Michigan.

In 1930 a group of Slovenian Catholics in the Chicago area began the Bishop Baraga Association to promote knowledge of the life and work of Bishop Baraga and to promote his canonization. The official Cause for canonization opened in 1972 and has made slow but steady progress. Recently the Bishop Baraga Association and Diocese of Marquette acquired the house in Marquette in which Bishop Baraga died. Eventually it will house the Baraga archives and museum.

Regis M. Walling

# CHRONOLOGY OF
# THE LIFE OF FREDERIC BARAGA

| | |
|---|---|
| 1757, May 8 | Birth of John Nepomucene Baraga at Preserje |
| 1759, March 21 | Baptism of Catherine Jencic at Dobernig |
| 1792, May 16 | Marriage of John Baraga and Catherine Jencic Residence at Mala vas |
| 1793, March 13 | Birth and death of Maria Baraga |
| 1794, January 11 | Birth of Vincent Baraga |
| 1794, February 24 | Death of Vincent Baraga |
| 1795, July 6 | Birth of Amalia Baraga |
| 1797, June 29 | Birth of Frederic Baraga |
| 1800 | Baraga family moved to Trebnje |
| 1803, February 4 | Birth of Antonia Baraga |
| 1803–1806 | Frederic at school at Belnek |
| 1806–1816 | Frederic at school at Ljubljana |
| 1808, October 10 | Death of Catherine Jencic Baraga |
| 1812 | Birth of Mary Baraga to Amalia |
| 1812, October 18 | Death of John Nepomucene Baraga |
| 1816–1821 | Frederic Baraga at University of Vienna |
| 1818, October 18 | Marriage of Amalia Baraga to Joseph Gressel |
| 1821, November 2 | Frederic Baraga entered seminary in Ljubljana |
| 1823, September 21 | Frederic Baraga ordained to the priesthood |
| 1824, May 31 | Marriage of Antonia Baraga to Felix von Hoeffern |

| | |
|---|---|
| 1824–1828 | Fr. Baraga at St. Martin Parish at Smartno |
| 1828–1830 | Fr. Baraga at St. Nicholas Parish in Metlika |
| 1829, March 18 | Leopoldine Society begun |
| 1829, August 10 | Fr. Baraga asked permission to apply for the missions |
| 1830 | First printing of *Dushna Pasha* |
| 1830, February 6 | Death of Felix von Hoeffern |
| 1830, September 22 | Fr. Baraga received acceptance to Cincinnati diocese |
| 1830, October 18 | Fr. Baraga left Metlika to begin journey to America |
| 1830, December 31 | Fr. Baraga arrived in New York |
| 1831, January 18 | Fr. Baraga arrived in Cincinnati |
| 1831, April 21 | Fr. Baraga left Cincinnati |
| 1831, May 27 | Fr. Baraga arrived at L'Arbre Croche |
| 1832 | Published first Indian book: *Otawa Anamie-Masinaigan Wawiyatanong* |
| 1832, April | First priest at Beaver Island |
| 1832, mid-May | First priest at Indian Lake (U.P.) |
| 1832, September 13 | Death of Fr. Gabriel Richard |
| 1832, September 26 | Death of Bishop Fenwick |
| 1832, December 17 | First mention of desire to go to Lake Superior |
| 1833, March 5 | First mention that Antonia wanted to join Fr. Baraga |
| 1833, March 8 | Detroit diocese created; Frederic Résé named bishop |
| 1833, June 15 | Fr. Baraga visited Grand Rapids |
| 1833, September 23 | Fr. Baraga arrived "permanently" at Grand Rapids |
| 1833, October 6 | Consecration of Bishop Frederic Résé, Detroit |
| 1833, October 13 | Consecration of Bishop John Baptist Purcell, Cincinnati |
| 1835, February–July | Fr. Baraga at Cottrellville (Marine City) |
| 1835, July 10 | Fr. Baraga left Sault Ste. Marie |
| 1835, July 27 | Fr. Baraga arrived at La Pointe |
| 1836, September 29 | Fr. Baraga left La Pointe for Europe |
| 1837, October 8 | Fr. Baraga returned to La Pointe |
| 1843, May 24 | Fr. Baraga visited L'Anse |
| 1843, October | Fr. Baraga arrived "permanently" at L'Anse |
| 1847, February 8 | Marriage of Mary Baraga (daughter of Amalia, adopted daughter of Bartholomew Pengov) to John Koroshin |

| | |
|---|---|
| 1850 | Publication of the Grammar |
| 1852, June 27 | Fr. Baraga began his Diary |
| 1853, July 1 | First mention of deafness |
| 1853, July 8 | Publication of the Dictionary |
| 1853, July 29 | Rome approved the establishment of the Apostolic Vicariate of Upper Michigan and appointed Frederic Baraga as Bishop |
| 1853, October 9 | Fr. Baraga received official notification of his appointment as Bishop |
| 1853, November 1 | Consecration of Bishop Frederic Baraga |
| 1853, November | Wrote English and Chippewa Pastoral Letters |
| 1853, November 26 | Departed from New York for Europe |
| 1854, April 24 | Marriage of Emperor Francis Joseph and Duchess Elizabeth of Bavaria |
| 1854, August 21 | Returned to Sault Ste. Marie |
| 1854, October 18 | First Ordination, Rev. Henry Louis Thiele |
| 1855, May 13–29 | First Provincial Council of Cincinnati |
| 1856, May 31 | First edition of Diocesan Statutes |
| 1857, January 9 | Diocese of Sault Ste. Marie approved |
| 1858, May 2–9 | Second Provincial Council of Cincinnati |
| 1860, October 19 | First hint of illness (slight stroke?) |
| 1861, April 28–May 4 | Third Provincial Council of Cincinnati |
| 1862, August 10 | Death of Amalia Gressel |
| 1863 | Second edition of Diocesan Statutes |
| 1863, July 16 | Last entry in Diary |
| 1866, May | Moved to Marquette |
| 1866, October 7 | Opening of the Second Plenary Council of Baltimore; attack by Bishops |
| 1866, October 9 | Fall and possible stroke |
| 1867, November 10 | Last public appearance, Negaunee |
| 1868, January 19 | Death of Bishop Frederic Baraga |
| 1871, May 21 | Death of Antonia von Hoeffern |

# *ABBREVIATIONS*

| | |
|---|---|
| AAC | Archives of the Archdiocese of Cincinnati |
| AAM | Archives of the Archdiocese of Milwaukee |
| AAQ | Archives of the Archdiocese of Quebec |
| ACHR | *American Catholic Historical Researches* |
| ACQR | *American Catholic Quarterly Review* |
| ACSJ | Archives of the Congregation of St. Joseph, Carondelet, Missouri |
| ACSM | Jesuit Archives of the College Sainte Marie, Montreal |
| ADBA | Archives of the Archdiocese of Baltimore |
| ADM | Archives of the Archdiocese of Montreal |
| ADQC | *Acts and Decrees of the Four Provincial Councils of Cincinnati* |
| AFC | American Fur Company |
| AFML | Archives of the Franciscan Monastery, Ljubljana |
| ALJ | Aljancic Manuscripts |
| AMK | *Ave Maria Koledar*, Lemont, Illinois |
| AR | Article in the Bishop Baraga Archives |
| ASSJN | Archives of the Sisters of St. Joseph, Nazareth, Michigan |
| BB | *Baraga Bulletin* |
| BBA | Bishop Baraga Archives |
| BBC | Bishop Baraga Collection |
| BLR | Baraga, "Letters Received by Me" |

| | |
|---|---|
| BLS | Baraga, "Extracts of Letters Sent" |
| BNB | Baraga Notebook |
| CAA | Archives of the Archdiocese of Cincinnati |
| CALM | *Catholic Almanac* (Directory) |
| CCHS | Chippewa County Historical Society, Sault Ste. Marie, Michigan |
| CHC-CMU | Clarke Historical Collection-Central Michigan University |
| CLSSM | Carnegie Library, Sault Ste. Marie, Michigan |
| CPL | Chicago Public Library |
| CT | *Catholic Telegraph*, Cincinnati |
| D | Diary of Bishop Frederic Baraga |
| DAL | Diocesan Archives, Ljubljana |
| DCV | *Detroit Catholic Vindicator* |
| EJP | Edward Jacker Papers, Burton Historical Collection, Detroit Public Library |
| HODA | Hamilton, Ontario, Diocesan Archives |
| JAR | Jesuit Archives, Rome |
| KK | *Katholische Kirchenzeitung*, New York |
| LMV | Ludwig Mission Society, Munich |
| LMVA | Ludwig Mission Society Archives |
| LS | Leopoldine Society, Vienna |
| LSA | Leopoldine Society Archives |
| LSB | Leopoldine Society Berichte |
| LZ | *Laibacher Zeitung* |
| MADA | Milwaukee Archdiocesan Archives |
| MHS | Minnesota Historical Society |
| MPHC | *Michigan Pioneer Historical Collections* |
| MQDA | Marquette Diocesan Archives |
| MVHR | *Mississippi Valley Historical Review* |
| NA-OIA | National Archives-Office of Indian Affairs |
| NAL | Yugoslav National Archives, Ljubljana |
| NCE | *New Catholic Encyclopedia* |
| NDUA | Notre Dame University Archives |
| PFAP | Propagation de la Foi, Paris |
| PFAR | Propaganda Fide, Rome |
| RML | Ryan Memorial Library, Philadelphia |
| RS | "Reputation of Sanctity," Bishop Baraga Archives |
| SBL | *Slovenski Biografski Leksikon* |
| TAA | Archives of the Archdiocese of Toronto, Ontario |
| UAC | Ursuline Archives, Chatham, Ontario |

| | |
|---|---|
| V | Vault, Bishop Baraga Archives, Marquette |
| WF | *Wahrheitsfreund*, Cincinnati |
| WHC | *Wisconsin Historical Collections* |
| WHS | Wisconsin Historical Society |
| ZD | *Zdognja Danica*, Ljubljana |

# A NOTE ON THE TEXT

Only words that Baraga underlined in the text are underlined in this edition of the Diary. Other symbols are

* *   An unusual feature about the specific entry
< >   Text added at a later time
//    Indicates a new thought within an entry (Baraga's own marking)

The primary language of the Diary was German. Baraga's use of other languages is indicated by superscript letters: L = Latin; F = French; E = English; S = Slovene; I = Italian; C = Chippewa.

Letters found in the Bishop Baraga Collection are designated "A," letters by Baraga; "B," letters to Baraga, which mention his name or are of primary significance in Baraga's life and work; and "C," letters of secondary importance. The letter *following* the file number indicates the original language of the letter or source.

When Baraga named a ship his punctuation was irregular. In this text quotation marks indicate the names of ships. The punctuation in the Diary reflects Baraga's style.

In the Diary Baraga mentioned many persons for whom no biographical information is available.

# The Diary of
# BISHOP FREDERIC BARAGA

## JUNE 27, 1852–JULY 16, 1863

# PURPOSE OF THE DIARY

*On the inside of the front cover of Volume I, Baraga pasted a printed excerpt from an unidentifiable source. It suggests some of the reasons why he kept the Diary. In addition to the practical result of remembering details, Baraga's motivation included increased personal awareness and deliberation in choice and action.*

ᴸAll persons, who [wish to know] themselves,ᴸ in German: every parish priest who does not want to conduct his life in ambiguity, ought to write a diary, first of all, for not doing things without knowing why and for thinking over his actions, if not before and during them, at least after they have been done, that is at evening time, when he writes them in the notebook. Moreover, there are some more or less important reasons which oblige us to keep a diary, such as to have a memo for confession, or a guide in some entangled cases, or for being stimulated to humility, since many times the most stupid things occur; it could give some hints for pastoral theology or for journalists as reminders for the incomplete page.

# VOLUME I

## JUNE 27, 1852–OCTOBER 31, 1856

June 27:
M.T.[1]

Today I received the first report of my nomination for the Bishopric of Sault[2] Sainte Marie. I received the first report in a letter of June 7 from the Rt. Rev. Bishop Henni,[3] where he states that "Providence appears to want to call me to the chief <u>pastorship</u> on Lake Superior; where I may then also feed his (too much neglected) sheep!"[4]

The second report I received from the Kirchenzeitung[5] of June 10; where it states: "About the election of the new bishops, there is, of course, nothing definite as yet to report. However, it is certain that

---

[1]"M. T.," a German abbreviation for "noteworthy day," was inserted later.

[2]Baraga usually used the proper French word, "Saut." This text uses the current spelling of this and all other place names.

[3]John Martin Henni was born in Switzerland on June 15, 1805. Bishop Edward Fenwick ordained him on February 2, 1829, in Cincinnati. It was there in 1837 that he founded the *Wahrheitsfreund*, the first German Catholic newspaper in the U. S. Henni was consecrated the first bishop of Milwaukee on March 19, 1844, and became its first archbishop on February 12, 1875. He died on September 7, 1881, in Milwaukee. Code, p. 131.

[4]Baraga used the first person where a direct quotation would have had the third person.

[5]Catholic newspaper published in New York City.

the Rev. Dr. Baraga, in L'Anse,[6] Michigan, that worthy missionary to the Indians, was appointed Bishop of Sault Sainte Marie."

*The third report I received from Mr. Crebassa,[7] indirectly, namely, that Upper Michigan will get a bishop.*[8]

Whether this now is really so very "certain,"[9] the future will show. <Alas, it has proven to be certain.> ᴸMay God's will be done. Not to us, O Lord, not to us, but to Your Name give glory.ᴸ[10]

June 28:        ᴱAnswer to W. Wade's letter, in regard to the Chippewa[11] Dictionary.[12] It cannot be finished this summer; it will hardly be ready for next summer.ᴱ

Two accounts sent to P. B. Barbeau,[13] besides $23.84. With it gave a memorandum to Crebassa (20 # coffee).

---

[6]Baraga often wrote "Anse."

[7]"Creb." in text. Pierre [Peter] Crebassa was born in the Red River County of Canada, August 15, 1807, and raised and educated in Montreal. In 1829 he became the agent of the American Fur Company at Mackinac. From there he travelled Lake Superior and, in 1837 at La Pointe with Baraga presiding, he married Nancy Roussain. In 1838 they moved to L'Anse where Peter established his own trading post and served as postmaster. The Crebassas brought their first three children to La Pointe so Baraga could baptize them. The Crebassas raised their large family at L'Anse where many of their descendants still reside. *History of the Upper Peninsula*, p. 199. In 1850 Crebassa's holdings were valued at $4000. Federal Census, 1850, Houghton County, #3. Crebassa died on April 25, 1898.

[8]This text was added vertically in the upper left corner.

[9]Refers to the item in the June 10, 1852, *Katholische Kirchenzeitung*.

[10]Ps. 115:1.

[11]"Otch." is an abbreviation of Otchipwe or Ojibway, i.e., Chippewa.

[12]Due to Baraga's efforts in composing a Grammar and Dictionary, Chippewa is one of the few Indian languages with written resources from the nineteenth century.

[13]Peter B. Barbeau was born at La Prairie, Quebec, on June 29, 1800. He came to Sault Ste. Marie in 1822 and married Archange La Londe on August 9, 1831. They had three daughters, the oldest of whom married James P. Pendill. Barbeau was originally a trader for the American Fur Company in Wisconsin but he left the company in 1842, purchased the old Indian Agency at the Sault, and set up his own trading business. He served in many elected positions. Barbeau died at Sault Ste. Marie on October 17, 1882. Baraga conducted much of his business and made his purchases through Barbeau. Baraga employed him to repair and construct churches at the Sault and at Payment. Barbeau was also a trustee in the parish at the Sault. Barbeau died at Sault Ste. Marie on October 17, 1882; his wife died there on July 24, 1895. Both were 82 at the time of their deaths. Bayliss, pp. 283–85. By 1860 his real estate was valued at $20,000. Federal Census, 1860, Chippewa County, #117. In the census of 1850 (#39) Barbeau's age is 45, in 1860 it is 57. This is just one of numerous discrepancies, ranging from 7 to 12 years, between ages given in the two census documents.

June 29:     Today is my 55th birthday.[14] ᴸThanks be to God.ᴸ

June 30:     Wrote two letters. One to Rt. Rev. Bishop Henni. The second to Chr. Wieckmann.[15] See Letter Register.[16]

July 1:      Wrote two letters (Bishop Henni — copied, Bishop Lefevere).[17] See Letter Register.

July 2:      Letter to M. Örtel.[18] He should cite the source from which he quoted.[19]

July 6:      Today I have transcribed an entire notebook, the 22nd (16 pages).[20] ᴸThanks be to God!ᴸ I H S[21] This evening I heard the news of the unfortunate death of Benjamin Morin,[22] while intoxicated.[23]

July 10:     Journey to Quincy Mine.

July 11:     Sunday at Quincy Mine. — ᴱMarriage of John Ryan.ᴱ[24] —Difficulties with C. C. Douglass.[25] — ᴱGolden Rule

---

[14]Baraga always considered June 29 his birthday. However, his full name, Irenaeus Frederic Baraga, suggests that he may have been born on June 28, the feast of St. Irenaeus.

[15]Editor of WF.

[16]This "see" reference is Baraga's. He kept notebooks for "Letters Received by Me" and "Extracts of Letters Sent." Both of these records omit some letters known from other sources. Occasional discrepancies in dates also occur. The extant registers begin in 1854.

[17]Peter Paul Lefevere was born in Belgium on April 29, 1804, and ordained by Bishop Joseph Rosati in St. Louis on November 30, 1831. He was consecrated bishop on November 21, 1841, and appointed administrator of the diocese of Detroit. Bishop Lefevere died in Detroit on March 4, 1869. Code, p. 164.

[18]Editor of KK.

[19]Baraga asked for the source, which said that he would "certainly" be bishop.

[20]The twenty-second fasciculus of the Dictionary.

[21]Iesus Hominum Salvator ( Jesus Savior of Mankind).

[22]Benjamin Morin was a 38-year-old laborer, born in Canada, and husband of Harriet. Federal Census, 1850, Houghton County, #9.

[23]Death while intoxicated was not unusual. Baraga mentions others who also met their death in this condition. Some died in fights; others, losing their sense of balance, direction, and common sense would wander off, become disoriented and lost, and, in winter, starve or freeze to death.

[24]John Ryan, born in Ireland in 1829, emigrated to the United States in 1848 and was a pioneer in the Hancock area. He and his brother, Edward, were partners in numerous mining ventures in the Keweenaw area. In 1852 John became an "explorer" at the Quincy Mine. He later held the position of captain at the Pewabic and Hecla Mines. He and his wife, Johanna McDonald, had two daughters and three sons, among whom were Mother Agnes Gonzaga Ryan, fourth General Superior of the Sisters of St. Joseph of Carondelet, and John Ryan, copper industrialist and benefactor of the Sisters and of St. Joseph Hospital in Hancock. *History of the Upper Peninsula*, pp. 296–97.

[25]C. C. Douglass was born in Springfield, New York, but moved to Mt. Clemens,

|            | of prudence: <u>Say and write nothing that can be of any possible use to anybody against you!</u>[E26] |
|------------|----|
| July 12:   | Return to L'Anse.—Rev. N. Barnum's[27] and Mr. Brown's[28] visit. |
| July 13:   | [E]Note to C. C. Douglass. Had I known on the 6th of July what I know now I would have written otherwise.[E] |
| July 14:   | [E]I would have written this:[E] See <u>Summary</u> in the Letter Register. |
| July 20:   | Today I completed the <u>first half</u> of transcribing Chippewa words from the First Part[29] of the Dictionary. |
| July 22:   | Today more than half of my Indians went [F]fishing to Bete-grise.[F30] |
| July 29:   | Today I received a letter from Rt. Rev. Henni in which he says that it now depends only on the Holy Father whether or not Upper Michigan will become a Vicariate Apostolic; whereupon I then immediately, etc. — He says further: "I already believe you may assuredly count upon it, that you will have to take also this burden on your shoulders." — *<u>Done first, and then considered, to many has brought regret.</u>*[31] |

---

Michigan, as a youth. In 1844 he assisted Dr. Douglass Houghton in the geological survey of the Upper Peninsula. As a pioneer in the copper region, he owned and organized many mining companies and was a business partner of Ransom Shelden. He was also a member of the Michigan Legislature. He died in London, England, after 1863. *History of the Upper Peninsula*, p. 278.

[26]This is a variation of one of Baraga's favorite expressions. It first appeared on November 2, 1818, in a diary-notebook that he kept as a college student in Vienna. Cf. D, July 29, September 7, 1852. Baraga underlined this sentence twice, first in blue-green ink and then in red ink.

[27]Nelson Barnum was a 34-year-old Methodist clergyman, born in Vermont. He and his wife, Natio, had a 15-year-old son, Edwin. Federal Census, 1850, Houghton County, #12.

[28]John Brown was a Methodist missionary in the northern Keweenaw area. He was in L'Anse in 1843 when Baraga arrived there.

[29]Part I of the Dictionary is Chippewa-English; Part II is English-Chippewa.

[30]Bete-grise is near the northeast tip of the Keweenaw peninsula.

[31]Baraga underlined this sentence and added in the margin [L]"Whatever you do, do prudently."[L] These annotations are in blue-green ink.

Aug. 12: Today Leclair's[32] small boy burned himself. The best remedy is: wax, butter, incense, gaume.[33] (NB)

Aug. 22: My days pass by so uniformly one after the other, (in transcribing the Second Part,) that I find nothing at all to enter in the diary. (The copies, or at least excerpts of the letters I write, are in the Letter Register).

Aug. 29: Sunday. One of the most noteworthy days of the year. — 3 hours![34] — A real <sup>C</sup>Sunday!<sup>C35</sup> — Received good news in the letters. See Letters.

Sept. 1: Today I have finally completed transcribing the Second Part. <sup>L</sup>Thanks be to God!<sup>L</sup>

Sept. 7: From the 7th until 22nd Sept[ember] I was on a mission tour in the <sup>E</sup>Ontonagon [copper] Mining Region.<sup>E</sup> On Sept[ember] 8 I got lost in the woods, and had to spend the night out in the open, without fire, without blankets.[36] —It was my own fault. —<sup>L</sup>Whatever you do, do prudently.<sup>L</sup> I certainly know that I am not in a position to go straightway through the woods; I should always keep to the marked trail. NB.

[32]Francis Leclair, 32, was a Canadian-born fisherman. Federal Census, 1850, Houghton County, #7.

[33]A gum or resin.

[34]Baraga habitually arose at 2 or 3 A.M. for meditation and on this occasion he prayed for three hours.

[35]Literally, "a day of praise and thanksgiving."

[36]"One morning my father left his cabin looking for small game for his dinner. As he walked he noticed a man's tracks. Thinking Indians were lurking about, since they were moccasin tracks, he followed them for some distance. He was indeed surprised to come upon a man, cold, wet, and exhausted, sitting on a log; and more surprised to find his old friend, Father Baraga, the missionary. . . . On this occasion he was walking from Houghton to Rockland. The road was a mere trail in the dense forest and while on his way it rained, then turned to snow, and in the dark he lost the trail and wandered about in the woods, wet, hungry, cold and exhausted. My father took him to his cabin, gave him a hot meal, dry clothing and a dry bed. The next day Father Baraga, refreshed, prepared to leave again for Rockland. Before leaving he thanked my father for saving his life, saying he surely would have perished had he not been found. He wished to show his appreciation in some way, so he gave him, as a memento, the Crucifix he was wearing. This was prized very highly by my father until his death, when it came into my possession." This statement by Mrs. Adeline Le-Moine Halter and the crucifix are in the Ontonagon County Historical Museum. Undated. Mrs. Halter died c. 1940.

Sept. 28:      Today is <u>Election Day</u>. I wanted to vote for Ab[ner] Sh[erman],[37] but I was ashamed, and gave it all up and went away without voting for anyone. This was my last walk to any <sup>E</sup>election.<sup>E</sup> I will not go to any <sup>E</sup>election<sup>E</sup> anymore, no matter for whom it may be. — <sup>L</sup>God help me!<sup>L</sup>

Oct. 6:      From the 6th until 22nd Oct[ober] I was on a mission tour in <sup>E</sup>Point Keweenaw Mining Region.<sup>E</sup> — Nothing unusual. — In Eagle Harbor I purchased a <sup>E</sup>lot<sup>E</sup> to place a church on it in time with a priest.[38] (Oct[ober] 20, 1852).

Oct. 30:      Today we received the report that the "Baltimore"[39] is wrecked. — Misère![40] — <It is not true! — <sup>E</sup>Bravo!<sup>E</sup>>

Nov. 5:      Today John Hotley[41] moved into my big house.

Dec. 30:      For a long time I have not entered anything in this diary. My days passed by so uniformly, and monotonously, in the nerve racking copying of the Second Part, that I found nothing remarkable to enter. — Now I once more finished, but not finished for good.

---

[37]Abner Sherman was a trader at L'Anse, although the 1863 *Michigan Manual*, p. 136, lists his profession as "wanderer." As a member of the Michigan House of Representatives, in 1853 he introduced the resolution that protected the rights of the L'Anse Indians to vote, own their property in L'Anse, and to receive their annuities at L'Anse. *Acts of the Legislature of the State of Michigan*, February 9, 1853. In BBC-B 1260. He also sponsored legislation to bring railroad lines to Ontonagon. In his newspaper, the *Upper Peninsula Advocate*, he promoted statehood for the Upper Peninsula, and in 1857 he introduced a petition for separation from the Lower Peninsula. *Michigan House Journal*, January 13, 1857. According to the *Grand Rapids Enquirer* of November 24, 1852, he was a Democrat; however, in 1860 he cast an electoral vote for the Republican candidate, Abraham Lincoln. *Journal of the* [Michigan] *House of Representatives*, January 26, 1864. State Senator Sherman and his son were lost when the steamer *Sunbeam* sank on August 28, 1863.

[38]Baraga anticipated his appointment as bishop by making provisions for future parishes.

[39]The name of a Great Lakes ship. In this case Baraga also underlined the name of the ship.

[40]An untranslatable all-purpose idiom, usually expressed under duress. J. G. Kohl explained: "Ah, misère! I naturally mention all this . . . to throw a light on their favorite expression, 'Ah, misère!' which has become in this helpless country such a permanent interjection, that it supplies the place of all others." Kohl, p. 176.

[41]John Hotley was a 40-year-old, Michigan-born carpenter. He was married and had five children. Federal Census, 1860, Houghton County, #1183. The same census (#575) also lists an 80-year-old, Michigan-born fisherman of the same name.

## 1853

Jan. 4:     Now at last I am completely finished with my diction-
            ary. God be thanked!

Jan. 7:     From the 7th until 26th Jan[uary] I was on a mission
            tour in the Ontonagon Mining Region. — On
            Jan[uary] 11 I received a ᴱtown lotᴱ in Ontonagon Vil-
            lage as a present from James Paul,[42] to build a church
            thereon.[43]

Jan. 27:    NB[44] for Detroit. Charles Frejeau, Ontonagon Village,
            found $78 last Sept[ember]. Three tens.

Jan. 28:    From Jan[uary] 28 to Feb[ruary] 16 I was on a mission
            tour in Keweenaw Point Mining District, and an-
            nounced to everyone that this would be my last mis-
            sionary visit. — <I don't know.>

[42] James Kirk Paul [Paull] was born near Richmond, Virginia, on March 20, 1813. He was the first white settler in the village of Ontonagon. After a very colorful life, he died there on May 1, 1881. *History of the Upper Peninsula*, pp. 542–43.

[43] Baraga omitted mention of a trip to Fond du Lac during this time. Benjamin Armstrong, a trader and son-in-law of Chief Buffalo at La Pointe, gave the details: "One incident which came directly in my way, in the winter of 1853, that shows one man at least whose heart was true to his teachings. It was a very hard and cold winter and many Indians were poor and destitute, particularly so at Fond du Lac at the head of Lake Superior. By some means Father Baraga, a Catholic priest located at L'Anse Bay, a distance by trail from Fond du Lac of about two hundred and fifty miles, heard of the great suffering there and that one family in particular, a widow and her children, were all sick. He provided himself with such medicines as could readily be had and set out on snowshoes to make the journey in dead of winter, with the snow several feet deep. About the 20th of January, 1854 [sic], I left La Pointe for Ontonagon, some ninety miles away in the direction of L'Anse. About half-way between La Pointe and Ontonagon I met Father Baraga on his way to Fond du Lac, as he said, to assist the distressed and needy there, and I am quite positive that he would have perished that night but for our meeting. His snowshoes had given out and it would have been impossible for him to have proceeded far without them on account of the deep snow. Our party made it comfortable for him that night and one of my men repaired his snowshoes and in the morning returned with him on the perilous journey. Some months after I met him when he told me of his trip and how he had found the family sick and destitute; that he had given them medicine and otherwise provided for them, and when he left them they were doing well and were comfortable.
     "I do not mention this incident for the purpose of drawing a line between any two or more denominations that had missionaries in this country but to state the plain facts for history. Any denomination that secured such a martyr as Father Baraga would be fortunate indeed, for his manly and upright disposition would have prompted him to such acts wherever placed." Armstrong, II, p. 57. The date *must* be 1853 because Baraga was in Europe in January 1854.

[44] NB, "northbound." The ship was northbound from Ontonagon to Eagle Harbor but southbound for Detroit.

March 2:     Today I left L'Anse to go overland to Detroit and have my dictionary printed there. On the 6th I reached Bay des Noques, from there I rode in 3 days to Green Bay. On the 9th I broke through the ice, 9 miles from Green Bay, and was almost drowned.[45] — However, God the Lord has graciously saved me also from this peril as He had from many others.[46]

[45]A member of the party, Captain John G. Parker, recalled: "In driving across Green Bay the horses broke through the ice at a drift of snow on the ice. The crack was about 20 feet wide. Simon Mendlebaum and Father Baraga were sitting on the bottom of the sleigh in the after end so they did not get hurt, but stepped out behind. Mr. Burtenshaw, C. C. Douglass and myself sat on the bottom of the sleigh and were tipped in the water. I got out after a while and pulled Burtenshaw out and then Douglass. They all started for the lighthouse, about a mile away. The teamster got out on the ice over the horses, and all helped to get the horses and sleigh out of the water before they left. I helped the driver hitch up and then followed. We cut through a crack that hove up fifteen feet high. It was a cold and freezing day. Father Baraga was on his way to have his Chippewa book translated into English." Parker, p. 584.

The account of this incident in Verwyst, pp. 225–26, is incorrect in locating this event on Lake Huron.

[46]Fr. Chebul described another occasion: "One time F[ather] Baraga was going to Ontonagon in company with an Indian half-breed in the month of March or April. At that season of the year the ice, though thick, becomes honey-combed and rotten. Some say that Baraga's companion was a man named Newagon. They went on the ice at La Pointe Island. As the walking on the sandy beach would have been very fatiguing and long, they determined to make straight for Ontonagon over the ice. By so doing they would not only have better walking, but also shorten their way a great deal. A strong southwest wind was blowing at the time, and the ice, becoming detached from the shore, began drifting lakeward. After they had traveled for some time, they became aware of what had happened, for they could see the blue waters between them and the shore. Newagon became greatly alarmed, for almost certain death stared them in the face. Had the wind continued blowing in the same direction, the ice would have been driven far out into the lake and broken up into small fragments. They would surely have perished. To encourage the drooping spirit of his companion, F[ather] Baraga kept telling him that they would escape all right and that they must trust in God, their loving Father and Protector. He also sang Chippewa hymns to divert Newagon's attention and calm his excitement. Finally the wind shifted and blew the field of ice back towards the shore. They landed near Cadotte Pointe, near Union Bay, a short distance from Ontonagon, which they reached that same day. 'See,' said the missionary to his companion, 'we have traveled a great distance and worked little.' The distance from La Pointe to Ontonagon is about sixty or seventy miles by an air line. Had they been obliged to walk the whole distance around the bend of the lake, it would probably have taken them two or three days of very hard and fatiguing traveling. So what at first seemed to threaten certain death was used by God's fatherly providence to shorten and facilitate the saintly priest's journey." Verwyst, pp. 221–22.

March 11:     This evening I arrived in Milwaukee, and went immediately to the Rt. Rev. Bishop Henni, with whom I intend to stay for a few days.

March 17:     This evening, at 8 P.M., I arrived in Detroit where I intended to have my dictionary printed. However, the local print shops do not have the equipment for the job.[47] I cannot have it printed here. I must travel to New York in order to have it done.

March 24:     I will not have to go to New York, but to Cincinnati to have the dictionary printed, and I hope to travel there on Easter Monday. — 'We shall see.'

March 28:     Today, Easter Monday, I sailed on the "Bay City" from Detroit to Sandusky, where I arrived at 5 P.M.

March 29:     Today I arrived in Cincinnati, and with Rev. Cl[ement] Hammer[48] found a hospitable shelter. The printing of the dictionary will not begin until Tuesday, April 5.

April 11:     Today I finally receive the first proofsheets of the Dictionary for correction. — Misère! When will it be finished! —

In April:     I spend my days very uniformly in correcting the proofsheets. It progresses slowly; much slower than I wish.[49]

May 12:     Today the Rt. Rev. Bishop Lefevere came from Detroit and stayed here a couple of days.

In May:     I am still occupied with the continuous, tedious correcting of the proofsheets for the Chippewa dictionary, and it will probably go on so until <u>July</u>.

---

[47]The Dictionary was a much larger work than could be printed in Detroit at the time.

[48]Clement Hammer was born in Bohemia, November 7, 1804. He graduated with a degree in mining engineering before he was ordained in Prague on July 15, 1836. In 1837 he came to Detroit with Baraga when he returned from Europe. Hammer transferred to Cincinnati in 1839 where he worked until 1866. He returned to Prague as rector at the Cathedral, where he died in 1879. Kummer, p. 198.

[49]As summer neared Baraga was anxious to return to the missions.

June 13:     Today Rev. Kundeg[50] [sic] arrived here from his European trip, and told me that Cardinal Franzoni told him in Rome that my confirmation as Vicar Apostolic and Bishop of Upper Michigan is not subject to any doubt; only one cannot say when the bulls from Rome will arrive. — <sup>c</sup>Well, let it be so — Then so it shall be, O Lord, then it shall arrive.<sup>c</sup>

June 17:     Today <sup>c</sup>two teeth<sup>c</sup> were set up for me by Dr. J. Taylor, whom the Lord may bless and keep for a long time. —

June 27:     Today it is already a year since I have heard it for the first time: but I am no further ahead than I was then. — Stop!

June 29:     Today is my 56th birthday, which I am spending sadly here in this dreadful heat.

July 1:      Last night my left ear plugged up tight so that I can not even hear my pocket watch when I press it tightly against it. — Misère! If it should remain so. <(It really remained so! Aug[ust] 2)> <(Still so, April 21, 1856)>

July 8:      Today I finally made the last corrections for the Chippewa Dictionary, and that difficult task is now at an end.[51] — God be thanked a thousand times for that! —

July 26:     Today, finally, (misère!) I am leaving this . . . Cincinnati.

July 27:     This morning I arrived in Detroit, and on Aug[ust] 2 journey from there to Sault Sainte Marie:[52] and arrived

---

[50]Rev. Joseph Kundek came from Croatia to the United States in 1839. He worked primarily in Vincennes, Indiana. He died at the age of 47 on December 4, 1857, at Jasper, Iowa. CALM, 1859, p. 246.

[51]"The Very Rev. Frederick [sic] Baraga has brought to a happy termination his great work, a dictionary of the Language spoken by the four, or five Indian tribes on Lake Superior, whom he has spent the last twenty-two years of his life in evangelizing. The labors of the printing room, where he has had for several months to remain a close, but willing prisoner, watching the forms as they come from the hands of the compositor, and correcting the proofs, have pressed somewhat heavily on the never robust constitution of the good Missionary." CT, xxii, 30, p. 4, July 16, 1853.

[52]Here Baraga met Mother Mary Xavier. On May 24, the first woman religious in the diocese, Mother Mary Xavier (Yvonne) Le Bihan, O.S.U., arrived at Sault Ste.

on the 4th. *On July 29, 1853 my name went before the Consistory in Rome*[53]

Aug. 5:  Today I went from Sault Sainte Marie to Eagle Harbor where I arrived on the 7th; and on the 9th I went to L'Anse, where I remained only 2 days.

Aug. 12:  From Aug[ust] 12 until Sept[ember] 26 I was on a mission tour through all the ᴱMining Locationsᴱ in the District of Keweenaw as well as in Ontonagon; and in various ᴱlocationsᴱ selected suitable sites for churches and future priests' houses. On this mission tour I baptized 56 children.

Sept. 29:  Today I arrived again at L'Anse, but left on Oct[ober] 3, to go to Europe.[54]

Oct. 6:  Today[55] I finally learned with certainty that my nomination as Bishop of Upper Michigan has been confirmed by the Holy Father in Rome.[56]

Oct. 9:  Today I arrived in Sault Sainte Marie.[57] On the 12th I left Sault Sainte Marie and arrived in Detroit on the 13th, where I learned from the Rt. Rev. Bishop Lefevere that on Nov[ember] 1 I will be consecrated in Cincinnati as Bishop of Amyzonia[58] and Vicar Apostolic of Upper Michigan.

Oct. 25:  Today I journeyed from Detroit to Cincinnati. On the 26th I arrived. Here I made a 3 day retreat at Mr. Hammer's, and on Nov[ember] I received the Episco-

---

Marie. She was born at Caudan, France, on April 18, 1814, entered the Order of St. Ursula on May 22, 1835, and professed her vows on December 11, 1838. A multitalented woman, she held numerous positions of authority from her first years as a religious. She came to the Sault in 1853 at the invitation of Fr. Menet who served as Superior of the community in Sault Ste. Marie. In 1860 the community moved to Chatham, Ontario, where a flourishing community remains. Mother Mary Xavier died on May 22, 1896. Her spirit of gentle and generous holiness still inspires the community. St. Paul, pp. 98–233.

[53]Written upside down at the top of the page.

[54]Baraga had determined to go to Europe for priestly and financial assistance for the Indian missions, whether he became a bishop or not.

[55]Baraga was probably in Eagle Harbor.

[56]Pope Pius IX, pontificate (1846–1878).

[57]At this time Mother Mary Xavier mended his only coat. St. Paul, p. 132. She may also have designed and/or prepared his coat of arms.

[58]A city in Caria, Asia Minor.

pal consecration[59] from the hands of Most. Rev. Archbishop Purcell,[60] with the assistance of the Rt. Rev. Bishop Lefevere and Henni.[61]

Nov. 6:    Today, in St. Mary's Church, Cincinnati, I held my <u>first</u> pontifical high mass.[62]

Nov. 10:   Today, at Stonelick, Ohio,[63] I administered holy confirmation for the first time.

Nov. 14:   Today at last, I departed from Cincinnati.[64] On Nov[ember] 21 I arrived in New York. I had to wait 5 days in Dunkirk for my trunk which has been mislaid.

Nov. 26:   Today I sailed on the "U.S.M.S. Pacific" for Liverpool.

Dec. 7:    Today I arrived in Liverpool after a successful and pleasant voyage of less than 11 days; and set out on the same day for Dublin.

Dec. 8:    ᴸOn the feast of the Immaculate Conception of the Blessed Virgin Maryᴸ — Arrived in Dublin where the Most Rev. Archbishop Paul Cullen[65] took me into his house with great kindness and hospitality.

Dec. 20:   From Dublin via Holy Head and London to Paris, where I arrived on Dec[ember] 22, in the company of

[59]George A. Carrell, S.J., 1803–1868, was consecrated Bishop of Covington, Kentucky, at the same time. Code, pp. 135–36.

[60]Bishop John Baptist Purcell was born in Ireland, February 26, 1800, ordained in Paris on May 20, 1826, consecrated second bishop of Cincinnati on October 13, 1833, and made Archbishop on July 19, 1850. He died on July 4, 1883, at St. Martin, Ohio. Code, p. 243.

[61]The consecration was reported in: DCV, November 5, 1853; in BBC-B 804 E; in CT, November 5, 1853; in BBC-B 1011 E; in WF, November 3, 1853; in BBC-B 860 G.

[62]WF, November 10, 1853, reported that the new bishop performed the ceremonies of the pontifical mass with such precision and exactness that it was difficult to believe that he had been a missionary among the Indians for so many years and so far removed from the splendor of Catholic worship.

[63]At St. Philomena Church in Clermont County, now Holy Trinity Church, Batavia, Ohio. WF, November 17, 1853.

[64]During his stay in Cincinnati, Baraga wrote Pastoral Letters in Chippewa and English to his flock. The Chippewa Pastoral Letter is the only such document written in a Native American language.

[65]Primate of Ireland. Baraga "first visited Ireland, because the greatest portion of our Catholics in the mining community are Irish people." Baraga to the *Tablet*, Dublin, December 9, 1853; in BBC-A 742 E.

Rev. Lawrence Dunne[66] whom I lodged at the Ecclesiastical Retreat[67] until I come back to Paris to take him with me.

## 1854

Jan. 3:     From Paris via Brussels to Malines, in Belgium, where I found a very friendly and honorable welcome by his Eminence, the Most Rev. Cardinal and Archbishop Englebert Sterckx.[68]

Jan. 5:     Journeyed from Malines via Louvain, Aachen to Cologne, where I lost my travelling bag through the punishable carelessness of the railroad officials.

Jan. 6:     Journeyed from Cologne via Dusseldorf to Cassel.

Jan. 8:     Said mass in Cassel at the Rev. Dean's, God be thanked! Then via Darmstadt and Bruchsal, Stuttgart, Ulm, Augsburg to Munich, where I arrived early on Jan[uary] 10, and stayed with the court chaplain Müller.[69] — On the same day I came to the Benedictine monastery of St. Boniface where I intend to remain for some days. A revoir![70]

Jan. 16:    Today I set out from Munich. On Jan[uary] 17 I offered mass in the ancient Chapel of Grace at Alt-Otting, in Bavaria. On 18th I came to Linz, where I found a very friendly welcome with the Rt. Rev. Bishop Rudiger.[71]

---

[66]Lawrence Dunne was born in Dublin c. 1824 and was ordained in 1846. He had spent five years as a missionary among the Kaffirs (Cape of Good Hope) before Baraga recruited him. In May 1854, he accompanied Baraga back to New York and, upon their arrival, was sent directly to Ontonagon where he worked until 1858. At that time he transferred to Illinois. He died in Chicago in 1894. Rezek, I, pp. 374–75.

[67]Residence for clergy visiting Paris. Dunne studied French while he waited for Baraga.

[68]Englebert Sterckx was born on November 2, 1792, ordained on January 18, 1815, consecrated archbishop of Malines on February 24, 1832, and elevated to the cardinalate in 1838. He died at Malines on December 4, 1867. NCE, 13, p. 703.

[69]Head of the Ludwig Mission Society, Munich, which sent generous donations to Baraga.

[70]Baraga made a seven-day retreat at the monastery.

[71]Franz Josef Rudiger was born on April 7, 1811, ordained in 1835, and consecrated

Jan. 20:    Today I set out from Munich. Here I live with the Rev. Director Widemer[72] at the Augustinaeum, or the Frintanaeum.

Jan. 27:    Arrived in Ljubljana.[73] On the 29th preached in the cathedral.[74]

Jan. 30:    Arrived in Trebnje.[75]

Feb. 1:    Offered mass in Dobernic. There said a prayer of thanksgiving at the baptismal font for the infinitely great grace of my own regeneration on June 29, 1797, at this baptismal font.[76]

Feb. 2:    Preached, pontificated in Trebnje, and then confirmed my grand nephew, Joseph Frederic Gressel.[77]

Feb. 5:    Pontificated and preached at Metlika.[78]

Feb. 12:    Pontificated and preached at St. Martin.[79]

Feb. 14:    Today departed from Trieste for Ancona in a miserable little steamboat.

---

bishop of Linz in 1852. He died on November 29, 1884. His cause for beatification was introduced in 1905.

[72]Rev. Bartholomew Widemer, later Bishop of Ljubljana.

[73]"We have just learned that our countryman, Rt. Rev. Bishop Frederic Baraga, will come this afternoon at five on the railroad to Ljubljana from Vienna." ZD, VII, 16, January 26, 1854; in BBC-B 726 S.

[74]"Last week the Rt. Rev. Frederic Baraga, Bishop of Amyzonia, (so named after a city in the country of Caria, Asia Minor), and Vicar-Apostolic of Upper Michigan in North America, came from Vienna to Ljubljana where a very large throng eagerly awaited him. . . . How the people of Ljubljana respect him was shown especially on Sunday at the cathedral which was fully packed with listeners of all classes, who were present at his German sermon which he gave with all apostolic zeal and in it earnestly recommended to avoid, with all strength, sin, which is the greatest evil." ZD, VII, 19–20, February 2, 1854; in BBC-B 756 S.

[75]The Baraga family lived in Trebnje, 1800–1806.

[76]After an extended meditation at the font, he preached a long, moving sermon on the sacrament of baptism and regeneration in the Lord. ZD, VII, 27–28, February 16, 1854; in BBC-B 891 S. Baraga had done the same in 1837 when he visited Dobernic.

[77]The son of Karl Gressel and the only grandson of Amalia and Joseph Gressel, Joseph Karl Gressel was born in 1847. After thirty years of service in the imperial infantry, he received the title of baronet. ALJ, January 17, 1898.

[78]Baraga was curate at St. Nicholas Parish in Metlika, 1828–1830.

[79]Baraga was curate at St. Martin Parish in Smartno, 1824–1828.

Feb. 17:         Offered mass in Loretto, in the Holy House.[80]

Feb. 21:         Arrived in Rome.[81] On the 27th had an audience with the Holy Father, Pius the Ninth,[82] and on March 5. In Rome I offered mass in St. Peter's, St. Paul's, in Mary Major and in the Lateran, etc.

March 8:       Set out from Rome for Trieste, via Bologna, Florence, Padua, Venice.

March 16:     Arrived in Ljubljana. On the 19th ᴸ(feast of St. Joseph),ᴸ preached and pontificated in Loka.[83] On March 25 ᴸ(on the parish feastday)ᴸ preached and pontifi-

---

[80]An old tradition says that the "Santa Casa" is the stable in which Christ was born.

[81]Baraga's sister, Amalia Gressel, traveled with him. Together they visited their sister, Antonia von Hoeffern, who was living in Rome at that time.

[82]Baraga wrote: "I was in Rome and had two audiences with the Holy Father. He is as good and amiable as a mortal can be. He is far too good for the age, and especially for the Italians. To my great pleasure he gave me a beautiful chalice, which will be to me a continual memorial of the kindness of our Holy Father." Baraga to Lefevere, April 8, 1854. Orig. in NDUA; in BBC-A 132 E. When he was in Rome, Baraga gave the Holy Father a gift of an Otchipwe Grammar and a Dictionary. Rezek, I, p. 125.

[83]Baraga was in Loka on March 18 and at Stara Loka on the 19th: "On Saturday before St. Joseph, at half past four in the afternoon, the thundering of cannons and the joyful ringing of the bells in all the churches began to announce to us his sincerely desired arrival. Stepping out of the carriage, he first went into the beautifully decorated convent church of the Immaculate Virgin Mary to adore the Blessed Sacrament, with which he also blessed a very large group of people present.

"After this holy service, he spent some time in the sisters' convent and then received the clergy and the Capuchin Fathers, conversed very pleasantly with them and related to them many an interesting thing about his Indians. . . .

"Toward evening the Rt. Reverend Bishop set out for Stara Loka, where with the gathered crowd he prayed the rosary in the church with great inspiration for all present. Then he gave them benediction with the Blessed Sacrament. How great also was the joy of the inhabitants of this parish because the Rt. Reverend Bishop had deigned to visit them at least for a few moments and to bless them, may be deduced from the fact that for the returning Rt. Reverend Bishop, in the complete darkness of the night, amid the joyful ringing of bells, they lighted his way on the road with lights set in the windows, which was something really stirring to see.

"On St. Joseph's day the Rt. Reverend Bishop had high mass in the parish church of St. James, at which he was assisted by eleven priests. He preached before the holy mass. . . . The cordial sermon as well as the truly pious demeanor of the Rt. Reverend Bishop has inspired and moved many a person, especially since nothing like that has ever happened here before, that an American bishop would preach and sing high mass." ZD, VII, 51–52, April 23, 1854; in BBC-B 1049 S.

cated at the Franciscans in Ljubljana.[84] On the 26th preached in St. Peter's.[85]

March 28:
From Ljubljana to Celje. On the 29th to St. Andrew[86] and the Most Rev. Prince Bishop Slomsek,[87] where I accepted the Roesch brothers.[88]

March 31:
Arrived in Graz where I found hospitality with the Franciscans and many courtesies with the Schusters. — On April 2 preached in the Cathedral of Graz.

April 4:
Today at 5 A.M. arrived in Vienna[89] where I again stay with the Augustinians.

---

[84]On this occasion Baraga gave holy pictures with handwritten inscriptions to the people. On those which still exist the inscriptions are: "If God takes anything from you, be convinced that you do not need it any more. What God does, is well done"; "He who is born only once, will die twice. On the contrary, he who is born twice will die only once"; "You are weak, the Tempter is strong; therefore be vigilant and pray"; "Many are called, few are chosen; therefore be vigilant and pray"; "Life is short, death is certain, all the rest is uncertain; therefore be vigilant and pray"; "Man dies but once; as the tree falls so it lies; therefore be vigilant and pray"; "There are two eternities; one of them must be your portion; therefore be vigilant and pray." Orig. in possession of Baraga family members and ADJ; in BBC-A 700 G; A 704 G.

[85]Baraga preached with "all the fervor of a Catholic bishop" by "recommending that we should imitate dear Jesus in his meekness, humility, patience, prayer and love for God. . . . He was here among us only a short time. But who can describe all the good which his apostolic conduct has produced." ZD, VII, 54, March 30, 1854; in BBC-1038 S.

[86]Seat of the Diocese of Savant.

[87]Martin Slomsek was born on November 26, 1800, at Slom in Styria. He was ordained in 1824, and in 1829 he became the spiritual director at the theological seminary at Klagenfurt. In his talks to the students he often cited Baraga as an exemplar of missionary zeal and encouraged their generosity to the missions. Slomsek was personally generous, both financially and materially, to Baraga. Cf. Harastelj, pp. 8–10. In 1846 Slomsek became archbishop of the Levant Valley (Carinthia) and, in 1859, of Maribor where he died on September 24, 1862. NCE, 13, p. 292.

[88]Joseph (November 1, 1819–October 12, 1884) and George (April 12, 1822–April 6, 1877) Roesch came to New York in July 1854. They were dissatisfied, and Baraga released them that same month. Baraga later defended them, writing to H. H. Muller that "the reprimand of the brothers Roesch was not deserved." BLS, March 2, 1855. Joseph served as a diocesan priest in New York, Illinois, Indiana, and Ohio. George became a Redemptorist in 1859 and made his vows on June 21, 1860. He worked in Philadelphia, Chicago, and Baltimore. BBC-"Roesch" file.

[89]The Leopoldine Society, directed by Baraga's former classmate, Archbishop Othmar von Rauscher, was located in Vienna. Baraga requested travel money for three missionaries, the Roesch brothers who were traveling with him, and Rev. Lawrence Lautishar, who would follow later. Baraga to LS, Vienna, April 15, 1854. Orig. in LSA; in BBC-A 409 G. Baraga received 600 florins from the soci-

April 27:   This morning, at half past five I finally left Vienna,[90] and the following morning at 10, I arrived by steamboat in Linz. From there immediately on a mail coach to Munich, where on April 29 I happily arrived.

May 3:   From Munich to Augsburg. Spent the night with Count Taufkirchen in Augsburg.

May 5:   Arrived in Paris where I again reside at the Foreign Missions.

May 20:   From Paris,[91] through Brussels, Malines, etc., to Antwerp. On [the] 21st arrived in Antwerp.

May 24:   From Antwerp, via London, to Liverpool.[92]

May 27:   From Liverpool on the British Steamship "Niagara" to Halifax, where I landed on June 6, (10 days ᴱfrom shore to shoreᴱ).

June 6:   From Halifax to Boston, then to New York.

June 9:   At 2 A.M. arrived in New York where I again live with the Redemptorist Fathers (ᴱ53 Third St.ᴱ).

June 12:   Father Dunne to Upper Michigan, I to Washington.

June 13:   Said mass with the Jesuit Fathers in Georgetown. And then to the ᴱCommissioner of the General Land Of-

ety for the travel expenses of the Roesch brothers. He also received 5000 florins for his diocese. Baraga Receipts, Vienna, April 26, 1854. Orig. in LSA; in BBC-A 427 G; A 428 G.

[90]Baraga remained in Vienna to represent the American church at the wedding of Austrian Emperor Francis Joseph. Baraga to Lefevere, Vienna, April 8, 1854. Orig. in NDUA; in BBC-A 132 E. Archbishop von Rauscher of Vienna, the celebrant at the wedding, was a long-time friend and classmate of Baraga at both the University of Vienna and at the seminary. He had also been a tutor of Francis Joseph and, with his outstanding interest in the African and American missions, had probably introduced Francis Joseph to the letters of Baraga and other missionaries. The Emperor gave Baraga a chalice, engraved with the name of the Emperor. This chalice is on display at the Pastoral Office Building in Marquette and is used for masses of ordination and diocesan celebrations.

[91]On the day of their departure from Paris, Baraga, with his priests and seminarians, attended a general meeting of the Propagation of the Faith in the church of St. Roch. The Archbishop of Paris, many priests, and laity were present. The Archbishop addressed the meeting. Lautishar to ZD, VII, 140-43, July 26, 1854; in BBC-B 1034 S.

[92]Rev. Lawrence Dunne accompanied Baraga, while the others sailed from Antwerp on May 31. Lautishar to ZD, VII, 140-43; in BBC-B 1034 S.

fice, Honorable <u>Wilson</u>, to seek the grant of that strip of land where the Catholic Church stands at Sault Sainte Marie.[93] Then to the Secretary of the Treasury, Honorable <u>James Guthrie</u>,[E] about the free passage of my religious articles.[94]

June 14:     In the evening, at 11, again arrived in New York at the Redemptorist Fathers.[95]

June 27:     Today it is two years since I have begun making entries in this booklet. Since then I have seen much, heard much, learned much, received much. God be thanked for all!
[C]Would that you take care of me * * *[96] that I take good care of all you have given me — that I do well and always, as it is pleasing to you, Jesus, whom I love exceedingly.[C] I H S m. 3 × 7 g.f.[97]

June 29:     Today is my 57th birthday. [L]Thanks be to God.[L]
[C]How many years shall I still live? Well! I cannot know. Only one knows this.[C]

July 15:     Today my Missionaries[98] arrived from Antwerp, in 44 days. [L]Thanks be to God.[L]

July 17:     Today I received $50 from Mr. O'Brien, making $528 in all + 3 = 531 + 5 = 536[99] And today I also sent Mr. Barth[olomew] Pierz[100] to the seminary in Cincinnati.

---

[93]The mission property was requisitioned by the War Department by an act of Congress, September 26, 1850, for the expansion of Fort Brady so that the mission no longer owned the church property. No satisfaction came from the Land Office in Sault Sainte Marie. Baraga appealed directly to the commissioner but received no satisfaction from him either. Baraga then authorized Fr. Menet to purchase from Placidus Ord lots adjacent to the church for $400. BLS, July 3 and August 10, 1854.

[94]Guthrie refused Baraga's request. Cf. D, July 29, 1854.

[95]During his stay in New York Baraga frequently preached at the Redemptorist churches. BLS, June 29, 1854. The Redemptorists took a special collection of over $500 for him. Isaac Hecker, who later founded the Congregation of St. Paul, was a member of the community at this time. Baraga ordered two paintings from Europe for Hecker. BLS, July 21, 1854.

[96]Manuscript mutilated. Possibly the monogram I H S has been excised.

[97]Meaning unknown.

[98]Revs. George Steinhauser, Lawrence Lautishar, Timothy Carie, and the Roesch brothers.

[99]These gifts completed the collection by the Redemptorists. Here the manuscript is mutilated (excised from the front).

[100]Bartholomew Pierz was a nephew of Rev. Francis Pierz (cf. D, February 1, 1859). He was skilled in household tasks and prepared all the meals for the travelers

July 18:    Today Charles Jaboeuf[101] departed for Cincinnati.[102]

July 21:    I released the 2 Roesch brothers, because of dissatisfaction.

July 29:    Today is the first anniversary of my consistory in Rome.[103] — And also had much grief at the customs office, and had to pay $310 duty for my effects. Misère!

July 31:    Today I finally left New York, and on Aug[ust] 2 arrived in Detroit,[104] where I have to wait again for my trunks.

Aug. 10:    Departed from Detroit and on Aug[ust] 11 arrived in Mackinac.[105]

---

on the ship. Lautishar to ZD, vii, 140-43; in BBC-B 1034 S. Baraga sent Pierz to Cincinnati to study theology. Baraga to Purcell, New York, June 12, 1854. Orig. in NDUA; in BBC-A 134 E. However, Pierz went to Minnesota to study with his uncle. Realizing that he had no vocation to the priesthood, he married and lived in various locations in Minnesota, Colorado, and New Mexico. In the Sioux rebellion of 1862 he suffered much property damage. In 1864 he organized the first school district in Minnesota where he taught. In 1872 he was elected to the Minnesota state legislature, an office he held until his death in 1896. Jaklic, pp. 483–84.

[101]Baraga approved Jaboeuf's "desire to enter the sanctuary" and then required that he pay for his own education. BLS, March 26 and April 4, 1855. Never ordained, Jaboeuf later married. Baraga wrote to him that he approved his decision. BLS, June 25, 1859. Jaboeuf returned to France shortly afterwards.

[102]On the following day Baraga wrote to Sister Celestine of the Sisters of St. Joseph of Carondelet, Missouri, to remind her of her promise to provide sisters. BLS, July 19, 1854. He later wrote: "For a third time I beg you to send me six of your Sisters, [there are] 100 children without a school at Mackinac." BLS, August 13, 1854. He also wrote to the Sisters' chaplain, Fr. Paris (August 21, 1854). The Sisters of St. Joseph finally came to the diocese in 1866.

[103]Baraga was named a bishop on July 29, 1853. Rezek, i, pp. 99–100.

[104]On August 4 Baraga and Bishop Lefevere agreed that Baraga would tend the Indian missions in the northern part of the Lower Peninsula. Baraga and Lefevere, Detroit, August 4, 1854. Orig. in NDUA; in BBC-A 135 E.

[105]Fathers John G. Steinhauser and Lawrence Lautishar were with Baraga. Steinhauser, a Swiss, went to Little Traverse until 1856. He was at St. Joseph Parish in Detroit in 1857; at Muskegon in 1859; Conowingo, Maryland, in 1864–1865; and at Havre de Grace, Maryland, 1886. There is no record of the intervening years nor after 1866. CALM, 1859, 1865, 1866. Lautishar continued to the Sault where, for a month, he studied English under Father Thiele. Lautishar was born on December 11, 1820, in Carniola. He was ordained on August 3, 1845. Canon Novak recommended Lautishar to Baraga: "Although by nature he is small and homely, his heart and intellect are formed harmoniously and justify the fairest promise." Novak to Baraga, Ljubljana, May 9, 1854. Orig. in MQDA; in BBC-B 1056 G. In September Lautishar went to Arbre Croche to learn the Indian language from Fr. Mrak. On June 14, 1858, Lautishar left Michigan to join Fr. Pierz. On December 3, 1858, a week before his thirty-eighth birthday, Lautishar froze

Aug. 14:    Arrived in Cross Village, and there, on the 15th offered mass and preached.

Aug. 16-17:    Offered mass and preached at Little Traverse.

Aug. 18:    To Chaboigan;[106] on the 19th about midnight, returned again to Mackinac.

Aug. 20:    In the evening left Mackinac, and on

Aug. 21:    the next morning arrived at Sault Sainte Marie where I received many letters, etc.[107]

Aug. 25:    Today I sail for Lake Superior on the "Samuel Ward".[108]

---

to death on Red Lake, Minnesota. He is buried at Calvary Cemetery in Duluth, Minnesota. His death was a great personal sorrow for Pierz and Baraga.

[106]Also called Sheboygan, it is located on the western side of Burt Lake in Cheboygan county. From Little Traverse one could canoe via Round Lake and Round River, Crooked Lake and the Maple River, which empties just south of the Indian village. The location was a permanent settlement since c. 1720. H. F. Walling, p. 59.

[107]One letter was from a French priest, Fr. Sebastian Duroc, whom Baraga immediately answered, assuring him of admittance to the Vicariate and giving him instructions for traveling to the Upper Peninsula, where "you will be able to do much good." Baraga to Duroc, Sault Ste. Marie, August 21, 1854. Orig. in PFAP; in BBC-A 495 F.

[108]Upon his return to Sault Ste. Marie in October, Baraga wrote an account of his missionary visits to his sister, Amalia Gressel, to ZD, to the Leopoldine Society, to PFAP, and to the WF. His accounts read: "After many tedious but unavoidable delays, Bishop Baraga, on August 21, arrived safely here in Sault Ste. Marie, in his see and future place of residence, to the most sincere contentment of his good children in Christ. But when they heard that he will soon go ahead again, they became sad. He knew that his poor children on Lake Superior also awaited him with yearning for a long time, and so he continued his journey at once on Aug[ust] 25, and arrived on the 27th at La Pointe, in this, his first mission on Lake Superior. Already for many years he had not been at all in La Pointe, and it was already a year since the Rev. Father Skolla had departed from there. The poor people were then so glad to see him once again, and that as a Rt. Rev. Bishop. At the same time they were also very grateful that he had brought them a missionary [Father Carie] with him who will stay with them.

"The Right Reverend stayed eight days in La Pointe, and during the entire time he was very intensively and very usefully occupied. There were nearly 100 confirmees, and these he had to prepare himself for confirmation by daily instruction, and had to hear all their confessions because the new missionary cannot as yet speak Indian. These eight days he gave instructions for confirmation, and most of the remaining time he spent in the confessional, because not only the confirmees, but nearly all the others came to confession. — This confirmation of his at La Pointe was the first in his own diocese.

"From La Pointe he went to Ontonagon which now is already a rather important little town on Lake Superior, and stayed there 12 days so as to bring the affairs of this very poor station somewhat in order. Also here he installed a new priest, an Irishman [Father Dunne], but who speaks also French well so that he

Aug. 27:     At noon, arrived at La Pointe.[109] Preached in the after-
             noon and announced confirmation. The entire week
             each evening, I instructed for confirmation, and al-
             ways heard confessions.

Sept. 3:     Confirmation at La Pointe; nearly 100 were con-
             firmed.

Sept. 4:     Arrived in Ontonagon.

---

also preaches in French. Here the Right Reverend Bishop also administered confirmation. But here he had only to hear the confessions of the Indians, of whom
there are only a few, and Germans. The priest heard the confessions of the Irish
and French. Here we had still another solemnity, namely, the blessing of the
nice and spacious church which the Catholics have built during his European
journey in the hope that he would bring them a priest with him, which, to their
great satisfaction, he also had done. This little town of Ontonagon is increasing
rapidly, and it is believed that it will become the most important town in Upper
Michigan.

"From Ontonagon he again came here [Sault Ste. Marie], but again for
only a short time, 4 days, during which he conferred tonsure and 4 minor orders on Mr. Thiele, a very promising incipient missionary. And then he went to
L'Anse, where for 10 years he had labored as a missionary. Here again the joy
of his dear children was great when their anxious wish, to see him as a bishop,
was finally fulfilled.

"In L'Anse he stayed 12 days, and, as at La Pointe, he again had to perform everything himself, instruct the confirmees and hear confessions himself,
because the missionary [Father Lemagie] who is now there was sent there just
to help, since he does not speak Indian. The one at the head [of the lake, Fr.
Angelus Van Paemel] had asked to be transferred to Arbre Croche. —

"Also here in L'Anse, all, or nearly all came to confession, and on October
1, in this mission of the Most Holy Name of Jesus, so dear to him, he administered confirmation, at which all were very much moved, his dear children as
well as the Right Reverend Bishop himself, so that he cried from emotion. The
emotion and edification with which they saw their Father and missionary, who
now stood before them with crozier and mitre, and heard him deliver before
them words of sincerest consolation in their language, was noteworthy and consoling. Most of our Indians have, indeed, seen bishops before, but they have
never heard one speak in their language.

"On the 7th inst[ant] he again arrived here, now to stay a longer time. Until now he was only on the journey and had no permanent place. Everywhere
he was only for a few days. Finally he is at home. It was a long journey.

"On the 11th inst[ant] the first ordination in Upper Michigan took place.
The Right Reverend Bishop conferred the sub-diaconate on the above mentioned Mr. Thiele. On the 18th inst[ant] he will receive the diaconate and on the
21st the holy priesthood; and on the 22nd he will celebrate his solemn first
mass here in our St. Mary's church, at which the Right Reverend Bishop will
preach. — All this is very noteworthy, for the Right Reverend as well as for
Sault Ste. Marie in general, because these are the first ordinations which he has
conferred in this newly established diocese.

"Yesterday were here confirmation and a solemn pontifical mass, the first
that have ever been celebrated in Sault Ste. Marie. There were 85 confirmees,
French, Irish and Indian." Baraga to WF, Sault Ste. Marie, October 16, 1854.
Printed in WF, xviii, 98–99; in BBC-A 685 G.

[109]Baraga accompanied Rev. Timothy Carie whom he placed at this mission.

| | |
|---|---|
| Sept. 10: | Administered confirmation, 20 persons. |
| Sept. 18: | Returned to the Sault where I received many letters, both good and bad. *On Sept[ember] 20, conferred the 4 minor orders on Mr. Thiele.*[110] |
| Sept. 22: | Went to L'Anse with "Captain Slow", and on |
| Sept. 25: | early morning arrived. |
| Oct. 1: | Confirmed 43 at L'Anse. |
| Oct. 6: | Today I departed from L'Anse on the "Baltimore" (after [attending] the [E]Payment of the L'Anse Indians[E]), and on the evening of |
| Oct. 7: | again arrived at the Sault. I H S Letters. |
| Oct. 11: | Today I administered to Mr. Thiele the sub-diaconate. |
| Oct. 15: | Today is noteworthy for me and for Sault Sainte Marie. I celebrated my first pontifical mass here (the first which has ever been celebrated here), and for the first time administered confirmation to 85, French, Irish, and Indian. |
| Oct. 18: | Mr. Thiele received the diaconate. (Johnson[111] has moved into my house.) |
| Oct. 21: | And today the priesthood. |
| Nov. 1: | [L]Anniversary of my Consecration.[L] Celebrated solemn pontifical mass. |

[110]Written in left margin. Henry Louis Thiele, a classical scholar, was born in Osnabruck, Hanover, in 1819. He had taught English and French and had worked for the *Wahrheitsfreund* in Cincinnati for five years by the time he met Baraga. His ordination was Baraga's first. Thiele served impressively in Eagle Harbor and its missions until the early 1860s. The isolation and loneliness of a remote station led to personal problems. In October 1862, he left the diocese for Cleveland. However, he returned in July 1864 and worked in Marquette and Rockland (including Ontonagon and the mining locations) until the fall of 1871. He went to Notre Dame, Indiana, where he taught for thirteen months until his death on August 17, 1873. Jacker wrote that his friend Thiele's story was too long and too sad to tell. Thiele always had a great devotion to Mary, Refuge of Sinners. EJP; in BBC-AR 13, pp. 7, 150.

[111]A year later Fr. Menet described Johnson as a "small boy." Menet to Hus, Sault Ste. Marie, September 27, 1855. He wrote that Baraga had paid "nothing for an orphan whom he brought along with him, and who has been here for over a year." Menet to Hus, Sault Ste. Marie, October 18, 1855. A few months later Menet, suggesting that Johnson was no longer with them, wrote: "We had in our care a child of 13 or 14 years of age." Menet to Hus, Sault Ste. Marie, March 30, 1856. Origs. in ACSM; in BBC-mss. 26.

Nov. 3:  Today the Rev. Thiele departed for his mission at Eagle Harbor.

Nov. 17:  Left the Sault for Mackinac[112] where I arrived on the 18th. — Misère! Three hundred thousand Misère!!![113]

Nov. 25:  Today for the first time I used E"burning fluid".E Excellent! <Not at all!>

Dec. 3:  Today I introduced here in Mackinac, at St. Ann's Church, the Archconfraternity of the Immaculate and Holy Heart of Mary for the conversion of sinners, and for the first time said mass on the altar of the Blessed Virgin Mary.

Dec. 12:  Today, finally, the Rev. Mr. Sebastian Duroc[114] arrived here, thanks be to God! I H S; and on the 13th, I took him to Pointe St. Ignace.

Dec. 20:  Today the Rev. Mr. Duroc has again returned to Mackinac to celebrate the Most Holy Nativity. I H S

Dec. 29:  Unpleasant gossip. Left [Samuel] Ab[bott]'s[115] boarding house; now taking board with Mrs. Todd.

## 1855

In Jan.  Busy with writing the "Kagige Debwewinan",[116] and the days pass by pleasantly and quickly for me; often Lfull days.L

Jan. 13:  This morning with a prayer and an address, I inaugurated the Society of St. Vincent de Paul,[117] which the

---

[112]Baraga had promised the Indians that he would return for an extended visit. He remained at Mackinac for the entire winter.

[113]Baraga found difficulties with the priests in the Mackinac–St. Ignace area (cf. D, June 27, 1855 ff.). This fact may explain his exclamation.

[114]Sebastian Duroc was from the Vosges area of France. He was the first pastor in Marquette, 1855–1864, after which he went to Bay de Noques (Escanaba). As administrator, Jacker dismissed Duroc who went briefly to France. Rezek, II. pp. 194, 365. In 1871 he returned to Ishpeming where his nephew, Honoratus Bourion, was pastor. Shortly afterwards they both left the diocese for Golden City, Colorado. Duroc was chaplain at St. Joseph's Home for Invalids in Denver Colorado, 1883–1886, his last known address. CALM, 1883–1886.

[115]Samuel Abbott was a convert of Fr. Mazzuchelli when he was stationed at Mackinac.

[116]*Eternal Truths Always to be Remembered by a Catholic Christian*, Cincinnati, 1855, 337 pp.

[117]The Society of St. Vincent de Paul was founded in Paris in May 1833 by Antoine

Rev. Mr. Jahan[118] had initiated, and which hopefully, will do much good. ⁵May God grant it!⁵

Feb. 1: Always engaged in writing the "Kagige Debwewinan," 6 or 7 or 8 pages a day.

Feb. 4: Today, the first Sunday of the month, we celebrated in pontificals the first procession of the Society of St. Vincent de Paul.

Feb. 10: Today I went to Pointe St. Ignace, and on the 11th gave confirmation there. Very many Indian confessions ———

March 4: Today, on the first Sunday of the month, ᴸpontifical massᴸ for the first general communion of the members of the Society of St. Vincent de Paul. And I also completed the "Kagige Debwewinan". 328 pages.

March 7: Today I began to translate the catechism into English for the schools, on the suggestion of Mr. Mrak.[119]

March 10: Today I again went to Pointe St. Ignace and confirmed 18 people, and on

---

Frederic Ozanam, a professor at the Sorbonne. Its members are lay men and women who practice the corporal and spiritual works of mercy. Each conference is organized within a parish.

[118]Eugene Jahan, a Frenchman, ordained on March 27, 1853, in Detroit by Bishop Lefevere, was assigned to Little Traverse, Chaboigan, Grand Traverse Bay, and finally at Mackinac where he was stationed when Baraga became bishop. He also established perpetual adoration of the Blessed Sacrament. BLS, January 16, 1856. Although he was unable to learn English or Ottawa, the Indians appreciated him for his excellent singing ability. In the fall of 1857 he transferred to the Diocese of Sandwich (Windsor, Canada) and worked with Canadian Indians until the 1880s when he returned to Paris.

[119]Ignatius Mrak was born in Carniola on October 16, 1810. He was ordained in 1837 and came to the United States in 1845 where he worked at Arbre Croche with Fr. Pierz. His entire missionary career was in the Arbre Croche–Grand Traverse area. Baraga regularly sent his new priests to work with Mrak to learn Ottawa and practical ministry. On November 20, 1859, Baraga made Mrak his vicar general. Twice, in 1860 and 1863, he wanted to return to Europe, although in 1861 Baraga named him as a possible successor. After his stroke, Baraga recommended Mrak as his co-adjutor with right of succession. Rezek, I, p. 194. Mrak was consecrated the second Bishop of Sault Ste. Marie and Marquette on February 7, 1869. In 1870 he attended the First Vatican Council. He retired for health reasons in 1879 although he continued to work, first among the Indians of Grand Traverse, then in some of the diocesan parishes and as chaplain for the sisters at the Marquette orphanage. Mrak died on January 2, 1901, and is buried in the Bishops' crypt at Saint Peter's Cathedral in Marquette.

March 11:    Third Sunday of Lent, founded the Society of St. Vincent de Paul, to which God the Lord may give his holy blessing.

March 24:    The translation of the Indian catechism is completed. ᴸFor whose advantage?ᴸ — ᴵWe shall see.ᴵ

April 8:     Easter Sunday. Pontificated, poorly, with only one untrained priest [Piret?], and he will always remain willingly untrained.

April 18:    Rode to the Bois Blanc Island in a sled; firm ice.

April 22:    Today I delivered my ᴱfarewell sermons in Mackinac.ᴱ

April 27:    Today we saw the first steamboat ("Michigan") arrive from Detroit, and it went to Green Bay. Mr. Theodore Wendell[120] brought good news [from Washington] about the government's continuation of the Indian payment.[121]

April 29:    (Sunday) Today the first propeller[122] from Chicago arrived at Mackinac and went to Detroit. But since it was Sunday I did not want to go aboard.

April 30:    Today another propeller came, ("Nile") and on this I arrived ᴱvery comfortablyᴱ on

May 2:       in Detroit, where, God be thanked a thousand times, I again found my trunk which had been lost.[123] I H S (ᴱ$600 in gold for Indian schools.ᴱ $600 still remains with Moore and Foote for the end of June or the middle of July.)

---

[120]Jacob A. T[heodore] Wendell (c. 1823–November 25, 1879) was a merchant at Mackinac, a state representative, collector of customs, and county supervisor. He accompanied a delegation of Ottawa to Washington in March 1855; he was also a protector of Indian property rights. *History of the Upper Peninsula*, p. 366. Wendell was often host to Baraga. In 1861 Napoleon III stayed with him; in the 1870s Fr. Jacker was his frequent guest. In 1850 his real estate was valued at $1500. Federal Census, 1850, Mackinac County, #290.

[121]Annual payments to the Indians were for land ceded to the United States by various treaties.

[122]Around 1840 "propellers" (steamboats propelled by a screw propeller in the water rather than paddle or side wheels) began appearing on the Great Lakes. They were small and efficient and were used primarily for transporting passengers. Quaife, *Lake Michigan*, p. 161.

[123]Since the previous August.

| | |
|---|---|
| May 4: | Today, at 10 A.M. arrived in Cincinnati, where I again found a hospitable welcome with F[ather] Hammer. |
| May 9: | Today I received the first proofsheets of the first version of "Kagige Debwew:[124] |
| May 13: | This Sunday the first Provincial Council of Cincinnati opens. |
| May 20: | Today the Provincial Council was solemnly concluded. |
| May 25: | Timothy McNamara[125] reported to me as schoolteacher for Little Traverse Bay. I H S |
| May 26: | Today I corrected the last sheets of "Kagige Debwewinan". Now I have only the title page, etc. (17 days)[126] |
| June 9: | I received the finished 14 Stations of the Cross. The pictures cost $12, and the pasting on the linen and varnish, $7. Altogether $19.00. |
| June 14: | Today my portrait from Lang[127] has been completed. $50. |
| June 20: | Journey from Cincinnati, via Sandusky to Detroit, with six school teachers.[128] |
| June 24: | Arrived at the Sault about 10 P.M. on the 23rd, and on the 24th preached in English and French. |
| June 26: | Arrived in Mackinac (stupidity because of Dousman's[129] house for $500). |

[124]Baraga came to the end of the line and apparently did not want to put only a few letters on the next line. Such a decision would reflect his carefulness to waste nothing. Baraga also had a fifth edition of the Indian prayerbook, *Anamie Masinaigan*, printed at this time. Pilling, p. 24.

[125]Hired as a teacher by Baraga in Cincinnati.

[126]Begun on May 9, the task of proofreading took seventeen days.

[127]Mateus Langus was a Slovenian artist and friend of Baraga. This portrait is the lithograph that Baraga mentioned in a letter to Amalia Gressel: "So now a lithograph of me has been arranged, with the inscription, 'Premier Eveque du Saut Ste. Marie.'" Baraga to Gressel, Mackinac, April 19, 1855. Printed in LZ, No. 162, July 28, 1855; in BBC-A 771 G.

[128]Baraga strove to provide English-speaking teachers for the Indian schools as the government required and the Indians had requested.

[129]Dousman is the name of a wealthy fur-trading family that still lives on Mackinac Island.

June 28:    Arrived at Cross Village, and on the following day
            immediately press [sic] on.[130]

June 29:    Arrived in Little Traverse.[131]

July 1:     Confirmation at Little Traverse.

[130]Lautishar described this visit: "On the afternoon of June 28 he [Baraga] came from
Mackinac in a canoe; a number of Indians were with him. The canoes of the Indians are very much like the boats on the Ljubljana river. Since he was not expected on this day, not many Indians were at home. As many as there were
came hastily as soon as they heard the bell ring and knelt to receive the blessing
of their dear bishop. In the evening all the men gathered in the school where
they wanted to talk with the bishop. The next day at 6 he said mass and
preached; it was the feast of Sts. Peter and Paul, but, in the 'United States' it is
not a holyday. Then we went to Little Traverse (Crooked Tree), and I accompanied him. Since the wind was contrary, the Indians had to pull the boat by a
rope for the distance, 7 hours. Between Cross Village and Arbre Croche is Middle Village with a church; it is in my mission; all the Indians gathered on the
shore because they had learned that the bishop was to pass by. We all went into
the church where the bishop gave them a short speech and then we went further. In the evening at 6 we came to Little Traverse. There the bishop preached,
confessed, taught the children and some of them he confirmed. Then he went to
another village where there is also a church. Friday, July 6 he again returned
and in the afternoon he came to Middle Village where I was waiting for him
and preparing a class for holy confirmation. He remained there Saturday and
Sunday; he preached and confessed, and on Sunday, the 8th, he administered
holy confirmation. On Monday we set out towards Cross Village. The next day
we went on an island . . . ; we left at 9 and in the evening at 6 we were there.
Also here he labored as usual; he administered holy confirmation to 44, most of
whom were adults. A bishop was never here before. Father Fred[eric] Baraga
was the first priest to announce the holy gospel on this island and he was also
the first bishop to come there. Here poverty is especially great. In the church
there was not even a stool on which the bishop could kneel; he had to kneel on
the floor. We returned Friday afternoon. On Sunday he administered holy confirmation in the home church [Cross Village] and on Monday he returned to
Mackinac, to where I accompanied him." Lautishar to ZD, VIII, 185–86, September 6, 1855; in BBC-B 590 S.

[131]Baraga also described the journey in four identical letters. The letter to the *Wahrheitsfreund* is as follows:
    "To comply somewhat with the wishes of the Catholic friends of the mis-
sions, I give here a brief report of my visitation journey of this year to the missions in and around Arbre Croche which I had established and attended more
than twenty years ago. Since that time these missions have increased very much
and now, in most of them, there are no more pagans. But in some there are one
or more pagans who still stubbornly resist all efforts of the missioners and the
influencing examples of the converted Indians that surround them. However,
these pagans have become very rare. In these missions almost all are converted.
    "On June 29th, (on my 58th birthday), I arrived at Arbre Croche which
was my first mission station. On May 25th, 1831, 24 years ago, my first bishop
in America, Edward Fenwick, brought me to this mission, which I took over
with a grateful heart and deep emotions.
    "Now I remained here several days and during the entire time I instructed
the Indians and heard confessions, and on Sunday, July 1st, I administered holy

July 3:   Arrived in Chaboigan, and on the 4th heard confessions the entire day.

July 5:   Returned to Little Traverse where I found Flinn to whom I gave $100.

---

confirmation for the first time in my first mission. True, I was here last August, but I did not confirm because only a short time before Bishop Lefevere of Detroit confirmed here.

"I arranged for confirmation on the next Sunday in a mission that I have founded 24 years ago, but where this holy sacrament has as yet never been administered. In the simple mission church, built by the poor Indians themselves, they saw, with great spiritual joy, their bishop, in full vestments, preach to them and administer the holy sacrament of confirmation.

"From here I once more sailed in an Indian boat, after so many years, to Beaver Island which lies in the middle of Lake Michigan and is so far from firm land that it is scarcely visible as a streak of mist. As I was the first priest who 24 years ago stepped on this island, so now I was the first bishop who ever visited it. All the inhabitants of this island, who live very simply and peacefully, are now converted to the Catholic religion, because the missioners who were my successors in this mission have visited them frequently and have preached to them until all were converted.

"My visit to this romantic island was joyful and stirring for me and these simple children of nature. Many old Indian men and women came to me, knelt down to receive the bishop's blessing and then with gratitude and deep emotion said to me: 'Father, you baptized me, you certainly did, long, long time ago.' Others said: 'My parents have told me that you had baptized me, but at that time I was yet a very small child.' And now they themselves have several small children around them. They now were very pleased to receive the bishop's blessing from their old missioner, from whom they or their parents first learned to pronounce the holy names of Jesus and Mary. And now I began with instructions and hearing of confessions, and administered to them, with deep emotion, holy confirmation. At this time forty-four received this holy sacrament on Beaver Island. Next time I come here those who are not yet well-enough instructed will be confirmed. In one house two Indian women were sick in bed. They were sad because they could not come to the church and receive holy confirmation. — I therefore went into their house, heard their confessions and instructed them, and the next day, I administered to them, on their sick-bed, and to their great consolation, this holy sacrament.

"From Beaver Island I went to a mission known as Cross Village and where the Rev. Father Lawrence Lautishar is missioner. At the time I took care of these missions the converted Indians erected a large cross in their village, which since has often been renewed. From this cross the village received its name. Until now Father Mrak had been there for many years, but this spring, at his own request and with my consent, he has moved to another mission which I will mention later.

"The Indians of Cross Village are well instructed and good Christians; they are the best Indians that we have. Father Mrak was here nine years and has conscientiously fulfilled his duties as a missioner, for which may God the Lord bless him. Father Lautishar, his successor, is a zealous and pious missioner who makes a great effort to continue the good work begun by his predecessor. The short time in which he has learned the Indian language is astonishing. He came to this mission last fall and with great diligence he immediately began to study the Indian grammar and to translate the Indian books we have. And now for 2

| | |
|---|---|
| July 6: | To Abitawaiing,[132] where on the 7th, I was ready all day for confessions; on the 8th, Sunday, preached and confirmed. |
| July 9: | Arrived at Cross Village, and on |
| July 10: | sailed to Beaver Island[133] (in 8 hours). Here I remained 3 days and heard everyone's confession, and on |
| July 13: | confirmed 44 Indians on Beaver Island. Then on the same day returned to Cross Village. |
| July 15: | Confirmation at Cross Village, about 20. |
| July 16: | Again arrived at Mackinac, and on |
| July 17: | departed for Grand Traverse on the propeller "Stockman". |
| July 18: | Landed at Grand Traverse, at <u>Northport</u>. On the following day journeyed to and arrived at Pishabetown. |
| July 22: | Confirmed at Grand Traverse, Pishabetown, 31 people. |
| July 24: | Returned to Mackinac where I await with longing for an opportunity to go to the Sault. Alas, little chance, misère. |
| July 29: | FUnfortunatelyF just on <u>Sunday</u>, after I had waited in |

---

months he is alone in his mission, without an interpreter, (whom he has never used), and catechizes, hears confessions and preaches better than I could at the end of my second year as a missioner. (To be sure, at that time there was no grammar, no dictionary and no book from which one could have learned this entirely peculiar language). Father Lautishar's progress is a surprise to all. He now speaks also English with some fluency and could very well hear English confessions; however, he seldom has occasion for this.

"The last mission station I visited was Grand Traverse where Rev. Father Mrak is now stationed. Previously, a missioner had never settled here, although I and all my successors came here frequently until now, but only for a few days or weeks. The Indians of this mission are very humble and willing. I hope that the meritorious and experienced missioner Mrak, who now lives with them, will instruct them in everything that is good and keep them in a good christian disposition. On July 22nd I administered confirmation there to 31 persons, children and adults. On the 30th I returned to Saut Ste. Marie from where, in a few days, I shall undertake a visitation journey to the missions on Lake Superior." Baraga to WF, Sault Ste. Marie, August 4, 1855. Printed in WF, XVIII, 616–17; in BBC-A 706 G.

[132]Middle Village.

[133]The Indians were actually on Garden Island, a short distance northeast of Beaver Island.

vain all week, an opportunity presented itself [to sail] on the "Illinois" for the Sault.

July 30: Arrived at Sault Sainte Marie where I received many letters, both good and bad.

July 31: Today I conferred the minor order on Mr. Jacker.[134]

Aug. 1: Mr. Jacker received the sub-diaconate.

Aug. 4: Mr. Jacker received the diaconate, and on the 5th, priesthood.

Aug. 8: Today Rev. Mr. Dunne departed from here for New York, Louisville, Boston.

Aug. 9: Sailed from the Sault on the "Illinois", and on the 10th, via Marquette,

Aug. 11: arrived in Eagle River, and departed at once for Eagle Harbor, where on the 12th, (Sunday), I offered mass and then departed.

Aug. 14: Arrived at L'Anse with Rev. Mr. Jacker and Mr. Branen.[135]

[134]Edward Jacker was born in Ellwangen in the diocese of Rottenburg, Germany, on September 2, 1827. Although he came to the United States to become a Benedictine at St. Vincent Abbey in Latrobe, Pennsylvania, where he received the name of Brother Bede, he responded to the need for missionaries to the Indians. Baraga accepted him and ordained him on August 5, 1855, and sent him to L'Anse. He worked in the L'Anse-Houghton-Hancock area until 1866 when Baraga called him to Marquette to administer the diocese while he was at the Second Plenary Council of Baltimore. Because of Baraga's stroke at Baltimore, Jacker remained administrator and assistant. He was present at Baraga's death and gave the eulogy. Upon Mrak's consecration in 1869, Jacker was made Vicar General until 1873. During Mrak's absence for the Vatican Council in 1870, Jacker administered the diocese. Upon Mrak's return, Jacker was sent to begin the new parish in Calumet. In 1873 he went to St. Ignace, where he researched and discovered the grave of Fr. Jacques Marquette. Upon Mrak's resignation, he was again diocesan administrator. After Vertin's appointment, Jacker went to Hancock. He resigned the parish in the spring in 1886, going to Detour and Marquette, where he died on September 1, 1887, a day before his sixtieth birthday. He was buried in the Catholic cemetery in Hancock. In 1862, he had adopted Philomena (Millie) Mertz, upon the death of her parents, and supported her until 1872 when she married Peter Ruppe, Jr., in Calumet. Throughout his life he was especially interested in nurturing young clergy; he was also a researcher and writer. His notes on the first thirty-five years of the diocese are invaluable. His library was esteemed as one of the most complete in the region. Rezek, II, pp. 376–80. EJP, in BBC-AR 13, passim.

[135]Thomas Branen was the schoolteacher in L'Anse from August 1855 until July 1858.

Aug. 16:      Departed from L'Anse with Rev. C. Lemagie,[136] and on the 17th arrived at Eagle River, where I wait for a steamboat for La Pointe.

Aug. 18:      Today I sailed on the "Northerner" for La Pointe, and on the 19th, afternoon, (misère), arrived here.

Aug. 23:      Today Rev. Mr. Carie[137] left La Pointe, and Rev. Mr. Van Paemel[138] arrived to take his place on the same day.

Aug. 26:      Confirmation at La Pointe, 37 people.

Sept. 1:      Mr. Hickey[139] has begun boarding with Ant[oine] Gaudin,[140] (even before the 1st); Rev. Mr. Van Paemel somewhat later, but cost begins for both from Sept[ember] 1.

Sept. 4:      Today I left La Pointe[141] at 4 P.M. on the fast moving

---

[136]In July 1854 Rev. Charles Lemagie joined Baraga in New York, and in August Baraga brought him to L'Anse. Lemagie built a sawmill in L'Anse and apparently stole boards from Captain Bendry. BLS, July 25, 1855. Baraga sent Lemagie his Exeat on June 25, 1855. BLS. From L'Anse he left the diocese. On November 12, 1858, Baraga wrote to him, "I owe you nothing. You have caused enough damage." BLS. Lemagie is listed at New London, Wisconsin, in CALM, 1868.

[137]Timothy Carie was born in Montpelier, France. In 1854 Baraga took him to La Pointe. After leaving La Pointe he went to the Mackinac–St. Ignace area. He was erratic in both his private and public conduct, and Baraga finally dismissed him in the spring of 1858.

[138]Angelus Van Paemel, a Belgian, was ordained in Detroit in 1850. In 1853, after Van Paemel had spent two years among the Indians in Arbre Croche, Baraga asked Bishop Lefevere to send him to L'Anse. He tended both L'Anse and La Pointe from the fall of 1853 until August 1855, when he was permanently assigned to La Pointe. In September 1859, after violence and threats upon his life in Bad River, he returned to Belgium for health reasons. Van Paemel returned to the Sault in the summer of 1861. In November he returned to Belgium. In 1868 he became a "Gentleman's chaplain" and pastor of a small congregation in Leicestershire, England.

[139]Michael Hickey was one of the six English-speaking teachers whom Baraga hired in Cincinnati. Cf. D, June 20, 1855.

[140]Gaudin was a 33-year-old clerk in La Pointe. He was married and, by 1850, had three children. Federal Census, 1850; La Pointe File in BBC. He served as interpreter for Fr. Skolla at La Pointe, 1845–1853. Acta et Dicta, VII, No. 2 (October 1936), pp. 217–68. He also assisted Fr. Van Paemel and Fr. Chebul.

[141]Great Chief Buffalo of La Pointe died on September 7 at the age of 96. Richard Morse wrote that: "During the life of the great chief, if importuned in regard to his religious belief and duty, he has been known frequently to say, 'he would be baptized when he died.' Truly was his saying verified. Two days before his death, he received the baptismal rite in the Catholic faith. Three days after baptism, funeral dirges for Ke-che-waish-ke were sung at the Cathedral [sic] of La Pointe, and within the cemetery of that church repose the earthly remains of the

"Northstar",[142] and at 9 P.M. (5 hours) came to Ontonagon!

Sept. 5: Arrived at Eagle River at 4 A.M. and that same morning departed overland for L'Anse, where on

Sept. 6: I arrived at noon.[143]

---

most illustrious chief of the Chippewas." Morse, p. 366. The La Pointe Baptismal Registry contains no entries between September 2 and 9. Conjecture continues about whether he was baptized by Baraga, Carie, Van Paemel, or by a lay
person. The chief's gravestone, chipped on the top, stands within a few yards of
the historical marker on the site of Baraga's first church on La Pointe.

[142]The *Northstar* was placed in service in 1854. She was one "of the most lavishly fit-
ted out steamers on the Great Lakes" and "the fastest, being the first to make
sixteen miles [sic] per hour." She left from Cleveland on July 15, 1855, the same
day that the Sault Ste. Marie Canal was open, on her first through trip to Duluth, stopping at Ontonagon and other ports. Heyl, III, p. 259. In August 1861,
Prince Napoleon and his entourage sailed on the *Northstar* from Cleveland to
Bayfield and to Mackinac Island. Pisani, pp. 163–229.

[143]The German cartographer, John G. Kohl, described this trip: "Bishop Baraga and I
left La Pointe and arrived at Eagle River the next evening, or I should say at
3:00 A.M. They came to get us in a canoe and shortly we were on the shore of the
desolate peninsula of Keweena[w] Point. We immediately went to the hut of a
poor Canadian fisherman, a former so-called 'Voyageur' whom my bishop
knew. We convinced him to accompany us on our trip across the peninsula. His
wife, an Indian woman, prepared breakfast which consisted of boiled fish fresh
from the water and the water in which the fish was cooked, which these good
people call 'tea'. Since the liturgical objects of my beloved companion (crosses,
crozier, vestments, chalice, silver vessels for the 3 oils, etc.) are quite heavy, and
since we could get no one to accompany us, we had to limit ourselves to the es-
sentials, what we were able to carry. We left behind our capes and coats, and
buried all unneeded things in the sand along Magnant's hut (that was the Canadian's name). At 6:00 A.M. we were on our way. To the place where we could
begin our travel by canoe at Torch Lake we had a trek of 22 miles. A good part
of the trip was through unbroken forest such as one finds everywhere in America and in which one always finds oneself with one foot in the mud while the
other searches, (often in vain) for a solid footing on some wooden tree limb.

   "Our shoulders laden, the Canadian Magnant, cheerful as usual, led the
way, then came my bishop, and I behind them. Below the bishop wore his high
boots, smeared with grease, for use in the water. Above he wore a gold chain,
with a large gold cross on his chest, and a large brilliant fisherman's ring on his
finger. I myself was burdened with a few books, maps, papers, tobacco pouch,
etc. We cut long poles for ourselves in the woods. The patience which a person
must exercise on such a footpath exceeds all imagination. At times we waded
for whole hours through bottomless mud. Occasionally every vestige of any
path disappears beneath the boughs which had been gathered by the wind (the
so-called 'renversis' of the Canadians). We nevertheless crawled through and
over this underbrush, not knowing at times, whether to call this the most tiring
or the most comical and entertaining experience that we underwent.

   "In regard to the bishop, the most interesting individual of these areas, I
must tell you that he had lived up here 25 [23] years already and that he has
covered, as an Indian missionary, all the wilderness in and around Lake Superior. He is small but sturdy, already 60 [58] years old. They had spoken to me

Sept. 10:       Departed from L'Anse overland; on the evening of the 11th I arrived at Eagle River, and from there on

Sept. 12:       arrived in Eagle Harbor, where I did not find Rev. Mr. Thiele since he had departed on Sept[ember] 2 for Detroit.

Sept. 16:       Early in the morning sailed from Eagle Harbor on the "Manhattan", and on

---

about him previously: Bishop Baraga is made of iron. Nothing holds him back and he lives even in places where an Indian would die of starvation. I didn't believe any of this till I saw it for myself. In the 25 years he has never been sick. With all this, he doesn't have much physical strength but he does have an iron will. He even fell in front of me a few times and occasionally I was fearful for him and had to help him. Despite his weak constitution he goes everywhere straight ahead and Providence, which is always with him, helps him everywhere. After various experiences we arrived on the shores of Torch Lake at 5:00 P.M. This lake is 25 miles long and with its inlets is about the size of Badensee, perhaps larger. Three persons live along its shores: the Scotchman Beasely, the Indian 'Little Frenchman' and the Canadian Picard, all three single, living in poor huts as hunters of wild game. From Beasely we got a canoe, while Picard loaned us an oar and some woolen blankets. Laden with these we made another 15 miles, through the quiet and solitude of the night, to the hut of the 'Little Frenchman'. During this trip my good bishop mostly dozed over his breviary. As for me I had enough chores that I can now recall and jot down my impressions of the phenomena about me. Unfortunately my travelling companion was far from receptive of the impressions of nature. . . . In that regard I was surprised that he did not know too much about the history of the region and was completely indifferent to the ethnographic origins of the Indians. All that was not Christian among them or capable of becoming such, did not interest him. Yes, all that concerned them, even their remarkable Monotheism, was the devil's work. At first we even had some heated discussions over this. But I soon realized what I shall have to forego completely in my relations with this outstanding travelling scholar. To this day we have had a good rapport and I hope he is as satisfied with me as I am with him. . . .

"At the Catholic Mission the small church bell rang out. All the Indians fired a salvo then knelt down along the shore to receive the blessing of their good bishop. He arrived totally unexpectedly since he apparently did not have himself announced. In his house, a wooden annex which had been built against the church, nothing else was prepared except the Indian bed such as we had the night before (boards, a mat and a blanket). . . . For breakfast, noon and evening I met with the bishop in the hut of the Indian with whom I was staying and whose wife prepared our fish for us. My good bishop, in regard to taste, has become such a good Indian, that he doesn't salt his fish. Indians do not use salt. Instead they sometimes pour some maple syrup over the fish. . . . In the evening . . . my good bishop returned early to his cell. . . .

"We returned to Eagle River . . . There I stayed with my dear bishop for 3 days at his modern church." Upon the return to the Sault, Kohl added the comment: "With good Father Baraga who in regard to politics is completely neutral, I greatly missed this sympathy." Kohl to his sister, Grand River, September 24, 1855. Printed in AMK, 1977, pp. 128–31; in BBC-B 1278 G.

Sept. 17:     before noon, arrived at the Sault, where I received many letters.

Sept. 18:     Conferred on Mr. Fox[144] the minor orders, and on the 19th the subdiaconate, on the 21st, the diaconate.

Sept. 20:     Today before noon, Mr. Auguste Eugene Benoit[145] arrived.

Sept. 23:     Mr. Fox received the priesthood, and on the 24th he sailed on the "Northstar" for Ontonagon, where he will celebrate his first holy mass and then labor as a missionary. May God's blessing be with him.

Sept. 24:     Mr. Benoit received the subdiaconate;

Sept. 29:     the diaconate, and on

[144]Martin Fox was the third priest ordained by Baraga. He was born in Koenigsberg, Prussia, c. 1825. As a seminarian, he was studying in Paris for the foreign missions when Baraga recruited him in 1854. Baraga sent Fox to Dublin to complete his theology and to learn English. Immediately after his ordination Baraga sent him as assistant to Rev. Dunne in Ontonagon and Minnesota Mine (the "Irish Hollow" or Rockland). In March 1856, Baraga divided the jurisdiction and appointed Fox pastor of the "Mine" where he served until 1868. His zeal, learning, and life-style occasioned Baraga to send newly ordained priests to work under his direction. In 1858 he had the distinction of being the first pastor to have a real pipe organ, which Baraga ordered for his church (an instrument still in use). In 1861 Baraga proposed his name as a future bishop. The following year Fox also became chaplain for the Ursuline Sisters who came from New York to Ontonagon where they conducted a girls' academy until 1867. After Baraga's death, Jacker appointed Fox pastor of the Cathedral in Marquette. On October 18, 1870, he left the diocese for Iowa but returned in 1872. He served in Menominee, Escanaba and the Lake Michigan shores, Stephenson, Spalding, Champion, Ishpeming, and Republic, where he died on March 21, 1881. He is interred at Holy Cross Cemetery in Marquette.

[145]Benoi[s]t was recruited when Baraga was in Europe. He was intended eventually for the Indian missions at Fort William but was sent to learn Indian with Van Paemel at La Pointe. He remained there until he returned to Europe in July 1858. He retained his interest in the missions and sent an organ from Paris to Father Chebul. Chebul to Globocnek, Bayfield, March 4, 1865. Chebul MSS, AR 29, p. 45; in BBC-B 1292 S. Antoine Gaudin respected Benoist: "Mr. Pamel [sic] and I often go there [Bad River] and at times, also Mr. Benois [sic], a truly fine priest. I am concerned since Mr. Benois is going to go to Grand Portage. Even though there are priests there, I am afraid his efforts will be extremely limited because so few Indians are there. He is a tremendous speaker and I have much affection for him." Gaudin to Manypenny, La Pointe, March 24, 1856. Orig. in NA-OIA; in BBC-A 446 C (enclosure).

Sept. 30:     the Priesthood, and on

Oct. 2:       offered his first holy mass.

Oct. 3:       I founded here in Sault Sainte Marie the Archconfra-
              ternity of the Most Holy and Immaculate Heart of the
              Blessed Virgin Mary.

Oct. 12:      To Marquette. Confirmed 30 persons. On Oct[ober] 15
              I returned to the Sault.

Oct. 16:      Mr. Thiele arrived from Cincinnati and went on to
              Eagle Harbor.

Oct. 23:      Mr. J. B. Weikamp[146] arrived and promised that possi-
              bly yet this year or certainly by next spring, to come to
              Little Traverse with his entire community.

N.B. on Oct[ober] 21 (Sunday) it began to snow ᴸabundantly.ᴸ The snow
              remained on the ground and increases. <(Oct[ober] 29.
              Already all the snow is gone, but soon more will be
              coming. None arrives until Nov[ember] 7.>

Oct. 29:      Mr. Steinhauser, who came here with Mr. Weikamp,
              has departed for Mackinac.

Oct. 30:      Mr. Benoit has left for La Pointe and from there to Fort
              William.

Nov. 7:       Today Mary Joseph Henry[147] was invested.

Nov. 9:       Departed from Sault Sainte Marie, and on

[146]John Baptist Weikamp, O.S.F., a native of Bocholt, Westphalia, Germany, came to
    Chicago in 1850, to Little Traverse in 1855, and to Cross Village in 1856. He
    was superior of the "Benevolent, Charitable, and Religious Society of St. Fran-
    cis," a community of ten men and eleven sisters. Although Baraga suspended
    him as pastor at Cross Village at the end of 1861, he resided there until his
    death on March 9, 1889.
[147]Miss Mary Henry [Mother Mary Joseph] was born on January 6, 1823, the daugh-
    ter of James and Ellen O'Regan Henry of Drumegarner, Londonderry County,
    Ireland. She came to the Sault, via Philadelphia, in 1855. Although she suffered
    grave illnesses in the 1860s, she regained her health and after a lifetime of
    teaching and service within the community she died at the age of 89, at
    Chatham, Ontario, on March 4, 1915.

Nov. 10:        arrived in Mackinac.

Nov. 14:        Arrived in Pointe St. Ignace.

Nov. 26:        From Pointe St. Ignace to Island of St. Helena, where I remained on the 27th and on

Nov. 28:        left by small boat and on the evening of the same day arrived at Little Traverse Bay, where I met, to my great joy, Rev. Fr. Weikamp who had arrived only a short time before.[148] I H S

---

[148]Baraga expressed his satisfaction with this development in a letter to the *Detroit Catholic Vindicator:* "Dear Sir: — As I suppose that whatever regards the prosperity of our Indian missions, is interesting to yourself and to many of your readers, I send you for insertion in your valuable paper, the following statement of a happy event in the Mission of L'Arbre Croche, or Little Traverse Bay. This was my first mission among the Indians, which I commenced in the Spring of 1831. When I was here last summer, I promised that I would come again soon and stay some time with them. I intend to remain here until the end of January, next, and then return to Sault St. [sic] Marie. On my arrival here I felt truly happy, when I saw that the Rev. Father Wiecamp [sic] had already arrived here with his religious community. Father Wiekamp [sic] has been in America a long time, and belongs to the third order of St. Francis. He lived before, in Chicago, where he gathered around him a considerable Society of Brothers and Sisters of his Order. His desire has been for some time past, to establish his community rather in the country than in a large city; and when he heard of our missions, he came to me at Sault St. [sic] Marie and consulted me in regard to his plan. I at once invited him to come and settle down in our missions with his whole society, consisting of ten brothers and eleven sisters; and to that purpose I ceded to him a portion of land which I had bought last year, in the vicinity of Arbre Croche. On this land he intends to settle permanently, to cultivate the soil with his brothers, and to establish a new mission. Two of his brothers wish to become missionaries, and will be ordained in due time. Next Saturday, on the feast of the Immaculate Conception of the Blessed Virgin Mary, they wil receive in our Missionary Church Tonsure, and the four minor Orders.

"When I was a Missionary here, I never thought that a time would come when I should confer minor Orders on anybody.

"The whole community will remain here in the mission-village this winter, and some of the brothers and Sisters are keeping separate schools for boys and girls.

"The land I ceded to them lies about five miles from here, on the southern side [Petosky] of Little Traverse Bay, and as they cannot move there this winter, they will move next spring, and build a church and several houses.

"I consider the arrival of the religious community as a most happy event for the L'Arbre Croche Mission." Baraga to DCV, III, 35:2; in BBC-A 659 E.

Dec. 8: *Tonsure and minor order to Frater Ludwig (Sifferath)[149] and Frater Seraphine Zorn.[150*151]

Dec. 28: Spent the evening and night at Little Traverse Bay. The ice froze so hard that on

Dec. 29: There were many skaters on the ice in the bay. <(On the following day the ice broke up again.)>

N.B. Dec[ember] 25 — First communion for 18 Indians, and 22 confirmations.[152]

[149]Nicholas Louis Sifferath, O.F.M., was born on December 12, 1828, at Beckendorf, Germany. He was ordained at Sault Ste. Marie by Baraga on August 23, 1857. He was sent to Little Traverse to work with Lautishar and to be his successor. In 1863 he went to Cross Village. Sifferath composed *A Short Compendium of the Catechism for the Indians*, to which Baraga gave his approbation in 1864 although the book was not published until 1869. BBC-V77-48. In 1868, after Bishop Lefevere resumed jurisdiction, Sifferath was suspended for refusing to shave his beard and to accept a new assignment. Under Bishop Borgess he was reinstated in 1877 and assigned to various hospital and religious chaplaincies in southern Michigan. He died at Kalamazoo, Michigan, on March 11, 1898. Sifferath had a brother, Phillip, who was a brother in the Franciscan community. In 1877 Phillip died a tragic (though unexplained) death. EJP; in BBC-AR 13, p. 160.

[150]Philip Seraphin Zorn, O.F.M., was born on August 15, 1825, at Bernfelden, Germany. Baraga ordained him to the priesthood on January 20, 1856, at Little Traverse. When the community moved to Cross Village in 1856, Zorn remained at Little Traverse for a year to learn Ottawa and ministry from Lautishar. Zorn then went to Cross Village, and in 1861 Baraga removed Weikamp as head of the mission and placed Zorn in charge. For twenty years he served all the Indian missions of the region; the 1881 *Almanac* noted his asignment to one parish (Little Traverse), four missions, and nine stations. His dismissal from the Franciscan Community in 1883 caused him great pain for the rest of his life. The newly created Diocese of Grand Rapids accepted him and assigned him to the Indian Mission of Elbridge and later to the chaplaincy of Mercy Hospital in Big Rapids. Zorn died on April 14, 1900, in Manistee where he is interred. Jacker wrote often and with admiration of Zorn's zeal. The Indians called him Wassigijig, "Bright-Heaven."

[151]The entire entry was written in the left margin.

[152]Baraga wrote an account of the Christmas festivities: "Dear Sir — Please insert in your valuable paper, the following brief report: Yesterday was a most remarkable day for our mission; it was the most glorious day it ever saw. The Right Rev. Bishop Baraga spends with us the first half of this winter. On Christmas night, soon after midnight, he celebrated pontifical mass, Rev. Mr. Wiekamp [sic], who came to this mission lately with his community of the Third Order of St. Francis, served as Deacon, and Rev. Mr. Steinhauser, the missionary of this

## 1856

Jan. 1–7:      At Chaboigan, where on Jan[uary] 6 I had 10 first communions and 4 confirmations.

Jan 15:      Mr. Seraphine Zorn recevied the subdiaconate. On the 18th he received the diaconate, and on the 20th Septuagesima, the priesthood.[153] Established a scapular confraternity. O.A.M.D.G.[154] I H S

---

place, as Sub-Deacon. The church was so crowded that we were apprehensive of some accident; the Indians from all the surrounding places flocked to Little Traverse Bay, to witness a ceremony such as they never saw before. We had regular church music, and most edifying singing by the Sisters of the Third Order, who brought a large melodian [sic] with them. At four o'clock there was another high mass, with an impressive and appropriate German sermon, by the Rev. Mr. Weikamp, for his community. Afterwards the other masses were celebrated till after nine o'clock. At ten o'clock the Rt. Rev. Bishop sung [sic] another pontifical mass, with the same assistant. At this solemn mass first communion was given by the Bishop to 18 persons, whom he had been preparing for it every evening since his arrival amongst us. Before communion he made them a touching sermon in Indian, from the bottom of his paternal heart. — After mass the Bishop called to the rails those that he had prepared for confirmation, and after making them another paternal admonition, he administered this holy sacrament to 22 persons. The church was again overcrowded to its utmost capacity, and all were edified and delighted by what they saw and heard. In the afternoon Vespers was in Indian, as usual, alternately by the Indians and the sisters of the Third Order, who accompanied the singing with their delightful melodian [sic]. Such was the religious performance on the most solemn day of the Little Traverse Indian Mission." Baraga to DCV, Little Traverse, December 26, 1855. Printed in DCV, III, 39:2; in BBC-A 661 E.

[153]Baraga described the event: "An extraordinary solemnity took place yesterday in our Missionary Church at Little Traverse Bay, which caused much spiritual joy to the Indians of the whole surrounding country. One of the members of Rev. Father Weikamp's religious Society . . . was raised yesterday to the dignity of the Priesthood, by the Rt. Rev. Bishop Baraga. The spacious Missionary Church of Little Traverse was over-crowded on this occasion. — The Indians from the southern side of Little Traverse Bay, those of Shaboigan, of Middletown, and of Mr. Lautishar's Mission at Cross Village, came in great numbers to our Mission to witness a ceremony which none of them had ever seen before. Even many people from Mackinac, over 50 miles distant, honored our Indian Mission with a visit on this solemn occasion. This morning the newly ordained priest, Rev. Father Seraphin Zorn, celebrated his first mass, and the church was again crowded. . . . Our good Indians were quite delighted and thankful to see a worthy religious man become a Missionary, who intends to devote his whole future existence to the Indian Missions." Baraga to DCV, Arbre Croche, January 21, 1856. Printed in DCV, III, 42:2; in BBC-A 440 E.

[154]"Omnia ad majorem Dei gloriam" — "All for the greater glory of God."

| | |
|---|---|
| Jan. 21: | Left Little Traverse Bay. Remained in Cross Village until the 27th, Sexagesima. Established a scapular confraternity also in Cross Village on Jan[uary] 27. |
| Jan. 28: | From Cross Village to Pointe St. Ignace. Very dissatisfied with the crazy T[imothy] C[arie]. . . . |
| Jan. 29: | From Pointe St. Ignace up to Bellanger,[155] by ᶠdogsledᶠ. |
| Jan. 30–31: | From Bellanger to Sault Sainte Marie. |
| Feb. 1: | Arrived at the Sault.[156] I H S |
| Feb. 13: | Investment of Miss Doyle.[157] |
| Feb. 20: | Rev. F. Carie came here. Perhaps needlessly. Or not. Misère. |
| Feb. 22: | This morning at half past seven my right ear plugged up so that now I hear just as little with it as with the left. If it should remain so, then I can no longer hear |

[155]Andre Bellanger was the first settler at Carp River, fourteen miles north of St. Ignace. Fr. Jacker wrote that he "was French Canadian, an ancient voyageur, and uncommonly monosyllabic for one of his race." His lodgings were "festooned with bunches of corn ears. Downstairs bed music . . . there are French, Irish and Indian ingredients in their voices. The old folks make arrangements as to the division of available space and bed-clothes for the night, all in excellent humor." Jacker to Finotti, St. Ignace, October 10, 1878. EJP; in BBC-AR 13, p. 165.

[156]Among the letters waiting for him was one from the Propagation of the Faith in Paris with 1357 francs and the promise of 12,000 francs for 1855. In his letter of thanks Baraga also mentioned: "The first provincial council of Cincinnati has given me (upon the suggestion of Cardinal Fransoni) the name of 'Episcopus Sanctae Mariae'; in French; Bishop of Sault Sainte Marie." Baraga to Choiselat, Sault Ste. Marie, February 5, 1856. Orig. in PFAP; in BBC-A 473 F.

[157]Catherine Doyle [Mother M. Angela], the daughter of Thomas and Anne Kensella Doyle, was born on May 18, 1836, in Dublin, Ireland. In 1852, after the death of her mother and sister, Louise, she and her father came to Philadelphia. After the community moved to Chatham she became the General Mistress of the Boarding and Day School, a position she held for thirty-five years. In 1896, when Bishop Vertin invited the Sisters to St. Ignace, Mother Angela came with her former pupil, Mother M. Augustine McCabe, to establish the Academy of Our Lady of the Straits. After sixteen years there she died on September 23, 1912. She is buried in the old cemetery in St. Ignace. *Règistre de l'entrèe de Novices.* Orig. in UAC; in BBC-Mss. 48. St. Paul, pp. 176–83.

<u>quiet</u> confessions. — I do not hear in the least my loud pocket watch.[158]

March 1: Today I already hear it fairly well. I H S Also yesterday I already heard a little.

March 7: I hear well enough for ordinary conversation, even by a person speaking to me some distance away; God be thanked a thousand times! However, to hear <u>quiet</u> confessions in the <u>confessional</u>, I am not able. I hear all confessions in my room.

March 7–8: The night of the 7th was probably the <u>coldest</u> of this winter, the 8th was one of the coldest days.

March 16: *See next page.*[159]

March 20: Two ᴱdrunkardsᴱ arrived from Pointe St. Ignace and received [my] permission for Fr. Piret[160] to [come] to Pointe St. Ignace to hear their Easter confession; and that Fr. Carie must go away (!!!)

March 21: Graveraet[161] came with 2 Indians and asked that Fr. Carie remain.

March 16: Palm Sunday. <u>Confirmation</u> — about 70. About 30 <u>First communion</u>.

---

[158]At this time Baraga wrote to Archbishop Purcell: "[I]n the first days of May next I hope to <u>see</u> you at least, if not to <u>hear</u> you. I will scarcely be able to hear you, if my present deafness continues. By a frightful rheumatism and cold, which almost rent my head asunder, and which is yet severely upon me, my ear got so incumbered, that I am almost stone-deaf. We hope that with the cold & rheumatism, this deafness also will disappear. But should it be permanent, it will be a great affliction for me. — I request you very humbly, my lord, to make a Memento for me at the Altar." Baraga to Purcell, Sault Ste. Marie, February 24, 1856. Orig. in NDUA; in BBC-A 143 E.

[159]Written between entries.

[160]Andrew D. J. Piret was born in Belgium c. 1802. He was a physician and continued to practice medicine throughout his priesthood. On May 31, 1846, he arrived in New York, came to Detroit, and was assigned to Mackinac. Piret was a poor linguist and ministered only to the French-speaking people around Mackinac and St. Ignace. His relationships with his bishops and fellow priests were irregular; twice Baraga dismissed him and Mrak dismissed him once. It is said that every night he placed a lighted candle in his window as a beacon of welcome for travellers. Praus, pp. 229–35. Piret kept a diary, which, in 1920, belonged to the Charlevoix, Michigan, Historical Society but has since been lost. Patton, p. 512. Piret is buried at Cheboygan, Michigan, where he died on August 22, 1875.

[161]Henry Graveraet was a fisherman and a leader of the St. Ignace community. His wife, Sophie, taught in the Catholic school.

| | |
|---|---|
| On April 29 | the "Superior" should have arrived, however, it was stranded 30 miles from here (Little Anibish) and finally arrived on May 5. Meanwhile the "Manhattan" and "Northstar" came up on |
| May 4: | and they were the first steamers of the spring. |
| May 9: | Departed from the Sault and on |
| May 10: | arrived at Detroit, where on |
| May 11: | I preached in the Cathedral at 11 o'clock, and at half past 7 at St. Joseph. |
| May 12: | I celebrated pontifical mass in St. Mary's Church and confirmed 103 persons. |
| May 13: | From Detroit via Sandusky to Cincinnati, where on |
| May 14: | I arrived at 10 A.M. |
| May 24: | Journeyed to Detroit for the dedication of St. Joseph's Church.[162] |
| May 25: | Preached at St. Joseph's and |
| May 27: | at 6 P.M. arrived again in Cincinnati. |
| May 31: | Now the printing[163] is finished, but I will wait here another week for the collections. |
| June 1: | At 10 A.M. preached in the Cathedral. After the ser- |

---

[162]"On Sunday Morning last, the several Catholic Societies and Military Companies of Detroit . . . and others, accompanied by bands of Music assembled in Randolph Street, in front of the Bishop's residence, and from thence proceeded in order to the Church. They were met by a procession from the school of young girls beautifully dressed in white, and teachers, carrying small baskets of flowers with garlands on their heads, attended by the Pastor. The Bishops and Priests then alighted from their carriages, vested themselves, and preceded by these children singing hymns and strewing flowers along the way, entered the Church which was handsomely and appropriately decorated outside and in, with trees and flowers. When the ceremony of blessing the Church was over, Pontifical High Mass was celebrated by the Rt. Rev. Bishop Lefevre [sic] assisted by Rev. Messrs. Kindekens and Wurley as Deacon and subdeacon — many other clergymen were also in attendance. The venerable Bishop Baraga of Saut St. Marie preached in the German language, and the Rev. Father Francis in the English language. After Mass the Bishops and Priests were escorted to the residence of the Pastor by the Yager Guard.

"In the evening the Pontifical Vespers was sung by Bishop Baraga, and thus ended the day devoted to Almighty God, and the dedication of his temple." DCV, IV, 6:2; in BBC-B 809 E.

[163]Statutes of the Diocese, first edition.

mon a collection was taken up, about \$150. — In the evening at 8 P.M. I preached at the Jesuits. — Collection, about \$60.[164]

| | |
|---|---|
| June 11: | Departed from Cincinnati with William O'Donovan and Tim Hegney.[165] |
| June 12: | Arrived in Detroit. |
| June 13: | Sailed from Detroit at 2:30 P.M. on the "Northstar", and on |
| June 14: | at 5:30 P.M. arrived in the Sault. |
| June 26: | Again departed, at 6 A.M. and on |
| June 27: | at 11 A.M. arrived in Ontonagon. |
| From June 27 to July 6 | remained in Ontonagon (Misère) waiting for a steamer. On July 6 the "Manhattan" came, I boarded it and on the 8th arrived in La Pointe, and on the 9th in Superior, and on the 10th in Grand Portage. |
| *June 29: | Anniversary of these entries.*[166] |
| July 10: | From Grand Portage in an Fordinary canoeF on the 11th, and after a rainy but otherwise, God be thanked, successful and speedy journey arrived at Fort William,[167] where on |
| July 13: | I confirmed 77 people. |

[164]Baraga also preached and received a collection at St. Patrick's Church. DCV, IV, 8:2; in BBC-B 798 E.

[165]William O'Donovan and Timothy Hegney were English-speaking teachers whom Baraga hired for the schools at Garden Island and Grand Portage.

[166]Written in left margin. The Diary began on June 27, 1852.

[167]The Jesuit missionary at Fort William, Fr. du Ranquet, wrote to his Superior: "Bishop Baraga arrived, unexpected, July 11th. On the 13th he gave confirmation to 77 Indians. On the 14th he left for Grand Portage. I accompanied him to prepare for the confirmation. On the 20th, 54 Indians received this sacrament in our small log chapel. The Bishop left on the 21 for Fond du Lac. He expressed the wish that I wait for the school-teacher [Hegney] to introduce him in his work.". During the following month he wrote again: "Bishop Baraga['s] first Pastoral Visit in July 1856 has produced a beneficial impression. Unfortunately a good number of our Indians were absent, and especially our youth, who would have needed to be revived and confirmed in their faith." Du Ranquet to his Superior, Grand Portage, July 26 and August, 1856. Du Ranquet's journal (July 11–August 6, 1856) gives the details of long hours of instruction, confessions, Mass, Vespers, meetings, etc., in which he and Baraga participated. Origs. in ACSM; in BBC-Mss. 26.

| July 14: | From Fort William with Fr. Du Ranquet[168] and on |
|---|---|
| July 15: | arrived at Grand Portage. |
| July 20: | Confirmed 53[169] at Grand Portage. |
| July 21: | Sailed from Grand Portage in a canoe to Superior (misère! why not directly to La Pointe!)[170] where on |
| July 24: | I arrived at 6 P.M., and stayed 4 days with Francis Roy.[171] |
| July 27: | (Sunday) In Superior preached five times, and strongly recommended to the people that they should try soon to have a church. |
| July 28: | Sailed on the "Manhattan" from Superior, and on |
| July 29: | arrived at La Pointe, where I found many letters waiting me (8400 francs) |
| Aug. 3: | Confirmation at La Pointe for 46. |
| Aug. 7: | Left La Pointe on the "Superior" at 3 P.M. and by 11 P.M. arrived in Ontonagon. |
| Aug. 10: | Confirmation at Ontonagon, only 12. |
| Aug. 13: | Arrived at <u>Minnesota</u>. |
| Aug. 17: | Confirmed 27 at Minnesota. |
| Aug. 20: | Arrived at Norwich, and on |

[168]Dominique Chardon Du Ranquet was born at Chalut, France, on January 20, 1813. He entered the Society of Jesus in 1838 and was ordained in 1842, the same year he came to Canada. He resided at Fort William from 1852 until 1877. From there he attended the Indian Missions of Grand Marais, Grand Portage, Isle Royale, Lake Nipigon, and Long Lake. The journal that he kept from 1853 to 1877 contains much information about customs of the Indians as well as the details of the Jesuit endeavors among them. Du Ranquet died at Manitoulin Island on December 19, 1900. Cadieux, p. 886.

[169]After the high mass Baraga confirmed a group of persons and, after Vespers, he had a second confirmation of "10 newly arrived and a few children." Du Ranquet Diary, July 20, 1856. Orig. in ACSM; in BBC-Mss. 26.

[170]In 1847 he nearly lost his life by taking the "direct route" in a canoe. A monument at the mouth of the Cross River at Schoeder, Minnesota, commemorates his safe arrival at the shore.

[171]At La Pointe on December 25, 1835, Baraga had baptized Francis Roy, then 39 years old. That Baraga stayed with him suggests that they had remained friends.

| | |
|---|---|
| Aug. 24: | I confirmed 33 there. On the 25th arrived at Ontonagon. |
| Aug. 28: | Left Ontonagon with Mr. Murray[172] for Chaboigan school, and on |
| Aug. 29: | arrived at the Sault. |
| Sept. 4: | Departed from the Sault. |
| Sept. 5: | Arrived at Eagle Harbor. |
| Sept. 7: | Confirmed 15 in Eagle Harbor. |
| Sept. 8: | From Eagle Harbor to Fulton Mine. |
| Sept. 10: | At 2 A.M. arrived in L'Anse. |
| Sept. 14: | Confirmed 11 persons at L'Anse. |
| Sept. 15: | At 2 P.M. sailed from L'Anse on the"General Taylor". and on |
| Sept. 16: | To the Cliff, where on |
| Sept. 20: | I preached in 3 languages and confirmed 26. |
| Sept. 22: | Returned to Eagle Harbor. |
| Sept. 23: | This morning there are some more confirmations, so that in all there were 20 confirmations at Eagle Harbor. |
| Sept. 24: | Sailed at noon from Eagle Harbor on the "Manhattan", and on |
| Sept. 25: | at 7 P.M. arrived (at the Sault.) |
| Oct. 3: | Nothing special to enter. N.B. From Nov[ember] 1 I will enter some thing every day. |
| Oct. 5: | Sunday. Today was a noteworthy sad Sunday: 6 vessels passed through the canal, 4 steamers and 2 schooners. |
| Oct. 18: | On this day of sad memories[173] Mr. Thiele passed |

---

[172]Nicholas Murray was an English-speaking schoolteacher whom Baraga hired for Chaboigan ( Jaboigan) near Burt Lake.

[173]Baraga made the same observation on October 18 in 1860 and in 1862. His father died on October 18, 1812. R. Walling, AR 91, p. 2. Also on this same date, in 1818 his sister, Amalia, married Joseph Gressel, and in 1830 he left St. Nicholas Parish in Smartno to begin his journey to the United States.

through on his way to Germany.[174] (It was on the 17th, not on the 18th.)

Oct. 21:     Today before noon, about 10 o'clock, it became so dark that I had to light my lamp in order to read.

Oct. 22:     Fr. Chone[175] sailed on the "Manhattan."

This has not been a real diary because I did not record something every day. From Nov[ember] 1 I intend to record something every day.[176]

Oct. 30:     "Superior" shipwrecked.

---

[174]Baraga gave Thiele approval to go to Germany to seek financial aid for the missions, with promises of prayer for those who made contributions. Baraga Approbation, Sault Ste. Marie, October 1, 1856. Orig. in LMVA; In BBC-A 732 L.

[175]John Peter Chone was born in Metz, France, on August 4, 1808, and ordained in 1832. He entered the Society of Jesus in 1837 in Switzerland. He came to Canada in 1843 and to Lake Superior in 1844 (Manitoulin Island, 1844–1847, 1860–1878; Pigeon River, 1848–1849; Fort William, 1849–1860). He died at Manitoulin Island on December 14, 1878. Cadieux, p. 885.

[176]Baraga kept this pledge until January 9, 1857. He made an entry every day, even if only about the weather or the names of ships passing through the canal or the condition of the ice on the St. Marys River.

*On the inside of the back cover of Volume I, Baraga pasted a printed excerpt from an unidentifiable source. It is a meditation that summarizes the essence of true religion and how it must be lived in everyday life.*

There is no doubt that the love of God consists neither of sweet tears nor inner comfort and sensitivity, but rather in that we serve Him with righteousness, <u>fortitude</u>, and true <u>humility</u>.[177]

A truly loving soul finds its greatest peace by expending everything that it is, has, and is capable of, for the Beloved, and the more dear and admirable something may be, the more readily it is given.

The highest and truest perfection of the spiritual life consists not of inner charm or comfortable sentiment, nor of raptures, appearance and offering of prophecy, but rather of the uniformity of our will with the will of God.

Whoever adheres to that which is mortal, everything that he does under those circumstances will be for him incomplete. Whoever follows that which is lost, also will be lost.

Whoever owns such mortal things to the extent that his whole will is possessed by them, he has and owns nothing. Rather those things will imprison, own and torment him.

[177]Baraga underlined these words.

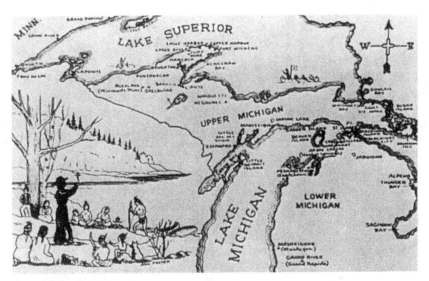

*Great Lakes Missions served by Baraga—1831–1868.*
*(Courtesy of Janet Foster, Ishpeming, Michigan.)*

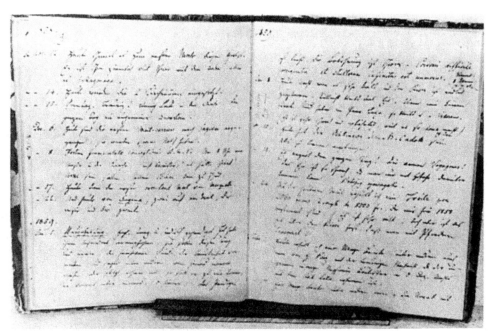

*Bishop Baraga's Diary, Vol. II, November 12, 1858–*
*February 17, 1859.*

*St. Ann Church and priest's residence/school, Mackinac Island. On the left is the home of Madame Magdelaine Laframboise. Drawing by Fr. Otto Skolla, OFM, c. 1845.*

*Holy Name of Jesus Mission L'Anse. Drawing by Fr. Otto Skolla, OFM, c. 1845.*

St. Mary's Church and Rectory, Sault Ste. Marie, 1853.

Residence of Bishop Baraga at Sault Ste. Marie,
1864–1866.

*Baraga during early morning prayer. Painting by Robert Bochy, Newberry, Michigan.*

*Chalice presented to Bishop Baraga by Emperor Francis Joseph of Austria, 1854.*

# *VOLUME II*[1]

## NOVEMBER 1, 1856–OCTOBER 8, 1860

Nov. 1:[2]   Today is the 3rd anniversary of my consecration. A
very sad day. I could almost say: $<$[L]"May gloom and
deep shadow claim it for their own, clouds hang over
it, eclipse swoop down on it."[L]$>$[3] Today there were
very few people at the high mass, which grieved me
very much; and I even expressed this grief in the sermon. //[4] After Vespers I asked Fr. Menet[5] to finish

---

[1]Bishop Frederic Eis, Baraga's third successor, added the following comments on
the inside cover of Volume II: "Remark: The late Bishop Frederick [sic] Baraga
had a special devotion to the Holy Name of Jesus. Hence you find frequently
I H S. He also died on the feast of the Holy Name of Jesus." "N.B. Bishop Baraga all this time resided at Sault Sainte Marie, his 1st See." "'Mr.' often pre-
cedes a priest's name instead of 'Rev.'" Eis, who made many annotations to the
Diary, was born at Arbach, Germany, on January 20, 1843. In 1855 his family
came to the United States and finally settled at Rockland where Fr. Fox taught
him French and Latin. On October 30, 1870, Bishop Mrak ordained him and
appointed him rector at the cathedral. Eis also served the parishes in Calumet,
Hancock, Negaunee, and Bessemer. He was consecrated fourth Bishop of Marquette on August 24, 1899. On July 8, 1922, Eis resigned and he died on May 5,
1926. He is interred in the Bishops' Crypt in the cathedral in Marquette.

[2]Cf. D, November 1, 1858.

[3]Jb 3:4–5.

[4]Baraga uses this symbol, which first appeared in Volume II, to indicate a new
thought or topic.

[5]John Baptist Menet was born at Nantes on March 6, 1793. He entered the Society
of Jesus in Russia in 1815 and was ordained in 1825. He taught French litera-

singing the "Divine Praises" before placing the Most Holy Sacrament in the tabernacle. // The weather is mild; the snow that fell yesterday and the day before has disappeared. // This morning I was a little indisposed; probably I ate too much yesterday or the day before and my weak stomach can not bear it. I should eat just a little to remain healthy. As soon as I eat according to my full appetite, I am not well. // I preached only in French because of the few people who were there.

Nov. 2: Sunday. Before noon I preached in English and Indian, and in the afternoon, about purgatory.

Nov. 3: This morning the "Mineral Rock" arrived from below but did not bring any mail. (Not the "Mineral Rock", but the new propeller "Webb" arrived). John (?) Baras left for Chicago on the "Lady Elgin" which arrived at 11 A.M. // At Barbeau's I cashed Gilbert's[6] check for $275 in gold. // I was called to Mrs. Barry but went only on the third call.[7]

Nov. 4: Today is election day for the new President. An extremely snowy day; it snowed all last night and it snows all day. It seems that we will have a snowy November.

Nov. 5: Today it was extremely cold; it has frozen hard // The poor novice[8] with our Sisters, who has been found unfit and without vocation, had to be compelled to leave today by the sheriff. She decided to go to Superior. // The "Illinois" came down the lake.

Nov. 6: Today we began to say mass in the sacristy,[9] however,

---

ture, church history, and canon law until 1845 when he came to Canada. He was pastor at Sault Ste. Marie, 1846–1860 and 1864–1868. Menet died in Quebec on June 24, 1869. Cadieux, p. 891.

[6]Henry C. Gilbert was Indian agent for Mackinac and vicinity, 1853–1857. MPHC, 6, p. 348.

[7]Such hesitation was atypical of Baraga.

[8]Sister St. Anne (Katharine Gordon) was the daughter of Georges and Agatha Landry Gordon. Of Scotch and Indian ancestry, she was born at Penetanguishene, Ontario, on May 17, 1829. She entered the community on May 24, 1853, the day that Mother Mary Xavier arrived at Sault Ste. Marie. On July 26 she entered the novitiate and received the habit.

[9]Because it was a much smaller room it was easier to heat.

needlessly, because it is not as cold anymore as it was on the 5th of the month, (yesterday). This morning the "Manhattan" left from here.

Nov. 7:    This afternoon I had a sad Indian confession. The Indians of this mission are, for the most part, very negligent, very poorly instructed Christians.[10]

Nov. 8:    Today I began to read *The Dictionary of Theology*[11] by Fr. [Nicholas Sylvester] Bergier. // It snowed all day and we had a blizzard like in winter.

Nov. 9:    Sunday. Preached in English and French. // The forenoon was nice and summerlike; in the afternoon it snowed again, and it was very winterlike. // The propeller "Webb", which passed up the canal on the 3rd of this month, came back today to be repaired. This evening we heard that Buchanan[12] was elected president. Thanks be to God, if this is true.[13] // "Northstar" passed up the canal. // Nothing is heard from the steamer "Superior". It is feared that she has perished.

Nov. 10:    "General Taylor" has arrived and brought the sad news that the Steamer "Superior" has foundered on the Pictured Rocks, whereby 55 persons have lost their lives.[14] Fr. Kohler[15] has just now arrived from Garden River.

---

[10]This statement reflects on Fr. Menet who had labored at Sault Ste. Marie since 1846.

[11]*Dictionaire theologique* (3 vols.) published in 1788. NCE, 2, p. 323.

[12]James Buchanan, fifteenth president of the United States, was born near Foltz, Pennsylvania, on April 23, 1791. He identified with the Federalist party and, upon its dissolution, with the Democratic party. Although he felt that slavery was morally wrong, he believed that the Constitution precluded congressional or presidential action on the issue. A man of unimpeachable honesty, patriotism, and considerable ability, he died on June 1, 1868, at Lancaster, Pennsylvania. He was the only unmarried American president.

[13]Millard Fillmore, the candidate of the anti-Catholic "Know Nothing" party, received 22 percent of the popular vote.

[14]Baraga wrote that some of his portraits were aboard the "ill-fated 'Superior'" and that he now has none to send to those who have asked for them. Baraga to John Foley, Sault Ste. Marie, November 17, 1856. Orig. in BBC-A 369 E.

[15]Auguste Kohler was born at Colmar, Upper Rhine, on August 10, 1821. He entered the Society of Jesus in 1842 and came to Canada in 1846 where he worked as missionary and physician with the Indians to the north (Lake Superior) and east (Lake Huron) of Sault Ste. Marie, Ontario. In 1868 he was a candidate to

Nov. 11:    Fr. Kohler has left again for Garden River. The weather is mild. // Today I received six cords of wood from Mr. McKnight.[16] // The storm shed was put up this evening. <(No!)> // "General Taylor" came up again, probably with the cargo of the "Mineral Rock", which is grounded on the "Flats".

Nov. 12:    Today the "General Taylor" went down. // Crochiere began to saw, split and tie my 6 <[F]cords of wood, at 10 francs per cord[F]> = $7.50. // We just heard that the propeller "Webb" was destroyed by fire in Weshking Bay, Lake Superor. Today the storm shed was set up.

Nov. 13:    Finally the "Mineral Rock", which was grounded for 6 days on the "Flats" came up here and went on to Ontonagon. // It snowed again.

Nov. 14:    Nice, clear weather. // "Mineral Rock" left only today, at 8 A.M. // Today it is nice all day. // This evening I received the gold bank notes from Nurre.

Nov. 15:    At 8 A.M. the "Northstar" came up. // It snowed considerably all day, but the snow melts away immediately. There is no Indian summer.[17]

Nov. 16:    <u>Sunday</u>. Today I preached in French and Indian. It snowed again heavily, but the weather is mild. // About the children, who die without baptism, I say: [L]Where they do not go, I know; where they do go, I know not.[L] That they do not go to heaven, that I know, this is certain. But where they actually go, that no one knows. The opinions of the Holy Fathers and the theologians differ widely on this point.

Nov. 17:    [E]The "Lady Elgin" came up on her last trip.[E] // [C]It is

---

succeed Baraga as bishop. Kohler died in a shipwreck north of the Bruce Peninsula in Ontario on October 15, 1871. Cadieux, p. 889; Rezek, II, p. 54.

[16]Sheldon McKnight was born in New York, c. 1812. He established a "forwarding house" at Sault Ste. Marie in 1846 in partnership with Lowell Tinker. In 1850 they organized the Chippewa Portage Company and built a tramway connecting the upper and lower landings. McKnight was the president of this company. MPHC, XXI, p. 358. In 1850 he was 38 years old and had $20,000 in real estate. Federal Census, 1850, Chippewa County, #164.

[17]French. Baraga called it "St. Martin's summer."

only this now that I shall write about. Well it is only this.[c]

Nov. 18: Today I gave the Sisters my new mitre to sew. There will be a lot of work on it. // I received 7 letters, one sadder than the next. There was not a word of consolation and not the least word of joyfulness in them. And such are, by far, most of the letters that I receive.

Nov. 19: Today I gave a frame to Jo[seph] Meniclier[18] to make. This is the beginning of the altar work which will probably cause me much unpleasantness and many expenses.

Nov. 20: A poor Indian came here and begged for charity. I gave him a dollar; but, perhaps, I have thereby done more harm than good. — It is a pity that in the performance of a good work, one does not know whether it is right or wrong, whether it is pleasing or displeasing to Thee. — // Today Meniclier brought me the lower or inner frame for the picture of the Blessed Virgin.

Nov. 21: This was confession day, [L]on account of the plenary indulgence granted after the recitation of the (prayers) of the three theological virtues.[L] The next confession day will be during the octave of the Immaculate Conception of the Blessed Virgin Mary, when another plenary indulgence is granted.

Nov. 22: Today I mailed 10 [copies of the] "Statutes" to the Rt. Rev. Bishops: Henni [Milwaukee], De St. Palais [Vincennes], Carrell [Covington], Spalding [Louisville],[19] Rappe [Cleveland], Neumann [Philadelphia],[20] Cretin

---

[18]Joseph Meniclier, 48, was a Michigan-born farmer. Federal Census, 1850, Chippewa County, #128. The 1860 Census lists two persons by this name, both coopers by occupation, one 25 years old and the other 50 years old. Federal Census, 1860, Chippewa County, #189, #201.

[19]John Martin Spalding was born on May 23, 1810, in Kentucky. He was Bishop of Louisville, 1850–1864, and Archbishop of Baltimore, 1864–1872. He had deep affection for Baraga. Baraga was Spalding's guest in 1866 when he had his debilitating fall. Spalding's letters to Baraga before his death were warm, affirming, and encouraging. Jacker wrote that Spalding "is one of the Bishops I love without knowing. How he loved Bishop Baraga!" Jacker to Finotti, St. Ignace, November 19, 1875. EJP; in BBC-AR 13, p. 82. Spalding died on February 7, 1872.

[20]John Nepomucene Neumann was born in Prachatitz, Bohemia, on March 28,

[St. Paul], O'Connor [Pittsburgh], Young [Erie], Timon [Buffalo]. — Perhaps it is foolishness. If word comes from Rome that I am not to be called Bishop of Sault Sainte Marie, <$^{L}$what will I do? (I will prepare a new edition, which I have already done.)$^{L}$>

Nov. 23:    Sunday. At the high mass I preached in English, French and Indian about the particular and general judgment. // In the evening the propeller "Ogans" came up, and Desrosiers from Mackinac brought me a letter from Mr. Jahan in which he communicates to me the news that Carie has arrived. — — —

Nov. 24:    This morning at 8 A.M. the propeller "Ogans" left for Chicago. // All the snow is gone.

Nov. 25:    Steamer "Lady Elgin" came down today. // Mrs. Johnson[21] came in with Charles McFalen. Then again I proposed to her some foolish questions because I did not recognize her.

Nov. 26:    "General Taylor" came in today from Detroit. // Very sad news regarding the school at Grand Traverse. We will receive nothing more for this school. I fear something sad will come out of this also for the Little Traverse school. // Also received news from

---

1811. After completing seminary study, he was inspired by Baraga's letters in the *Berichte* and migrated to New York City. There he was ordained on June 25, 1836, by Bishop John Dubois who sent him to the German families in western New York State. In 1840 Neumann entered the Congregation of the Most Holy Redeemer and on January 16, 1842, he was the first Redemptorist professed in the United States. He labored in Pittsburgh and Baltimore until March 28, 1852, when he was consecrated Bishop of Philadelphia. He became the "father" of the parochial school system in the United States and friend of many religious communities of women. His love of the Holy Eucharist led to the establishment of the Forty Hours Devotion, first in Philadelphia and then in most other dioceses. On January 5, 1860, while hurrying on an errand, he collapsed and died. He was canonized by Pope Paul VI on January 5, 1977.

[21]Probably Polly Johnston. Cf. D, December 24, 1856.

<sup></sup><<sup>E</sup>Manypenny[22] that my claim is rejected.<sup>E</sup>>[23] Cro-chiere filled my wood box. // I became provoked with Fr. Menet and reproached him for the many unnecessary expenses for the "<u>Academy.</u>"

Nov. 27:   "Mineral Rock" came down this morning. // Today I gave the <sup>L</sup>Dimissorial Letter<sup>L</sup> for Carie to the <sup>E</sup>mail-carrier<sup>E</sup> who is going on the "Mineral Rock" to Detroit. He will receive it late, which is unpleasant to me. If I had considered the matter better, I would have given it immediately to Desrosiers to take with him. <<sup>L</sup>Whatever you do, do prudently.<sup>L</sup>>

Nov. 28:   The "General Taylor" went through the canal and on to Ontonagon, and the "Mineral Rock", going to Detroit, came down through the canal. // Six mail carriers have taken passage today for Detroit.

Nov. 29:   This is butchering day. // It snows hard. // Mr. Ord[24] came and told me that only 5 Catholic children go to

---

[22]George Manypenny (1808–July 15, 1892), a Democrat from Ohio, was commissioner of Indian affairs, 1853–1857. He personally visited and defended the western reservations against further encroachment, resisted fraudulent claims upon Indian annuities, advocated quarterly payment of annuities to discourage white exploitation and whisky trade, and advocated a cabinet-level Department of Indian Affairs under civilian control. Manypenny, a Methodist, advocated the involvement of religious denominations in the administration of Indian affairs. However, Rev. Selah B. Treat of the American Board of Commissioners for Foreign Missions wrote that Manypenny had "no special fancy for Catholic, neither has the chief clerk [Charles E. Mix, later commissioner of Indian affairs]." Treat to S.R. Riggs, February 17, 1854. In his book, *Our Indian Wards* (1880), Manypenny blamed the Indian wars on the white man's greed and the army's control over the Indians. Kvasnicka, pp. 57–67.

[23]On November 4 Baraga reminded Commissioner Manypenny of his claim for expenses for the L'Anse Indians. Baraga to Manypenny, Sault Ste. Marie, November 4, 1856. Orig. in NA-OIA; in BBC-A 574 E. Manypenny answered: "Your claim is rejected." Manypenny to Baraga, Washington, November 18, 1856. Orig. in NA-OIA; in BBC-B 849 E.

[24]Placidus Ord, the son of James Ord, was a leader in the Catholic community at Sault Ste. Marie. Gilbert hired him for the school on Sugar Island. Gilbert to Ord, Detroit, August 7, 1856. Orig. in NA-OIA; in BBC-C 1690 E.

the free school, viz.: Nugent's two boys, Francis For-
neau's girl, P. B. Barbeau's orphan girl, and Green's
girl. — I thought there were more. <(Actually there
are many more.)>

Nov. 30:  <u>Sunday</u>. Today I again preached in English, French
and Indian, and began with the Indian catechism,
which I will continue every Sunday, all winter. // In
the evening I was called to the other side, to Francis
Grant, whom Fr. Menet had visited not long ago. //
The old Marie received the last sacraments today.

Dec. 1:  This morning Fr. Menet told me that last night the
brother of Francis Grant had come to bring me or him
to his seriously ill brother. However, Fr. Menet told
him: "Do you think that the bishop will go to your
brother at midnight?" And so the young man left
without calling me. — As soon as I heard of this, I
immediately carried the Most Holy Sacrament to the
sick man and also administered Extreme Unction to
him. // Today it snows heavily, but it is not cold.

Dec. 2:  It was a <sup>c</sup>cold<sup>c</sup> night. Today the weather is very nice
and sunny; but only in the morning; in the afternoon
it clouded over. The canal is closed.

Dec. 3:  St. Francis Xavier. // Today it is very stormy and
cold. Poor people on the "General Taylor" who are on
Lake Superior! // Today I went to Nugent and recommended to him that he ought to send his two boys to
our school, not the Protestant free school. He said that
our teacher does not give instructions in studies
higher than reading and writing. I then told him that
he ought nevertheless to send his boys to us. I would
tell Brother Lacoste[25] to instruct them according to
their abilities and proficiency. — Now I will see
whether Nugent sends his boys to our school or not.

[25]Adrien Lacoste was born at Lacombe, France, on March 20, 1820. He entered the
Society of Jesus as a brother in 1841. In 1842 he came to St. Mary College in
Kentucky, filled several posts at Fordham College in New York, and then came
to Sault Ste. Marie. After leaving the Sault he worked at Montreal and Guelph.
Lacoste died in Montreal on December 31, 1896. Cadieux, p. 890.

Dec. 4:  It snows very heavily. // Today I began to copy the Gagikwe-Masinaigan[26] with the task of three pages daily. <ᴸO God, come to my assistance, O Lord, make haste to help me.ᴸ> O.A.M.D.G.

Dec. 5:  It again snows heavily. // Fr. Menet had a ꜰ"requiem high mass"ꜰ on the other shore. // Fr. Kohler has arrived this evening with 2 [people] from Payment.

Dec. 6:  Again snowing very hard. // Fr. Kohler returned, but will come again Tuesday, as least so I hear.

Dec 7:  Sunday. I gave three very short sermons, English, French, and Indian. I announced to the people that tomorrow is the feast of the Immaculate Conception of Mary, our special diocesan and patronal feast, but which will be solemnly celebrated next Sunday. I also announced that throughout this entire Octave a plenary indulgence may be gained. // In the afternoon the church pews were auctioned for $400 and over. However, probably all will not pay what they have pledged.

Dec. 8:  ᴸFeast of the Immaculate Conception of the Blessed Virgin Mary.ᴸ This morning at 8 I said mass, at which there were many people, after my announcement yesterday and urgent invitation. The Ursulines sang very delightfully. // Today Fr. Kohler came again and will remain here the entire week.

Dec. 9:  Jo[seph] Meniclier came to make the ᴱ"four boxes"ᴱ [27] for the altar; he brought the wood from Trempe,[28] 200

---

[26]"Sermon Book."

[27]Rectangular sections of the altar. Cf. Gregorich Mss. xlii, p. 23.

[28]Louis P. Trempe was born at St. Ambrose, Quebec, on February 25, 1829. He came to Sault Ste. Marie with his father in 1847. After the death of his father in 1849, he took over the general store his father had begun. In addition to the store, he operated a number of the larger lake tugs, held numerous public offices, and was a trustee at St. Mary's Church at the Sault. He was beloved by the Indians and respected by the white people for his practical assistance to the poor. He married twice and left six sons and four daughters. Trempe died at the Sault on January 5, 1892. It was Louis Trempe who officially welcomed all notable visitors to the Sault. Bayliss, pp. 289–90. According to the 1860 census, he was 39 that year, making his date of birth c. 1821. Federal Census, 1860, Chippewa County, #96.

feet and some paneling. // Someone came to tell me that the German Lutheran who lives at Morningstar is breathing his last. I sent Fr. Kohler there.

Dec. 10: Have been with Jo[seph] Meniclier to see the wood, and to tell him that he should not make the ᴱ"four boxes"ᴱ four inches wider and longer. // Today I did not complete my task because I worked on a plan for the altar, which however I did not make right; ᶜa little later somewhat better I shall make it.ᶜ

Dec. 11: I have nothing to enter. It was an ordinary day, nothing special.

Dec. 12: This morning I was called to the other side of St. Mary's River, to old Labate. She is very old and entirely childish. I gave her Holy Communion and Extreme Unction.

Dec. 13: Rather many confessions today, also some in French and one in English. Fr. Menet did not hear confessions because of his ᶠ(poorly timed)ᶠ retreat. Fr. Kohler had perhaps nearly 100 confessions; ᴸ(because of the plenary indulgence).ᴸ

Dec. 14: Sunday. ᴸSolemnity of the Immaculate Conception of the Blessed Virgin Mary.ᴸ Pontifical mass, at which functioned Fr. Kohler as Deacon and Br. Lacoste as sub-deacon. — Poorly done! — At the pontifical mass there were nearly 70 communions (because of the plenary indulgence) which I had announced for this octave. // This evening it is rather cold. I believe we shall have a cold night, ᶜit will be a cold night.ᶜ <ᴱIt will be a cold night.ᴱ>

Dec. 15: ᶜIndeed it was a very cold night.ᶜ // Today I placed fresh relics in my pectoral cross. // Yesterday and today I again had thoughts of resigning — If I could only perceive or recognize the will of God in this matter, then I would soon be at peace, and resolve for one side or the other.

Dec. 16: The female Indian singers complained that last Sunday they were chased from the choir. Therefore, I went to the Sisters today and learned that they were very politely <u>requested</u> to make room. — I then told Mrs. Cotte[29] that she should leave the <u>first long pew</u> to the sisters; and they themselves should sit in one of the <u>short side pews</u>.

Dec. 17:   Today I wrote nothing; I made a new plan for the altar which at first did not please me at all; but now that it is finished, it pleases me very much. Thanks be to God! // Jo[seph] Meniclier brought the four boxes. // Crochiere filled the small wood box.

Dec. 18:   I am daily instructing two small Indian boys, Louis and Charles, whom I began to teach the day before yesterday, and [I] will instruct them the entire winter if they continue to come. // Today Fr. Menet's retreat is over; he came to me Ein regard to the singers.E I was displeased when he said to me: F"Do not concern yourself with that."F And I said to him Fthat the pastor is under the bishop, not vice verse.F

Dec. 19:   LWhat shall I write?L — The two boys came again for instructions. // Today I am already in the CJesus, his life on earth.C

Dec. 20:   Nothing special. My task completed. Instructed the 2 boys and the Indian woman. // It snowed the entire day and was very windy.

Dec. 21:   <u>Sunday</u>. Preached in English, French and Indian. // I was indignant with Fr. Kohler because he did not wait for me before the Asperges.

Dec. 22:   Finally, Fr. Kohler went home again to Garden River. This morning 2 sweet little hours.[30]

Dec. 23:   A small examination was held today in our boys' school and small awards distributed. // Catherine Richards came to instructions for her first holy communion and confession. She was baptized by me at

---

[29]Mrs. Henry (Isabella) Cotte was the daughter-in-law of Peter Cotte, who, with his wife, Margaret, assisted Baraga at Fond du Lac, La Pointe, Grand Portage, and L'Anse. The Cottes had five children, John, Charlotte, Josephine, Louis, and Amos. Federal Census, 1850, Chippewa County, #82.
[30]Early morning meditation.

L'Anse and is now here with her mother and cousin. // [E]Mail arrived from above, Lake Superior.[E]

Dec. 24:

Vigil. Polly Johnson[31] [L]and other women[L] are preparing a small crib for tomorrow. // Today they brought me the trimming for the altar baldachino.

Dec. 25:[32]

[L]Nativity of the Lord[L] Pontifical mass, at which Mr. Menet and Br. Lacoste assisted. // After the mass I wanted to give instructions in Indian [C]as I do repeatedly,[C] but no one [C]came forward[C] and so I left disappointed. [C]I don't know that I did well.[C]

Dec. 26:

The 2 [E]Indian boys[E] came, for the last 3 or 4 days they did not come.

Dec. 27:

The mail arrived today from Mackinac with 15 letters for me; some sad and disagreeable; some of them I answered immediately. // Crochiere filled the woodbox.

Dec. 28:

Sunday. English and French, and after the high mass I explained the Indian catechism. // Again answered some letters, and then sent them all to the post office.

[31]Polly (Marie) Johnston, was 31 years old according to the 1850 Federal Census (#101) and 44 according to the 1860 Census (#152). The latter is correct, making her date of birth c. 1816. She was 48 when she married Amos Stiles, 41, at Sault Ste. Marie on June 28, 1865. Legally she and her older sister, Sophia, were the children of Jean-Baptiste Cadotte and his wife, Janette Piquette, who had three older children still living. However, the two girls were also known as Johnston because, after 1823, Janette, now widowed, kept house for George Johnston and raised them in the Johnston household. Schenck, p. 43. "The other possibility is that their father really was the oldest Johnston son, Lewis, not Jean-Baptiste II. When Polly finally got married in 1865 at St. Mary's she gave her father's name as Lewis Johnston. Now Lewis died young (in 1825) but from the family letters I gather that he was a bit wild. One letter, in fact, makes mention of 'continuing his late connection with that abandoned woman (Janette was abandoned by JB) and his unblushing fatherhood which makes me fear he has lost all sense of shame and honor.' John [Johnston] Sr. to George [Johnston], 15 June 1817." Johnston Papers, BHC-DPL. "In the Library Archives [Sault Ste. Marie] I found a court record from 1844–1846. In Nov[ember] 1844 Polly Cadotte accused Eustace Roussain of rape and getting her pregnant. She had lots of witnesses who spoke for her. Roussain had only one. She won of course." Letters of Schenck to Walling, August 30, July 28, 1988. In BBC-Cadotte File. The only Johnston who was 5 years old at the time of the 1850 Census was Mary Ann, the daughter of John M. Johnston (#176); in 1860 the name Marie, age 15, appears in the John Johnston entry. Federal Census, 1860, Chippewa County, #186. Cf. D, January 20, 1860.

[32]This was the first year in which Christmas was a civil holiday in the United States.

Dec. 29:

Today Catherine Richards and her cousin Marie came for instructions. Catherine will receive first holy communion on New Year's Day, and Marie will be baptized.

Dec. 30:

I was at Barbeau's today to order ᶠ12,000 shinglesᶠ and to ask him to take over and supervise the work on the church next summer. // Last night I had become quite deaf, but in the morning it disappeared again, and I hear as usual. I H S

Dec. 31:

I was deaf again this morning, but before mass I was again well. // Confession day. // The last day of the year 1856. In some ways, this was a very unpleasant, but in some others, a rather joyful year.

## 1857

Jan. 1:

New Year's Day. I began this day, and therefore this year, very sadly. During the night I was stone deaf, did not even hear the Brother when he came in to make the fire and missed the entire morning prayer. Towards 7 A.M. the deafness, however, went away again. // Preached in English and French, and taught the Indian catechism.

Jan. 2:

Again the old misère with the deafness. Every night I become deaf, and in the morning it goes away again. Mr. Barbeau came and promised to have a nice gilded frame made for the altar piece for me in Detroit.

Jan. 3:

Same misère, the deafness began last night at 7 P.M. and continued until this morning. // In the afternoon I visited Mr. and Mrs. Barbeau and Trempe. In the evening I felt very well after a short stroll. I should go out a little every day.

Jan. 4:

Sunday. Today I preached only in French, because the day before yesterday Barbeau made the remark that some find it too long when I give two sermons. // ᴵWe shall see.ᴵ //

Jan. 5:

Today I was called to Francis Grant; I went there and said several prayers for him, etc. // Now the deaf-

|  |  |
|---|---|
|  | ness, thanks be to God, does not come to me any more during the night. |
| Jan. 6: | <u>Epiphany</u>. Today I preached only in <u>English</u>, but I read the Gospel in French and remarked that for the time being I will preach only in one language, and perhaps later again in two. // Held the Indian catechism class as usual. |
| Jan. 7: | Crochiere filled the woodbox. That is the most noteworthy [thing] that has occurred today. // It is very cold. There will be a very cold night. |
| Jan. 8–9: | Nothing![33] — It is foolishness to want to enter something everyday. Sometimes I really find nothing to enter. Henceforth I will make entries when I have something to enter. As for example = |
| Jan. 10: | Henry Graveraet[34] who was expected, came with letters from Mackinac. He surprised me also with the report that McNamara[35] is coming behind. — Misère! Perhaps he comes with a purpose. |
| Jan. 11: | <u>Sunday</u>. Preached in French; Indian catechism. // Instead of the announced McNamara, 4 Canadians came today from Mackinac and Pointe St. Ignace; and I have decided to go with them the day after tomorrow to Mackinac, etc. in order to dispose of some foolishness.[36] |
| Jan. 12: | Today I left the Sault and spent the night with Sobrero.[37] |

[33]Baraga later learned that it was on this day that the vicariate became a diocese and he was named its first bishop. Pope Pius IX to Baraga, Rome, January 9, 1857. Origs. in MQDA; in BBC-B 841 L; B 842 L.

[34]Henry Graveraet was a 34-year-old fisherman, born in Michigan. Federal Census, 1850, Mackinac County, #265. His wife, Sophie, was the Catholic teacher at St. Ignace.

[35]McNamara had taught at Little Traverse and Cross Village. Baraga sent him to La Pointe.

[36]At this time there was extensive conflict concerning Fathers Piret, Jahan, and Carie. In the midst of the troubles, the Graveraets were in danger of being evicted from the home which belonged to the church at St. Ignace.

[37]Francis Sobrero, 40, was a farmer. There were eight additional Sobreros but the ages preclude certitude about their relationship. Federal Census, 1860, Chippewa County, #91. Cf. D, April 1, 1861.

Jan. 14:  Spent the night with Bellanger.

Jan. 15:  Arrived at Pointe St. Ignace and at Mackinac, where immediately my trouble and foolishness began.

Jan. 18:  <u>Sunday</u>. In Mackinac preached a reconciliation sermon, whereby at least for the time-being peace has been restored. Mr. Carie promised to leave for Chicago at once.[38]

Jan. 19:  <sup>E</sup><u>Great Affront</u>.<sup>E</sup> — Went from Mackinac to Pointe St. Ignace. Borrowed $55 from McNamara.[39] From Pointe

---

[38] "At once" did not mean immediately, but as soon as shipping began in the spring. Fr. Carie continued to upset the peace, causing Baraga to write the following letter: "Mr. Wendell. I think you have some influence on Mr. Carie; for that reason I address you these few lines. — He wrote me of late <u>three</u> furious and most abusive letters; and one to Father Menet, in which he puts me on a level with the most common scoundrels. I sent him back all these four letters. — I wrote him today to keep quiet two months more, or else, I will not be able to give him letters of recommendation for his future Bishop. — I request you, sir, to speak to him and make him keep still and quiet. The more he makes noise, the worse for <u>him</u>. But if he keeps quiet, he will find a good place, through my recommendation; for instance at New Orleans, where there are so many Frenchmen longing after priests, whom they pay well — Or elsewhere. Please answer by the next opportunity." Baraga to Wendell, Sault Ste. Marie, February 20, 1857. Orig. in CMU-CHC; in BBC-A 522 E.

[39] This money was to pay a debt Baraga owed. Just as Baraga was about to leave the altar after Mass, Richard M. Smith, Indian agent at Mackinac and a longtime acquaintance of Baraga, publicly accused him of deliberately withholding money. In a rare revelation of his feelings, Baraga wrote to Wendell: "I just now received $5.00 from Mr. Wood of this place. I see you send me back the whole amount. I thank you for that; not so much for the money, which is a trifle, but for the friendship, which is dear to me. Yes, you are my friend, and have always been so, although my duty does not always permit me to act as you would wish me to do. <u>You</u> are my friend; but <u>that man</u> whom I have considered as my friend, and my <u>old</u> friend, since I first saw him at L'Anse and treated him as hospitably as I possibly could in my poverty, that man, to my most bitter sorrow, turned out to be my most atrocious and cruel <u>enemy</u>, who, on that unfortunate day (Jan[uary] 19) inflicted upon my heart a wound which, I am afraid, will never heal. It is as fresh and bleeding today, as it was on that unfortunate morning, when he committed towards me that shameful affront, treating a Bishop as they treat the most notorious scoundrels and thieves, — in the sight of a Catholic Congregation, — immediately after I had celebrated the Holy Sacrifice of Mass! —— Since that unfortunate hour, to this very hour, I never had a light heart, or a contented happy moment. —— I never in my life of 60 years had such a bitter moments, hours, days, and nights, as I have them constantly since that most unhappy hour! —— If that man who inflicted such a deep and never healing wound upon my heart, knew what I suffer, and if he has any kind or gentle feelings yet in his breast, he would be sorry for what he did to me. The loss of a thousand dollars, if I had them and should lose them, would soon be forgotten, and peace and contentedness would be restored to my heart. But the

St. Ignace to Bellanger, where I spent the night with 6 Canadians who were going to Sault Ste. Marie.

Jan. 22: Camped in a forest in a −40° F. cold, or −32° Reaumer. I was in danger of freezing my face.

Jan. 23: Arrived at the Sault where I received many letters, but none pleasing.[40]

Jan. 25: <u>Sunday</u>. Preached in English; Indian catechism.

Jan. 28: Crochiere filled the woodbox today. <(That is the most noteworthy even today, for the entire week.)>

Feb. 1: <u>Sunday</u>. Today I let Fr. Menet preach, and now we shall alternate, he in <u>French</u>, I in <u>English</u>.

Feb. 2: This afternoon I was called, at 1 o'clock, to a sick woman at Garden River. I went immediately, but I was too late; she had already died.

Feb. 3: Spent the day at Payment;[41] in the evening prayed and preached in French, at Payment.

Feb. 4: Buried the deceased woman; first offered mass and preached at the church at Garden River. — Again arrived here at the Sault.

---

loss <u>he</u> caused me will, I am afraid, never be forgotten, and the contentedness <u>he</u> deprived me of, never regained. ⸺ I never refused to pay that money; I only delayed because I received nothing, and because he told me repeatedly that he was in no hurry for it. — Had he come to me on that unfortunate morning, and told me earnestly that he will sue me if I don't pay him before I return to the Saut, I would have paid him immediately afterwards. But without trying first friendly and kind ways, he immediately resorted to the last extreme, by which <u>criminals</u> are compelled to do what is right. — Had such an atrocious stroke come from a man who was my enemy, I would not have felt it so painfully; but to receive it from a man, who at that time was my friend, and my <u>old</u> friend; this pierced, to the very center, my heart which is naturally friendly and benevolent, and opened a wound which is bleeding ever since! — If that man finds pleasure in my pain, he may have the assurance that he made a man who was his friend, unhappy for ever. ⸺ God forgive him, as I forgive him." Baraga to Wendell, Sault Ste. Marie, March 7, 1857. Orig. in CMU-CHC; in BBC-A 523 E.

[40]Two letters were "sad" communications from Henry and Sophie Graveraet (BLR). Baraga also learned that government payment vouchers for his schools and teachers were lost when the *Superior* sank. He requested repayment. Baraga to Gilbert, Sault Ste. Marie, January 30, 1857. Orig. in NA-OIA; in BBC-A 607 E.

[41]Payment was a rapidly growing community on the northern part of Sugar Island in the St. Marys River between the American and Canadian shores.

Feb. 8:    <u>Sunday</u>. Preached in English. That is all.

Feb. 10:   Thursday [Tuesday]. Evening = wood.

Feb. 15:   <u>Sunday</u>. Preached in French because Fr. Menet was somewhat hoarse.

Feb. 16:   This morning I had a very sad discussion with Fr. Menet about my <u>debts</u>, into which I am continually thrust after so much money received! That is also very surprising to me. However, my <u>accounts</u> show that I never spend anything uselessly.

Feb. 19:   Have been at Wilson's[42] with Fr. Menet, very unnecessarily, I will not go again so very soon, or never.

Feb. 21:   Saturday. Wood. // Today again I had a very unpleasant discussion with Fr. Menet because of the report at the dance. — I resolve, and firmly resolve, never again to say anything to him, because it is entirely useless, he never accepts anything. And it is worse than useless, because it gives him occasion to lose his temper, like today, and every time I say something to him. —

Feb. 22:   <u>Sunday</u>. Preached in all three languages and announced Lenten Regulations. // I will never again preach in all 3 languages; it is of no use, because it makes the people, ( <u>including the religious</u>,) bored and annoyed.

March 1:   <u>Sunday</u>. Preached in French on ᶠsudden death.ᶠ In the afternoon again in French on the Passion of Our Lord Jesus Christ. How nice and true are these verses:

> ᴱ"With peaceful mind thy race of <u>duty</u> run;
> God nothing does or suffers to be done
> But what thou wouldst thyself, if thou
>     couldst see,
> Through all events of things as well as he."ᴱ

---

[42]Thomas Wilson was 56, a Scottish-born farmer. Federal Census, 1860, Chippewa County, #295. He lived on Sugar Island. Brother Donovan, S.J. stayed overnight with him (D, January 31, 1860). In 1863 Wilson tended Caspar Schulte when he was ill (D, February 11, 1863).

| | |
|---|---|
| March 10: | From this morning on = Cabinet full of wood. We shall see how long it will last. |
| March 15: | <u>Sunday</u>. Preached in French and English. I have again begun to preach in both languages. I should never have done otherwise. |
| March 18: | From this morning on = woodbox full. <(It lasted 13 days, until March 30, inclusive.) From 31st new cabinet.) // 11 April = new cabinet.> |
| April 12: | <u>Easter Sunday</u>. Pontifical mass. Now probably I will not celebrate any more until Immaculate Conception, Dec[ember] 11, if the Blessed Hour[43] does not come before. |
| April 23: | Today at last, the bulls arrived which make this church the <sup>L</sup><u>Cathedral of Marianopolis,</u><sup>L</sup> and gives me the title: <sup>L</sup><u>Bishop of Marianopolis.</u><sup>L</sup>[44] |
| April 29: | This morning — new, fresh woodbox, probably the last <sup>E</sup>before navigation opens.<sup>E</sup> |
| May 8: | Finally this afternoon the first boat arrived, "Northstar", and right after it the second, "Illinois". — The poor "Manhattan" struck a rock on its way up here and sank right at the wharf;[45] Captain Ripley, <sup>I</sup>the poor man!<sup>I</sup> |
| May 9: | McNamara came up this afternoon on the "Lady Elgin", and I sent him immediately to La Pointe, instead of Mr. Hickey. |
| May 10: | It snowed heavily all day. We shall see how long this |

---

[43]Death.

[44]Baraga received this news from Archbishop Purcell, and two days later answered, making a few remarks about the inaccuracy of the newspaper report: "My Lord. The day before yesterday I had the pleasure of receiving your communication together with the Roman Bulls and Powers. I am sorry to see how the Editor of the <u>Catholic Telegraph</u> has constructed the news concerning me. He says: 'The Rt. Rev. F. B., DD., hitherto Vicar Apostolic of Upper Michigan, is now bishop, and Sault Ste. Marie the see of the new diocese.' What nonsense! — Is <u>now</u> Bishop. That means that he was not Bishop <u>before</u>, till now; and that he was consequently a usurper of the mitre, as often as he put it on. . . . I don't intend to go to Cincinnati this year, I have nothing to do there." Baraga to Purcell, Sault Ste. Marie, April 25, 1857. Orig. in NDUA; in BBC-152 E.

[45]The *h* in "wharf" was added later in pencil.

charming spring snow will remain. <(It stayed two days.)>

May 13: We heard today that all the steamers are still lying in Weshking Bay, waiting for a "Northern Passage" through the ice, wherefore they probably will be waiting 8 or 10 days. — ¹We shall see.¹ — Today also the last little pile of winter snow in front of my window has finally melted away.

May 16: Today it is again snowing heavily. Bravo spring! O you delightful, charming month! — Month of ice!

May 21: Today the river is full of floating ice. The steamers are probably still all in Weshking Bay.

May 22: The "Illinois" came up. She had time to make the trip, but she will wait before she proceeds up on Lake Superior.

May 23: No! Because today the "General Taylor" came down and brought news that steamers can at last continue their journey. Still floating ice in St. Mary's River. // Today for the first time, I made a fire only in the morning.

May 24: Especially today I have had lingering definite, resolute thoughts and plans of resigning, and (again become) an Indian missionary.[46] ᴸThy will be done, O Lord God!ᴸ <(And so continually and everywhere.>

May 25: The soldiers[47] arrived today.

May 26: Left the Sault and arrived at Mackinac.

May 28: To Pointe St. Ignace where I remained until Pentecost Sunday. There I had unpleasantness because of the ᴱBishop's land."ᴱ [48] I told Sophie Graveraet that after

[46]The original German is abbreviated and unclear but the sense of the statement accurately represents Baraga's mood.

[47]The summer contingent for Fort Brady.

[48]Bishop Résé had acquired extensive land for the church at St. Ignace. Wood from the property provided income; some buildings were used as residences, i.e., for the teachers in the Catholic schools at St. Ignace. Rezek, II, 148–50. In 1857 Baraga wrote to Résé: "Please send me a certificate that you bought your prop[erty] at Pointe St. Ignace for the use of every Pastor there." BLS, July 14, 1857. There is no record of a response from Bishop Résé.

August 1 she can remain in the "Bishop's house" only under sentence of <u>great excommunication</u>.

June 1:     Arrived at Cross Village. (Grief because of Weikamp.)[49]

June 4:     Arrived at Garden Island. The teacher O'Donovan is like a missionary, especially against drunkenness.[50] On June 7 I had all the men sign the temperance pledge.

June 8:     Arrived again in Cross Village, where I remained until the feast of Corpus Christi.

June 12:    Arrived at Middle Village, and stayed until the following Sunday.

June 15:    Arrived in Little Traverse, but stayed only <u>one</u> night, and on the 16th departed.

June 17:    Arrived at Grand Traverse. There especially I had firm resolutions of <u>resigning</u> the entire, or at least this troublesome appendix. <Mr. Mrak, 15 Cof.>[51]

June 22:    Arrived back in Little Traverse. Left the following day.

June 23:    Arrived in Chaboiganing.[52] The teacher is very good and satisfied. For $30 I bought the school house, for which previously I had to pay $15 annual rent.

June 26:    Arrived <with Laut[ishar]>[53] in Little Traverse, where on Sunday, June 28, I preached and had some confirmations. Also here I again encouraged temperance. God grant success.

June 29:    My <u>sixtieth</u> birthday. A day of fatiguing trip from Little Traverse via Middle Village to Cross Village, where on June 30 and July 1 I had to remain, exhausted.[54]

---

[49]Fr. Weikamp was eccentric in many ways and caused Baraga much anxiety.

[50]While Baraga was on Garden Island, fifty-four Indians signed a letter to Agent Fitch in which they praised O'Donovan's teaching and actions against intemperance and for their rights. Chippewas to Fitch, Garden Island, June 6, 1857. Orig. in NA-OIA; in BBC-C 3593 E. O'Donovan to Fitch, May 15, 1857, and September 27, 1858. Origs. in NA-OIA; in BBC-C 4067 E; C 1193 E.

[51]Added later in pencil. Probably means fifteen confirmations.

[52]At Burt Lake.

[53]Added in pencil.

[54]Lautishar sent an extensive account of this visitation to his friends, Little Traverse, August 11, 1857. Printed in ZD; in BBC-B 1044 S.

July 2:        Arrived at poor Mackinac,[55] and on

July 3:        sailed on the "Adriatic" at 7:30 A.M. and on

July 4:        at 10 P.M. arrived in Detroit.

July 5:        Sunday. Blessing of the church and bells in St. Philip's German Church,[56] where I preached in German and English, at the request of Bishop Lefevere. — I am glad I came to Detroit at this time of the change of agents.[57] The entire week I did much running around in order to receive from the agent my money loaned to the teachers.[58] It is well that I came myself to Detroit, otherwise I would have lost at least $275. (— 2nd quarter of 1856 for Hickey and Carpenter, and Branen.)

July 12:       In St. Joseph's preached in German. I told Fr. Francis[59] outright that he should not come to my diocese.

July 13:       Only today did I receive all the money which I had paid out in advance for the teachers in 1856. — Thanks be to God.[60]

July 14:       Departed from Detroit at 10 A.M. on the "Northstar".

July 15:       At 2 P.M. arrived in Sault Ste. Marie with the cleric John Paul Stenger.[61] May God grant that he will be-

---

[55]Cf. D, January 15 and 18, 1857.

[56]St. Philip Beniti Church at Columbus, Michigan, thirty miles northeast of Detroit. It is now St. Philip Neri Parish in Richmond. It was established as a mission in the 1840s and became a parish in 1907. Fr. Lawrence Kilroy, Baraga's friend, was serving the entire area at this time. Cf. D, August 1, 1862.

[57]Rev. Andrew M. Fitch replaced Henry C. Gilbert as Indian agent at Detroit, 1857–1861.

[58]As a regular practice Baraga paid the teachers from his own pocket and waited for the reimbursement from the government for himself.

[59]Francis Edward van Campenhoudt (c. 1825–September 26, 1880), a Belgian, was the first pastor of St. Joseph (German) Parish in Detroit (1855–1859). In 1859 he transferred to the Diocese of Albany. He was the pastor at St. Mary's Parish in Baldwinville, New York, when he died. CALM, 1857, 1859, 1881.

[60]In a memorandum to Fitch, Baraga listed the schools, teachers, and amount due yearly: Timothy Hegney, Grand Portage, $200 for first and second quarters; William O'Donovan, Garden Island, $100 for first quarter; Mr. Dillon O'Brien and Mrs. Elizabeth O'Brien, boys' and girls' schools at La Pointe, $100 and $75 respectively for third quarter. Baraga to Fitch, Detroit, July 13, 1857. Orig. in NA-OIA; in BBC-A 611 E.

[61]On August 14, 1857, Baraga wrote to Lefevere: "I send you back Mr. Stenger, he cannot be alone on a mission." BLS. Later Baraga explained to Henni: "Here is the promised letter [from the Benedictines] which testifies to the unfitness of the

come a good and zealous missionary! I H S <(He is a simpleton.)>[62] *On the 19th I conferred on J. P. Stenger the four minor orders.*[63]

| | |
|---|---|
| July 20: | Sailed from the Sault on the "Illinois" at 3 P.M. |
| July 21: | Remained in Marquette for a few hours, and on |
| July 22: | towards evening arrived in Superior, without calling on La Pointe. |
| July 23: | At 2 A.M. arrived in La Pointe where I stayed with Mr. V. Paemel over Sunday (the 26th), and confirmed 24 people. (Brought the family of school-teacher O'Brien[64] to La Pointe.) |
| July 27: | Sailed from La Pointe[65] on the "Northstar" to Ontonagon. |
| July 28: | Arrived on Ontonagon; very much displeased because of the disunity of the two priests, Dunne and Fox, and because Dunne did not appear satisfied to go to Mackinac. On the 31st Mr. Fox came to Ontonagon, and returned again to Minnesota [Mine] on Aug[ust] 1. |
| Aug. 4: | Arrived at Eagle Harbor at 4 A.M. on the "General Taylor". Fortunately, Mr. Jacker was just there, and on the 6th he again returned to L'Anse. |

---

poor Stenger for the priesthood. He had surreptitiously received ¹· minor orders¹· from me before I had received this letter. Your Episcopal Grace may keep this letter for future use: I do not need it any more." Baraga to Henni, Sault Ste. Marie, May 31, 1858. Orig. in MADA; in BBC-A 671 G.

[62]Baraga used the word *prismojenz*, which means "crazy" or "crack-brained."

[63]In left margin.

[64]Dillon O'Brien (1818–1882) was born in Roscommon, Ireland, where he received a Jesuit education. In the late 1840s he and his wife, Elizabeth, and their four children migrated to Detroit. Baraga advanced the third-quarter salary to the O'Briens. He also gave them $50 of his own money because of their extreme need. Baraga to Fitch, La Pointe, July 24, 1857. Orig. in NA-OIA; in BBC-A 612 E. They taught in La Pointe until 1863 when, with six children, they moved to St. Paul, Minnesota. Here O'Brien edited the Catholic weekly, *The Chronicle*, led the Father Matthews Temperance Societies and headed the Catholic Colonization Bureau to encourage and assist Irish immigrants to Minnesota. He was also a speaker, writer, and humorist and a revered friend of Bishops Grace and Ireland. Acta et Dicta, VI, No. 1 (October 1933), pp. 35–53. Verwyst, pp. 290–94.

[65]Before he sailed on the 27th, Baraga baptized a newborn girl. Cf. La Pointe Baptismal Registry.

Aug. 8:    At 11 A.M. left Eagle Harbor on the "Northstar", and at 10 P.M. arrived in Marquette. Here I was very much disappointed because of the complaints about the drinking and harshness of the priest.[66] Here I had only 4 confirmations.

Aug. 13:   Arrived again in Sault Sainte Marie on the "Lady Elgin" at 11 A.M. There to my great joy, I found Br[other] Ludwig who came for ordination I H S — On the other hand, sorrow because of the poor apostate Stenger, whom I am compelled to dismiss, as well as another student, <u>Mayer</u>, who came here on his own.

Aug. 15:   <u>Sunday</u>. At 8 A.M. I conferred the subdiaconate on Ludwig Sifferath. At half past 9 I was called to old Mrs. Biron.[67] At 11 I preached in English and French, and after the mass in Indian.

Aug. 20:   Today Mr. Sifferath received the diaconate.

---

[66]Fr. Duroc, who had just returned from France, was to have brought Rev. Mr. Martin Marco to the diocese. However, "Mr. Marco, who is of a tender & delicate conscience, having, on his journey been much scandalized at the improper conduct of his Companion, & besides, understanding, that, if ordained priest at Sault St. Mary, he must, of course, expect to be sent to some mission alone far distant from any other priest, has become so frightened that he is determined not to go farther & begged me to receive him for the Diocess [sic] of Detroit." Lefevere to Purcell, Detroit, June 10, 1857. Orig. in NDUA; in BBC-B 930 E. In August Baraga asked Lefevere to reimburse him for the $100 he had paid for Marco's passage. BLS, August 14, 1857.

Baraga omitted mention of these difficulties when he wrote: "On the annual visit of my diocese I have arrived here in Marquette . . . where I found the Rev. Mr. Duroc who has just arrived from his journey to France. . . . I attest . . . that he has great need of the assistance which he requests . . . and I hope, Mr. Choiselat, that you will have the kindness to forward to him the sum which he asks." Baraga to PFAP, Marquette, August 11, 1857. A week later Baraga again wrote: "Fr. Duroc has never sent me the 1000 francs that he has received from you; on the contrary, he is asking the Propagation for 1500 more, as you perhaps already know by his letter. I ask you, (if that is feasible,) to grant him that sum, without charging it to my account." Origs. in PFAP; in BBC-A 490 F; A 489 F.

[67]Probably the wife of "old Biron," an erratic parishioner at the Sault (cf. D December 8, 1858; January 11 and November 4, 1860). Thomas Biron, carpenter, was 33 years old, and his wife, Margaret, was 22. They are the only Birons in the census records but would hardly be "old" in 1857. Listed with them are two girls, Francis [sic], 1 year old, and Julia, 9. Federal Census, 1860, Chippewa County, #94.

Aug. 21:  The canal broke today, which perhaps cannot be repaired for a long time. Misère! (on the 24th it was finished.)

Aug. 23:  Mr. Sifferath received Holy Orders. On the 24th he sailed on[68] the "Collingwood" for Mackinac.

Aug. 26:  Mr. Jahan came up and remained here until the 31st.

Sept. 2:  Today Mr. Piret came and brought evidence that proves the unfortunate Catherine Plante named several men as fathers of her children; by which she proves that she deserves no credence. Misère!!!!!!

Sept. 4:  This morning at 7 Fr. Menet went to Detroit, and on his way back will spend a week or 2 in poor Mackinac. ([He will do this] later)

Sept. 8:  Jo[seph] Meniclier began his work on the church today. The scaffolding was erected. Tomorrow they will start painting the vaulted ceiling.

Sept. 11–12: On the 11th John Porter's sister died, and on the 12th she was buried.

Sept. 18:  Fr. Menet has left for Mackinac. (Misère!) and on

Sept. 29:  he has returned again.

Oct. 5:  Agent Fitch[69] arrived here today, and immediately continued on to <u>Pointe Iroquois</u>[70] where he takes over the payment. *And today William Kelly,[71] who was here a week, went on to Cape Girardeau.*[72]

Oct. 13:  Gave Mr. Barbeau $110 in banknotes which he is [to] make available at my ᶠdemand.ᶠ I drew $55 from P. B.

---

[68]In the original German Baraga wrote *auch* instead of *auf*.

[69]Rev. Andrew M. Fitch was Indian agent for the Mackinac Agency, 1857–1861. MPHC, 8, p. 230.

[70]Baraga anticipated that Agent Fitch would not stop at the Sault. He wrote to Fitch, requesting his money, and asked Barbeau to give it to Fitch at Mackinac. Baraga to Fitch, Sault Ste. Marie, September 24, 1857. Orig. in NA-OIA; in BBC-A 613 E.

[71]Baraga received Kelly into the diocese and sent him to Cape Girardeau, Missouri, to learn French. BLS, October 4, 1857. Kelly did not return to the Sault although, on July 20, 1858, Baraga sent him $20 to "come immediately; you will study here." BLS. In 1864 Kelly was the first priest ordained in Nebraska. He died in Omaha on October 23, 1907. Catholic Directory, CALM, 1908.

[72]Written in the left column.

Barbeau for D. O'Brien. Barbeau received from me, <sup>F</sup>at my demand:<sup>F</sup> $90 = Carolina[73] check, $450 = Rothchild, $275 = Fitch, $110 = bills, making $925. Now to keep an accurate record of it all that I have with him or will take from him.

Oct. 19:     Last night it snowed for the first time. Misère! (On the following day the snow melted.)

Oct. 25:     Mr. Patrick Bernard Murray[74] has arrived, with the intention of being incardinated in this diocese. On the 27th he received tonsure and the 4 minor orders; on the 28th the subdiaconate; on the 30th diaconate, and on the 3rd of November the priesthood.[75]

Nov. 1:      Fourth anniversary of my consecration. Pontifical mass at the new altar.

Nov. 7:      Rev. P. B. Murray offered his first holy mass. And I broke my topaz ring. — What kind of an omen is this?

Nov. 12:     Today, finally, Rev. Murray has sailed on the old "Michigan"[76] to Mackinac. // The "City of Superior", on her 4th trip, is stranded in the entrance of Copper Harbor.

N.B. Nov. 11 Pontifical mass and profession of Mary Henry: in religion <u>Mary Joseph</u>.[77]

---

[73]Carolina Augusta, dowager queen of Austria.

[74]Patrick Bernard Murray was born in June 1824 at Ballygovern, North Ireland. He studied in the United States and Canada and Baraga ordained him on October 31, 1857. His assignments included Mackinac, Beaver Island, Sheboygan, and Alpena. Upon Baraga's death he became part of the Detroit diocese; in 1883 Bishop Grace requested that he come to St. Paul where he worked until his death in Wabasha, Minnesota, on January 29, 1908, a few months after his Golden Jubilee of ordination. He avidly advocated temperance and was a great consolation to bishops Baraga, Borgess, Grace, and Ireland. He is the only priest who preserved many (thirty-five) of the personal letters he received from Bishop Baraga and was one of the few priests to visit Baraga in Marquette during his final illness.

[75]Baraga corrected the date of ordination to October 31 when he wrote accounts for DCV, WF, and KZ. BLS, November 3, 1857. The official diocesan records also give the date of October 31, 1857. Vertin to Murray, Marquette, March 7, 1893. Orig. in MQDA; in BBC-B 81 E.

[76]The U.S.S. *Michigan* was the first iron-hulled warship built on the Great Lakes. She sailed from 1844 to 1923. The *Michigan* was used on July 9, 1856 by the assassins of James Jesse Strang, leader of the Mormon community on Beaver Island. Howard-Filler, pp. 44–48.

[77]"On Oct[ober] 31, the Rt. Rev. Bishop Baraga has conferred the holy priesthood on

Nov. 15:    The church stoves heated for the first time. ——

Nov. 17:    Today the stormshed[78] was set up. // The "Lady El-gin", which went up on Oct[ober] 30, is not yet back today — 19 days! What is that! — No! She and the "Iron City" came down day before yesterday, Sunday the 15th.

Nov. 19:    Today the "Mineral Rock" went up. Probably the last boat. It is a very stormy day, north wind all day long.

Nov. 21:    The "Mineral Rock" went through the canal to Lake Superior. N.B. On Nov[ember] 19 Br[other] Donovan[79] put away approximately ½ cord of wood.

Nov. 27:    Today I broke my pectoral cross, like my pastoral ring on the 7th. What kind of omen and sign is this again? — It is a certain sign of ineptitude and imprudence.

Nov. 30:    The "Mineral Rock" came down entirely unlooked for and unexpected; went successfully through the canal and sailed away Dec[ember] 1.

Dec. 17:    Today the first ᴱover-land-mailᴱ arrived from Sagi-naw, etc. —

Dec. 31:    The last day of a splendid December. Having pleas-ant, mild weather; it does not[80] freeze at all and it is always calm. The river is as clear as in summer, not a piece of ice on it. — But the poor mail carriers, espe-cially those from Marquette, who probably have no ice on the shore and in the bays.

---

the Rev. Patrick Bernard Murray. On the 11th inst[ant] the bishop invested Miss Mary Henry with the black religious veil of the Ursuline order. Since this was the first religious profession that has taken place in this diocese til now, it was performed in a solemn manner. In an appropriate address the bishop spoke about the happiness of a religious vocation, and then sang a solemn pontifical mass, and before it as well as during and after it the ceremonies of the religious profession were performed." Baraga to WF, Sault Ste. Marie, November 13, 1857. Printed in WF, xxi, 163; in BBC-A 719 G.

[78]Translation *stormshed* inserted by Bishop Eis.

[79]William Donovan was a Jesuit brother. He came to the Sault in January 1856, and replaced Brother Harney in the kitchen and for the farm work. Later he also as-sisted with the teaching duties at the Sault. In 1860 he was 38 years old. Federal Census, 1860, Chippewa County, #158.

[80]*Not* is missing from the original German; the context would indicate that its omis-sion was inadvertent.

# 1858

Jan. 5:  Always fair weather, still no snow, nor is it windy; what snow there was is almost melted.

Jan. 12:  Had a few days and nights of some coldness, and the river is finally frozen.

Jan. 13:  Today it is very ᶜslushyᶜ again. The poor wayfarers.

Jan. 16:  Last night it snowed considerably but today is nice again, and not cold.

Jan. 21:  Had a dispute with Fr. Menet today, because I invited for a meal two poor Indians who arrived here late, bringing mail from Manitowaning.[81] And today he himself treated the two sons of Major Raines.[82] — ᴸRespector of persons.ᴸ — ꟳHospitality is lacking, which is a branch of charity.ꟳ — Christ the Lord said that it is better to treat the <u>poor</u> hospitably than the <u>rich</u>.

Jan. 24:  All day long thawing weather and rain. Everything is under water. It seems that the cold of last winter was <u>equal to two winters</u>. The poor ᴱmail-carriers!ᴱ <We

---

[81]Manitowaning is a settlement on the southeast coast of Manitoulin Island.

[82]Tudor and Hoel D. Rains were the sons of Major William Kingdom Rains of Neebish Island. Major Rains was born in Wales on June 2, 1789. A graduate of Woolrich Military Academy in June 1805, he served under Wellington. He came to Canada in 1830 and from 1834 was a partner in several business ventures on islands in the St. Marys River. Rains was an accomplished linguist and scholar; he trained each of his children in history, literature, and politics. He died in October 1874 and was interred at Sault Ste. Marie, Ontario. Bayliss, pp. 126–28, 167, 170. In the introduction (p. 5) to Grace Lee Nute's *Lake Superior*, Milo Quaife wrote of Rains: "On the rocky Island of Malta a century and a quarter ago a British officer pored over a collection of maps and charts. Fascinated by the conception he derived from them of the St. Mary's River as one of the world's great waterways, he determined that someday he would view it with his own eyes. Years passed and at length his dream came true. Resigning his commission he migrated to Canada to spend the remainder of his life beside the majestic river which conducts the waters of Lake Superior to their wedding with those of Lake Huron. Superior's basin was still a wilderness when Major William Kingdom Rains thus succumbed to the spell of the great inland sea." Sometime during 1858 Rains's 7-year-old daughter became a boarder at the Ursuline Academy. St. Paul, p. 139. In 1860 Rains was 71; his wife, Frances, was 50. Their children, Arthur, Hosea, Alice, Constance, Rupert, Lindah, William, and Almah, lived with them. Federal Census, 1860, Chippewa County, #252. Another son, Owen, 29, and his wife, Victoria, 19, lived nearby. Federal Census, 1860, Chippewa County, #253.

heard a rumor that Fr[ancis] Lalonde[83] and ———[84] Poisson foundered in the Straits of Mackinac. Hope it is false. — <u>False!</u> — January 26.>

Jan. 25:  I received the Ordo today, besides many rather pleasing and interesting letters.[85]

Jan. 30:  The past night was very cold. Moreover, it had been cold for 3 days already and I hope that the ice will soon be strong enough to carry me to Pinatangwishing.[86]

Feb. 3:  The mail carriers from Manitowaning arrived. They say the ice is now good, at least for foot and dog, perhaps not yet for horses. Those from Pinatangwishing have come also on good ice to Manitowaning.

Feb. 12:  Departed for Cincinnati,[87] via Pinatangwishing, Canada West. From the Sault to Mis[s]isagi[88] I rode with Mr. Sayer. From Missisagi to La Cloche[89] and on to Jibaonaning[90] I hope to ride with Mr. McTavish. From the Sault to Bruce Mine; remained overnight with Plante. (With Mr. Simpson, McTavish, Old Sayer, George Sayer, Edward Sayer). In the evening I said the evening prayer with the family, and baptized 3 children.

---

[83]Francis LaLonde, a farmer, 54, and his wife, Louisa, 36, had five children. Federal Census, 1850, Chippewa County, #117.

[84]Baraga could recall the first name.

[85]He received letters from Francis Joseph Salomon (a prospective teacher), Pierz, Lautishar, and Bishop Luers, Bishop of Fort Wayne. BLR.

[86]Penetanguishene is located on the tip of a peninsula in Georgian Bay, a few miles northwest of the Martyrs' Shrine at Midland, Ontario. It is one of the most ancient historic sites in Canada. Cadieux, p. 901.

[87]For the Second Provincial Council. Fr. Menet wrote: "The Bishop left yesterday for Cincinnati, where he must attend the Provincial Council, and have his Indian books printed. He will go Penetangushene [sic], Hamilton, Buffalo, etc. God only knows why he chose that way, which is long and tiresome. He'll have to suffer to get to Penetangushene [sic]." Menet to Tellier, Sault Ste. Marie, February 13, 1858. Orig. in ACSM; in BBC-Mss. 26. This out-of-the-way route gave Menet the suspicion that Baraga was going to Hamilton to see Bishop Farrell.

[88]The Mississagi is a river that flows into the North Channel of Lake Huron at a site two miles west of Blind River, Ontario. Cadieux, p. 900.

[89]Fort situated adjacent to the Spanish River Indian Reservation, nine miles north of Little Current, Ontario. Cadieux, p. 899.

[90]Probably Shebahonaning, the Indian name for Killarney, Ontario, located across the North Channel of Lake Huron from Manitoulin Island. Cadieux, p. 878.

Feb. 13: From Bruce Mine to Missisagi. In the evening we said evening prayers with the Sayer family, and I preached in French.

Feb. 14: Sunday. I asked Mr. Simpson and Mr. McTavish not to travel on Sunday, so we remained in Missisagi with Mr. Sayer, where we said prayers in common in the morning and in the evening I preached. One child baptized.

Feb. 15: From Mississagi to La Cloche, 54 miles. There again I said prayers in the evening with the family and preached and baptized one child. Here I left Mr. Simpson and McTavish.

Feb. 16: In a dog sled with 3 dogs from La Cloche to Jibaonaning, where, in the chapel that they have there, I prayed and preached in the evening. Here I was very well received by postmaster Johnson. From here we went Etogether with the mail-carriersE to Pinatang-wishing.

Feb. 17: From Jibaonaning to French River, somewhat further, where we spent the night in a very small Indian house.

Feb. 18: Next night in an Indian lodge, which was just a little better than outdoors.

Feb. 19: Spent the next night in an abandoned Email-carrier'sE house, without a door or windows, where I spent the night miserably in a dog sled.

Feb. 20: From here over Labatte's portage to Pinatangwishing, where we only arrived about 8 P.M. and turned into Louis Corradi's, here I paid Edward Sayer, Sunday inclusive.

Feb. 21: Sunday. I spent this day with Rev. Mr. Lebaudy.[91] At 8 I offered holy mass and at 10 preached in French and English, and in the afternoon assisted at vespers. I slept at Corradi's.

[91]Later Baraga aided Lebaudy in acquiring an Otchipwe grammar and dictionary from Bellecourt, the New York publisher. BLS, June 18, 1859.

| | |
|---|---|
| Feb. 22: | Left at 8 on the ᴱstageᴱ to Barrie, but because of the tardiness of the drivers I arrived just after 4 P.M. and the ᴱcarsᴱ[92] were pulling out for Toronto. |
| Feb. 23: | From Barrie to Toronto, where I did not stay long because the bishop [Charbonnel] was not there. In the evening I continued my journey and came to the ᴱSuspension Bridgeᴱ where I spent the night. This ᴱSuspension Bridgeᴱ over the St. Lawrence [Niagara] River, ᴱat the foot of Niagara Fallsᴱ is a ᴱstupendous work so solidᴱ that the heaviest train runs over it in safety. |
| Feb. 24: | From Suspension Bridge to Buffalo, where I remained all day and sought Bishop Timon[93] three times at his house, but never did meet him; he had gone to a nearby mission. |
| Feb. 25: | Arrived in Cincinnati[94] at 7 P.M., and stayed a night with Fr. Kroeger.[95] |
| Feb. 26: | Moved in with Fr. Hammer, where I shall remain until my works[96] are printed. |
| Feb. 28: | Very cold. The canal[97] is frozen shut. |

[92]Train.

[93]John Timon was born on February 12, 1797, at Conewago, Pennsylvania. He professed his vows as a Vincentian on June 10, 1825. On September 23, 1826, he was ordained. Timon became the first provincial of the Vincentians in the United States on November 16, 1835, and first prefect apostolic of Texas on April 12, 1840. He was consecrated bishop of the new diocese of Buffalo, October 17, 1847. Timon died on April 16, 1867. Code, p. 283.

[94]The newspaper reported: "Rt. Rev. Bishop Baraga in Cincinnati: In these days we had the great pleasure of seeing here the Rt. Rev. Bishop Baraga of Sault Sainte Mary, the Apostle of the Indians of North America. The Rev. indefatigable prelate will stay here some weeks in order to have several books in the Indian language printed in the office of the WF. The Rt. Rev. Bishop left Sault Sainte Mary on Feb[ruary] 12, rode in those cold regions 8 days long in a dog sled pulled by 3 strong dogs, hitched one behind the other, over the ice and frozen snow . . . to Pinatengwishing [sic], in Canada, covering 40–50 miles, once even 54 miles and arrived here via Toronto, Hamilton, and Buffalo on Thursday, Feb[ruary] 25, in good health even though somewhat affected by the cold." WF, xxi, 430 (March 4, 1858); in BBC-B 1061 G.

[95]Peter Kroeger was the theologian who assisted Baraga during the Second Provincial Council, May 2–9, 1858. CT, xxvii, May 2, 1858; in BBC-A 149 E.

[96]Gagikwe-masinaigan (sermon book); Anamie-misenagan (prayer book, Ottawa); Anamie-masinaigan (prayer book, Chippewa).

[97]The Miami-Maumee Canal, built in 1830, went from Cincinnati on the Ohio River to Toledo on Lake Erie. Lamott, p. 124.

March 6: Today I finally received the <u>first proof sheets</u> of Ga-gikwe-masinaigan; and today — misère!!! — B. L.[98] was imposed upon me. — <(Later: Thank God a thousand times for that!)>

March 14: My work progresses despairingly slow. In two weeks I have only gotten out 2 sheets.

March 29: Today I finished 10 sheets. I hope to be finished by Easter with the Gagikwe-masinaigan.

April 3: Now, finally Gagikwe-masinaigan is completed. Next week, Easter week, I will begin Anamie-mis, and the Anamie-mas. It will be a difficult task to publish this prayer book in <u>two dialects</u>.

April 9: Thanks be to God, today I received the report from Mrs. Kreuzburg that the Ludwig Mission Society[99] of Munich has sent me 1500 florins, $600, which I may draw at Kruezburg and Nurre.

April 11: <u>Low Sunday</u>. Today I pontificated solemnly at St. Mary's Church, and distributed first holy communion to the children prepared for it. In the afternoon at 4 P.M. I administered holy confirmation to 75 children and adults.

<(N.B. On April 18 of this year the first steamboats arrived in Sault Sainte Marie, the "Northstar" and 2 others, never have they come so early before.)>

April 20–23: These days, at the request of Bishop Carrell, I con-ferred in St. Mary's church minor orders to Mr. Spitzlberger[100] and to Mr. Fuchshuber,[101] and to Mr. Spitzlberger the subdiaconate, diaconate and priest-hood.

April 25: Today I performed for Bishop Carrell the laying of the corner-stone of a new German church on St. John's

---

[98]"B. L." is an abbreviation for *Bogen-Lesen*, reading the galley sheets.

[99]The Ludwig Mission Society, founded in Bavaria in 1828, was a German benevo-lent society formed to advance the missionary activities of the Catholic Church and German missionaries in the United States.

[100]Rev. Lawrence Spitzlberger served in Kentucky, Pennsylvania, Minnesota, and Wisconsin until his death at Appleton, Wisconsin, on August 19, 1905.

[101]Fuchshuber was later ordained but, after 1859, there is no reference to him in CALM.

Hill, 3 miles outside of Covington. A solemnity such as this, will never happen to me <sup>c</sup>it is far from being the case<sup>c</sup> in my diocese.[102]

May 2: <u>Sunday</u>. The Second Provincial Council of Cincinnati began, and on May 9 it was concluded.

May 14: Today I finally finished the editions of Anamie-<u>mis</u> and <u>mas</u>.

May 16: At Gallipolis,[103] in place of Archbishop Purcell, I blessed the church and then went to Pomeroy,[104] to Mr. Albrinck,[105] from here I left on May 18 and on

May 19: Arrived in Cincinnati.

May 23: <u>Pentecost Sunday</u>. In St. Mary's church I solemnly pontificated, and preached a sermon of farewell.

May 25: Finally, after 3 months, left Cincinnati.[106] I received there over $400 for mass intentions and from collections.

[102]Baraga blessed two cornerstones in the diocese. The first was at Marquette in the spring (possibly Easter, April 16) of 1865. The second, at St. Paul's Church in Negaunee on November 10, 1867, was Baraga's last appearance at a public function before his death.

Baraga wrote an extensive description of the event at Marquette: "[T]his spring a solemnity has come up which in this poor, remote diocese has as yet never taken place, namely, laying the corner stone of a new church. . . . [N]ow, in an important location on Lake Superior, a big church is being built, which, although it will also be built only of wood, its foundation, however, has been laid deep in the ground and regularly built with stone. The foundation alone costs 1200 dollars.

"The laying of the corner stone, which I performed precisely according to the rules of the Roman pontifical, was as solemn as it could be. A very large group of people assembled to be present at this solemnity, most of whom have never before witnessed it. We placed a document in the corner stone on which the usual data are recorded, namely, the names of the acting bishop, and of the pastor [Henry L. Thiele] of the church, as well as the name of the president of the United States [Abraham Lincoln] and of the governor of our State of Michigan [Kingsley S. Bingham]. Also various new coins were laid inside. After the solemnity I delivered an address to the assembled multitude in which I explained the meaning of this solemnity. The heavens favored our solemnity with as beautiful weather as one could have wished." Baraga to LS, Sault Ste. Marie, June 8, 1865. Orig. in LSA; in BBC-A 113 G.

[103]Gallipolis is on the western shore of the Ohio River, 175 miles east of Cincinnati.

[104]Pomeroy is twenty miles north of Gallipolis.

[105]Rev. John C. Albrinck, pastor at Pomeroy, also served Gallipolis. CALM, 1859.

[106]"May God grant the humble spiritually zealous disciple of the apostles a safe journey." WF, XXI, 474 (May 27, 1858); in BBC-B 394 G.

May 26:    At 3 A.M. I arrived in Detroit, where I live with the Redemptorist Fathers.[107] (Mr. Fitch has paid me the debt of Dillon O'Brien with $191 in silver.)

May 28:    At 11 A.M. sailed from Detroit on the "Northstar", and on the 29th at 1 P.M., 26 hours later, arrived at Sault Sainte Marie.[108]

June 7:    Early this moning, at 8 A.M., sailed from the Sault with Mr. Dunne and at 4 P.M. we arrived at Mackinac, where I heard nothing but good about Mr. Murray; thanks be to God!

June 8:    At 8 A.M. sailed from Mackinac and at 3 P.M. arrived at Cross Village.[109]

---

[107] The Superior-Pastor at St. Mary's, Rev. John Hespelein, C.Ss.R., frequently sent mass stipends to Baraga.

[108] Baraga wrote: "My return voyage was happy, and at my arrival here I found all in good order. Next week I intend to start for my Indian Missions on Lake Michigan, and will not be back again for 5 or 6 weeks." Baraga to Purcell, Sault Ste. Marie, May 31, 1858. Orig. in NDUA; in BBC-A 157 E.

[109] It is possible to follow this voyage in greater detail using this article Baraga wrote: "Since many readers of the Wahrheitsfreund know the Indian-bishop Baraga, either personally or through his letters, a report from my mission may perhaps interest them, and that is why I ask you to accept this letter in your widely circulated and much read Wahrheitsfreund.

"I have just returned from a long and fatiguing mission visitation journey, but I hope a useful one. I was on the journey for a month and a half. I have visited all the missions in the southern part of my diocese and in each mission I stayed at least a week. Some of these missions I have founded and established 27 years ago, and some I have continued, and at that time I have had many conversions and baptisms. For a long time all these Indians have been converted and now live by agriculture, like other civilized people. If here or there a pagan is still about, then he is a stubborn individual from whom nothing good can be expected.

"I first visited a mission which we call Cross Village and which is the mission of Rev. Seraphin Zorn. Here we have two small convents for Brothers and Sisters of the Third Order of St. Francis. The superior of this congregation, Father Weikamp, had built a conventual church, which he had dedicated during my presence. On the Sunday that I had spent at Cross Village I preached twice to the Indians, (which I did almost everywhere), and confirmed 27 Indians.

"From Cross Village I was given a ride to Beaver [Garden] Island which lies far from land, in the middle of Lake Michigan. When I came on this island for the first time, 27 years ago, where before then no priest had ever set foot, all the inhabitants were pagans, and I had the consolation of converting many to christianity and baptizing them. In the course of time all have been converted to the christian catholic religion, and now diligently visit the church on Sundays and feast days, even when no missioner is there. They assemble themselves in the church in the morning and in the afternoon to sing holy hymns and to pray the rosary in their own language. If possible, a missioner visits them every

June 13:     Blessed Fr. Weikamps's church, consecrated his ceme-
             tery, confirmed 27 persons and preached twice to the
             Indians.

June 14:     Today I sailed to Garden Island and remained there
             on the 15th and 16th, ᴸin the bitterness of my heartᴸ110
             because of the general drinking of the local Indians.

June 17:     Early in the morning after mass, confirmed 30 per-
             sons, young and old. After the ceremony I left and by
             evening arrived in Cross Village.

---

month, but sometimes the elements will not permit him to come. And when he does come, they usually all come to confession. We have here a good school-teacher [William O'Donovan], (such as we have in all missions); he is very zeal-ous and accomplishes much good among the Indians by his example and with his exhortations. My reception here was very friendly and at the same time edi-fying. They rang the bell, all came to me on the shore and knelt down to receive the bishop's blessing; and then they accompanied me to the church, where, af-ter a brief speech, I again gave them the holy blessing.—I came to them with the missioner Rev. Father S. Zorn, who generally visits them. I remained there a few days and on the morning of my departure I administered holy confirmation to 30 Indians.

"From Beaver Island I returned to Cross Village and the next morning I went to another Indian village which we call <u>Middle Village</u>. There is a small church here which the missioner Zorn visits once every 14 days; and on the Sundays when the missioner is not there, the Indians assemble themselves in the church, in the morning and in the afternoon, and then sing and pray. Also here some had been prepared for holy confirmation, 11 persons.

"My next station was my old Arbre Croche, where in May, 1831, I began my Indian missions under the saintly Bishop Fenwick, the first Bishop of Cin-cinnati, to whose diocese all these missions belonged at that time. He himself accompanied me to this mission and stayed there for a few days. The present missioner [Sifferath] has not been long among the Indians and still knows little Indian. And so, during my stay, I took over all the missionary labors and every evening heard confessions until 10 or 11 o'clock, and once until 11:30.

"From here I went to Grand Traverse, where the Rev. Ignatius Mrak has already labored for several years. In his mission district Father Mrak has also many whites, more and more of whom are settling on the spacious shore of Lake Michigan, Irish, French, German and Bohemians. Here I have confirmed 20 Indians.

"From Grand Traverse I went to Mackinac. This is an old mission of the Jesuits, which they had founded more than 200 years ago. After the dissolution of the Jesuit order, other missioners visited this mission from time to time, until, finally, the late Bishop Fenwick stationed a resident missioner here. The present missioner, the Rev. Patrick Murray, an Irishman, is a very zealous and active priest, who also takes great pains with the school and the Sunday instructions of the Christian Doctrine. He had prepared 45 persons for holy confirmation whom I have confirmed on the Sunday that I spent there.

"Now I again returned to Saut-Sainte-Marie, and in a few days I will leave for the missions on Lake Superior." Baraga to WF, Sault Ste. Marie, July 22, 1858. Printed in WF, xxi, 690; in BBC-A 687.

110Is 38:15.

June 18:     Rode from Cross Village to Middle Village.

June 20:     Sunday. Confirmed 11 persons in Middle Village and preached twice to the Indians.

June 21:     Arrived at Little Traverse, where the good humble Fr. Sifferat[h] serves God.[111]

June 22:     Departed for Shaboigan. There I heard confessions for 2 days in such terrible heat that the candles in the church melted.[112]

June 25:     Returned to Little Traverse Bay.

June 26:     Heard many confessions, until 11 P.M.

June 27:     Preached two stirring sermons; in the evening heard many confessions. Terrible heat — day and night.

June 28:     Have been in Agaming [Petosky] where I promised Trotochaud[113] board and nails. In the evening heard confessions until 11:30 P.M.

June 29:     ᴸMost celebrated day.ᴸ[114] I spent it sadly on the lake,

---

[111]Fr. Lautishar left for Minnesota on June 14. He had trained Fr. Sifferath since his ordination. Lautishar described the mission: "It is something like it is in Carniola, now and then some sinner becomes converted or one of the faithful falls. Some are pious, some lukewarm, some of the villages are better and some are not so good, — but all catholic Indians, except a small number, are of a catholic mind. Last fall the former minister (protestant teacher) took leave from my mission, as he said, because of the illness of his wife, (poor preachers who bear the marital burden!). But I believe he left for a different reason. It is well, thanks be to God! A protestant school in one of the villages of my former mission [Cross Village], which, up to last winter, I frequently visited, is also now abandoned. However, the small number of Indians is in great danger because of the whites. But God will watch over them." Lautishar to Volk, Little Traverse, June 10, 1858. Printed in ZD, 1858, 115; in BBC-B 603 S.

[112]On June 24 the fourth and final member of the nucleus of the Ursuline community made her vows. Irmine Bedard [Mother M. Augustine], daughter of Francis and —— Payment Bedard and niece of Michael Payment of Sugar Island, was born on February 24, 1836, at Regaud, Quebec. She served in the position of Depository, having charge of the temporal affairs of the community. In 1871 she came to Marquette to arrange for the departure of the Ursuline sisters who had taught at the cathedral school since 1865. On September 1, 1877, at the age of 41, she died from the complications of appendicitis. "Formulary Ledger." Orig. in UAC; in BBC-Mss. 48. St. Paul, pp. 183–88.

[113]Trotochaud was a carpenter. Baraga hired him to build a church at Agaming, present-day Petosky, then also known as Bear River. Trotochaud later gave Baraga an acre of land upon which to build the church, further removed from the hostile Protestant mission. Cf. D, June 6, 1859.

[114]It was Baraga's sixty-first birthday.

sailing to Grand Traverse. In the evening slept out in the open, however without mosquitoes.[115] (Terrible heat all day long.)

June 30: At 8 A.M. arrived at Eagletown where I remained until Sunday.

July 4: <u>Sunday</u>. In Eagletown — 20 confirmations. Peter Terhost[116] was almost sent away by Mr. Mrak, and then I would have had to take him with me to Mackinac.

July 5: Rode to Northport, where to my great displeasure, #but to my good luck, Rev. Mr. Moyce#[117] laid over at Dame's for 6 days.

July 11: Offered mass at Cat-head,[118] and preached twice in French and twice in Indian. On the same day, at 5 P.M. sailed on the propeller "Troy" for Mackinac.

July 12: Early in the morning, at 3 A.M., arrived at Mackinac. I sailed over to Pointe St. Ignace, where I remained 2 days, like my Jesus in Samaria.[119]

July 14: Confirmed 4 persons and then crossed over to Mackinac.[120]

---

[115]It was exceptional *not* to be pestered by mosquitoes.

[116]Gerhard Terhorst was born in Westphalia, Germany, on October 3, 1829. He studied with Fr. Mrak until Baraga sent him to the Sault in July 1860, where he was ordained on December 23, 1860. In May 1861, he was assigned to the Indian mission at L'Anse where he worked until his death on his seventy-second birthday (1901). A simple wooden cross marked his grave in the old mission cemetery at Assinins. Rezek, I, pp. 390–93.

[117]Venantius Moyce later went to Brooklyn where Bishop John Loughlin received him upon Baraga's recommendation: "How I found Mr. Moyce. He was dissatisfied with our poor M[issions] / No <u>intemp</u>[erance] or <u>immor</u>[ality]." BLS, November 2, 1858. Moyce was pastor at St. Mary's Church, Northhampton, Massachusetts, when he died on August 5, 1872. CALM, 1873.

[118]On the northwest coast of the Leelanau peninsula.

[119]Jn 4:40.

[120]From Mackinac Baraga asked Lefevere to cash a draft from PFAP for 7600 francs. Baraga to Lefevere, Mackinac, July 14, 1858. Orig. in NDUA; in BBC-A 158 E. He also informed Fitch that he "could not prevail on Mr. [Nicholas] Murray to remain at Sheboygan . . . [H]is immediate successor is Mr. Patrick Smyth, a good and practical teacher, a man of family. I always prefer married teachers, when I can have them." Baraga to Fitch, Mackinac, July 15, 1858. Orig. in NA-OIA; in BBC-A 616 E.

July 17:     #Mr. Patrick Venantius Moyce, cleric, arrived here to-day, and I won him over, God be thanked, for my diocese.[121] This occurred to me, praise God, during my delay of 6 days at Grand Traverse, because if I had been finished here in Mackinac last Sunday, then on the 14th I would have gone ahead on the "Illinois", and I would not have made, as I hope, this good acquisition. I H S m.d.s.g.J.[122] # <Great multi-sided misfortune!>

July 18:     Sunday. Preached in English and French, and after the high mass, confirmed 45 persons; and in the evening I went with Mr. Moyce on the steamer "Planet".

July 19:     At 10 A.M. I arrived at the Sault, and immediately had difficulties with Fr. Menet about Branen.[123] / Mr. Moyce is preparing himself for ordination, which he will receive this week.

July 21:     Mr. Moyce received the subdiaconate.

July 23:     Mr. Moyce received the diaconate.

July 24:     Mr. Moyce received the priesthood. This afternoon, on Ordination Day, Mr. Moyce and I boarded the propeller "Northern Light" to sail for Superior: however, I soon regretted this foolishness and we got off again at the head of the canal, thanks be to God!

July 25:     Rev. Moyce celebrated his first mass. // Received many consoling letters,[124] God be thanked! I H S m.d.s.g.J.

---

[121]Baraga was eager for an additional priest on Lake Superior. Fr. Dunne had just left Ontonagon and the diocese. See D, June 7, 1858.

[122]# . . . # indicates text that was crossed out. This five-letter abbreviation is used again on July 17 and 25, 1858, and on July 3, 1859. Its meaning is unknown.

[123]Baraga assigned Branen to teach at the Sault. He explained: "There is another change of teachers in your School-district. Mr. Jacker takes Mr. Branen's place at L'Anse. May Mr. Branen tell you what he pleases, I am very satisfied with the change. Mr. Jacker is as good an English scholar as Mr. Branen, if not better; and secondly, Mr. Jacker, being the missionary of that Band, will better be able to compel the children to come to school, than any other person." Baraga to Fitch, Sault Ste. Marie, July 20, 1858. Orig. in NA-OIA; in BBC-A 618 E.

[124]One of these letters was from Lefevere with the money Baraga had requested. Baraga to Lefevere, Sault Ste. Marie, August 26, 1858. Orig. in NDUA; in BBC-A 159 E.

July 29:  ·Today I finally sailed with Mr. Moyce for Superior on the "City of Cleveland", however, when we arrived in Ontonagon, Captain Lundy did not intend to continue sailing and I had to remain there 2 days.

Aug. 1:  Sunday. While passing the time in Ontonagon, preached in French and English, and at 11 P.M. sailed on the "Iron City" for La Pointe; but we were brought against our will to Superior, where however I could not remain because Mr. Van Paemel was not there. Thus we sailed on the same boat back to La Pointe, where we arrived after mid-night, Tuesday morning.[125]

---

[125]Baraga wrote a detailed account of this visitation: "On August 1st I came to La Pointe. This mission is always dear to me, because it was the first that I had established on that lake. On July 29 [27], 1835, I landed there for the first time and was received with great spiritual joy by the few Catholics who were there at the time. To my great consolation I found much occupation in the instruction of the catechumens who came here in large groups; baptisms of new converts were numerous. — On my present visit I remained there 12 days, preached, baptized and administered confirmation. Thirty Indians were confirmed here.

"From La Pointe I went with the zealous missioner Father Van Paemel to Fond du Lac, which I also established and visited for the first time in the year 1835. On my first visit here I had many baptisms and then in each of my succeeding visits. On August 15th of this year I administered here the holy sacrament of confirmation and forty of my dear Indians were confirmed. This is the first confirmation ever to have taken place at Fond du Lac. One can imagine the feelings and the mood of the bishop, who, surrounded by these simple, believing Christians, administered holy confirmation in a mission in which this holy and strengthening Sacrament had never been administered! —

"The next station I then visited was Portage Lake, a mining station, consisting of Irish, Canadians and many Germans. Father Jacker of L'Anse regularly visits this station. On the Sunday that I spent there, after preaching in English, French and German, and after having administered confirmation, also for the first time in this station, I made provisions for the building of a church on a site that we already had purchased in this mining station. I started a collection, or a subscription, and I myself signed first with a sum of money. And in a short time, I might say in a few moments, 130 dollars were subscribed. We now have a spacious school house where the missioner, when he comes, offers mass and preaches, but it is too small for the many Catholics who are here. I hope that we will soon have a proper church.

"The next mission I visited was L'Anse. I founded this mission in the year 1843 and was a missioner here for ten years. It is under the spiritual care of Rev. Edward Jacker who makes great efforts to preserve the Indians already converted in a genuine Christian life and to instruct them more and more in the Christian Catholic religion, and also to bring the unconverted into the Holy Church of God. Father Jacker deserves much praise especially for keeping the school himself, 5 to 6 hours every day. — To this mission are bound some of my most consoling recollections. Whenever I enter into the small room assigned to the missioner, (now occupied by the extraordinarily zealous Edward Jacker), I am reminded of the many consolations and spiritual joys I enjoyed when I saw

Aug. 8:

<u>Sunday</u>. Preached, etc. Confirmations — 30. / Mr. Moyce did not want to remain at La Pointe, so I appointed him to Ontonagon, at least for 1 year.

Aug. 13:

From La Pointe to Superior on the "Northstar", at 2 P.M. arrived.

---

that a savage band of Indians, degenerated by being sunk deep in drunkenness, would be transformed into a zealous Christian congregation through the powerful and benevolent influence of the Holy Words about the Cross, which God the Lord, by his boundless mercy, let be announced to them in their own expressive language. — In this little room I have also done much work for Indian literature. Here I have composed the Indian grammar and the dictionary as also one widely circulated work for our Indian missions. — On Sunday, September 12th, I preached to the Indians in the morning and in the afternoon, and administered holy confirmation to thirty Indians who were prepared for it.

"Another mission station that also gives me much consolation and spiritual joy is the mining station of Minnesota. Here and in the nearby surrounding mines is the largest congregation of Catholics in the entire diocese, Irish, Canadians, or the French from Canada, and especially many Germans. Here works and labors, with tireless zeal, Rev. Martin Fox, a Prussian. He is the builder of three churches, two of which are especially nice and roomy. Although they are built only of wood, the interiors are plastered so that they appear as if they were of masonry and vaulted. The entire architecture of same is so nice and symmetric that it is a joy to look at them. The persevering zeal with which Father Fox labors, not only for the building of churches, but mainly for his various mission stations, deserves unstinted recognition. Although he is German, he speaks and preaches fairly well in English and French and he is well liked by the French and Irish as he is by the German people. — Here 45 persons were confirmed.

"Now I visited again another mining station where another missioner, the Rev. Louis Thiele, labors so energetically with indefatigable zeal, in word and deed. He attends to various mission stations, the most important of which are named Cliff Mine and Eagle Harbor. He always preaches in three languages, English, French and German, because his congregations consist of Irish, Canadian and German people. Father Thiele is also occupied with the building of his second church. The first, at Eagle Harbor, is very big and very nice and to this church a very nice and roomy residence for the missioner has been built. With the small means available to him, he has worked hard to build a church so nice and big and also a residence, for which may God the Lord reward him in eternity! Father Thiele works hard for the conversion of the Protestants. At the time I was with him he again baptized 4 Protestants, English people, whom he had previously sufficiently instructed and then solemnly accepted in the Holy Church.

"The heretofore mentioned mines are <u>copper mines</u>. But we also have a very productive and really inexhaustible <u>iron mines</u>. At Marquette is such an iron mine and here we have a church and a congregation which is cared for by a French priest, Monsieur Duroc. He, too, has built a small church with a residence; but since the church soon became too small, he therefore had it enlarged last summer.

"So our missioners are at work, do as much as they can, for the greater glory of God and for the eternal salvation of their own souls and the souls entrusted to them." Baraga to WF, Sault Ste. Marie, October 24, 1858. Printed in WF, xxii, 151; in BBC-A 699 G.

Aug. 15:    Preached in English, French and Indian, after high mass confirmed 26 persons.

Aug. 17:    Today I have confirmed 5 more = 31 confirmed. Here in Superior I had the defective pages[126] 31 & 32 of <u>Anamie-mis</u> and <u>Anamie-mas</u> printed. // Confirmed 9 more, = 40 confirmed.

Aug. 24:    Early this morning sailed from Superior, and traveled non-stop to the Sault, where I arrived on the 26th, at 12 o'clock, on the "Northstar".

Sept. 1:    Again sailed on the "Northstar" to L'Anse, and on Sept[ember] 2 ᶠpassed the entry,ᶠ and during the night arrived at L'Anse.

Sept. 3:    Left for Portage Lake with Mr. Jacker.

Sept. 5:    Preached in English and French, and confirmed 12. I appointed Michael Finnegan[127] as collector for the new church there, and I myself signed up for $20.[128]

Sept. 6:    Returned to L'Anse.[129]

Sept. 12:   Preached and confirmed 30 persons. I wanted to leave the same evening but wisely remained and on

---

[126] Apparently the printer in Cincinnati made an error on these two pages.

[127] Michael Finnegan was an Irish-born farmer, 37 years old, married and the father of five children. His real estate was valued at $7000. Federal Census, 1860, Houghton County, #55. Earlier Baraga had charged him with the solicitation of funds to build the church in Eagle Harbor. BLS, July 10, 1854.

[128] Subscription List, St. Ignatius Church, Houghton, September 5, 1858. Orig. in MQDA; in BBC-A 342 E.

[129] From L'Anse Baraga sent a school report: "As I don't know whether I shall have the pleasure of seeing you here or not, I will write you these few lines, in order to tell you that I am very much satisfied with the change in our school. Mr. Edward Jacker, who is now our schoolteacher, is by far better qualified for teaching school, than Mr. Branen was; and the school is now much better attended than it was before, and the progress of the scholars is visible. I can confidently say, (and this is not <u>my</u> saying only,) that the number of regularly attending scholars is at present greater on our side of the Bay, than on the other (run by Protestants), as also the general number of the Indians is larger on this side than on the other.

"I also (in the name of our Indians,) remind you, dear sir, of your kind promise to build a new school-house also on this side, as you did on the other. I am sorry I cannot stay long enough here to see you. I have many other places yet to visit." Baraga to Fitch, L'Anse, September 11, 1858. Orig. in NA-OIA; in BBC-A 619 E.

Sept. 13:     Early in the morning went to the Entry where at 3 P.M. I boarded the good "Northstar".

Sept. 14:     Arrived on Ontonagon at 3 P.M., and remained with Rev. F. Moyce until the following Monday. (He was dissatisfied with this place, and with the entire diocese. He will not even go to Sault Sainte Marie.)

Sept. 19:     <u>Sunday</u>. Had a small confirmation of about 9 people.

Sept. 20:     Today I went up the river to Minnesota Mine and arrived there about 4 o'clock, and remained there the entire week with the good, zealous Fr. Fox, who is building a nice large church.

Sept. 26:     Preached in three languages; confirmed 30 in the new although still unfinished church of St. Mary. (I was very pleased with Fr. Fox and with his activities.)

Sept. 28:     Today I received 13 letters, both good and bad. In the afternoon I went to Maplegrove. Here in Maplegrove I was also very pleased with everything that Fr. Fox is doing, and how he treats the people. I stayed with Mr. Flanagan[130] where I was very well treated.

Oct. 4:     Rode the stage to Ontonagon Village. I took Esther Coll[131] with me for the Sisters at Sault St. Marie. The small Mary McCabe[132] came down here[133] a few days later. I was very much displeased in Ontonagon because I was compelled to pay Rev. Moyce $200 annually, otherwise he would not live there. // On the same evening I went aboard the "Northern Light", and arrived on

---

[130]Captain James Flanagan (variant spellings), born in Ireland, was 44 years old, married, and the father of nine children. Federal Census, 1860, Ontonagon County, #418. One son, Patrick, was ordained by Baraga on November 16, 1862, at Minnesota Mine.

[131]Esther Coll became a boarding student at the academy at the Sault. St. Paul, p. 139.

[132]Mary McCabe, later Mother Mary Augustine McCabe, was nine years old when she became a boarding student at the Sault. In 1881 she entered the novitiate. In 1897, with Mother M. Angela Doyle, she founded the Academy and Day School at St. Ignace where she died in 1927. St. Paul, p. 266.

[133]Such phrasing suggests that Baraga filled in some of the diary entries when he had completed his travels.

Oct. 5:        in Eagle Harbor at 11 A.M.

Oct. 10:       <u>Sunday</u>. Preached in English and German and confirmed 12.

Oct. 12:       Closed the contract with Nicholas Grasser for the church at Cliff, for $1860.

Oct. 14:       Fr. Thiele baptized 4 Protestants who came back to the Catholic Church.[134]

Oct. 15:       Sailed on the "Iron City" to Eagle River with Mr. Thiele, and from there to the Cliff, where we were hospitably received and treated by the good Anton Grewe. He gave $65 for a bell in Eagle River; for that he has a mass offered annually on Sept[ember 25] for his deceased mother and for himself and his wife Josephine.

Oct. 17:       <u>Sunday</u>. Preached in French, English and German, and confirmed 11 persons. Fr. Thiele bought a nice and good horse for $60 from John Slawson.[135]

Oct. 18:       Today we returned to Eagle Harbor from the Cliff.

Oct. 19:       Sailed on the "Northern Light" at 7 A.M. and by 3 P.M. arrived in <u>Ontonagon</u>!!! where I found that Mr. Moyce, who is not qualified for our poor missions, had departed with bag and baggage on Oct[ober] 11.

Oct. 20:       This evening at 8, we arrived in Marquette, and lingered here 2 hours. I saw Rev. Mr. Duroc and promised him to pay Bisson $50 and Meneely's Sons[136] $60.

Oct. 21:       At 12 noon arrived at the Sault, where among many letters I found one from Munich with $609.13. I gave dimissorials to the Rev. Moyce without further ado, because he is not in the least qualified for our poor missions.[137]

---

[134]To be understood in a broad sense, not that they had once been Catholic.

[135]John Slawson was born in Ohio. He was a mining agent. In 1860 he was 37 years old with property valued at $8000. Federal Census, 1860, Houghton County, #724.

[136]Meneeley and Sons was a company in New York that sold church bells. Baraga did business with them often.

[137]Bishop Eis added in pencil to this comment of Baraga's one of his own: "The German priests were better qualified."

Oct. 24: <u>Sunday</u>. Today Susan O'Brien[138] came from La Pointe to enter the Sisters; and the wretched Moyce finally went away.

Nov. 1: The fifth anniversary of my consecration. — Sad! — ᴸSee the same date in the year 1856.ᴸ — The past saddens me; the present torments me; the future frightens me.[139]

Nov. 12: It snows today for the first time, this fall. There is already quite a bit of snow on the ground, but it is ᶜsoft and watery.ᶜ

Nov. 14: The 2 church stoves were used today.

Nov. 15: <u>Sunday</u>. Sad! Few people in church. All day an unusual snowstorm.

Dec. 6: Today the first ᴱmail-carriersᴱ left for Saginaw. They will have a hard time.

Dec. 8: ᴸFeast of the Immaculate Conception of the Blessed Virgin Mary.ᴸ At 8 o'clock the mass was in church, (not in the sacristy), there should have been a high mass, but Biron came too late.

Dec. 17: The first overland mail arrived from <u>Marquette</u> today.

Dec. 22: And today from <u>Sagina</u>,[140] two at once, the first and second.


# 1859

Jan. 1: <u>New Year's Day</u>. Preached in English, French and Indian. I recommended to them especially that on this first day, and <u>for ever</u>, they should renounce the terrible sin of drunkenness, and told them, among other things, if any one wanted to make a <u>promise</u>, or to

---

[138]Susan O'Brien was the 16-year-old daughter of the Dillon O'Briens. She became a boarder at the Sault. St. Paul, p. 140.

[139]In the left margin this unidentifiable newspaper clipping is attached: "<u>Past, Present and Future</u>. Look not mournfully into the past; it cannot return. Wisely improve the present — it is thine; go forth to meet the shadowy future without fear and with a manly heart."

[140]Margaret Sagima of Little Traverse entered the Ursuline community in June. D, June 5, 1859.

take the <u>pledge</u>, he should come to me but no one comes. *(Jan. 3). To preach is easy, the conversion is difficult. ᴸ"The perverse are hard to correct, and the number of fools is infinite."ᴸ [141] (No one! Jan. 8–Jan. 19 — etc. . . . . . . )*[142]

Jan. 8:
Last night it was very cold, the river is finally frozen over. Perhaps the ice will remain. If we have no strong wind for a few days, then it will remain. ᴵWe shall see.ᴵ <(It is very weak and dangerous, because the weather is mild. Jan. 19)>

Jan. 10:
Today the ᶜyoung man,ᶜ John B. Cadotte has begun to learn his ABC's. *<Jan[uary] 13 received the <u>Ordo</u>.>*[143]

Jan. 19:
It is raining all day. The poor travelers! The ice is so weak the canal can be crossed only with danger. ᶜAlone I walked across the ice.ᶜ [144]

Jan. 24:
With today's mail I received a draft for 2560 francs, on account of 8500 francs which is allotted to me for 1858.[145] It is very mild, yet the ice over the river is so firm that it can be crossed with horses.

Feb. 1:
I received letters today,[146] among them also one from

[141]Eccl 1:15.

[142]Baraga added these observations in the right margin as the days went by.

[143]In left margin.

[144]In view of the previous sentence Baraga was either extremely imprudent or strongly and apostically motivated.

[145]Baraga immediately sent a letter of appreciation to the PFAP. In the letter Baraga detailed some of the needs for which he would use the money—a new roof, steeple, and bell for the cathedral; the five churches then under construction in the diocese; and the needs of the schools. Baraga also reported that the recent Jubilee "has done good also in my little diocese, thanks be to God! The letters that my missionaries write me, are full of consolation. It was truly a time of grace. Some hardened sinners, who no longer had approached the Holy Sacraments for a number of years, were brought back to 'the word which inspires the world' and to its echo which makes itself heard in the most extended corners from the Center. The churches were filled, the confessionals were besieged, and our indefatigable missionaries cooperated with the Master of the Vineyard while doing the most divine work on earth: 'for of all the divine things, the most divine is to cooperate with God in the salvation of souls.'" Baraga to PFAP, Sault Ste. Marie, January 24, 1859. Orig. in PFAP; in BBC-A 591 F.

[146]One of the letters contained a Catholic *Hymn and Prayerbook* by B. H. Franz Hellenbusch, for which Baraga wrote an approbation. Baraga to WF, Sault Ste. Marie, February 2, 1859. Printed in WF, xxii, 330; in BBC-A 651 G.

Fr. Pierz[147] with the sad report that the extra-ordinar-
ily zealous missionary Lautishar, on the night of
Dec[ember] 3, froze to death on Red Lake.[148]

Feb. 17:     Many letters, among them one from Canon Novak[149]

---

[147]Francis X. Pierz (also Pirec or Pirc) was born on November 20, 1785, at Godec in
Carniola, Austria. After ordination in 1813 he worked in numerous parishes. He
was skilled in the arts of fruit growing and homeopathic medicines. After reading Baraga's letters in the *Berichte,* he came to the Indian mission in 1835.
Bishop Résé assigned him to Arbre Croche/Cross Village. Pierz made occasional visits to Sault Ste. Marie and Grand Portage. In 1852 he went to the Indian missions in Minnesota. He also encouraged Germans to settle in the area
and the Benedictines from Latrobe, Pennsylvania, to establish St. John's Monastery and University (Collegeville, Minnesota). Pierz retired from the missions in
September 1873 at the age of 88; he died at Ljubljana on January 22, 1880.

[148]Baraga wrote the following obituary: "Our north mourns the loss of its most zealous and most hopeful Indian missioner! On December 3d of last year, the Rev.
Lawrence Lautishar has ended, in the 38th year of his life, his missionary activity, so zealously and successfully begun, with an early death. He was born in
Carniola, a province of Austria, and in the year 1854 came with me to America
to devote himself to the Indian missions for the remainder of his life. His first
station was Little Traverse Bay, among the Ottawa Indians. Here he learned the
Indian Language in a short time, so that in the second year of his residence
there he already could preach in Indian. After he had learned the language well,
he earnestly wished to go up further north where there are still so many pagans.
Not to restrain his pious zeal, I released him last summer to the diocese of St.
Paul, Minnesota, where the old missioner, Rev. Pierz, labors tirelessly already
for a long time. Rev. Lautishar went further to the north, up to <u>Red Lake</u>. Here
are still many unconverted Indians and among them the zealous young missioner intended to spend the winter. But the wisdom of Providence decided otherwise. In his report to me, the Rev. Pierz writes as follows:
    "'To emulate the great patriarch of the missions, the Rev. Lautishar de-
cided on December 3d, the feast of St. Francis Xavier, to make a visit to a sick
pagan on the other side of Red Lake, with fasting and praying, all alone, over an
extremely difficult way of twelve miles over the ice. Deceived by the mild
weather of the morning, too lightly clothed, he wanted to make the difficult
journey to there and back with uninterrupted prayer and corporal denial in one
day. He did not want to take with him a companion, nor a sled with dogs, nor
better clothing or food. On his return journey the southwind changed and in the
night came a terrible northwind over the lake with severe cold in which the
good heavenly messenger, in his zeal for penance in his apostolic labors, succumbed; and next morning, very near the mission house, he was found frozen
to death. Several knee traces on the snow over the ice on Red Lake sufficiently
testify how often ascended the pleasant odor of his devout prayers to the heavenly throne, even on the last day of his life, on his journey to there and back,
for the conversion of the pagan Indians, and certainly they will be heard.'
    "Although the untimely death of this missioner, so zealous and saintly,
grieves us deeply, so, on the other hand, consoles us [with] the assured hope
that he now prays to God for our poor Indians." Baraga to WF, Sault Ste. Marie,
February 8, 1859. Printed in WF, XXII, 326; in BBC-A 444 G.

[149]Canon of the cathedral in Ljubljana, a friend of Baraga, Lautishar, and the other
Slovene missionaries.

with 300 florins from Amalia[150] and 120 from himself = 420 florins = $205 through F. L. Brauns and Co., Baltimore.

Feb. 19: Rained all day, in the middle of winter. But on the whole, we have had very little cold this winter, but rather much snow and blizzards.

March 4: Last night I felt severe rheumatic pains in my back; and could not even say mass on 4th, 5th and 6th. On March 7 I again offered mass; the pains were gone.

March 10: Mild weather; it rains frequently instead of snowing. This is the mildest winter that I have seen in this country.

March 13: ᴸI Sunday of Lent.ᴸ Today we had the children's first communion, and confirmation. About 30 were confirmed.

March 14: Invited Julia Ward family to be converted. She came and promised a sincere and permanent improvement. Likewise did Angeline Lafond . — May God grant them both perseverance in their good intentions. ᴸ"The perverse are corrected only with difficulty" — "With God nothing is impossible."ᴸ[151]

March 29–30: Today and yesterday there was a terrible ᴱsnow storm.ᴱ More snow fell in these two days than in the entire winter. On the whole, last fall was, and the present spring is, worse than the real winter (from ᴱChristmas to Annunciation.ᴱ)

April 1 & 8: ᴱExamination for the boys and girls.ᴱ — The examination for the boys was too early on April 1; they were too long without school.

April 15: Today we already pass mid-April, and we are still in severe winter. It snows nearly every day; we have much more snow now in springwinter than in winter proper. Also the ice in the river, especially in Mudlake,[152] is still thick and solid. I believe navigation will be late this year.

[150]Bishop Eis added in pencil: "His sister in Austria."
[151]Eccl 1:15; Lk 1:37.
[152]A settlement on the west shore of Sugar Island.

April 26:  Today the ᶠstorm shedᶠ¹⁵³ was taken down.

April 25:¹⁵⁴  <u>Easter Monday</u>. Today I sent Charles Ebert with a letter for Rev. D. O'Neil¹⁵⁵ to Mackinac, and this morning (29th) he is not back yet. God save us from misfortune! —

May 3:  This morning between 7 and 8 o'clock, 3 boats arrived: the "Northstar", the "Lady Elgin", and the "Iron City". (The "Northern Light" is aground.) The "Illinois" will arrive perhaps tomorrow.

May 15:  <u>Sunday</u>. At 4 A.M. I departed from the Sault¹⁵⁶ on board the "Lady Elgin," and the same day at noon ar-

---

¹⁵³Bishop Eis wrote in a translation: *storm shed*.

¹⁵⁴Baraga had the dates in this reverse order.

¹⁵⁵Baraga accepted Dennis O'Neil from the Milwaukee diocese on April 24, 1859 (BLS) and assigned him briefly to Ontonagon and then to Portage Lake with Fr. Jacker. Because of the problems caused by O'Neil's drinking, Baraga planned to dismiss him in November but, because of the lateness of the season, did not send the dimissorial letter. BLS, November 15, 1859. Later, although Baraga wrote to Jacker: "O'Neil must go away. Give him the document" (BLS, March 23, 1860), O'Neil did not leave. Baraga then placed him under interdict but refused to give him an Exeat. BLS, May 4, 1860. O'Neil forged Baraga's name on documents when he left the diocese during the summer of 1860.

¹⁵⁶Baraga wrote an extensive account of this visitation: "A few days ago I have again returned from my visitation journey to the missions, and now I wish to insert this brief report on the same in your esteemed periodical if you will obligingly accept it.

"From this journey I returned half sick and exhausted, because it was a difficult circuitous journey through all our missions among the Ottawa Indians. In these missions one must either go from one mission to another on foot or sail on the stormy Lake Michigan in a small Indian boat, which is often connected with danger to life, and which would be even more dangerous if the Indians were not so skilled in guiding their boats. On these journeys one must also spend the night at times on the shore, and this spring the nights here were very cold.

"I set out on a visitation this spring at the first opportunity that I could find to Mackinac and St. Ignace. However, this opportunity did not come before May 15, because the ice remained in our St. Mary's River a very long time this year. And when I came to these two mission places, the people, whose occupation and service consist mostly in fishing, had already sailed for their spring fishing grounds. These poor people are hired by white employers to catch fish. The employers provide them with empty barrels, nets and salt, and pay them 4 or 5 dollars for each barrel which they fill and salt. Among these fishermen there are many who are already adults and have not yet been confirmed, because they are never there when the bishop comes on a visitation. Therefore the missioners said to me that I should come in winter in order to meet them. Therefore, in winter, in the first days of the month of February, 1860, I shall have to make a journey on foot, on snowshoes, to Mackinac and St. Ignace. These winter journeys on foot are now difficult for me, first, because I am now already somewhat out of practice, and, secondly, also because of my age, since next February, if I live, I will be in my sixty-third year. In these years, (especially when one in past years has suffered hardships,) one is already somewhat stiff and feels the cold.

"The marching throughout the day is still tolerable, but when it comes to the evening, to spend the night on the snow under the open sky in this northerly climate, that does not go well. By the tiresome walking on snowshoes, over hill and dale, one is in a sweat the entire day, despite the cold, so that all the underwear becomes wet; and in the evening, when one comes to a halt, he then soon feels extremely cold and begins to shiver as if he had a fever. If on these winter journeys I could come every evening to a house, then they would not be difficult for me. But in this desolate country one must often travel many days before he again comes to a house. Such is the lot of a missionary bishop, which, however, I do not find hard, because I have been a missioner in this dreary country for so many years; only the years oppress me somewhat.

"From the St. Ignace mission I sailed in an Indian boat to Cross Village, where a worthy German missioner of the Third Order of Saint Francis, Father Seraphin Zorn, who in a short time had learned Indian well, works zealously for the honor of God and for the salvation of his Indians. This is a pure Indian mission. Mackinac and St. Ignace are mixed missions. There they are Indians, half-Indians, Canadian French and Irish, but in Cross Village all are Indian. The Indians were glad to again see their old missioner and bishop. As soon as they saw the boat coming from afar, they rang the mission bell, and all assembled. The schoolteacher, who is a brother of the Third Order, came at the head of his school children who carried two flags and whom the Indians joined down to the shore in order to welcome the bishop. They all knelt down to receive the bishop's blessing, and then with salvoes and the ringing of the bell, accompanied me into the mission church, where, after a short address, I again gave them the holy blessing. In general, the Indians everywhere welcome the bishop thus. — In this mission I always have much consolation, because the poor Indians there are good and very diligent in attending church; and the missioner is exemplary and zealous.

"From there I sailed to the Beaver Islands, which are situated in the middle of Lake Michigan, between the Upper and Lower Michigan. Two of these islands are inhabited, one by Indians and the other by whites, mostly Irish. When I came to these missions for the first time only Indians lived there, but some years ago the whites began to settle on the large Beaver Island, and certainly the worst kind of whites, namely, the Turkish-minded Mormons with their numberless wives, and in a short time there were more than 300 families there of these abominable people, and they applied such an absolute rule over the entire beautiful island that none other could settle there. Besides their Mohammedan polygamy, they were also kind of pirates and thieves, and caused so much disturbance that, finally, the neighboring settlements, especially the inhabitants of Mackinac, united themselves against them, hired a large steamship [U.S.S. *Michigan*] and with armed forces drove the thieving Mormons from Beaver Island. Now this beautiful and large island, which for many years was the seat of the cruelest, devil-worship, is populated almost entirely by Catholics, mostly Irish, some German and French, who sincerely wish nothing more than to have a church and a priest soon in their midst. — On May 27, on the 4th Sunday after Easter, I said holy mass there in the spacious school house, and preached in English for the first time on this island. And after the holy mass I administered holy confirmation to 24 persons. All these persons, with the exception of only one boy, were adult people, among them were also old men and women who never before had an opportunity to see a bishop in their midst. After the divine service the women and children went out and I held a conference with the men, how and where a church on this island was to be built, which they all want very much.

"After that I sailed to the smaller Beaver Island, named Garden Island, which is inhabited by the Indians, who from time to time are visited by the Reverend Missioner Zorn. These Indians are now all Catholics and hold firmly to the faith, despite the evil examples with which they were surrounded when the Mormons lived in their neighborhood. Until now they still had their old chapel, put together with tree bark. But now they are about to build themselves a regular church out of the nicest cedar wood that I have ever seen, and which is already all hewn and ready for the building. Such building, entirely out of cedar wood, can last more than a hundred years, if only the roof is repaired from time to time.

"Then, in company with the zealous Missioner Zorn, I visited two other mission stations, and on June 3 I reached the mission of Little Traverse, the former Arbre Croche. This was my first mission among the Indians which I began on May 28, 1831. Here the Indians have a beautiful and spacious church which they have built themselves. In general, these Indians are already rather advanced in civilization. Nearly all are cabinet-makers and carpenters, and they also make their own boats. When I came here for the first time, the Indians had only canoes from birch-bark; now such canoes are not seen anymore.

"At this visitation of mine an incident occurred to me which previously had not happened in our Indian missions. A young Indian girl of 18 or 19 years [Margaret Sagima] according to the testimony of the missioners, leads a pious life for many years and every Sunday goes to communion, came to me and urgently begged me to accept her into the Ursuline convent at Sault Ste. Marie. I was surprised by such a request from an Indian girl, because this nation, as well as the Hebrew and other ancient nations, esteem and desire only the married state. To proceed safely, I called her parents and asked them about their daughter, and they testified that several youths have already asked her to marry them, but she refused any offer, and always said that she wants to remain single all her life. Then I questioned her repeatedly if she really wants to leave everything and go in the convent, and she assured me that this was her only wish. Therefore I took her with me and she was accepted in our Ursuline convent as a novice. If she will only remain persevering.

"In Little Traverse Father Louis Sifferath is missioner, a conscientious, zealous and pious German priest, who in a short time has learned the Indian language fairly well, and who is still perfecting himself in it daily.

"After I had visited two more small mission stations, in company with Father Sifferath, and everywhere preached to the Indians, I arrived, on June 9, in Grand Traverse. This is the mission of Father Mrak who labors already for many years as a zealous and judicious missioner among the Indians. There I was very pleasantly surprised when I saw how nicely Father Mrak has repaired and improved his mission church from the outside and inside.

"On the return trip, in the night, which was stormy and cold, we had to disembark and spend the night on the shore. I had no blanket with me, but, fortunately, my cloak. I had laid down on the cold sand and spent the night shivering. On the following morning I could scarcely speak and also could scarcely get up. I caught a bad cold.

"On the 17th inst[ant], I finally arrived again, to my joy and that of others, here in Sault Ste. Marie, where I shall remain a few weeks and then undertake a new visitation journey on Lake Superior which will last about two months." Baraga to WF, Sault Ste. Marie, June 24, 1859. Printed in WF, xxii, 546; in BBC-A 668 G.

rived at Mackinac, *<where I found D. O'Neil and sent him to Ontonagon.>*[157]

May 17: Went to Pointe St. Ignace. But since the fishermen were already all away, I promised to come in February 1860. Misère!!

May 19: Arrived in Cross Village, and took the necessary measures in Fr. Welkamp's convent.[158]

May 20: This morning at 8 o'clock, I sailed from Cross Village to Garden Island, and arrived there at 2 P.M., thanks to a good wind.

May 22: Sunday. Offered mass in <u>Beaver Harbor</u>[159] and confirmed 24 persons. After mass we discussed building a church and priest's residence, Lwhom the Lord of the Vineyard may send to me.L

May 26: At 8 A.M. embarked at Garden Island and reached Cross Village at 1:30 P.M.

May 29: Sunday. Preached twice in Cross Village, but no confirmations.

May 31: Sailed with a good wind to Middle Village, and preached there on June 2, Lon the Feast of the Ascension of Our Lord . . .L

June 3: With a good wind sailed in 2½ hours from Middle Village to Little Traverse Bay.

---

[157]In the right margin.

[158]There is no record of what situation required "necessary measures" or what action Baraga took.

[159]From Beaver Harbor Baraga sent the following report: "Sir. I came hither some days ago on a Missionary visit to the Indians, and to my great sorrow I find that they are drinking liquors more and more, notwithstanding our prohibition. But I am very glad to see the efforts of our school-teacher, who labors very fruitfully indeed, though his efforts are not always crowned with success, through the fault of the parents who don't compel their children to attend regularly to his school. — I understand that a petition was sent against him by some Indians who were pushed to it by some liquor-seller who hate [sic] Mr. Donovan. I request you, Mr. Fitch, not to heed that petition, if really one has been sent to you, and to believe me when I tell you, that you could hardly find a better and more industrious and able teacher, than Mr. Donovan. So I respectfully request you, not to remove him." Baraga to Fitch, Beaver Harbor, May 22, 1859. Orig. in NA-OIA; in BBC-A 622 E.

June 5:    Sunday. Preached twice in Little Traverse and confirmed 8 children. <(N.B. There I accepted Margaret Sagima,[160] misère!!!)>

June 6:    To Sheboygan, where I met poor John Heaphy,[161] to whom I advanced $40 more; in all $70.[162]

June 7:    Again back to Little Traverse Bay in a terrible rain storm.

June 8:    To Bear River, where I offered mass at Trotochaud, and preached. Trotochaud gave me an acre of land on which I shall build a small church,[163] E30 by 20 and 12 feet high.E

---

[160]"Marguerite Sagina, [a] young indian of the tribe of Otawata left on the 27th of the same month and of the same year. She did not know her age. I would have given her about 20 years." Memoirs of Mother Mary Xavier, p. 18. "Margaret Sagima, daughter of Mr. Sagima and of, I do not know the name of her mother. That sister was of the tribe of the Otawata and spoke only indian. She was eighteen years of age, her birthplace was little Traverse, on lake Michigan. She entered the novitiate on the 17th of June and left on the 27th of the same month and year 1859." *Règistre de l'entrèe de Novices.* Origs. in UAC; in BBC-Mss. 48.

[161]Teacher at the Sheboygan (Burt Lake) location.

[162]From Sheboygan Baraga sent another report: "Dear Sir. You promised me once at your office in Detroit, that you will let me appoint teachers for this school here. So I did, and the last whom I appointed was Mr. Patrick Smith. But he left last winter and put his boy in his place as teacher without asking me, but the Indians are not willing to have a boy to teach their boys and girls, they prefer to have a married man, and so also you told me yourself that you preferred married teachers. They are certainly better, and especially for this so lonely place it requires a man of family to resist [sic] here, and to be able to stay here all the time, because in the season of sugar-making there is not one living soul in the whole village for about two months. Only a man with a family could bear it to remain here, when the village is entirely deserted for two months.

"I then appointed a married man, John Heaphy, who is now here and already commenced keeping school. The Indians are satisfied with him, he is an able teacher, and has been keeping school for twenty years past. The Indians don't wish a single man for their teacher, they prefer a married one, of course. I hope, dear sir, you will keep me [sic] your word and promise. Relying upon your word of honor I appointed Mr. Heaphy, who would be left in the greatest distress, if not confirmed by you in his present situation." Baraga to Fitch, Sheboygan, June 7, 1859. Orig. in NA-OIA; in BBC-A 623 E.

[163]Andrew Porter, the Protestant missionary and teacher at Bear Creek, wrote to Fitch: "[Y]ou will remember that two years since the papists began to build a house of Baal on our side, our Indians petitioned you, & you stopped the proceedings; you are aware also of the sneaking course pursued by Baraga in aiding Trotochaud to build a dwelling house designed, & since used as a church. The bishop has been here again, and has obtained a lot in our village from this same ignorant Frenchman, upon which he designs raising a church at once. Will you allow him thus to set aside (Mormon like) your authority? When the above facts were known, our Indians came to me and proposed a council for the purpose of

June 9:         At 10 A.M. departed for Grand Traverse, and arrived there just before midnight on a cold night.

June 12:        <u>Sunday</u>. Preached in Grand Traverse in the morning and afternoon and confirmed 7 persons. Fr. Mrak has repaired the church outside and inside, very nicely.

June 13:        About noon departed Grand Traverse and at 1:30 A.M. arrived at Green River, where I spent the night on the sandy shore in considerable cold, since I was without a blanket.[164]

June 14:        At 3 P.M. arrived at Cross Village, and there met Margaret Sagima ready to go with me to the Sault and enter the convent.

June 15:        With a good wind in five hours sailed from Cross Village to Mackinac, and on the following day (June 16) continued with Anna Lorch[165] and Margaret Sagima.

June 17:        Friday. Arrived at the Sault at 8 A.M. aboard the steamboat "Illinois", and brought <u>Anna Lorch</u> and

---

petitioning you; I rather objected . . . but they proceeded alone, and having drawn up a petition, obtained the names of almost all the Indians in this immediate vicinity, when they brought it to me, asking me to transcribe and forward it to you.

"The case on the part of the bishop is mean and arbitrary, since he <u>knows</u> that his party is a small minority . . .

"You know there is no need for a church here, since they have one only 4 miles off; they had 20 years before we came, why did not they build a church during that time; but no, they choose rather, when we have formed a little nucleus, to come with their tares; [s]hall they come with their wolf teeth and devour the bones & marrow?

"The paper they (our Indians) signed is simply this, 'We whose names are annexed do not wish to have a church (Catholic) built here on this side.'" Thirty-one persons, 25 Indian and 6 white, signed this petition. Porter to Fitch, Bear River, June 14, 1859. Orig. in NA-OIA; in BBC-B 1320 E.

[164]Bishop Eis added: "Behold the missionary Bishop's misery!"

[165]Anna Lorch entered the community as a lay sister. She remained until January 3, 1860 (D). "Anna Marguerite Lorg [sic] was born at Bettigen in Germany and was 22 years old. She took the holy habit on the 17th of December of the same year [1859] with the names [sic] of Mary Ste. Barbara. She was sent [dismissed] the 3rd of January 1860." Memoirs of Mother Mary Xavier, p. 18. Orig. in UAC; in BBC-Mss. 48. She may have been associated with the German Franciscan community in Cross Village since it was from that location that Baraga brought her to Sault Ste. Marie. More likely she was the young woman of whom Baraga had written to Fr. John Albrinck of Pomeroy, Ohio: "Ask the German girl if she should like [to come] at once into the local Ursuline Cloister." BLS, May 31, 1858.

<u>Margaret Sagima</u> to the Ursulines. <(N.B. Anna M. Lorch will probably remain, but Margaret Sagima <sup>C</sup>wishes to go home. She will go home<sup>C</sup> on board the "Lady Elgin" on June 26.)>

June 26: <u>Sunday</u>. Today the good <u>Margaret Sagima</u> departed on the "Lady Elgin" for Mackinac, etc. .... —N.B. One should never try to train an Indian to be a priest or an Indian girl to be a nun.[166]

June 29: My 62nd birthday. <sup>F</sup>Thanks be to God!<sup>F</sup> — This afternoon I sailed on the propeller "Montgomery" for L'Anse, and the following day I arrived at at the Entry where I stayed for 2 days with Edgerton.

July 2: This noon I arrived in L'Anse.[167] Fr. Jacker was not there; he had sailed for Eagle Harbor to have Fr.

---

[166]Sentence underlined with red pencil and marked "F.E." i.e., Bishop Frederic Eis.

[167]Baraga wrote an account of this visitation: "On June 29, on my 62nd birthday, I set out on my journey and on July 2nd I arrived at my former mission station of L'Anse. This time I had much consolation in this mission. It has increased considerably, so that the mission church is now too small to accommodate all the people who assemble there on Sundays. But even more consoling and joyful for me was the assurance given to me by some pagans from the distant settlement of Vieux Desert. That is, they told me that they themselves and many of their relatives and acquaintances, all of whom are still pagans, will come to L'Anse next summer and be converted to the Christian Catholic religion. By this increase of the mission the church will now be entirely too small. I therefore promised the Indians that next year I will come to them earlier, remain with them longer and will have their church lengthened by almost a half. Of course, this will have to be done at my expense, inasmuch as the Indians have little or no money. — The zealous and exemplary missioner Jacker continues to labor at L'Anse. He works very hard and especially for the mission school.

"From L'Anse I went to Eagle Harbor and on the following day to a copper-mine known as Clark Mine. This copper-mine is being operated by a French company from Paris and all miners in its employ are Catholics. Rev. Thiele, the indefatigable missioner from Eagle Harbor, attends to these Catholics. He comes here from time to time, offers mass, preaches and hears the confessions of these miners, some of whom are French and some are Irish. I went in this mine to ask its directors if they would build a neat little church there, so that the priest, when he comes, will have a respectable place for the celebration of the Divine Service. It is hoped that this church will be erected next summer.

"After I had spent a Sunday with Rev. Thiele at his mission at Eagle Harbor, I went with him to the famous Cliff Mine from which millions of dollars of copper had already been taken and which is still so abundantly rich that it usually produces 150 to 180 tons, (about 300,000 pounds) of the nicest pure copper every month. — Here a new, nice and spacious St. Mary's church will be built this year. Preparations for the building of this new church have already been made a long time ago, and now it is completed, as is also the residence for the priest. Though no priest has as yet been stationed here, it is to be hoped, how-

---

Thiele treat his ailing foot. Thus I did not remain long in L'Anse.

July 3:      <u>Sunday</u>. Offered mass at L'Anse at 10 and preached. I promised the Indians to come about this time next

---

ever, that this will happen soon. In the meantime Father Thiele comes here every third Sunday from Eagle Harbor and holds the Divine Service, and when he comes he preaches each time in the English, German and French languages, and also hears confessions in these three languages, inasmuch as his congregation consists of Irish, Germans and French-Canadians. For the building of this church it was necessary for me to contribute 300 dollars, besides a nice bell which has cost me an additional 116 dollars. The directors of this copper-mine, although they are Protestants, have contributed 100 dollars to this church. This shows that they are inclined to be friendly towards us, although they do not belong to our religion. — It is very pleasing that we now have there a regular church, because the congregation is large and since its very beginning it has always shown a special spirit of piety and a great zeal for attending the Divine Service and for the reception of the Holy Sacrament. Every time that the priest comes here his confessional is besieged by the penitents of all 3 nations; and at the masses which he offers there they are present, if they only can come.

"Next I went to Marquette where a French priest, Mr. Duroc, is missioner. Here are the famous and inexhaustible iron-mines, the iron of which, as one generally reads in our newspapers, excels in qualities every other iron known previously. These mines are about 15 English miles away from Lake Superior, but a good railroad runs to there on which one comes there in less than an hour. In these mines a church is now also to be built, for many Catholic laborers are there, German, Irish and French from Canada. In the little city of Marquette, which lies by Lake Superior, a church has been built several years ago, at which Mr. Duroc lives; but now a church will also be built up in the mines, so that the priest, when he goes there, will no longer offer mass and preach in a house as previously, but in a regular church. It is really pleasing to see in these regions, so desolate, where only a few years ago nothing else stood but a dark primeval forest, new churches are being built for the glory of God and for the salvation of many souls.

"From there I went to Portage Lake, where five large copper mines are in operation, all of which are located close to each other. Here are now very many people and two-thirds of the population is Catholic. This is a newer location, because the mines here proved to be productive. This summer a very large, nice and sturdy church has been built here. Though it is only of wood, (as are all of our churches), it is very strong and durable. On July 31st, on St. Ignatius day, I have dedicated this house of God in the name of this same missionary saint whose spiritual sons were and still are the greatest missioners. I have dedicated this church of St. Ignatius with distinctive solemnity. I sang there a pontifical mass and was assisted by 3 priests, which, in these missions, so far distant from each other, cannot happen often. On the same Sunday I installed here a resident priest. Until now Rev. Jacker of L'Anse took care of this station and said mass and preached in the local schoolhouse, but which now is burned down.

"After I had visited some smaller stations, I came to the big and very productive copper-mine of Minnesota, where the distinguished missioner Rev. Martin Fox labors with saintly and persevering zeal. Besides the large congregation at Minnesota, which consists of German, Irish and French people, he has 3 other church congregations to care for, and which he visits from time to time. Besides a great, holy spiritual zeal, God has also given him a strong and durable

summer to enlarge their church, etc. Several pagans from Vieux Desert gave hope of being converted. I H S m.d.s.g.J.[168]

July 4:   Set out on the "Princess" from L'Anse to the entry, and on the "Mineral Rock" from Entry to Eagle Harbor, where I arrived the next morning at 5 A.M.

July 6:   Rode to Copper Harbor and Borie, etc., and the following morning returned to Eagle Harbor.

July 9:   Rode with Rev. L. H. Thiele to Cliff Mine.[169]

July 10:   Sunday. At the Cliff preached in 3 languages and suggested a collection be taken up after mass, which amounted to more than $400, including the $100 given by President Howe.[170]

July 11:   Rode[171] in the terrible heat from Cliff Mine back to Eagle Harbor.

July 17:   Sunday. Preached in Eagle Harbor in English and German. After the sermon Rev. Thiele took subscriptions at which $65 was pledged.

July 18:   At 10 A.M. I sailed with Rev. Thiele on the "Illinois" to

---

physique, which always triumphs victoriously over all hardship, of which there are many and which would tire and exhaust two ordinary priests. May God keep him with us for a long time and reward him for his indefatigable, salutary activity! — Last summer when I came to Rev. Fox, his nice, elegant and big church, (it is the nicest and biggest in the entire diocese), was not yet completed. Now it is almost entirely finished, and on Sept[ember] 4th, I dedicated it to the Almighty God in the name of the Most Blessed Virgin Mary; and also the nice organ, that Rev. Fox had sent from Buffalo, resounded for the first time. This is the first genuine organ in my entire, poor mission-diocese; here, in my cathedral as well as in all the other churches, we have only such organ-like instruments known as melodeons.

"From Minnesota I again returned to Saut-Sainte-Marie, where I arrived, thanks be to God, safe and well." Baraga to LS, Sault Ste. Marie, September 8, 1859. Printed in LSB, xxx, pp. 9–13; in BBC-A 672 G.

[168]While Baraga was in L'Anse he wrote to Agent Fitch on behalf of the Indians and asked for a flag. Baraga to Fitch, L'Anse, July 3, 1859. Orig. in NA-OIA; in BBC-A 627 E.

[169]Baraga did not spend Sunday in Eagle Harbor as his letter stated. He was there on Sunday, July 17. Writing nearly two months later he could easily err about his location on a specific day.

[170]Thomas M. Howe (1808–1877) was a financier and banker from Pittsburgh who became active in mining ventures in the Lake Superior district and in the Rocky Mountains. Chaput, p. 74.

[171]Bishop Eis inserted: "On horseback?"

Ontonagon where we arrived at 7 P.M. Heard terrible reports about the unfortunate[172] [Rev.] D. O'Neil.

July 20: Sailed on the "Northstar" from Ontonagon (with Rev. Thiele and the unfortunate D. O'Neil) and on the 21st arrived in Marquette where I heard many complaints about Mr. Duroc.

July 21: Went by railroad to Pioneer Iron Mine[173] where I made a deal with John Charles Mackenzie for a lot and building for a small chapel. That same evening I returned to Marquette. (Many complaints[174] about Mr. Duroc, especially from the Irish and Germans, sometimes also from the Canadians.)

July 24: <u>Sunday</u>. In Marquette preached in English, French, and German, and gave communion to many people, especially Germans, who would not or could not go to confession to Duroc, and who came to me.

July 29: At 1 A.M. sailed on the "Iron City" to Portage Entry, and from there to Portage Lake, or Houghton, where I met Rev. Mr. Thiele, who had arrived here an hour before I did. (I also found Rev. Dennis O'Neil here, contrary to my expectations.) The church was erected, roofed, the floor laid, but as yet no glass in the windows.

July 31: Solemnly blessed the church of Portage Lake to the name of St. Ignatius, whose feast is today, with the assistance of 3 priests: Rev. Thiele, Jacker and O'Neil. I sang the pontifical mass, and preached in English, French and German. The collection for the church to-day amounted to $304. — Because of a strong petition, I left Mr. O'Neil here conditionally, for one year only; if he does well, he may remain longer. The dissatisfaction of the Germans and French towards him showed itself immediately. Priests who speak English, German, and French are not easy to find.[175]

---

[172]"Unfortunate" usually indicated that the person had problems with alcohol.
[173]Bishop Eis added: "Now Negaunee."
[174]In addition to the problems which his drinking created, Duroc also lacked facility in English or German.
[175]Bishop Eis added in pencil: "And can speak English." It has been erased and is difficult to read.

Aug. 3:     At 3 P.M. departed on the "Northstar" and at 4 A.M. arrived at the Sault, where as usual, I found many letters waiting to be answered, for which reason I returned here <u>before</u> completing my Lake Superior Mission visitations.[176]

Aug. 9:     Sailed today on the "Lady Elgin" to Mackinac, in order to have the 2 pages, 31 & 32 of A. and AM printed. — $8.

Aug. 11:    Summoned as a <u>witness</u> by Patrick Smith ————[177]

---

[176]The letters omit mention of the interval at Sault Ste. Marie and Mackinac.

[177]As early as February 1859, Baraga seems to have communicated with Smith about replacing the Jesuit teachers if they left the Sault: "I regret to state that now I cannot employ you here at Saut Ste. Marie, because Father Menet and his two Brothers remain now here and will not quit the Saut, consequently I could not employ another teacher, as one of the Brothers will continue to teach in our boy's school. There you earn the same wages as would here — You owe me $30.00, which I lent you at Mackinac on the 15th of July last. This sum I make you a present of.

"Please tell me immediately, whether you intend to keep on the Sheboygan school, or not. If not, I must then look for another teacher." Baraga to Smith, Sault Ste. Marie, February 2, 1859. Orig. in NA-OIA; in BBC-A 620 E.

Baraga wrote to Smith, in care of Fr. Murray, about the controversy: "Sir. On my arrival here on the 14. inst[ant], I received a letter from John Heaphy of Sheboygan, in which he says: '<u>Mr. Smith filled the returns for three months, and has drawn three months money, instead of two.</u>' — What an injustice! You know that you have been disconnected with the Sheboygan school before the month of June, and your boy, whom you had no right to substitute for you, has kept that school for the last time of [sic] the 3d of June, and you had the temerity to fill the public Government returns for the <u>whole month of June</u>! This is a public fraud! I spoke of your proceedings to Agent Fitch on board of the Illinois; he knows you now, and he promised me repeatedly to confirm John Heaphy for the Sheboygan school.

"You are in conscience bound, before God and men, to pay over to John Heaphy $33 for his month of June. You acknowledged yourself disconnected with the Sheboygan school; by your engaging to keep the school at Mackinac, which you kept some days in May, <u>the whole month of June,</u> and some days in July, until Father Murray was obliged to dismiss you, on account of your neglecting that school, and not complying with the agreed condtions. You have been paid for the month of June for the Mackinac school: and now you rob poor Heaphy of his payment for the same month of June. What right have you to be paid <u>twice</u> for the same month? This is unjust, it is a roguish robbery, and it will leave a stain on your character, before God and men, until you make restitution of the ill-gotten $33. — I pity very much your poor soul!" Baraga to Smith, Sault Ste. Marie, August 16, 1859. Orig. in MQDA; in BBC-A 596 E.

The next day Baraga wrote to Fitch. After explaining the details and again asking Fitch to confirm Heaphy in the teaching position at Sheboygan, Baraga concluded: "1. John Heaphy is at this time very poor indeed, and he depends entirely on his present situation for a living; whereas Patrick Smith has his business at Mackinac, where he keeps a pretty large hotel which he leased for three years.

Aug. 13:       At 11 P.M. departed on the "Illinois" for the Sault and on

Aug. 14:       Sunday, at 9:30 arrived. Preached in English and French at the high mass.

Aug. 15–16:   On these two days I've been somewhat sick.

Aug. 19:       Sailed on the "Iron City" to Marquette, (with Julie W. Ward and Em. Chalut.)

Aug. 21:       Offered mass in Marquette, and at 10 preached in French and English.

Aug. 22:       Sailed on the "Northstar" at 6 A.M. from Marquette to La Pointe. (On this same day gave $100 to George Rice for Bernard in Eagle Harbor.)

Aug. 23:       At 4 P.M. arrived in La Pointe.

Aug. 28:       Sunday. Preached in English, French, and Indian, confirmed 17.

Aug. 30:       Departed from La Pointe for Ontonagon on the "Lady Elgin".

Aug. 31:       Sailed on a river boat to Minnesota Mine, and at 3 P.M. arrived at Fr. Fox's.

Sept. 4:       Sunday. Blessed the beautiful St. Mary's Church at Minnesota Mine, preached in English, German and French, and confirmed 14 persons.

Sept. 5:       Arrived in Ontonagon Village with Fr. Fox.

Sept. 6:       At 9 P.M. departed from Ontonagon on the "Northstar", and came

Sept. 8:       At 6 in the morning, to Sault Sainte Marie, where I was very sad because I did not find any of the 3 expected priests or the expected theologian Haller. <(Mr. Joseph Haller[178] will come at the beginning of Oct[ober])>

---

"2. I advanced to poor Heaphy more than $80, to buy provisions and other necessaries for his household. If he is turned out the money will be a dead loss to me." Baraga to Fitch, Sault Ste. Marie, August 17, 1859. Orig. in NA-OIA; in BBC-A 629 E.

[178]Joseph Haller was from Salk City, Wisconsin. He arrived for a few days at the end of October. Haller was never ordained. Cf. D, January 25, 1861 n.

Sept. 14:      Today we had our first snow, but it disappeared quickly.

Sept. 21:      36th anniversary of my ordination. ᴸThanks be to God!ᴸ — 18th anniversary of my meditative morning prayers. ᴸBoundless thanks to God!ᴸ —

Sept. 23:      I departed on the "Illinois" for Portage Entry, but this boat is so slow that I did not arrive there until late, the evening of the next day, and as a result of this slowness, I have lost the following Sunday.

Oct. 2:      <u>Sunday</u>. Consecrated the Cliff church, the reason why I undertook this short trip.[179]

Oct. 6:      Returned to the Sault on the "Iron City". — Sad, because neither Mr. Haller nor the 2 priests from Carniola have arrived.[180]

Oct. 13:      Today, on his <u>27th birthday</u>, Mr. John Chebul[181] arrived here, appointed for Minnesota Mine, and on

---

[179]Baraga wrote: "This year I went three different times to Lake Superior. My last journey, from which I returned a few days ago, I undertook alone to dedicate the nice new church, which, under the supervision and management of Rev. Thiele, has been built this summer at Cliff Mine. It is a Marian church and it was dedicated on Oct[ober] 2nd, the feast of the Holy Rosary of the Blessed Virgin Mary, to the Almighty God under the invocation of His Most Blessed Mother. The church was filled, especially with Germans, of whom there are many at this mine. For the celebration of the solemnity I sang the pontifical mass at which the Germans sang and answered; and after the gospel I preached in the three languages that are common here. The sermon in the German language was a Marian sermon that pierced deep into the hearts of the venerators of the dear Mother of God, and which also came from the innermost part of my heart. God grant that by the intercession of the Most Blessed Virgin Mary, the spirit of piety and of zeal, which has manifested itself in this congregation from the very beginning, be also always kept and may it increase more and more for the honor of God and His Most Blessed Mother and for the salvation of many souls!" Baraga to WF, Sault Ste. Marie, October 12, 1859. Printed in WF, XXIII, 98; in BBC-A 673 G.

[180]Baraga declined an invitation to attend the consecration of Bishop-elect Quinlan: "I daily expect three new laborers for my poor Diocese, two priests and one theologian, who will be ordained soon after his arrival; and as navigation will soon close on Lake Superior, I must be careful with my time." Baraga to Purcell, Sault Ste. Marie, October 6, 1859. Orig. in NDUA; in BBC-A 165 E.

[181]John Chebul was born on October 13, 1832, at Velesovo in Carniola, Austria, and ordained on November 3, 1855. In 8 months at Minnesota Mine he mastered English and French. He was transferred to La Pointe in June 1860, and for twelve years worked among the Chippewa as far west as Duluth/Superior and south to Chippewa Falls. After a brief vacation in Carniola in 1872, he worked with the Menominee at Shawano and Keshena, Wisconsin. Failing eyesight and ill health drew him to Arabia and later, for 3 years, to a parish at Versailles in

Oct. 14:      left on the "Mineral Rock" for his destination.

Oct. 15:      Today Fr. Menet became ill, (Angina,) Quincy,) [sic] and on

Oct. 16:      <u>Sunday</u>, he could not say mass, so I said both masses and preached from the altar.

Oct. 19:      Fr. Menet is still very sick, he can neither drink nor eat, an inflammation of the throat. // Today the first snow fell, which remains. We shall see for how long. <(Two days.)>

Oct. 23:      <u>Sunday</u>. Fr. Kohler sang the high mass, and I preached, but perhaps the last time until Advent.

Oct. 26:      Had two very sad reports today. Rev. Van Paemel[182] is leaving for home. // The Sisters are leaving, to Chatham, Canada West. /// Yes, the "Lady Elgin" came, but Joseph Haller was not on it. //// A three-fold day of misère!!!

Oct. 30:      Finally Mr. Haller is coming, via Detroit. On the next "Lady Elgin" he will go down to study with Mr. Mrak and qualify for ordination in a year or two. <(Nothing has come of it.)>

Nov. 4:      Mr. Haller went on the "Lady Elgin", first to Milwaukee, and from there to Grand Traverse, to Mr. Mrak. <(He has given up everything.)>

Nov. 11:      <u>St. Martin</u>. Today we began to say mass in the new winter chapel.

Nov. 30:      Madame Rouleau (Archange Gourneau) began to learn how to read (Indian). Misère.

---

France. In 1882 he returned to Upper Michigan (St. Ignace, Calumet, Manistique, Ironwood, Ontonagon, Iron River, Iron Mountain, Norway, St. Ignace, Newberry, Grand Marais, and Garden) where he died on August 3, 1898. In addition to being a superb linguist, Chebul was totally dedicated to his missions and people. He was able to walk sixty to seventy miles a day on snowshoes; trappers and Indians could follow the bloody tracks his feet left in the snow. He was loved for his music and song, for his stories, jokes, and whimsical humor. Chebul is buried at St. Ignace. Chebul Papers, BBC-AR 29.

[182]Bishop Eis added: "Rev. Van Paemel spoke the Chippewa like an Indian."

Nov. 27: The "Forrester" went up to Weshki Bay, carrying a new ᴱcylinderᴱ to the "Lady Elgin" (she broke her old one), and came on

Nov. 28: down again and through the canal. That was the last boat through the canal this year. The "Lady Elgin" will have to stay above.

Dec. 13: The first ᴱover(land) mailᴱ arrived today (only from Mackinac), and brought me 6250 ꟳfrancs from Parisꟳ . . . I H S . . . . . . . for 1859 ꟳon my allotment of 12000 francs;ꟳ but only for 1859. In the future I am to expect only 8000.

Dec. 18: The first and second mail arrived from Saginaw. Nothing special.

Dec. 28: The river is frozen; one can cross quite well, but there is always water on the ice.

Dec. 31: Coldest night, coldest day. The old 1859 is making a cold exit.

## 1860

Jan. 1: Sunday. A fair day, a good beginning for 1860. Many visitors,[183] especially from the other side, because the crossing is good. — Today Fr. Menet preached. I now like to let him preach.

Jan. 2: Poor old Madame Perault was here, begging, and I gave her $2, and a cotton bed cover. I must set myself the task of pasting 50 Ottawa booklets so that in 12 days I must complete, 50 X 12 = 600.

Jan. 3: Finally Bernier has arrived and brought a good mail, the Ordo and 2 Dunigan Almanacs.[184] / Mr. Barbeau was here, wishing me happy New Year. / This evening the lay sister [Anna Lorch] left the convent. Too bad! /

---

[183]Such visiting was a custom on New Year's Day.
[184]Metropolitan Catholic Almanac (CALM).

Jan. 4:    Trempe's 7 year old daughter was buried today. Happy angel! Fabian [Landreville][185] filled the wood-box.

Jan. 5:    I wanted to buy myself a pair of moccasins for my journey to St. Ignace, but Mr. O'Neil[186] gave them to me as a ᴱNew Year's present.ᴱ

Jan. 6:    Cadron's son,[187] from the other side, whom I had prepared last winter for first holy communion, and instructed in prayers, came to confession, and I found to my great disgust that for the most part he has forgotten ᶜI confess and the act of contritionᶜ because he seldom or never prays.

Jan. 7:    L. P. Trempe sent me $100 in silver today, ᶠon the account of myᶠ ᴱFrench draftsᴱ of 6250 francs. // — It is now very mild, perhaps it will be too mild for the roads, which until now have been very good. To the poor Bagage I gave $2.

Jan. 8:    Sunday.[188] Preached two short sermons: ᶠ"About the duties of fathers and mothers;ᶠ ᴱHappy is he who comes regularly to church every Sunday."ᴱ

Jan. 9:    Today Fr. Menet left for his ᴸyearlyᴸ mission at Sailors' Encampment,[189] where he intends to stay about a week. / From the other side a person came asking for something to eat for Thibault's children. I gave her $1.

Jan. 10:   Two foolish visits from the other side which needlessly took away a few hours of my time. // The ᴱmailᴱ arrived bringing me two ridiculous letters and a ᴱnewspaper.ᴱ // Loaned the ᴱIndian chief ᴱ $15.

Jan. 11:   Gave $2 to old Biron. In the afternoon I went down to John Johnston to have Mr. Fitch sign an order for the

[185]Fabian Landreville, 32, and his wife, Adaline, 20, had two children, Flavia, 4, and Louis, 2. Among his carpentry jobs was the construction of the church at Goulais Bay. Pat Landreville, 23, was a hostler who lived with Peter B. Barbeau. Federal Census, 1860, Chippewa County, #192, #117.

[186]Michael O'Neil, 39, a merchant, and his wife, Bridget, 35, lived in Sault Ste. Marie. Federal Census, 1860, Chippewa County, #110.

[187]This was Joseph, the 13-year-old son of Thomas Cadron. In 1861 Joseph became a canoeman for Baraga between the Sault and Goulais Bay. Cf. D, December 12, 1862. He left an account of his last visit with Baraga in Marquette, shortly before "his bishop" died. Lawrence, pp. 4–6.

[188]Feast of the Holy Family.

[189]Neebish Island.

$15. He was not at home, perhaps he will come to see me. — He did come and promised to procure for me a paper with which I will certainly get back the $15. This evening Cadotte brought my confessional: $3.50.

Jan. 12:    Mail arrived bringing me an Ordo, a letter and many newspapers.

Jan. 13:    At 10 o'clock Br. Donovan went to get Fr. Duranquet so that he can help here instead of Fr. Menet. / Gave wood to Polly until Monday, at which time she will have her own wood.

Jan. 14:    Nothing special. ᶠMy task of ᶠ 50 Ottawa booklets is again completed for today. Now I have to do it only on Monday and then 600 are corrected and only about 200 remain to be done.

Jan. 15:    <u>Sunday</u>. Preached in English and French with much sorrow, because I have new examples of how <u>many</u> do not come to the 10 o'clock mass, and how <u>few</u> attend the 8 o'clock mass.

Jan. 16:    This morning Mr. Montreuil came here and requested me to perform the marriage of his foreman with a daughter of Jos[eph] Meniclier, Misère!! — In my stupidity I said immediately that they should come this evening; but then I wrote him that they should come tomorrow to Fr. Menet.

Jan. 17:    Today I pasted and glued 109 Ottawa booklets, and have now corrected in all 709. About 130 still need to be corrected, but unfortunately I do not have any more "pages".

Jan. 18:    After all the gluing was finished, I still pasted today the 33 "Greetings to Jesus" in the booklets.

Jan. 19:    At 6:30 this morning a house in the village burned down; many more would have burned if there had not been ᴱperfectly calm.ᴱ — In the evening I gave the burned out Montferrat[190] $30 as some small assistance in his need.

---

[190] Also spelled "Montferret" and "Montferrand." After the fire Baraga gave him the position of teacher at L'Anse where he taught until the summer of 1863. He then returned to the Sault as teacher but remained in that position only a very short time.

Jan. 20:    ᴱJohn Johnston, the U.S. interpreter, expressed his great desire to have my portrait. So I made one up nicely in a gilt frame and gave it to Miss Polly to give to him.ᴱ

Jan. 21:    This was a quiet, visitless day, in the evening one person came and ᶠasked for holy pictures, and I gave him four.ᶠ / Today Br. Donovan had a sore throat; I hope it will soon pass away. / ᴱMild weather.ᴱ

Jan. 22:    Sunday. Preached in English and French. Glued a calendar together for Br. Hickey while little Bonneau was here, and so I lost no time with her visit. // Fr. Menet will begin his catechism classes late this year. He will first speak about it next Sunday.

Jan. 23:    This evening I made a sad discovery, which really proves Mr. Menet's lack of zeal. I went to J. B. Lalonde[191] to persuade his old ᶠmother-in-lawᶠ to come to church and learned that his wife [Victoria] also never comes to church, has never really been baptized, etc., and Fr. Menet has never spoken a word to her about religion, has never visited them.

Jan. 24:    Yesterday Fr. Duranquet came up here, partly by ᶠdog sled,ᶠ partly on foot; and very early this morning Br. Donovan drove him by cutter back to his mission. // The ᴱmail,ᴱ already expected last week, has finally arrived.

Jan. 25:    All last night and all day a terrible storm.

Jan. 26:    John Bolan from Pointe St. Ignace came today ᶠto get some holy pictures, and I gave himᶠ at the same time a letter for Fr. Piret, ᶠthat he should send his men to pick me up,[192] Jan[uary] 30.ᶠ

Jan. 27:    The unfortunate Abraham Boulet, who while drunk last December froze both of his hands, came to me ᶠto

---

[191]Baptist Lalonde, 32, and his wife, Victoria, 20, had a 2-year-old daughter, Maria. Federal Census, 1860, Chippewa County, #214. According to the 1850 census, his father, John Baptiste, then 52, and mother, Catherine, then 37, and two brothers and three sisters also lived at the Sault. Federal Census, 1850, Chippewa County, #118.

[192]To take him to St. Ignace.

ask my pardon for the insults he said about me (of which I know nothing),[F] and told me that tomorrow the doctor will amputate his decaying fingers. — He promised improvement. May God grant it to him! // In the afternoon I went to Victoria Lalonde and gave her instructions and encouraged her to accept formally the Christian Catholic religion.

Jan. 28:    Mrs. Trempe brought me $100 in gold, on the account of the 6250 francs which I had given Trempe in a draft. Later I went myself for $50 more.

Jan. 29:    Sunday. Preached in English and French. Pointed and blunt sermons. In the evening I was called to Francis [sic] Lalonde;[193] [F]she is really sick and deserves pity.[F] — My Jesus, graciously accept that which I have given her.[194]

Jan. 30:    Today Fr. Menet begins his catechism for the first holy communion, from 10:30 to 11:30 in the morning. Whether also about first confession as I recommended to him that I do not know. // A very stormy day. // Confession day.[195] // Br. Donovan went to Sugar Island right after dinner for dry wood and by evening has not returned.

Jan. 31:    Immediately after breakfast Fr. Menet went over to deaf Peter's to see what is the matter with Br. Donovan. He even went to the place where the Br[other] had loaded the dry wood, and was just about to drive home. [E]All right![E] Br[other] had spent the night with Wilson. Wood hauling day. // Fr. Duranquet is here on a mission journey to Goulais Bay.

Feb. 1:    A beautiful day for traveling. I too should have left today, but my people have not come; perhaps the storm the day before scared them.

Feb. 2:    Candlemas. I am still here, which is very unpleasant

---

[193]Possibly the mother of Francis and Baptist LaLonde, Sr.
[194]This unusual expression suggests that Baraga may have performed some act of penance on her behalf.
[195]Monday would not have been a day for confession by the people. Baraga may be indicating that on this day he himself went to confession.

for me, because yesterday and today were good traveling days. I don't know why the people don't come for me. // The mail arrived in the evening and I received 4 letters[196] and 5 newspapers.

Feb. 3: Finally 2 men came for me. Very awkward! Now they must remain here 3 days at my expense (because of Fr. Menet's inhospitality). They are at Polly's.

Feb. 4: Another good traveling day. Too bad the people didn't arrive on Thursday; then I would have been traveling yesterday and today.

Feb. 5: <u>Septuagesima</u>. Delivered two nice practical sermons. Whether they have done any good or not, only You know. I believe they will have no effect, as usual. It is snowing a bit; I'm afraid I am going to have a difficult journey — ᴸ"May Your will be done!"ᴸ

Feb. 6: <u>Departure</u>. God grant me a successful journey.[197] — I feel that my loins are a little tired; I do not know

---

[196]One letter was a request from a theologian, Erhard Buttner, to enter the Diocese. Baraga asked Bishop Lefevere, with whom Buttner was living, "tell me <u>sincerely and conscientiously</u> what kind of man he is, and whether you advise me, or not, to receive him." Baraga to Lefevere, Sault Ste. Marie, February 3, 1860. Orig. in NDUA; in BBC-A 167 E. Buttner did come to the diocese (D, April 27, 1860), but Baraga sent him back to Detroit. Baraga to Lefevere, Sault Ste. Marie, July 7, 1860. Orig. in NDUA; in BBC-A 170 E.

[197]Baraga gave the reasons for this winter mission: "Last spring when I held my canonical visitation at Mackinac and Point St. Ignace, (two missions in the southern part of this diocese), I learned that only a few persons had received the Holy Sacrament of Confirmation. And so it was every spring for several years. Then the missioners told me that most of the people in their missions, consisting of Indians, half-Indians and Canadians, are fishermen, and that as soon as the ice on Lakes Huron and Michigan thaws they go fishing, 50–80 miles away, and there they spend the entire spring and summer. The missioners endeavor to visit them on their fishing shores from time to time, to offer mass, preach and distribute the Holy Sacrament among them. Then last spring the missioners of Mackinac [Murray] and St. Ignace [Piret] said to me that it was useless to look for these fishermen in this mission in spring or summer, because then they are all on their fishing grounds; and at the same time they told me that I could find them at home only in winter, if it were possible for me to come in winter. I immediately promised to come, although the missioners were worried about me, because in winter, one can make the distance from Saut-Sainte-Marie to Pointe St. Ignace and Mackinac in no other way but on foot, and that is three and a half days down and just as long again back, during which one must endure 4 nights under open skies.

"With confidence in the support and help of God, I undertook this journey on foot last month. Early on February 6th I started out on this dangerous march with two companions who carried on their backs the necessary provisions and coverings for the night. It was very cold, but otherwise a good day for the jour-

whether it is fear, or a reality — I hope to God that all will go well. — From the Sault I rode in a dog sled for three miles, then I went a considerable distance on snowshoes, and then without snowshoes, and with

---

ney, because in the cold one marches better than when it is mild or warm. We tied the snowshoes on our feet; the two companions walked ahead, to trample the way a little, and I followed them close by. — A scene that would have moved to tears every friend of the missions, if he could have seen me there! — An old mission bishop [62] walking laboriously over deep snow, following two half-Indian guides who, worried, glanced back from time to time to see if the old bishop is able to follow them; and when they saw that I followed them actively they were satisfied and relieved. I soon began to sweat, although it was very cold. — And so we wandered on until noon. There we stopped; my companions started a fire and made tea; and this drink with a piece of bread was my midday meal. In the afternoon we wandered again ahead until evening; on this day we had gone about 20 miles on a fatiguing, difficult trail. I thanked God that I could do so much.

"That evening we were so fortunate as to find an old abandoned Indian hut, or lodge, and though entirely open, and also without a door, it was nevertheless better that the dusky, gray heavenly arches over us. My two companions cut wood and made a fire and I passed through a fairly warm night. The next morning I arose at 4 o'clock to read a part of my breviary before daybreak. (In this winter-time, the breviary can be read only in the morning and evening.) My companions made a frugal breakfast, which again consisted of tea and bread, as did generally all my meals on this journey. I marched fairly well all day, but towards evening I felt a terrible fatigue, so that I could scarcely keep myself on my feet. We now stopped and made camp. My two guides scraped away some of the snow with their snowshoes and then brought small pine branches, and that was my bed. They chopped wood and made a big fire, for it was very cold under the open skies, especially because our underwear was all wet from the sweat of the fatiguing day. After I had read my breviary and had drunk my tea, I laid down, in God's name, on my cold bed and slept only a little from time to time.

"Now came the break of the third day of my journey; I had hoped to arrive at the mission of St. Ignatius by noon, to my great consolation, as I was already tired — How age has had its effect on me! When I was a missioner on Lake Superior I could walk constantly all week long, without becoming tired. Now a journey of two or three days fatigues me. — We arose as soon as we could see the trail and at half past 9 o'clock we came out of the primeval forest, in which we had previously rested, on to the deeply frozen-over Lake Huron. From here we could already see the region of the mission of St. Ignatius, however, we were 15 miles away from it. But scarcely had we walked a short stretch over the ice, when an extremely welcome scene came before our eyes. More than twenty nicely decorated sleds from Pointe St. Ignace and from Mackinac were coming towards us over the ice at a brisk pace. The good people had learned about the time of my arrival and had shown me this favor and this honor. When they had come to us, they jumped out of their sleds, knelt down on the ice and asked for the bishop's blessing which I gave them with deep emotion. For the moment they could not have given me a greater pleasure. And now followed greetings and demonstrations of love. All wanted that I would partake of the refreshments that each one had brought with him. I took some, and then at the fastest pace we went over the nice ice to the mission of Pointe Ste. Ignace. We were soon there. The good missioner, Father Piret, rang the bell, the people assembled in the church and received the bishop's blessing.

moderate fatigue I reached the lodge of the chief and Fabian, but they were not in this lodge 20 miles from the Sault. I spent the night in this lodge very well, ᶠthanks to my double blankets, and the care of my guides.[F198]

Feb. 7:       Set out at 7 A.M. and marched all day fairly well, although towards evenings with considerable fatigue. In the afternoon the ᴱmail-carrierᴱ Miron caught up with us, and we remained in his company to Pointe St. Ignace. In the evening we camped ᶠ5 miles from this side of Pine River.ᶠ Had I known we were so near the lake, I would have insisted on reaching the lake that same evening.[199]

Feb. 8:       Wednesday. About 9 A.M. we arrived at the lake [Huron], and when we were 5 miles from Pine River, more than 20 dog sleds came towards us from Mackinac and Pointe St. Ignace to greet and welcome me. About 1 P.M. we arrived at Pointe St. Ignace.[200]

---

"I remained in this mission 8 days. The missioner, the people of the mission and I myself were very pleased that I came, for on the Sunday that I stayed here, I confirmed ninety persons whom in the summer I could not have found here. In large dioceses the confirmation of 90 persons is not much, but in this poor mission diocese it is very much. And I thank God that I could make this journey on foot to administer to these good people the Holy Sacrament of Confirmation. There were also a number of adults and old people among the confirmed.

"For the next week, (February 15th), I firmly decided for my arrival at Mackinac, 6 miles from Pointe St. Ignace. On this day 19 nice sleds from Mackinac and Pointe St. Ignace came together and drove me in triumph to Mackinac, where the zealous missioner, Father Murray, received me at the door of the church. The people came into the church and from the altar I gave them the bishop's blessing. In this mission I spent 7 days and on Sunday I confirmed eighty-two (82) persons, whom I could not have easily found in spring and summer. Therefore, on this winter mission journey of mine, I confirmed 172 persons, and for this we all in unison thank God. — On these two [missions] I also preached in the French, English and Indian languages in order not to leave out anyone; ᴸthat no one be sent away emptyᴸ [Mk 8:3].

"On February 23rd I started out on my return journey. The good people drove me again to the place on the ice where one enters the forest. After enduring two days and two cold and very unpleasant nights, I arrived, to my great satisfaction, at my residence on February 25th, and thanks be to God! I am very well." Baraga to WF, Sault Ste. Marie, March 3, 1860. Printed in WF, xxiii, 374-75; in BBC-A 674 G.

[198]Louis Rabeska and George Bourassa, cf. D, February 23, 1860.

[199]Bishop Eis added: "Certainly a big trip on foot for a man of his age."

[200]Bishop Eis added: "Halfbreeds met him with sleighs on the ice."

Feb. 9:    All day, from time to time, I had visitors, and in the meantime I read and discussed <u>all sorts of things</u>[201] with Fr. Piret. Wrote 2 letters, to Mr. Menard and Msg. Bourget.[202]

Feb. 10:   Went to an old sick Indian woman, who asked to be baptized. I instructed her a little and baptized her. — Today I also had some Indian confessions.

Feb. 11:   Wrote to Mr. Hennaert[203] regarding Fr. Piret's affairs in Belgium. Today I had many visits and Indian confessions.

Feb. 12:   <u>Sunday.</u> Preached in French, English and Indian, and after the high mass confirmed 90 persons. It was really worth the effort for me to come down here. — Many visits from Mackinac, where I intend to go on.

Feb. 13:   Today I had some Indian confessions and visits. I felt my rheumatic pains because of the draft in the parish house at St. Ignace.

Feb. 14:   Again Indian visitors and confessions; otherwise I read with great interest all day the booklet "Sure way to find out the true religion".

Feb. 15:   At 10 A.M. 19 ᶠdog sledsᶠ [204] came from Mackinac to accompany me there. At noon we arrived. In the afternoon I had some visits, otherwise discussed with Fr. Murray, who perhaps must remain here because I have no one better whom I could send here. (ᶜNo better could I send here.ᶜ)

Feb. 16:   A very cold day after a cold night, but bright and sunny. Today I paid $33 to Toll and Rice for J[ohn] Heaphy, which the miserable P[atrick] Smith should have paid to him for the month. — Received a petition from the Irish[205] for Fr. Murray; naturally, it was to be expected.

---

[201]Among the topics discussed were difficulties with the school. Tanner to Fitch, Pointe St. Ignace, February 12, 1860. Orig. in NA-OIA; in BBC-A 433 E. They also probably talked about Fr. Piret's personal situation. D, March 28, 1860.
[202]Bishop Eis added: "Montreal."
[203]Bishop Eis added: "Vicar General Detroit."
[204]Bishop Eis translated this word as "sleighs."
[205]Probably the Irish at Beaver Island.

| | |
|---|---|
| Feb. 17: | Today I made a visit to the Wendell ᴱfamily,ᴱ with the intention of strengthening his resolve to leave the Free Masons. — I also visited the poor, sick Mrs. Reinville, who will not be able to live much longer. |
| Feb. 18: | Many confessions today. Fr. Murray heard confessions for nearly 10 hours. I also had some, and many visits from all kinds of people. |
| Feb. 19: | <u>Sunday</u>. Very many communions at my 8 o'clock mass from yesterday's confessions. At the high mass I preached in French, English and Indian; after the high mass I confirmed 82 persons. — At noon I dined with Wendell, ᴸas the Lord dined with Zacheaus.ᴸ 206 |
| Feb. 20: | Visits and confessions. In the afternoon I heard the confession of poor Mrs. Reinville. — In the evening Theodore Wendell came (to whom I had written a note) and assured [me] that he intends to give up all connections with the Free Masons and make his ᴱEaster dutyᴱ this year. ᴸThanks be to God.ᴸ |
| Feb. 21: | This afternoon at 1, I rode to Pointe St. Ignace, from where I intend to set out early tomorrow morning for the Sault, if it is the will of God, if the loving God gives us favorable weather. |
| Feb. 22: | <u>Ash Wednesday</u>. It was <u>not</u> the will of God that I should depart today. It <u>rained</u> (!!!) and stormed all night and all day; it was by no means a traveling day. |
| Feb. 23: | Today at 5 A.M. I rode with Louis Rabeska and George Bourassa from Pointe St. Ignace to Pine River. Then we walked a good distance and camped about 3 o'clock,207 since the great ᶠburnt woodᶠ 208 prevented us from camping further in the interior. I spent a very miserable night in this camp.209 |

---

206Lk 19:1–10. Wendell was also a tax collector.

207At this time of the year the sun sets about 6:15 P.M. at this latitude. An early stop was required in order to prepare the camp, the evening meal, and the sleeping arrangements.

208*Brule* means heat or burned wood. There had probably been a forest fire which would explain a lack of boughs upon which to sleep or for a fire, causing a "very miserable night."

209Bishop Eis added: "From St. Ignace to the Sault on foot again."

Feb. 24: Walked all day rather well, and at 4 P.M. we camped about 12 miles from the Sault. Here I had a good night because I made my bed better than the night before.

Feb. 25: Started on our way at 6 A.M.,[210] walked rather quickly, and reached the Sault by 10:15, Eto my great satisfaction.E I received many newspapers and 7 letters, but alas, none with a check.[211]

Feb. 26: L I Sunday of Lent.L Today I preached in English and French, and also announced the LLenten RegulationsL which I announced after the high mass also in Chippewa, in the winter chapel. At the same time I said that from now on I will preach every Sunday in this chapel to Cthose who only speak Indian.C In the afternoon there were FStations of the CrossF and a sermon on the Passion of Our Lord Jesus Christ. And thus it will be on all the Sundays of Lent.

Feb. 27: An unusually nice day. — This afternoon I told Br[other] Donovan that I will come to supper only on Sundays, but never on weekdays, during the entire Lent.[212]

Feb. 28: Confession day. Visitors and confessions. Among others, John Boucher's wife. She complained bitterly about him. The other side must be heard too. I promised her that I will visit and reprimand him. FArchange Gourneau has resumed again herF EIndian spelling.E

Feb. 29: Dull day. Nothing special. Wrote 2 letters. Poor Mrs. Bagage came again begging. I promised her a quart of wine.[213] ETake care!E — In the evening Fr. Duranquet came for a short visit.

March 1: He really was here a short time; this morning he disappeared; I have not seen him at all. — Wrote 3 let-

---

[210]Sunrise was about 7:45 A.M. Perhaps the availability of moonlight affected the time of departure.
[211]Bishop Eis commented: "Too bad."
[212]Bishop Eis reflected: "Easy on the Brother cook."
[213]Neither the spelling nor the meaning of this word are clear. It appears to be *gamine*, which could come from the French *gamay*, meaning a tart sour wine of poor quality. It could also be from the Chippewa *Jamin* meaning *grape*.

ters. — From L[ouis] Trempe received $150 in coin, on my account. In the evening I received a consoling letter from Rev. Van Paemel, in which I note that he intends to return as soon as he gets well. Therefore I should pray to God for his health.

March 2: Wrote letters all day. A big letter writing day. ᴸThanks be to God!ᴸ Among them were useful letters, for instance: To Rev. Mr. Van Paemel, and to the Propagation of the Faith.[214]

March 3: Wood hauling day. This time the wood lasted a long time, since Jan[uary] 31, because I was in Mackinac; and I hope this load will also last due to ᶜmild weather,ᶜ ᴸas it is today.ᴸ // Another big letter writing day, Leopoldine Society,[215] and Ludwig Mission Society.

March 4: ᴸ II Sunday of Lent.ᴸ Terrible storm! 16 children for first communion. I preached in English and French after the Gospel, as usual. I also preached in French before the first communion and distributed it. After mass was confirmation for 22, without an address because the ceremonies were already long enough without it. // In the afternoon preached on the Passion in French. // In the afternoon the mail carrier Boucher arrived, perhaps faster than ever because next Sunday was ᴱ"his time".ᴱ [216]

March 5: Nothing special, only that I wrote many letters, especially to Frs. Piret and Murray that Eliza Jane St. Louis

[214]Baraga acknowledged receipt of a draft of 6250 francs and added: "I thank the good Lord and the two councils [Paris and Lyons] with all my heart for these great benefits which they have had the kindness to bestow on my poor Diocese. My Diocese gives me not a cent of revenue. The Leopoldine Society, although founded in my homeland, gives me little; in the six years since I have seen them in Vienna they have sent me aid only once. The Munich Association sends me 600 dollars, or 3000 francs per year. It is Paris which supports the bishop of Saut Ste. Marie. Without the aid that the Propagation of the Faith sends me so punctually every year, I would be obliged to resign." Baraga to PFAP, Sault Ste. Marie, March 2, 1860. Orig. in PFAP; in BBC-A 505 F.

[215]The Leopoldine Society, established in Austria in 1829 was a German benevolent society formed to advance the missionary activities of the Catholic Church and German missionaries in the United States.

[216]Bishop Eis added: "Mail came 6 days ahead of time — dog train."

remains excommunicated for 1 year from the day of her scandalous marriage.

March 6: A glorious spring day! Too bad it was not like this yesterday (Sunday), but of course it was not the Will of God. This afternoon I began to write a clean copy of the second edition of the Statutes:[217] ᴱTask: four pages of the old Statutes per day.ᴱ

March 7: Very mild weather. Everything is under water. The poor travelers at this time! Thanks be to God I am home! // In the evening gave a lecture on God's First Commandment.

March 8: A terribly windy day, otherwise nice and sunny. ᴱMrs. Galley[218] (?) came to tell me <u>stories</u> about Trempe's servant girl, but I stopped her, and would not listen to such stories.ᴱ

March 9: Today Fr. Menet rode to Garden River with Br. Donovan ᴱon a visit toᴱ Fr. Duranquet. I went to [John] Bapt[iste] Lalonde who promised me to come and take the ᴱpledge.ᴱ — I also heard the confession of old Mrs. Lafond, ᶠmother of Angeline Lafond.ᶠ

March 10: Today I carried the Most Holy Sacrament to old Mrs. Lafond, who is not able to come to church, although she is not sick, but weak from old age; and ᶠit was her first communion.ᶠ Poor old woman.

March 11: ᴸ III <u>Sunday of Lent</u>.ᴸ A well spent day, ᴸa full day.ᴸ Thanks be to God. Preached 4 times, English, French, Indian, and French, and I believe that they were useful, practical sermons.[219]

---

[217]In 1856 Baraga published *Statutes* for the governance of the diocese and the missions. These *Statutes* also gave motivation and encouragement for the clergy. The second edition (1863) added a few clarifications and modifications, which Rome had requested, but it was substantially the same as the original *Statutes*.

[218]Margaret Galley, 32, was the wife of Sgt. William Galley, 36, ordinance sergeant at Fort Brady. Their children were James, 7, and Mary Ann, 4. Federal Census, 1860, Chippewa County, #159. Sgt. Galley "fired the salute of welcome from Fort Brady upon the arrival of Bishop Baraga to the Sault [1854]." Rezek, I, p. 147.

[219]Bishop Eis observed: "Always practical." Jacker noted that every meditation in Baraga's Ottawa books concluded with some resolution. EJP; in BBC-AR 13, p. 52.

March 12:     Great grace! Three full hours.[220] — My task of 4 pages accomplished. — A fair sunny day, but very cold and windy; a real March day = <u>sunny, cold, windy</u>.

March 13:     [E]Last night[E] was the coldest night, at least for me, this winter. Because of the intense cold I could not sleep well. Nice day, [E]perfectly calm,[E] which is very unusual in March.

March 14:     [E]Examination-day at the Ursuline convent.[E] I accomplished my [E]task[E] today, which was very complicated, [E]notwithstanding the girls' examination, which lasted three hours.[E] // In the evening I went to Mary Briggs,[221] to hear her Easter confession, because she cannot come to church.

March 15:     [E]Midnight last night was mid-Lent.[E] Made 23 days, still 23 more to come — // After the mass I carried the Most Holy Sacrament to poor Mary Briggs for Easter. // More like a summer day than spring!

March 16:     A beautiful day. I stayed home all day and wrote. I have finished half the Statutes, (since the 6th of this month). Therefore still 10 more days.

March 17:     Again a warm, calm, sunny day; very unusual for March. // <u>Wood hauling day</u>. // I went to Polly and told her that her sister will not be able to go to communion as long as she sends her children to the [E]Sunday school.[E] // Already today I prepared all 3 sermons for tomorrow. I should always prepare them ahead on Saturday.

March 18:     <u>Sunday</u>. 3 sermons, English, French, French. The roads were bad, and thus very few people in church. // Last night the mail arrived and this morning I received the papers and letters all wet.

March 19:     My task of 4 pages accomplished. Today I received from Eb[enezer] Warner the $10 which Jo[hn Baptiste] Lalonde owed me. Again a warm day.

---

[220]Time of meditative morning prayer.
[221]Mary Briggs, 34, had four children. Federal Census, 1850, Chippewa County, #152. Only John Briggs, 21, a cooper, appears in the 1860 Census, #90. He lived with Louis Cotté.

March 20:     Paid Fr. Menet for the first quarter of 1860. — A rather nice day, the sunset was especially beautiful. — We shall see if this will make tomorrow nice.

March 21:     Yes! A glorious morning! I hope it will be nice all day. // Fr. Duranquet is here. He came last night and will remain here 9 days to make his retreat and also to conduct the sisters in theirs.

March 22:     A beautiful day; in the morning it was cold. — Fr. Duranquet began his retreat last evening, ᴸtherefore silenceᴸ ᶠfor 8 days.ᶠ Bravo!

March 23:     This morning I visited the chronically ill Mary Briggs, and read her a passage from Kagige Debwewinan to her great spiritual consolation, as I noticed. I should do her this charity often. It is snowing.

March 24:     Today I completed the copying of the second edition of the <u>Statutes</u>, which I began on the 6th of this month, thus 19 current days = 17 working days.

March 25:     ᴸPassion Sunday.ᴸ Preached 3 times, <u>English</u>, <u>French</u>, <u>Indian</u>. Extremely few people in church. The river is half open. No one can cross over.

March 26:     This morning I went to see the work on the canal.[222] In my opinion it will not be completed, NB., before the <u>middle of July</u>. Some say it will be finished by the <u>middle of May</u>.[223] ᴵWe shall see.ᴵ

March 27:     Read in Butler[224] all day. A nice but windy day. No one can cross the St. Mary's River; the middle of the river is open, and both sides are lined with dangerous, rotten ice.

March 28:     21 men arrived here from Mackinac to work on the canal. They were deceived; they were promised ᴱhigher wagesᴱ than they will really receive. Some

---

[222]In 1858 breaks of an "alarming character" occurred on the north bank of the canal. Due to delays in obtaining money, the repair was not begun until 1860. *History of the Upper Peninsula*, p. 216.

[223]The canal reopened on May 12 (D).

[224]Bishop Eis explained: "Life of the Saints." Bishop Alban Butler wrote, in four volumes, *The Lives of the Saints*. Baraga frequently marked passages that had significance for him. Cf. Kotnik. In BBC-AR 92.

will probably go back. // Rev. Fr. Piret informed me of his decision to leave the holy ministry.

March 29:   Several of the Mackinac people went home, 10 or 12, (all except 3) They find the work too hard and the pay too small. // Today I have corrected and numbered all the Statutes, and have already cut up paper for a second ᴱcopy.ᴱ <u>Confession day</u> for ᴸplenary indulgenceᴸ = ᴱMarch.ᴱ

March 30:   A warm, calm day. I went again to visit sick Mary Briggs, and again read to her ᶜconcerning sickness.ᶜ // Today I began to write the second copy of the Statutes; which I hope and intend to complete on April 13, ᴸwith the help of God.ᴸ // Fr. Duranquet has disappeared this morning. // I already prepared the 3 sermons for the day after tomorrow, Palm Sunday.

March 31:   The last day of March; a wonderful nice day! ˢ"<u>March has its tail twisted</u>." This year it was twisted for the better.ˢ — ᶜWould that every spring this would happen.ᶜ ᴸIt will be however God wishes it to be.ᴸ

April 1:   ᴸ<u>Palm Sunday</u>.ᴸ Gave 2 short sermons, because the blessing of the palms and the Passion were long enough. // I let Montferret[225] come today and I advised him that he should give up keeping the saloon[226] as soon as possible, and that meanwhile he should not sell on Sunday, etc.

April 2:   Again a beautiful day, but quite cold in the morning; later it warmed up nicely. // Received two bottles of syrup from Theresa Jourdain.

April 3:   <u>Wood hauling day</u>. A very nice day. Last night it snowed a little, but it has already melted. // Archange Gourneau did not come. ᴱShe misses many days.ᴱ ᶜSeldom she knows it,ᶜ[227] ᴱif ever.ᴱ

---

[225]The Montferrand (Montferret, Montferrat) name does not appear in the 1860 census.

[226]Bishop Eis translated this *saloon*. The original German meaning would be more like a *grocery store*.

[227]Her lesson for the day.

April 4:      Another summer day. It was nice all day. In the evening it rained considerably. [F]Poor travelers![F 228]

April 5:      <u>Holy Thursday</u>. Consecrated the Holy Oils. [E]Somewhat awkward with the assistance of only <u>one</u> priest. // Last night[E] it snowed a little, nevertheless it is nice again today.

April 6:      Again a beautiful day, like summer. Such a Holy Week I never before have seen. Today I again visited poor sick Mrs. Briggs, and read aloud, part of the Passion. // The poor [E]mail-carriers, last Saturday due[E] are still not here.

April 7:      The last day of Holy Week; again a real summer day. // The mail carriers have not yet arrived — at 2 P.M. Neither did they come all day.

April 8:      <u>Easter Sunday</u>. Pontifical mass, which perhaps I will not sing again until [F]Christmas.[F 229] [C]I don't know.[C 230] Fr. Menet preached.

April 9:      A very nice day. Today the stove will be removed from the church; and we also received the news that 300 men came on the "Seabird" to Detour, intended for work on the canal. — Received $250 in cash from L[ouis] Trempe. // 2 mails now arrived. One is still behind, perhaps in Mackinac. // Received good news from Schwarz,[231] that 303 Pounds will be sent to me.

April 10:     Yesterday's report of 300 workers for the canal now reduced to 60. It is hoped the work will be finished by

---

[228]Bishop Eis added: "The breakup in spring, hardest on the mailcarriers."

[229]Bishop Eis wrote: "Xmas."

[230]Baraga repeated, "I do not know" in Latin, below the Chippewa words.

[231]Johann Georg Schwarz was the son of a Viennese fur dealer. With his brother he came to Detroit in 1819 to establish ties with the Indian fur trade. Upon the death of his father in 1821, he returned to Vienna where he became the first American consul in Austria. He was one of the first officers of the Leopoldine Society. He received and preserved many Ottawa artifacts, which Bishop Résé and missionaries, including Baraga, sent to the society. Christian F. Feest, "Michigan Ottawa History—100 Years after Andrew J. Blackbird," lecture presented at Little Traverse Historical Society, Harbor Springs, MI, July 20, 1988. In BBC-AR 118. This money was only the second contribution Baraga received from Vienna since 1854.

May 15, which I still don't believe. ᴱLast nightᴸ it snowed considerably, but it has already turned to water.

April 11:     Today I completed my task and somewhat more than the task already before noon, which has never happened before. // This evening Fr. Duranquet came up here, all alone in a ᶠbirch bark canoe across the ice floes.ᶠ

April 12:     A very stormy day! First it rained, then it snowed, and a terrible wind. // ᴱThe chimney of the sisters' house caught fire. Great commotion for nothing.ᴱ // Fr. Duranquet is still here, ᶠtired.ᶠ

April 13:     This morning Fr. Duranquet went home, but he had difficult times. // I visited Mrs. Briggs again; and completed copying the 2nd copy of the 2nd edition of the Statutes, ᴸas I scheduled on March 30.ᴸ For the first time ᶠsupper <u>without candles</u>.ᶠ [232]

April 14:     I wrote the Appendix for the Roman ᴱcopyᴱ (of the Statutes) and began an index for mine, or the Cincinnati ᴱcopy.ᴱ // A very windy and cold day. // ᶠSupper without candles.ᶠ Now we will always be able to have supper without candles. <(ᴸBut not on April 18ᴸ)>

April 15:     <u>Sunday</u>. Great spiritual ᶠmisfortuneᶠ this morning! // Instead of 3 rose at 5. 2 hours absolutely lost![233] // Delivered 2 sermons to empty pews. I believe that the church was <u>never</u> as empty as it was today. // The mail which has been expected for the last 3 weeks has finally arrived.[234]

April 16:     Today Montferrat came, and I promised him the soon to be vacated teacher's post at L'Anse. . . . Perhaps misère! . . . Yes, if I had known!!! Terrible wind! Poor workers on the canal!

---

[232]Bishop Eis commented: "Supper by daylight."
[233]Bishop Eis added: "He rose regularly at 3 o'clock A.M."
[234]Bishop Eis added: "Mail 3 weeks late (sic)."

April 17:     ᴱLast night it blew a perfect gale;ᴱ it is also windy all day. March was not as windy as April. Now we have the equinoctial storms.

April 18:     ᴱYesterday poor Thomas Edwards died in the sugar-bush, and today they brought his corpse in. I spoke to Ellen, and wrote a letter to Clark.ᴱ Whether it will do any good, I don't know. ᴸThe perverse are corrected only with difficulty.ᴸ

April 19:     Late notice: Yesterday a Scotchman who worked on the canal was killed by a stone that fell on him. // Work is being done on McKnight's railroad. A bad sign! The canal will not be finished for a long time.

April 20:     ᴱPoorᴱ Edwards was buried at last. My two sermons are finished. <u>Wood hauling day</u>. — The Statutes are now completely copied, corrected, revised, and ready for printing. However, I will wait until the first copy comes back from Rome. Only if it should not return in a <u>year and a day</u>, ᴸwhich is not likely to happen,ᴸ then I will have the 2nd ᴱcopyᴱ printed.

April 21:     ᴸWhat shall I say?ᴸ — Today I know nothing.

April 22:     <u>Sunday</u>. Preached in French ᶠon sudden death.ᶠ ᴸIn English on the dignity and happiness of being a Christian.ᴱ

April 23:     Fr. Duranquet was here again, but returned at once. He related how sad the outlook is for the Catholic missions on the North shore of Lake Superior. All the Indians are becoming Methodist.

April 24:     Snowed a little ᴱlast night.ᴱ Very cold this morning. Today L[ouis] Trempe's tug boat left for Detroit. // Snowed again in the evening.

April 25:     ᴸ<u>Feast of St. Mark</u>. Day of the Major Litany.ᴸ // This afternoon I went to overlook the canal work. It certainly will not be open soon. // ᴱThis evening at 7 the first boat arrived, the propeller "Ontonagon."ᴱ

April 26:     A glorious day! // Wrote several letters. // We await with yearning a boat from above, on Lake Superior.

April 27:        The "Seabird" arrived from Detroit and brought many passengers for Lake Superior. Among them also Mr. Erhard Buttner, whom I designate for Portage Lake. <(Alas, as usual, I do not know what I am doing . . . Oh, if I had only known! . . . . ) (I did that poorly.)>

April 28:        Today I had a sad <sup>F</sup>scrape<sup>F</sup> with Fr. Menet on account of Fr. Duranquet because I had written to Bishop Farrell that he should recommend to him the instruction of the ignorant Indians on the other side of the Sault.[235]

April 29:        <u>Sunday</u>. Preached in English and French. In the evening the "Lady Elgin" came <sup>E</sup>in, and will leave the day after tomorrow at noon perhaps.<sup>E</sup> // I received the good news that O'Neil made himself scarce. // <u>Confession day</u>.

April 30:        Today we went to the "Lady Elgin" <sup>E</sup>[at] the head of the canal.<sup>E</sup> She will <sup>E</sup>probably<sup>E</sup> <sup>F</sup>leave tomorrow.<sup>F</sup> O, had I been able to go up before the scandals [of Fr. O'Neil] went so far.

May 1:        <sup>E</sup>Last night it snowed a little, so that this morning we had a nice white beginning of beautiful<sup>E</sup> <u>spring</u>! — Departed for Portage Lake with Mr. Buttner, Montferrat and family, on the "Lady Elgin".[236]

---

[235]Baraga merely intended that Bishop John Farrell of Hamilton, Ontario, should reaffirm Fr. Duranquet's task of catechizing the Indians on the Canadian side of Sault Ste. Marie. Baraga to Tellier, Sault Ste. Marie, April 29, 1860. Orig. in ACSM; in BBC-A 816 F. However, Fr. Menet would not accept Baraga's explanation nor his attempts to improve the situation. Menet charged that Baraga was trying to induce the Jesuits to withdraw from the Sault: "We would not be anymore at Sault Ste. Marie, if the bishop had been able to find priests to replace us; and in spite of the promises he made to keep us here, in spite of the change he shows in his conduct towards us, it would not be surprising if he sends us away as soon as he will be able to find others to succeed us." Menet to Tellier, Sault Ste. Marie, June 11, 1860. Orig. in ACSM; in BBC-Mss. 26.

[236]On this day Mother Mary Xavier and Sister Angela left the Sault, "not without regrets," for Chatham. They arrived there on May 9. Mother Mary Xavier Le Bihan to Ursuline community at Clermont, Chatham, c. 1876. Orig. in UAC; in BBC-Mss. 48.

Baraga gave the details of his trip to Houghton but did not mention the difficulties with Fr. O'Neil. In the same letter he described his second and chief visitation journey to Lake Superior for the summer of 1860: "On May 1st I boarded a steamboat and on the first day it went on very well and quietly, but on the second day we struck an incalculable floating ice-field which prevented us from sailing. We had to remain idle for 20 hours until the wind drove away the ice-field and provided us with a passageway. Similar incalculable ice-fields one sees on Lake Superior still late in May, and at times even in June. I recently read in a newspaper that in St. Petersburg, Russia, no more ice was to be seen since the end of April, and that at that time navigation could be continued unhindered and from this I conclude that the temperature on Lake Superior must be colder than there.

"The first mission that I visited was the mountain town of Portage Lake, or Houghton, where we have a very spacious church, but which already has become too small, inasmuch as the copper mines are very productive in that region and this draws the miners and other laborers to there. There are already about 4000 persons in this settlement, Irish, English, American, German and French, and almost half of the population is Catholic. A German priest, Rev. Edward Jacker is now there but he preaches and hears confessions also in English and French very well. When I was there we decided to build a second church, for the present one cannot accommodate all the Catholics.

"My next visit was to the city of Superior, at the westernmost end of the lake of the same name. There the people were extraordinarily pleased to again see a servant of God, because the pious and zealous missioner, Father Van Paemel, who attended this mission from La Pointe, has become so sick last fall that he could not work anymore and therefore returned to his native country, Belgium, to again restore his health, if possible. I see from a letter that he has written me that he wishes to return, but, until now, his shattered condition of health has not permitted it. His mission people, who are attached to him with much love, were very sad when they saw him go away, and sadder when throughout the winter they had to be without a priest, because the sick missioner went on the last steamboat and then one could not come to La Pointe and Superior anymore until May, when navigation is again open. That is why the people were pleased when they saw me. I remained 10 days in Superior and there I was once more a simple missioner. I often sat all day in the confessional and on other days I instructed the children and adults, baptized them, blessed their marriages, and performed, in general, all the functions of a simple priest.

"From there I went to La Pointe, about 80 miles this side of Superior. This was my first mission on Lake Superior which I had founded 25 years ago. Here, too, I stayed 10 days and performed all the functions of a simple missioner. There I was again right in my element, and very satisfied, for the Indian missions are truly my element. In these two mission stations I baptized 64 persons, some children, some adults, and only a few had died since the absence of the sick missioner. The members of our mission continue to increase, while among the wild unconverted Indians there are more and more deaths, so that now there are a few as yet unconverted. — On June 10th, I baptized 23 persons at La Pointe and preached five times, twice in the morning and three times in the afternoon.

"After I had performed everything I went to the mountain city of Minnesota [Mine], where Rev. Martin Fox is missioner. He has now entirely completed his nice and spacious church and has a large congregation of Germans, Irish and French. Although his church is the biggest in the diocese, it can scarcely accommodate two-thirds of his congregation. On Sundays many must stand outside during the Divine Service. Fortunately the church has three large doors which are left open so that the people standing outside can see the priest at the altar and hear the sermon.

"Throughout the past winter there were two priests at Minnesota Mine, Rev. Martin Fox, a Prussian, and Rev. John Chebul, a Carniolan from the diocese of Ljubljana. Immediately upon his arrival last fall, I sent the Rev. Chebul to Minnesota Mine, so that he would learn there English and French, and he has applied himself to these two languages with such diligence and with such wonderful success, so that since the last three months he hears confessions and preaches in the English and French languages. — In less than 6 months he has learned well these two languages, about which he previously knew almost

May 2:    Up to White Fish Point all went well; but there we were detained by the ice for about 20 hours. <Noteworthy for <u>Berichte</u>:[237] St. Petersburg[238] (in Russia) is already free of ice by this time in April.>

May 3:    Arrived at the Entry about 1 P.M. Went directly to L'Anse to introduce the Montferrat family, because I thought Fr. Jacker would still be there, but he had already gone to Portage Lake.

May 4:    From L'Anse to Portage Lake, where I arrived at noon, and immediately handed O'Neil his document of interdict, and removed him from the house.

May 5:    This morning I again offered holy mass. All day I have had mostly unpleasant visitors.[239]

May 6:    <u>Sunday</u>. Preached in English, French, and German, and described the unfortunate O'Neil acccording to his deserts,[240] and recommended that the people now come more regularly to church, etc.

May 7–8:  Always the same trouble. The miserable man wants to have his Exeat from me by force, and I do not give him one. He goes from house to house and gathers a following for himself; but also this will be of no use to him.

May 9:    Again the old song. I guess O'Neil acquired a few sig-

---

nothing, whereby we were all astonished because this has never before occurred to us. I have now sent him to La Pointe, from where he will also take care of Superior and other small mission stations. In Minnesota Mine he had no need for the Indian; at his present mission it will be indispensable to him. I hope that by his application, and with his talents for languages, that he will learn it sufficiently in a year to preach without an interpreter.

"After I had visited and taken care of these missions it was time for me to return to Sault Sainte Marie, because of my correspondence. And it was really about time that I came home, inasmuch as a large number of letters awaited me, some of which required an early reply.

"However, in 2 or 3 days, I will go again on another mission visitation journey, to the southern part of my extensive, but sparsely inhabited half-Indian diocese." Baraga to WF, Sault Ste. Marie, July 4, 1860. Printed in WF, XXIII, 559; in BBC-A 675 G.

[237]Publication of the Leopoldine Society in Vienna.
[238]Now Leningrad.
[239]Probably the Irish who supported Fr. O'Neil.
[240]Since July 3, 1859, O'Neil had been on probation (D).

natures but he mentions nothing about them to me. I composed ᴱa warning[241] to all the Rt. Rev. Prelates.ᴱ

May 10: Already yesterday evening we (I, Jacker, and Buttner) copied many copies of the "Warning" and this morning we completed them. // Departure from Houghton to Entry on Bendry's[242] scow. We found the "Lady Elgin" there, but she was going up.

May 11: All day[243] in tedious waiting for the "Mineral Rock", which was expected already yesterday. // Read Butler all day.

May 12: This mornig there is still no appearance of the "Mineral Rock" . . . just as I write this I hear the whistle of the "Mineral Rock" on which we sail for the Sault. // On this day the first boats passed through the repaired Sault Sainte Marie canal.

May 13: Sunday. I spent this day on the boat as well as I could, spent all day reading the long breviary and Butler.[244] At about 4 P.M. we arrived at the Sault where I received all kinds of letters, among them also a check for about $1450 from the Leopoldine Society. ᴸThanks be to God!ᴸ I H S

---

[241]Of the thirty-nine letters sent, only those to Archbishop Purcell and Bishop Lefevere remain: "My Lord. I most respectfully warn Your Grace, never to receive in your diocese one Dennis O'Neil, an Irish priest. He is a hard drinker and a most scandalous priest. He is now under the censure of Suspension or Interdict." Baraga to Purcell, Sault Ste. Marie, May 15, 1860. Orig. in NDUA; in BBC-A 168 E.

[242]Captain James Bendry was born on June 6, 1822, at Wootten Bassett, Wiltshire, England. When he was 12 he began sailing—the Mediterranean, West Indies, Africa. In 1841 he came to the Great Lakes and in 1845 became a deck hand on the *Independence*, the first steamer to traverse Lake Superior. At the Sault, in 1846, he married Charlotte Contoui, a woman of French and Indian blood. They had eleven children. His wife and two children were with him when he moved from Sault Ste. Marie on the *Siskowit* in 1850 (Federal Census, 1850, Chippewa County, #184). A severe winter storm stranded them in Keweenaw Bay. Thus they became the first settlers at the location now known as Baraga. Bishop Baraga and his priests did business at Bendry's sawmill and brickyard and sailed on his ships. Charlotte Bendry died on May 28, 1892, and James Bendry died on October 14, 1894. They were buried from the old Indian Mission Church at Assinins and are interred in the Catholic Indian Cemetery. Dompier, pp. 30–32.

[243]The word *day* was entered later in pencil.

[244]Bishop Eis added again: "Life of the Saints." See note 224 above.

May 14:  Had difficulties with the check. The <u>number</u> reads: 297 Pounds Sterling, and the letters say: ᶠtwo hundred <u>eighty</u>-seven, instead of <u>ninety</u>-seven.ᶠ [245] This is the first check, now I must wait for the second, hoping it will be more correct.[246] If the same fatal error also appears, then I will have to send the check back to Vienna, and with great delay wait for another.

May 15:  This morning at 6:30 Mr. Buttner went to Mackinac to learn the mass and breviary with Mr. Murray. (NB. Last evening I received $400 from Louis P. Trempe for the checking account.)

May 16:  Been home all day and read. // Among other things I have also looked for the O'Neil documents, but have found not a <u>one</u>. I can testify under <u>oath</u> that I have no documents from him. // Trempe sent me $100 more on the check; that now makes $500.

May 17:  ᴸ<u>Ascension of Our Lord Jesus Christ</u>ᴸ I kept a little fire burning all day; it is a bit rainy. // Towards evening I went to visit a sick Indian, and heard his confession.

May 18:  Today the unfortunate Dennis O'Neil passed through here on the "Fountain City". I do not know where he will turn. He will find his way blocked everywhere. He should mend his ways completely and resolutely, or become something else.

May 19:  I again visited the sick Indian at the canal, and brought him an Indian prayerbook, and also promised him a G[agikwe Masinaigan], which I still must bring to him, besides a "Flowers of Piety."

May 20:  <u>Sunday</u>. Today Fr. Menet preached, and I preached at the high mass. There were quite a few people from the other side.

May 21:  The "Northstar" is expected today but she probably will come only tomorrow. ᶦWe shall see.ᶦ // In the

---

[245]$1,450. Rezek, I, p. 159.

[246]Apparently two checks were mailed each time for security. Often the mail was lost so two separate letters provided more assurance that at least one letter would arrive safely.

evening we received the news that she is frightfully aground. The tug went down to loosen her.

May 22: Still no "Northstar". She is perhaps $^E$damaged.$^E$ // Paid a visit to sick Briggs and the sick Indian, but he is now on the road to recovery. He promised to drink no more and to come to church diligently. May God give him the grace for that!

May 23: At noon the "Northstar" arrived at the Sault, entirely unexpected, and I sailed on her for Superior. The journey is very pleasant, few passengers and fair weather, and cheap fare, only $13 to Superior.

May 24: The journey continues to be very pleasant; I have a splendid $^E$state room,$^E$ and am not sea-sick in the least. All day I read the life of St. Francis Xavier. // I saw Fr. Thiele and his nicely arranged church and residence.

May 25: Arrived at La Pointe at noon, where we scarcely remained 15 minutes. The same in Bayfield. I had no time to inspect the new church there.[247] I promised to come again in 12 or 14 days and remain for a few weeks. // In the evening I arrived in sad Superior.

May 26: I was in the house all day, waiting for people to visit me. No confessions; yet perhaps they will begin to come later in the evening. // Very few have come. I hope they will come during the week and next Saturday.

May 27: Pentecost. This morning there were a few confessions, and also a few communions[248] at the first mass which I offered at 7:30. // At the second even fewer, and also very few people. // Three short sermons at the mass, and three again after Vespers.

May 28: Today I visited poor Mrs. Danie and heard her confession. She has a terrible cancer sore around her nose

---

[247] "The church at Bayfield was a low but neat and well decorated frame building, 24 by 70 feet. It had been built in 1860 by Fr. John Chebul. It was used until 1898, at which time it was used as a church hall and eventually torn down and the good lumber used for construction of a school." Vogt, pp. 89–90.

[248] The custom required confession before reception of holy communion.

and mouth. Mr. Anglois gave me a "recipe" for healing cancer sores.

May 29: Last night it stormed and rained frightfully. Terrible roads in Superior! Fortunately there are sidewalks almost everywhere, otherwise it would not be possible to get around in this weather. Brought the Holy Eucharist to Mrs. Danie.

May 30: There were more confessions today and many communions this morning, as well as many candidates for confirmation at the instructions. // In the afternoon I heard the confession of sick Mrs. Ryan — ᴸ miserable afflicted humanity.ᴸ —

May 31: A very nice day! The old May wishes to coax us a little before it leaves us. // Brought Mrs. Ryan the Holy Eucharist. // Until now I have baptized 10 children, but there are perhaps more to be baptized. (Baptized one more today.)

June 1: June, my birth month, begins nicely; we shall see how it will behave in the future. // Many confessions. The people of Fond du Lac are beginning to come; even some Indians from Ishkonigan are coming.

June 2: An extraordinary day of labor! Continuous confessions and instructions for baptisms and confirmation, also ᶠfirst communion.ᶠ

June 3: Sunday. Today there were more people in the church than on Pentecost, because they have come here from different locations. A very intensive day of labor, but, alas, only up to 4 P.M. because then I had to leave. The "Northstar" arrived sooner that I expected. Confirmed 22. Confirmed all alone.

June 4: At 1 A.M. arrived at La Pointe. At 7 A.M. said mass and then heard confession of sick Tchetchigwaio. In the evening I had many confessions.

June 5: At break of dawn I brought only communion to Tchetchigwaio, offered mass, and then set out for Bad River and arrived there in 5 hours. Stayed with Nawadjiwans[249] where I found a neat chapel on his ᴱupper floor.ᴱ Immediately after my arrival I went to visit sick Wabada. In the evening said prayers and preached.

June 6:

ᴱLast nightᴱ I almost did not sleep at all because of the loud mosquitoes and the crying of children. After the mass I carried the Holy Eucharist to sick Wabada, to whom I also administered Extreme Unction. // It is raining terribly from time to time.

June 7:

Corpus Christi. I had mass at 10 o'clock and preached; after that baptisms, 2 adults and 4 children.[250] In the afternoon vespers and sermon. // Towards evening I called Nawadjiwans and made an agreement with him for the ᴱupper story of his house.ᴱ

June 8:

Departed from Bad River at 9 A.M. and by 2 arrived in La Pointe. Soon after that I went to a sick ᴱhalf-breed,ᴱ the pitiful Michael Basinet's son, and heard his confession. Then I went to Bayfield, to Colonel Drew,[251] who paid me $275 for Dillon O'Brien. In the evening many confessions.

June 9:

A great day of labor. I had confessions all day and some baptisms. // To Nawadjiwans I paid $40 for the upper part of his house, to be used as a chapel.

June 10:

Sunday. An extraordinary day of work! From 4 A.M. until 10 P.M. I had uninterrupted work, very many confessions, 5 sermons, 23 baptisms and 3 confirmations. The church was packed full.[252]

June 11:

Not so much to do today. In the afternoon I went to visit sick Dufant and sick Chalut and heard their confessions. In the evening there were some confessions.

June 12:

Still less to do today. I have made an agreement with Joseph Riel[le] for the addition to "Little Current's"

---

[249]"Little Current."

[250]The La Pointe-Bayfield Baptismal Registry lists only five names for June 7.

[251]Col. Cyrus Drew had replaced Gilbert as Indian agent. *History of Northern Wisconsin*, p. 83.

[252]Bishop Eis remarked: "What our priests do now in comparison."

house; and when I reached into my carpetbag to pay him $10 in advance, I discovered the very distressing fact, that about $65 had been stolen from me. John Cottons was accused. The suspicion is strong against him.

June 13: The unfortunate John Cottons is actually the thief; this morning he admitted that he stole $65 from my carpetbag. He was brought to justice and is now in custody, awaiting the circuit court.

June 14: Today I went to the agent [Drew] in Bayfield, to request him to indemnify me by paying the $50 which is still due to me. (Because yesterday I got back $15.) He gave me hope and the promise that he would do his best.

June 15: All day sadly waiting for the "Northstar." // Today I made an agreement with Perinier to repair the arches of St. Joseph church at $1.50 per day. // On the same evening boarded the "Ogans" and on

June 16: In the morning at 8, arrived at Ontonagon, where, thanks be to God, I have much consolation because I find Mr. Chebul with such excellent missionary dispositions.[253] // That evening I had Indian confessions.

June 17: Sunday. Celebrated the 8 o'clock mass and preached at the 10 in English and French at Ontonagon. The church was rather full; it is said that at times it is filled even more. In the evening I had Indian confessions.

June 18: Millette[254] is working on the transfer of the ᴱgarden fence,ᴱ ꟳat the enormous price of $2.25 per day!ꟳ The properties in Ontonagon are now worth nothing. // At first I had some Indian confessions, but now there is nothing to do here.

---

[253]"I am also rich, as rich as I have ever been in my life, for I have a satisfied and happy heart. Bishop Baraga said to me, as I was strumming a song on a guitar: 'It pleases me that you are so satisfied; a missioner must be of a happy heart.'" Chebul to Globocnik, La Pointe, December 1, 1860. Printed in ZD, 1861, pp. 54–55; in BBC-B 615 S.

[254]Thomas Millette was a Canadian-born carpenter, 33 years old. He and his wife, Sophia, age 23, had a 2-year-old son, Thomas. Federal Census, 1860, Ontonagon County, #646.

June 19:  Millette completed the fence in the afternoon and started transferring the stairs. // Learned from Lawyer Jones (?) that I still will have to wait a long time after the expiration of the mortgage term before I can sell the house; if some one will buy it then. —

June 20:  At 8 A.M. I wanted to ride to ᴱMinnesota landingᴱ on a riverboat, but I missed it. So I then rode the stage to Maplegrove and from there walked to Minnesota Mine in immense heat.[255]

June 21:  The church in Minnesota is now completed, but still deep in debt. // Read all day, or conversed with the good Fr. Fox. // Fr. Chebul returned to Ontonagon today, and from here continued on.

June 22:  An unusually hot day; I fear a thunderstorm. The clouds are piling up. // Read the ᶠLives of the Ancient Philosophersᶠ all day.

June 23:  Still continues to be sultry, but no rain comes out of it, only a few drops have fallen. // Bought Fr. Fox 4 pair of knives and forks and spoons.[256]

June 24:  Sunday. ᴸIn the church of the Blessed Virgin Mary,ᴸ celebrated at 8 o'clock, at 10 I preached in English, German and French. After high mass had about 20 confirmations.

June 25:  At 12 noon departed from Minnesota Mine, and at 7 P.M. arrived in Ontonagon Village with Patrick O'Flanigan[257] and Schulte,[258] the former intended for

---

[255]Bishop Eis added: "Six miles over big hills."

[256]Bishop Eis observed: "Poverty."

[257]Patrick M. O'Flanigan (with multiple spellings) came from Maple Grove. He began to study for the priesthood in August 1860, was ordained by Baraga at Minnesota Mine on November 16, 1862, and sent to Clifton. After an incident involving an Ursuline sister at Ontonagon and problems with alcohol, Baraga willingly gave him an exeat effective July 20, 1865. O'Flanigan went to the diocese of Chicago. He was pastor at St. Anne Parish in Chicago when he died on August 29, 1907.

[258]John Caspar Schulte, the son of John and Anna Marie Griffel Schulte, was born on September 25, 1827, at Westphalia, Germany. He had been a novice of the Brothers of the Christian schools. His name first appeared on the subscription list for the construction of St. Ignatius Church, Houghton, on September 5, 1858. He did not remain in La Pointe but, on September 3, 1860, he sailed from Eagle Harbor with Baraga. From then until Baraga's death, Schulte was his faithful servant. Schulte received Minor Orders on October 21, 1862, and five

theological studies in Cincinnati, and the latter for La Pointe.

June 26: Baptized Schiek's child. Millette made 2 bedsteads for the rectory. The plasterer demanded $4 for his work and said the materials would be another $4. I discharged him.

June 27: All day I improved the sacristy and put it in good order, as well as the church and the house. // In the evening I sailed on the "Ogans" for La Pointe alone, not with Mr. Chebul and his young man.[259]

June 28: At 7 A.M. I arrived at La Pointe, and was very pleased with Perinier's work. Towards evening I went to Bayfield, to Agent Drew, and received for Mr. Chebul the $75 which O'Brien still owed me, which he will be able to draw on July 2.

June 29: My 63 birthday. ˪Thanks be to God!˩ I offered mass very early, and then went to Bad River to see what is happening there. The chapel will be quite nice, but I hear it will cost much because Jo Rielle (?) is working desparingly slow. At 3 P.M. I was already back in La Pointe. The "Northstar" arrived and went on up to Superior, but Fr. Chebul was not on her; he imprudently went by schooner. // At 11 P.M. I boarded the "Northstar" and

June 30: At 4 A.M. was already in Ontonagon, where Patrick O'Flanigan embarked for Cleveland and Cincinnati. We had a very calm journey all the way, and on

---

days later he vowed perpetual celibacy. Later Baraga wrote: "I testify herewith that Caspar Schulte, the bearer of this, has been in my service for many years and has proved to be a devoted, trustworthy and obedient servant and has carefully fulfilled the office of sacristan. He has received the four minor orders. He wishes now to enter a Benedictine Monastery as a lay brother. I recommend him very much to the Rev. Father Superior of the monastery where he shall ask for admission." Baraga, Marquette, c. July 1, 1867. Orig. in NDUA; in BBC-A 396 E. Schulte was living in Detroit in 1889. Schulte to his brother [Henry], Detroit, March 25, 1889. Orig. in Mrak Papers, NDUA; in BBC-AR 14, #18.

[259]Baraga hired an interpreter for two years for Chebul. Chebul learned the Chippewa sufficiently to discharge the interpreter after three months. Chebul to Globocnik, La Pointe, December 1, 1860. Printed in ZD, 1861, pp. 54–55; in BBC-B 615 S.

July 1:     We arrived at the Sault. <u>Sunday</u>. There I entrusted the porter with a small box with $30 in gold for Perinier. I found many letters waiting for me, both good[260] and bad. // Good news! The <u>Sisters</u> will remain, and their number will be increased.[261]

July 2:     Theophil Trempe[262] brought me $300 for the checking account. // The "Lady Elgin" went down without my even knowing about it. In a way it is just as well since I have some business here to take care of.

July 3:     It rained a little, but not enough to suit the wishes of the people whose gardens and meadows are suffering from drought.

July 4:     <u>Day of general sinning and misfortune!</u>[263] Here it passes rather quietly, at least I hear no noise here, except for some firing of the cannon at the fort[264] at noon. A useful work day; report to the Leopoldine Society and the Ludwig Mission Society.

July 5:     Several boats came down, but none go to Mackinac. I am grieved. // In the evening I delivered to P. B. Bar-

---

[260]One of the good letters contained a check for 4800 francs from Paris. After thanking them for their support Baraga continued: "I was absent from the Sault for six weeks, and I was obliged to perform the functions of a simple missionary at several mission stations. The bishop was completely forgotten. I spent my days in the confessional, I instructed the catechumens who presented themselves, I baptized children and adults, and I sang the high mass every Sunday without an assistant just like I used to do before being bishop; because one of my best missionaries, Fr. Van Paemel, became sick last fall, and has left his missions in order to go and take care of himself in his country, Belgium. I was therefore obliged to perform his duties, and I will be obliged to return again this summer because the good missionary is not coming back, and the one that I have now sent in his place does not as yet speak the Indian language. When I am once again a simple missionary, I am in my element and happy." Baraga to PFAP, Sault Ste. Marie, July 2, 1860. Orig. in PFAP; in BBC-A 486 F.

[261]Baraga misunderstood the information he received. Mother Mary Xavier and Sister Angela had left the Sault on May 1 and immediately located a "convent" and began a school at Chatham. Sisters Mary Joseph and Augustine followed them in August. Mother Mary Xavier did mean "remain" but at Chatham, not at the Sault.

[262]Theophil Trempe was 22 years old, a bookkeeper. He lived with Louis Trempe. Federal Census, 1860, Chippewa County, #96.

[263]This expression was Baraga's usual way of describing the July 4th festivities. He opposed both drinking and dancing.

[264]Fort Brady.

beau the FFrench draftF for 4800 francs = $902. At the same time made arrangement to sail to Mackinac in a small boat.

July 6:    At 5 A.M. departed[265] from the Sault Fin a small river boat.F It was calm and extraordinarily hot all day. The

[265]Baraga gave the *Wahrheitsfreund* a detailed account of these travels: "This summer, with the exception of a few days, I have devoted entirely to mission visitation journeys. On July 1st I had just returned from a journey, and on the 6th, I set out again on another. I perceive the usefulness of these journeys, that is why I undertake gladly the hardships and dangers of the same, so as not to appear at some future time before the Lord as a useless servant and be an outcast.

"Therefore, on July 6th, I set out on a new mission journey. After I had waited in vain for a steamboat that would have taken me to Mackinac, I hired two Indians and started out on the journey, according to the old missionary custom, in a small fishing boat for Mackinac. The first day went well; we had quiet weather and the two Indians rowed the entire day. But on the second day we had a terrible wind; as it was favorable, we made use of it, and the light fishing boat, on which the Indians set sails, glided to their destination like a feather over the waves. We were already near the island of Mackinac, when suddenly the plank on which the mast was set broke into pieces. The sail fell overboard and we were in great danger of sinking; because if the mast, on which the sail was hung, would go under the canoe (which continued to speed fast), then we would unfortunately turn over. However, one of the Indians quickly grasped the sail and pulled it in and so saved us. This incident reminded me of the many perils, in which I found myself at the beginning of my missionary life, before our lakes were navigable by steamboats.

"In Mackinac I stayed only until I found the first occasion for travelling to the Indian mission of L'Arbre Croche. In this mission, all is progressing in good order. This year, nothing in particular has happened; except that on Beaver Island we are building quite a large church, which will be made of wood, but will be nice, and will cost about 2000 dollars, when it is finished next summer. After the Mormons departed from the island, many whites are settling here, who, however, are poor fishermen and cannot afford to build a sumptuous church. We wanted to have a church here for a long time, but the work could not start. I then advanced a considerable sum, from the contributions from Europe, thus allowing the purchase of timber and, to some extent, the remuneration of the carpenters. It stirred things to the extent that the indispensible church will be completed the next summer with minor contributions.

"On July 29, I arrived in Grand Traverse, in the mission of Mr. Ignatius Mrak, who was recently appointed Vicar-general of this diocese for his manifold, zealous, missionary activities. So we discussed, among other matters, the shortage of priests in my diocese. He proposed to go to Europe to find new missionaries for our growing missions. I approved his suggestion, and Mr. Mrak is now in Europe, and will return before winter, and bring, I hope, some missionaries with him.

"At the beginning of August I arrived in Saut-Ste. Marie, and after having answered the correspondence waiting for me here, I boarded a steamer and travelled on my visitation of the missions on Lake Superior, first of all to the Rev. Chebul, missionary of La Pointe, where I landed on the 4th of August. This was the quickest trip I ever made in this northern country. On Monday, July 30th, I departed from the mission of Mr. Mrak in Grand Traverse, and the same week, on Saturday, Aug[ust] 4th, I arrived at La Pointe. The distance between these two missions is 640 miles, and in the first years of my missionary

men had to row all day and by 8 P.M. we arrived at Detour and we stayed overnight with Gafney.

July 7:  Set sail at 4:30 from Gafney's place. At first progress was slow and we had to row, but by 10 A.M. and then increasingly so by noon we had a favorable wind and

---

life here, I employed nearly a month for travelling from Grand Traverse to La Pointe. Now I did the trip in 6 days, or better, in 4 days, because I stopped for two days in Mackinac and the Saut. So you can see that we have also made some advancements in the art of travelling in this inhospitable and half-Indian country. (In the more civilized countries, where you can travel for 300 miles in one day, this does not seem like very much.)

"The good, zealous missionary, Mr. Chebul, is pleased to stay at La Pointe, because he always wanted to be placed in an Indian mission. This year, I let this missionary church, which already was outdated, to be improved by renovation, which cost me more than 200 dollars, because all things are very expensive here. Besides, I allowed Mr. Chebul to build a pretty chapel at the branch mission in Bad River. I will have to pay much for it too, but the chapel was necessary, because the missionary at La Pointe often goes there, and until now it was necessary for him to say and preach the mass in an Indian's house.

"From La Pointe, I went to the missions of Rev. Edward Jacker, who has taken care of the mission in Portage Lake, and who will continue working in the Indian mission at L'Anse, until a new missionary will be appointed there, next spring. The copper mines in Portage Lake are very rich, and they attract so many people that on the census, taken this year, over 6000 persons were found there, of whom one-third are Catholics. There are an exceeding number of Germans here. Last year, we built quite a large church here, but it is now too small. This year, we will begin to build the second one. I would like to point out a remarkable fact: the zealous missionary, Mr. Jacker, who already hears confessions and preaches in 4 languages, is now going to learn the fifth, that is the Irish, or better, the Celtic language, because he has many Irishmen who only speak this language. It takes a heroic will for learning such a language. I procured him a Celtic grammar in New York. On the Feast of the Assumption, I stayed at my old mission in L'Anse. The church was crowded. These missions are growing more and more.

"In the missions of Rev. Mr. Thiele all is proceeding well. His two churches and parish houses in Eagle Harbor and Cliff are really nice and cozy. Each year I find them improved and embellished. Especially, this year, Mr. Thiele is worthy of consideration, because he succeeded in obtaining, free-of-charge, the legalized deeds of the mission of Cliff, which were delayed for many years. Our church now possesses an acre of the nicest ground, worth over 100 dollars.

"Then I proceeded to the famous iron-mines in Marquette. I boarded on the big, fine steamer, 'Lady Elgin', not having any presentiment of what was to happen to this ship within a few days. I stayed at Marquette for a few days, and was making preparation to travel again, and then I heard the terrible news (which now is generally known) that 'Lady Elgin' sank together with 300 persons: men, women, and children! It was a pleasure trip, and in the large cabin, the people were dancing to the sounds of music, when the death-blow came.

"After a few days, another nice steamer, 'Gazelle' sank in Lake Superior, without the loss of human lives. She foundered over a rock, broke and sank, but near to the shore. The men who pilot our ships are really guilty of carelessness and negligence. I feel fearful every time I board a steamer.

"At the remarkable and very rich iron-mines in Marquette, we began to

arrived at Mackinac by 2 o'clock. There I immediately told the poor Mr. Buttner that I do not need him in my diocese and that therefore I could not ordain him. He must go away.[266]

July 8: Preached in French and English at Mackinac. // In the evening Mr. Buttner left for Milwaukee; whether Bishop Henni will accept him or not, is uncertain.

July 9: Set out early in the morning for Cross Village, but it was too windy and rough on the lake, so we turned around and came back to Mackinac. Perhaps we will leave tomorrow.

July 10: Sailed for Cross Village and after a slow and tedious voyage arrived at Cross Village, where I had nothing but grief because of Weikamp.

July 11: Remained in Cross Village all day; in the evening the Indians held a meeting at which nothing but complaints against Weikamp were discussed, to which I made no other reply than that sad necessity so required it.

July 12: At 9:30 sailed to Beaver [Garden] Island in a contrary wind, so we did not arrive until evening, and immediately I had nothing but bitter grief because of the

---

build a pretty big church. This very summer, finally, we proceeded (after so many idle speeches going on for years) in buying all the necessary timber and shingles. Now, the building of this needful church is progressing rapidly.

"A few days ago, I finally returned home. I finished my missionary travels for the year." Baraga to WF, Sault Ste. Marie, October 5, 1860. Printed in WF, xxiv, p. 114; in BBC-A 746 G.

[266]Baraga sent Buttner to Lefevere: "My Lord. The bearer of the present, Mr. Erhard Buttner, came to me with an excellent letter of recommendation from you. I was just on the point of starting for Lake Superior, when he arrived at the Sault, and I told him that I would ordain and employ him, when I came back from Lake Superior. But on further consideration and consultation I found that there is not one place in my poor diocese which would suit him. So I cannot receive him. I send him now back to you with the request to receive him into your diocese, for some German congregation." Baraga to Lefevere, Mackinac, July 7, 1860. Orig. in NDUA; in BBC-A 170 E.

On the same day Baraga sent a short letter of instruction to Barbeau at the Sault indicating that he would pay the Indian rowers for four or five days, not including Sunday, or not over $5 each. Baraga to Barbeau, Mackinac, July 7, 1860. Orig. in CLSSM; in BBC-A 106 E.

wickedness of the local Indians; and no consolation whatever.

July 13:     Very few Indians at the holy mass; I recommended that tomorrow morning more should come and then I would preach to them.

July 14:     I had recommended that more come, but indeed still fewer came. However, I preached about drunkenness to which they are now terribly addicted. A few came to confession, and fewer to holy communion. The poor Indians on Garden Island are very demoralized. After the mass we sailed to Beaver Harbor.

July 15:     ᴸVII Sunday after Pentecost.ᴸ ²⁶⁷ Offered mass at 8 o'clock in the schoolhouse on Beaver Island, preached in English and confirmed 23 persons. In the afternoon we discussed the building of a church, but we could come to no agreement. Fr. Seraphin [Zorn] will take care of the construction.

July 16:     Said mass in the schoolhouse, and by 9 left Beaver Harbor; we had such a favorable wind that we arrived in Cross Village in 4 hours.

July 17:     Said mass at 6 and preached. The rest of the day was spent in making plans for the church on Beaver Island.

July 18:     Again at Cross Village, offered mass early and preached, after Mass confirmed 23 persons; by 9 sailed away from Cross Village and by 1 P.M. reached Middle Village. Here, it is said, things go fairly well.

July 19:     In Middle Village said mass early at 6 and preached. After mass²⁶⁸ I had different visitors and some confessions. Fr. Seraphin had very many confessions.

---

²⁶⁷Beginning here and used rather consistently hereafter is a clumsy way of designating each Sunday. Baraga gave it first in German and then in Latin. This edition of the Diary uses only the Latin designation.

²⁶⁸Here follows a long phrase that Baraga crossed out and wrote again in the entry of July 20. This is another example of how Baraga filled in segments of the diary from memory at a later date.

July 20: Mass at 6 with sermon, then confirmed 21. Then made preparations for departure and by 9:30 were on our way from Middle Village and at 2 P.M. arrived in Little Traverse, where I have some consolation from Fr. Sifferath, but much grief from the mission. It is getting worse and worse.

July 21: Said Mass at 7 in Little Traverse, at which quite a few people attended.

July 22: <u>Sunday</u>. Preached twice sharply and ᴱprofitableᴱ against all kinds of vices prevailing here.

July 23: Said mass, [at] Agaming, blessed the cemetery and church and preached twice. // In the evening Guibeault[269] signed the contract for the building of the church at Beaver Harbor for $250 plus $10, plus $12 for house rent.

July 24: Left at 9 A.M. for Sheboigan and arrived there at 5 o'clock. I inspected the new schoolhouse which is not yet completely finished. In any case, the schoolteacher [Heaphy] wishes to remain here.

July 25: ᴸFeast of St. James.ᴸ It is rather cold for St. James. I said mass in Sheboigan and preached, then read all day. // I visited the school where I found 23 children.

---

[269]Baraga and Guilbeault signed a hand-written agreement: "Alexander Guilbeault agrees to build a frame church at Beaver Island, Lake Michigan. The church shall be fifty feet long, thirty feet wide and fifteen feet high inside, with one double door eight feet high, and two windows in front, and three windows on each side. He agrees to make the door, but not the windows, except the frame of the same.

"He also agrees to ceil the church inside, three feet from the floor, all around, except on the side where the altar shall stand. He further agrees to match and lay the floor, and to put a good shingle-roof on the church with cornice all around, and to place and put on clapboards on all four sides. He also agrees to put a steeple astride on the roof of the church, according to plan and instruction.

"Behind the church there shall be an addition of ten feet, with a door from the church, and a door and two windows from outside, and one window in the loft of the church, according to plan and instruction.

"All the necessary materials will be furnished, he will have only the work to do; and for his work Bishop Baraga promises to pay him two hundred and fifty dollars, as soon as the work shall be done. This work must be finished before the first of December next." Baraga Agreement, Beaver Island, July 23, 1860. Printed in the *Detroit Free Press*, July 17, 1958; in BBC-A 791 E.

July 26:    Again offered mass and preached. I had trouble in finding 2 Indians who would drive me, so we set off late at 10:30 and only reached Little Traverse by 7 P.M.

July 27:    At 9 A.M. we sailed from Little Traverse, and with a favorable, but weak wind, arrived at 11 P.M. at Grand Traverse, Eagletown.

July 28:    Spent all day with Fr. Mrak, discussing the most distressing matters concerning the advancing deterioration at all the missions.

July 29:    Sunday. Offered mass at 7, and then before high mass received the distressing report from Fr. Menet.[270] This disturbed me so much that I could hardly preach at the high mass. // I have accepted Gerhard Terhorst and for the time being appointed him to the school at the Sault.

July 30:    After mass we went to Northport and as we were still 2 or 3 miles away from there we saw a propeller coming in, one which was going on to Mackinac fortunately, God be thanked. I immediately boarded it and we set sail at 12 noon; reached Mackinac by 8 P.M. I H S[271]

July 31:    Confession day. I am waiting here in Mackinac for the "Illinois", which according to the card, will be here tomorrow evening. 'We shall see.'

Aug. 1:    Right, this evening the "Illinois" came up from Detroit with a noisy pleasure party, and we sailed during the night from Mackinac in a nice moonlight.

Aug. 2:    At 10 A.M. arrived at the Sault where I found many pleasant and unpleasant letters; among them, one from Munich with $816.32. I H S // Today I received $200 from Trempe, and from Barbeau $300. // In the afternoon at 4 I boarded the "Northstar."[272]

---

[270]The Jesuits and the two remaining Ursuline sisters definitely would leave Sault Ste. Marie at the end of August.

[271]The monogram has been cut out.

[272]There is no record if any meeting took place between Baraga and the Jesuits. This was the only time Baraga was in the Sault in August before the Jesuits actually left.

Aug. 3:     Arrived quite early in Marquette, where I did not get off; instead wrote a letter to Fr. Menet about Gibbons. In Portage Entry I saw Fr. Jacker who told me that he was expecting his brother[273] on the "Illinois." // At Copper Harbor we remained 14 hours, lying at a very inappropriate time.

Aug. 4:     Did not sail from Copper Harbor until 8 A.M., and via Eagle Harbor, Eagle River, arrived in Ontonagon at 4 P.M. Here I saw Fr. Fox who very actively and industriously takes care of all 4 of his churches. He now has a horse. // At 11 P.M. we arrived at La Pointe.

Aug. 5:     <u>Sunday</u>. Perinier has arranged the church nicely, but it will cost much. // Today here in La Pointe I preached 4 short sermons, in French, English and Indian, and recited the Stations of the Cross.

Aug. 6:     I was in Bayfield with Fr. Chebul and <u>Henry M. Rice</u>,[274] who promised me to have a house built at once for the priest if he would live on that side. I promised him that the priest would live there.

Aug. 7:     I was again in Bayfield, and see that Rice actually has already started building a house for the priest.

Aug. 8:     Perinier was called to Bayfield to complete the church there. The church as well as the priest's residence will now be completed.

Aug. 9:     Today I sent the almanac report for 1861 to Murphy and Dunigan, with 11 priests!! // Had some confessions.

Aug. 10:    This noon I went to Bad River, to visit ailing Charlotte Haskin, and remained there overnight. On the same evening Jo[seph] Rielle brought the 18 pews for the chapel at Bad River.

[273]Francis Jacker and his family settled at Portage Entry. They are buried in the Indian cemetery at Assinins.

[274]Henry Mower Rice (November 29, 1817–January 15, 1897) was a businessman-entrepreneur in northern Wisconsin and Minnesota. He was a founder of the cities of Bayfield, Superior, and Duluth and connected these cities by railroad with St. Paul; to acquire the necessary lands he supported removal of the Indians to the west. He was a delegate of the Minnesota Territory in Congress from 1853–1857 and United States senator from 1858–1862. Rice was a friend of Fr. Chebul. He built the rectory at Bayfield and gave an organ to Chebul for the church.

Aug. 11:   At 6 A.M. I left Bad River and arrived at La Pointe towards noon, thinking I would find the "Lady Elgin" there, but I did not.

Aug. 12:   Sunday. Still at La Pointe. I preached 3 short sermons before noon and one in the afternoon. // In the evening I had many confessions, and at 9 P.M. sailed away on the "Lady Elgin".

Aug. 13:   Towards evening I arrived at Portage Entry and remained there overnight in order to go the following morning to L'Anse, where Fr. Jacker then happened to be.

Aug. 14:   At 11 A.M. I arrived at L'Anse and found everything in the old usual order. I took a document from Montferrand through which he wanted to place himself ᴱin "Possession of many acres of land" in L'Anse.ᴱ

Aug. 15:   Assumption of Mary. The church in L'Anse, thanks be to God, was packed full, although no one from the east side came to mass (ᶠbecause of bad weatherᶠ and lack of zeal.) I firmly resolved next spring to make the entire building into church ᶠby removing the partitions;ᶠ and to have the house ᶜsituated at foot of hill, on the top of hillᶜ moved.

Aug. 16:   Today I visited all the Indians in L'Anse in their dirty, neglected houses.

Aug. 17:   At 6 A.M. sailed from L'Anse, at 9 arrived at the Entry, and at 1 P.M. by tugboat, arrived in Houghton. // Fr. Jacker's house is very nicely arranged. // He is learning Irish, Old Celtic.

Aug. 18:   A noteworthy day for writing! Today I wrote 14 warning letters to the Canadian Bishops against O'Neil, who has forged an Exeat with my name.

Aug. 19:   Sunday. In Houghton said mass at 9 o'clock and preached in French and German. At 10:30 Fr. Jacker sang the high mass and I preached in English.

Aug. 20:   I was on the other side of Portage Lake to secure building sites for the new church. At the same time I made a very poor collection among the zeal-less Canadians.

Aug. 21:      Rev. Francis Fusseder[275] arrived in Houghton to take up a collection for a new church at the mines, but I gave him permission only to collect enough on Fr. Jacker's side to cover his traveling expenses, no more. // At 4 P.M. I left Houghton on the "Cleveland" and arrived

Aug. 22:      Early in the morning, 5 o'clock, at Eagle Harbor. Said mass at 7 and then discussed with Fr. Thiele all day and read.

Aug. 23–24–25:      Have been home and read, nothing in the least has occurred to enter.[276]

Aug. 26:      <u>Sunday</u>. There were many people in church, and even more would have come if the morning had not been dark and threatening to rain. // I said mass at 8 and at 10 preached in English and German. After the mass I confirmed 8 persons.

Aug. 27:      Fr. Thiele rode to Eagle River and I gave him a letter to take along for John Burns, whom I ask to state clearly if he wants to make the church at Hancock or not.

Aug. 28:      Read German and English newspapers all day; the latter for practice. We had tea with Mr. Bawden.[277]

---

[275]Rev. Francis Fusseder was born in Austria in 1825 and ordained in 1850 in Wisconsin. He labored primarily in the Diocese of Milwaukee. He retired for health reasons in 1876 and died in 1888. *History of the Catholic Church in Wisconsin,* pp. 1025–26.

[276]Baraga wrote one of his few "light" letters at this time: "My Lord. I have seen several priests wearing a long beard, and have heard of others who wear it, as for instance the Benedictines, the priests of Fr. Sorin, and many others in Wisconsin, Indiana and elsewhere; and my missionaries [Thiele and Jacker] also expressed a wish to wear it; they have commonly bad razors, and suffer a kind of martyrdom once or twice a week by applying those bad instruments to their faces. They say, if the bishop wore a long beard, they also would do so. <u>Query</u>. What would you say, dear Archbishop, if I appeared at the Third Provincial Council of Cincinnati with a long gray beard?" Baraga to Purcell, Eagle Harbor, August 23, 1860. Orig. in NDUA; in BBC-A 171 E.

    On the 24th the Jesuits made their last entries in the Baptismal Registry at the Sault. Rezek, II, p. 55. The last two Ursulines, Sisters Augustine and Mary Joseph, sailed with the Jesuits. They arrived in Chatham, Ontario, on August 28.

[277]James Bawden, age 45, was born in Cornwall, England. He came to Lake Superior in 1845 on a survey and exploring expedition, and was one of the first people to settle at Eagle Harbor. Besides being the captain of a mine, he also owned a dock and warehouse, and later also a hotel and a large general store in Eagle

Aug. 29: A very warm, yes even, a hot day, a rather rare occurrence this summer. Also the evening and night were unusually warm.

Aug. 30: At 10 A.M. we rode in a very good wagon to Eagle River where we arrived by noon, at 2 o'clock had dinner with John Kerry, and then we rode off to Cliff Mine. We met John Burns who solemnly assured me he wants to build the church in Hancock yet this fall.

Aug. 31: Confession day. Otherwise read all day. The food is brought to us here, which I like better.

Sept. 1: A rather cool morning, but the afternoon warmed up. Read all day.

Sept. 2: Sunday. At 8 o'clock offered mass in St. Mary's church at the Cliff. Preached in 3 languages and announced a collection, but it only brought in something over $100. To make a good collection, one must go around to the houses. // After mass I confirmed 9 persons.

Sept. 3: Left the Cliff at 9 A.M. and towards 1 we arrived in Eagle Harbor, where I scarcely had time to take a small mid-day lunch and left on the "Lady Elgin" where I met Caspar Schulte, and immediately took him with me and sent him to the Sault.[278]

Sept. 4: At 9 A.M. arrived in Marquette, where right away I heard sad reports about Duroc. For more than 3 months he had not been to the iron mines.

Sept. 5: I wrote to 3 French theological candidates[279] that they should come because I hope to establish a seminary at the Sault. ———

---

Harbor. He was married and had five children. His personal estate was valued at $8000. Federal Census, 1860, Houghton County, #864. He died in 1861.

[278] At the top of the page Baraga wrote in large letters, "Caspar Schulte, 3 Sept[ember] 1860."

[279] One of these theologians was Honoratus Bourion. He was born in Lorraine, France, on June 1, 1840. In 1861 he followed his uncle, Rev. Sebastian Duroc, to Upper Michigan. Baraga ordained him on December 1, 1861, and assigned him to Negaunee. In 1866 he accompanied Baraga to Baltimore and brought his stricken bishop back to Marquette. From 1871 until 1890 he worked in Colorado and Ohio. He returned to Ishpeming, Iron Mountain, and Menominee where he died on November 1, 1902. His brother, Alcide, a priest of the Cincinnati archdiocese, is buried at the same site.

Sept. 6:    Read all day. In the evening I closed the contract with Smith for the construction of a church at Nigani [Negaunee] for $250.[280]

Sept. 7:    Took the railroad to Negaunee, to find out about a church lot, but I could not determine definitely if the lot will be given to us or not; we must wait for the answer.

Sept. 8:    This morning I gave Dr. John McKenzie $102 Ffor his sawed wood for the Pioneer[281] church.F // I had many confessions, especially in the evening, nearly until 10 P.M.

Sept. 9:    Sunday. Offered mass at 8 and at 10 preached in 3 languages, had 3 confirmations after mass. Again several confessions, especially German.

Sept. 10:   Went to Pioneer again today and paid $25 to Agent Spilman for Elot 3, block 2,E as partial payment of the $100 which the lot will cost. Perhaps we shall get it gratis or at half price.

Sept. 11:   Read all day, waiting for a boat to go down, wrapped in a cloak because it was cold and stormy. I often mention to Duroc about calling him to the Sault.

Sept. 12:   By 9 A.M. = still no boat. And none all day. Read in Butler and waited. (The "Lady Elgin" is lost, more than 300 human lives.)

Sept. 13:   Again read all day, and with longing, or rather boredom waited for a boat.

Sept. 14:   Friday. Still no boat here. // Finally at 9 P.M. the "Illinois" arrived with the sad news that the "Gazelle"

[280]On this day Baraga wrote two letters. One letter was to Fr. Thiele to inform him that he could not send him the money he had promised for a gallery for St. Mary's Church at Cliff because he needed the money more urgently for the church at Negaunee. Baraga to Thiele, Marquette, September 6, 1860. Orig. in BBC-A 625 E. The other letter was to PFAP: "Mr. President. Have the kindness to give Mr. Honore Bourion 500 francs on account of my next allotment, for his journey into my diocese. If he has one or two companions (but not more,) please give to each one the same sum." Baraga to PFAP, Marquette, September 6, 1860. Orig. in PFAP; in BBC-A 471 F.

[281]St. Paul's Church was built on the corner of Pioneer and Case streets in Negaunee.

|            | was wrecked on a rock at the entrance to Copper Harbor, but without loss of human lives. |
| ---------- | --------------------------------------------------------------------------------------- |
| Sept. 15:  | At 4 P.M. I arrived at the Sault and saw the devastation[282] . . . // Gerhard Terhorst gives me consolation; I hope he will become a good missionary; and Casper Schulte a good servant. |
| Sept. 16:  | <u>Sunday</u>. Today I performed everything in our church, as a <u>simple priest</u> usually performs; and so it will probably be all winter because I have little hope of finding a <u>qualified</u> priest for the Sault this fall. |
| Sept. 17:  | Mr. Terhost keeps a well attended school for boys and girls, I only fear that he will not persist in it for long. |
| Sept. 18:  | Mr. Terhorst is beginning to complain that he is ᴱtired.ᴱ At the next opportunity I will write to Detroit and have a teacher come, if one can be found. |
| Sept. 19:  | Today I made large disbursements of money: Rev. Fr. <u>Weikamp</u>, $197, <u>Sifferath</u> $58.50, Murray $7.50 = $263 by L. Trempe-Duncan. (The day before yesterday by Barbeau's clerk to <u>Rev. Chebul</u> $50, Dr. <u>John McKenzie</u> $188.88, <u>Rev. Duroc</u>, $46 = $284.88) |
| Sept. 20:  | Bought provisions, cheap, which should last a long time. Now I will be able to live more economically. |
| Sept. 21:  | Today is the 37th anniversary of my ordination, and the 19th of my morning meditative prayers, for which I thank God most heartily in IHS. |
| Sept. 22:  | Received $100 ᴱin gold and silverᴱ from Scranton[283] ᶠfrom the two letters of exchange.ᶠ In the afternoon the "Northstar" arrived and I delivered to the porter: 2 packages for Fr. Jacker — ciborium, Celtic grammar and A.[284] and catechism, 2 packages for Rev. J. Chebul — candles, A. and ritual, 1 portrait for Rev. Thiele. *The 37th anniversary of my first mass in Ljubljana.* [285] |

[282]Because the Jesuits and Ursulines were gone.
[283]Myron W. Scranton was the son-in-law of Peter B. Barbeau.
[284]Anamie (prayerbooks).
[285]Entered in the left column under September 22.

Sept. 23:      <u>Sunday</u>. I said holy mass at 8 and Fr. Duranquet[286] at 10. Preached in English and French. Fr. Duranquet also sang the vespers. // I held the catechism class, and then told the children that in the future they should come by 1:30.

Sept. 24:      I saw Fr. Duranquet at the dock; I would have liked to go to confession, but I could not find a proper place for that. Perhaps he will come here again next Sunday.

Sept. 25:      The oddest weather in the world! All day first the sun shines and then it rains. The wind is very strong.

Sept. 26:      Same weather as yesterday. Today the Brothers[287] set up their stove, because early in the morning and in the evening it is rather crisp.

Sept. 27:      The stove in the school was also set up, and the classes for the boys as well as the girls, are now in the upper classroom. . . ᴸLord, what do you want me to do? Speak, Lord, for your servant is listening. . . I will listen to what the Lord God speaks to me.''ᴸ,[288]

Sept. 28:[289]      Cooked supper.[290] // In the evening the "Iron City" brought up a heavy mail, among others, a letter from Vicar-General Mrak, and one from Rev. Jos[eph] Ant[hony] Mary Gaess[291] of Baden, who probably will come to us next spring. ᴸIf it pleases the Lord.ᴸ

Sept. 29:      St. Michael. It snowed a little early this morning. // From L[ouis] Trempe I took $160, from Barbeau $200,

---

[286]The occasional presence of Frs. Duranquet and Kohler and the Jesuit Brothers indicates a positive relationship between these Jesuits and Baraga.

[287]Apparently these are Jesuit Brothers. Br. Hickey was in the Sault with Fr. Duranquet. D, October 1, 1860.

[288]1 Sm 3:30; Ps 85:8.

[289]Baraga wrote and then crossed out: "N.B. the above should have been noted here."

[290]Baraga had to do his own cooking after the departure of the Jesuit Brothers.

[291]Joseph Anthony Mary Gaess (Gaes) from Freiburg arrived at Sault Ste. Marie on August 31, 1862, nearly two years after his first contact with Baraga. On September 3, 1862, Baraga sent Gaess to Mackinac. In less than three months he transferred himself to Minnesota to work with Fr. Pierz. Fr. Jacker wrote that Gaess was an enthusiast who left Mackinac because there were not enough Indians for him there and who then went to Minnesota, but left that place because there were too many Indians. Jacker thought that Gaess had gone to England. EJP; in BBC-AR 13, p. 7.

and sent $400 to the zealous and active Missionary, Fr. Seraphin, for his church at Beaver Harbor. I hope it will be his church, if Mr. Gaess should come to Cross Village. I H S

Sept. 30: Sunday. Today Fr. Duranquet again sang the high mass, and I said the 8 o'clock and preached at the 10. Catechism at 1:30. Many children at catechism, if it will only continue this way.

Oct. 1: Today I numbered the church pews. In the evening Fr. Duranquet came over here with Br. Hickey, and remained here overnight. He missed the "Seabird" which went to Fort William.

Oct. 2: Fr. Duranquet hopes to sail today on a schooner, at least to Michipicoton, and from there in his barge to Fort William, with Br. Hickey.

Oct. 3: Last night Fr. Duranquet boarded a schooner and this morning it left. // A quiet, lifeless, rainy day. // ᴸGood work?ᴸ [292] Wrote a rather long and interesting report about the last missionary visitation journey.

Oct. 4: Went to visit poor Briggs, and told her that I would come tomorrow to hear her confession.

Oct. 5: A quiet, still day. Oct[ober] seems actually to want to be quieter than September. // This evening I heard the Canadian geese migrating to their southern winter quarters.

Oct. 6: All day I worked on numbering the pews. In the morning after mass I carried the Holy Sacrament to the sick Briggs.

Oct. 7: Sunday. Today I was alone and had to perform everything; first mass at 8, high mass and 2 sermons at 10. I believe that I never have seen so few people in church as today. This is the fruit of my frequent exhortations for diligent church attendance. — // In the afternoon catechism and Stations of the Cross.

Oct. 8: I sent Commodore Schwarz a small box with Lake Superior newspapers, and some minerals and coins. [293]

[292] 2 Cor 9:8.
[293] At the bottom of the page Baraga wrote: "Continued in Vol[ume] III."

*Fathers Martin Fox, John Chebul, and Edward Jacker,*
*c. 1860.*

*Rt. Rev. Ignatius Mrak at the time of his Episcopal*
*consecration, 1869.*

*Caspar Schulte, servant and handyman for Bishop
Baraga.*

*Mother Mary Xavier LeBihan, OSU, first Catholic sister
in Upper Michigan.*

*Coat of arms of Bishop Baraga, designed by Mother Mary Xavier, 1853.*

*Father Patrick Murray shortly before his death in 1908 at the age of 83.*

*Father Gerhard Terhorst, pastor at Holy Name Mission in L'Anse, 1860–1901.*

*Steamboat* Northstar. *(Photo courtesy of University of Detroit Marine Historical Collection.)*

*Looking south over Harbor Springs (Little Traverse)*
*Church and cemetery. Oldest known photo, c. 1858.*

*Bishop Baraga, 1867, after years of hardship and a series*
*of strokes.*

*Baraga catafalque, January 19–31, 1868.*

*Crypt chapel of Bishop Baraga, St. Peter's Cathedral, Marquette, Michigan.*

*Tomb of Bishop Baraga, St. Peter's Cathedral, Marquette, Michigan.*

# VOLUME III

## OCTOBER 9, 1860–JULY 16, 1863

Oct. 9:    I heard the Ursulines want to come again. — They should remain where they are. ᶠI do not like to have subjects who are not under my control, whom I do not control; who come and go as they wish.ᶠ

Oct. 10:   Today we took the partitions out of the schoolhouse and it is now one large schoolroom. // Received news that Rev. Andolshek[1] and Koshmerl are coming with Fr. Mrak.

Oct. 11:   It is snowing heavily and everything is already white. // NB. The first bill for Donahue's books is $9.79, the second $10.50. I sent this second payment today, besides the order for a Vesperal and Gradual.

Oct. 12:   I was called to old Mrs. Lafond who is very low ᶠand nearly unconscious.ᶠ Bought boards for ᴱa separate playing ground of [sic] the boys.ᴱ

---

[1]Baraga sent Andrew Andolshek to study with Fr. Fox. He was at Eagle Harbor from April to September 1861. He entered the Redemptorists but left them in August 1862. He went to Erie, San Francisco, and the Green Bay area and on November 16, 1879, returned to Eagle Harbor where he worked until his death on June 23, 1882. He is buried at Holy Redeemer Cemetery in Eagle Harbor. Rezek, I, pp. 165, 170, 173.

Oct. 13:    Francis Xavier now has 3 days at $10, Fabian has day, Cadotte and Son have 1 day at $1. // Today the slow "Illinois" came up and brought news that Mr. Thomas Levan is coming up as teacher.

Oct. 14:    Sunday. Said 2 masses, preached twice, catechism and vespers with benediction. ᴸThanks be to God!ᴸ // Gibbons came in and told me that John Burns did not yet commence building the church at Hancock.

Oct. 15:    Fabian began to make the ᴱschool-pews,[2] 16 in all; 8 for the boys, and 8 for the girls,ᴱ ᶠat 5 placesᶠ ᴱeach = 40 boys, 40 girls = 80 scholars. We will never have so many at once in the school.ᴱ

Oct. 16:    A very nice warm day. Today Fabian nailed the molding on the walls for the children's seats and writing desks in the school.

Oct. 17:    This morning Dr. McKenzie came, to whom I gave $41.14 for Flynn and Hageman; and Michael Finegan, to whom I gave $199, and with this I settled his entire debt at Houghton. Now this church owes me $781. // Today the schoolroom is being plastered. // I buried old Mrs. Lafond today.

Oct. 18:    Noteworthy and sad remembrances![3] // Today I was on the other shore, to bury a child, and there I saw the chapel, which leans to one side, and has not even a cross on the roof.

Oct. 19:    This noon the "Illinois" came down, and Rev. Thiele and Jacker came to me, both bearded. // At 5 P.M. the "Cleveland" came up and the 2 priests left for home. // Still no teacher. ᴸWhat is this?ᴸ [4]

Oct. 20:    Early today Peter Connell came down on his way to Ireland, and I gave him his $53. He missed the "Seabird", and is now waiting for the "Cleveland". In the meantime he is working a little for me.

[2]Benches and desks.
[3]Cf. 1856 and 1862.
[4]Baraga used this expression when he suffered paralysis in his hands. This may be the first such episode.

Oct. 21:     <u>Sunday</u>. Performed <u>everything</u>, as usual. // In the afternoon I made an agreement with Peter Connell that he will remain with me (or with other missionaries) all his life, <sup>E</sup>without wages but $300 at my death.<sup>E</sup> I H S <(Goes away.)>

Oct. 22:     Completed the school benches, and in the afternoon school was held for the first time on the new benches.

Oct. 23:     "Northstar" came up, but no teacher. // I sent a box of cigars to Rev. Chebul and $50.

Oct. 24:     Peter Connell decided to go to Ireland, and <u>perhaps</u> will return again. // In the afternoon, on the other side, I buried Blackwood's[5] child.

Oct. 25:     Peter left on the "Cleveland". // Many boats arrive, but no teacher. This places me in great danger of having no teacher this winter.

Oct. 26:     I began teaching theology to Mr. Terhorst. Otherwise nothing special has occurred. // Always in the unpleasant expectation of a school teacher.

Oct. 27:     Finally a teacher arrived, not Levan, but Seymour.[6] I do not know how he will be. May God grant that he will be <u>capable</u>. He has good <u>will</u>.

Oct. 28:     <u>Sunday</u>. The usual work. I said that almost $200 [pew rent] are <sup>E</sup>due<sup>E</sup> <sup>F</sup>for the pews.<sup>F</sup>

Oct. 29:     I heard there is a small bell at Payment for $15, and immediately asked Trempe to have it brought up here on the tugboat. // I told Seymour that he might better return to Detroit if he is not satisfied. But he said he was satisfied.

Oct. 30:     I forwarded to Fr. Seraphin Zorn, by the "Planet", a box of Anamiemas and a chalice for Beaver Harbor.

---

[5]James Blackwood, 48, a Scottish-born miner, and Margaret, 28, had four other children, John, 11, Mary, 8, William, 6, and Henry, 2. Federal Census, 1860, Chippewa County, #182.

[6]Maurice Seymour taught at Sault Ste. Marie until early 1861 when Baraga was forced to dismiss him. Baraga described Seymour as "a bad teacher, passioned & ignorant." BLS, January 9, 1861.

// I handed the ᴱRegulations for St. Mary's Schoolᴱ to the teacher.

Oct. 31:

Mr. Seymour began teaching school by himself; he was with Mr. Terhorst the last two days. // Many boats are coming up and going down, because the weather is unusually nice. Among others, the "Northstar" sailed down this morning.

Nov. 1:

<u>Seventh anniversary</u> of my consecration. // Performed everything. Mr. Barbeau has been installed as Syndicus[7] (syndic) of this church. — Is this good and right, according to the divine will? I H S?

Nov. 2:

<u>All Souls Day</u>. "Requiem" high mass at 8 o'clock. // Mr. Barbeau says he wants to go from house to house and collect the pew rent.

Nov. 3:

Several confessions, of young and old. // Trempe went to Garden River (Payment)[8] for the bell which is for sale.

Nov. 4:

<u>Sunday</u>. (Bell?) It is not there. // Everything performed. // I will remove the old boozer Biron from the church singing.

Nov. 5:

The bell seems to belong to Fr. Kohler, because it may be sold only on his order. Just the same, I could not have it sent to La Pointe because the "Northstar", which passed up today, goes <u>only</u> to Ontonagon.

Nov. 6:

Paid Fabian $5; I have to pay him $10 more. // A lifeless, quiet day, but rather cold. // Brought holy communion to old Vasseur, ᴸfor his devotion,ᴸ and to the sick Mrs. Cadotte.

Nov. 7:

A nice day, unusual for this time of year. Nearly every day boats come and go. With each boat I expect one or two priests, perhaps also Rev. Mrak.

Nov. 8:

Another beautiful day, ᴱa perfect summer day.ᴱ // The boats go busily up and down, but none brings a priest or theologian.

---

[7]Similar to a parish trustee.
[8]Garden River is on the Canadian side of the St. Marys River; Payment is on Sugar Island, which is on the United States side of the river.

Nov. 9:      Mr. Seymour disclosed that ᴱ45 bulk barrelsᴱ of his luggage are ᴱstill on board the "Seabird".ᴱ How much luggage this man has! // ᴱTo drunken Thiele, that he must leave next spring.ᴱ

Nov. 10:     Fabian and his brothers set up the 3 church stoves, in very nice weather. Perhaps we shall not use them yet tomorrow, but it is well that they are set up. // Wood hauling day. // Made a box in which to send paper and books to Mackinac with the "Planet". // In the evening Br. James Sweeney[9] arrived.

Nov. 11:     Sunday. A very nice day, and yet there were few people (especially few men) in church. // Br. Sweeney and I wrote a letter to Fr. Tellier,[10] asking him to release Br. Sweeney.

Nov. 12:     I brought this letter again to the post office and shall wait until ᴱnext spring,ᴱ to see how God will arrange it. Rev. Andolshek arrived in the evening on the "Northern Light," and I sent him immediately to Fr. Fox.

Nov. 13:     This morning Br. Sweeney went down on the "Northstar" to Gulf [Guelph], and will return if he receives permission and release, yet this winter. // In the afternoon I handed the porter of the "Ontonagon" my box for Mackinac.

Nov. 14:     The nice weather still continues, which is very extraordinary for this time of year. In the evening it rained a little.

Nov. 15:     Still nice weather, continually perfect calm. Almost

[9]James Sweeney was a Jesuit Brother. After speaking with Baraga, he requested and received his release from the Jesuits. He studied under Fr. Jacker, was ordained by Baraga on September 19, 1862, and assigned to Hancock. In 1869, Jacker, then administrator of the diocese, dismissed Sweeney. With a contingent of Irish farmers from Michigan, Sweeney moved to Iowa where he began the village of Sunny Side and, with the approval of Bishop Hennessy of Dubuque, a parish. After a visit in 1869 to the Trappists at New Melleray, Iowa, he resolved to enter that community. He finally became a postulant in 1880 but died on July 23, 1880. He is buried at the monastery. Rezek, I, pp. 165, 170, 176; II, pp. 262–63. New Melleray Archives, Account of the Founding of the Monastery; in BBC-Sweeney File.

[10]Remi Tellier, S.J., was the superior of the Canadian-American mission.

every day boats come and go; they seldom had such favorable weather even in the summer.

Nov. 16:     Nice, calm weather, however nothing to enter.

Nov. 17:     Last night it snowed a bit, and it remains on the ground, however it is not very cold, and [E]perfect calm[E] still [E]good steamboat-time.[E]

Nov. 18:     <u>Sunday</u>. Again snowed. Today we began to fire the church stoves. In the evening I was called to old <u>Masta</u>, who then admitted that he unjustly possesses the land of <u>Bonneau</u>.

Nov. 19:     I began to say holy mass in the winter chapel. All day it snowed a little and rained; it was real [S]slush of St. Elizabeth.[S] But [E]calm all day.[E]

Nov. 20:     A very nice but somewhat cold day, [E]according to the season. Very calm.[E] The [E]steamboats[E] busily go up and down. // It is snowing from time to time.

Nov. 21:     I went with Mrs. Bonneau to the other side to old Masta, whom we found dying. Mrs. Bonneau wanted to speak to him about the parcel of land which he unjustly possessed, and which belongs to the Bonneau family, but it was too late, he was in his agony.

Nov. 22:     2 boats went up today, "Planet" and "Cleveland". Perhaps still more will come yet this fall. Always calm, but it snows from time to time, for which we thank God; this makes good roads.

Nov. 23:     Today I was brought over to the other side, to bury old Masta. Before the ceremonies, I read a document which clearly expressed the unjustice [sic] which Masta and his family commit by keeping the land of J. B. Bonneau for themselves.

Nov. 24:     Last night was very cold and stormy. The 2 boats of the day before yesterday are certainly in great danger; it storms terribly all day. // [E]Kitchen stove-pipe changed at Mr. Seymour's.[E]

Nov. 25:     [C]It was a very cold night.[C] <u>Sunday</u>. A terrible stormy day; very few people at mass and few children at catechism. // The canal is frozen hard. The 2 boats will have to remain above. // The very costly ᴱgate, the "largest gate in the world,"ᴱ is useless this year, it cannot be closed.

Nov. 26:     ᶜAgain it was a very cold night.ᶜ In order to remember the name: Nibanabekwe (Kagigedwe), he[11] promised to go to Sugar Island this winter. // Just now, noon, the propeller "Globe" is coming up. Where does it want to go? Misère! The canal is froze hard. If it goes through the canal, then there is hope for the "Planet" and "Cleveland". — ᴵWe shall see.ᴵ —

Nov. 27:     ᴱSure enough!ᴱ The small propeller "Globe" has cut through the ice and is up above. // ᴱToday I bought a box of star-candles of 20 pounds.ᴱ

Nov. 28:     (Last year's closing of the canal.) ᴱT̶h̶i̶s̶ ̶m̶o̶r̶n̶i̶n̶g̶ ̶a̶ s̶t̶e̶a̶m̶e̶r̶ ̶c̶a̶m̶e̶ ̶d̶o̶w̶n̶;ᴱ No! // <u>Wood hauling day</u>. //

Nov. 29:     This morning both boats of 8 days ago came down, and just now are passing through the canal, with some misery, but still going. // John Boucher (Lacourse) took a package for me to Detroit, <u>Sealpress and Missal</u>. // Brought holy communion to old Mrs. Biron, ᴸfor her devotion.ᴸ

Nov. 30:     ᴸSt. Andrew.ᴸ A very nice winter day. Rather cold in the morning and evening. // Mr. Seymour says he wants to start a night school for young men. — Bravo! // Adieu, November! In general it was a nice month.

Dec. 1:     A very nice, somewhat cold day. // The piano[12] was

[11]There is no indication to whom Baraga was referring.
[12]Sarah Haynes [Hyens] Cadotte brought this piano, the first in Chippewa County, from London when she came to America with her half-breed husband, Alexander. She used it while she taught school at Sault Ste. Marie. The piano was of African rosewood; its sounding board had been planed out with a hand ax. When she died in 1851, the piano became the property of the Catholic church. Later it was sold at a church auction and was made into a handsome table; it graced the new owner's summer home at Sailor's Encampment. Anonymous account of the Cadotte Family, Bayliss Public Library, Sault Ste. Marie; in BBC-Cadotte file. Sarah Cadotte became a Catholic under Fr. Menet's instruction, and he hired her to teach the girls at St. Mary's. Although her husband, Alexander, was a "drunken brute," she remained gentle. The "fair, delicate London girl" nursed the sick, tending "their papooses, teaching the urchins, doing all

carried back into the school house, so Mrs. Seymour can play it.

Dec. 2: <u>Sunday</u>. Performed everything as usual. // At the first mass I conferred tonsure on Mr. Terhorst and the 4 minor orders. He held the English catechism class in the church, and I the French in my room.

Dec. 3: Today I paid $10 to Fabian ᴱand that's all.ᴱ NB. I gave him ᶠmy quart of fish for $5 of labor.ᶠ

Dec. 4: <u>Closing of the canal</u>. 2 boats remain on Lake Superior this winter: "Burlington" and "Globe". Visited sick Mrs. Dolman in Livingston's house.

Dec. 5: A very nice, but somewhat cold day. Baptized Dolman's little boy. // At 9 P.M. I was called over to Crochiere's daughter at Garden River, and I administered the last sacraments to her; then I went to Alfred Payment's.[13]

Dec. 6: ᴸSt. Nicholas.ᴸ Heard confessions at Payment, and remained until 11 A.M. Then I went to Garden River, to sick Mrs. Larose, whose confession I heard. Then I rode home and arrived about 3 P.M.

Dec. 7: A very nice, quiet day. // Bought oil for the consecration of holy Oils — ᶠMaundy Thursday.ᶠ

---

the work of a sister of Charity, and praying for her husband." Jacker to Finotti, Sault Ste. Marie, June 28, 1875. EJP; in BBC-AR 13, pp. 89–90. Emily Cadotte, 9, was living with Alexander and his second wife, Celenise, in 1860, suggesting that Sarah Cadotte may have died in childbirth. Federal Census, 1860, Chippewa County, #167.

[13]The Payment family is an old pioneer family of Sugar Island. The father and first settler was Michael G. Payment, born in Canada in 1814. Early in his life he was a New York merchant, and in 1827 he moved to Detroit. He became a partner in a dry-goods concern. In 1840 he married Catherine Edessa Riopelle, and in 1844 they moved to the Sault, eventually settling on the island at the site known as Payment's Landing where Holy Angels Church was built. He was the uncle of Sr. M. Augustine [Irmine Bedard]. He was the treasurer of Chippewa County and postmaster of Sault Ste. Marie from 1864 until 1876, when he moved to Bay City where he died in April 1891. The census of 1850, #78, gave his occupation as farmer and lists his sons, Richard, age 10, Clarence, age 8, and Alfred, age 5. The family of Philip Payment was also listed. He was a 26-year-old farmer. Living with him were Moses Payment, age 24 and Alfred, age 22. Federal Census, 1850, Chippewa County, #79.

| | |
|---|---|
| Dec. 8: | Mr. Terhorst began to read the breviary, and will stop when he stops breathing.[14] He studies every day, all day, the holy mass. |
| Dec. 9: | Sunday. ᴸPatron feast of the diocese and cathedral.ᴸ // At 8 o'clock, Mr. Terhorst received the subdiaconate. // 10 o'clock was pontifical mass, ᴸhowever it was,ᴸ Mr. Terhorst assisted. // ᴱThe church-pews were put to auction today.ᴱ |
| Dec. 10: | Wood hauling day. I was called to the other side, to the sick son of Alex Makey. // A dark and snowy day. |
| Dec. 11–12: | Two windy, snowy, cold days. Fortunately, there were no ᴱsick call(s)ᴱ these two days. // Mr. Terhorst diligently practices reading the breviary and the mass. |
| Dec. 13: | How many people are always and everywhere every morning at mass in Advent! Here two or three come. |
| Dec. 14: | Today there were a few more people at mass and — one communion. // ᴱLast night was the coldest night till now.ᴱ // NB. Only one communion till now. This is a nice ᴱindulgence-octave.ᴱ |
| Dec. 15: | A very cold night! The day is not so cold. The river is more than half frozen over. |
| Dec. 16: | Sunday. Diaconate on Mr. Terhorst. |
| Dec. 17: | Alexander Cadotte made a spectacle because of the ᴱ"dresses of his late wife,"ᴱ which I gave to Polly Johnson, whom he hates; and because of the piano, which he wants back. Windy and cold. |
| Dec. 18: | Again windy and cold. // This afternoon the first ᴱover-land-mailᴱ arrived, but brought in all only 6 letters,[15] three for me, and for all the other citizens of the Sault, three. |
| Dec. 19: | This morning I went to visit Archange Aiabens (Pi- |

[14]Bishop Eis commented: "Good!"
[15]Bishop Eis noted: "Six letters in mail for a whole town — not much."

quette),[16] but found her without her right senses. Perhaps she will die. // In the evening I was called to Mrs. Dolman, who, however, is not as sick as Mrs. Piquette.[17]

Dec. 20: A windy and snowy day. // After mass I carried the Holy Eucharist to the sick Mrs. Dolman.

Dec. 21: Brought the Holy Eucharist to a daughter of [Michael] Nolin,[18] at Grosse Pointe, 7 miles from here. A very fatiguing road over deep snow and bad ice. Although the distance is only 7 miles, we needed almost 3 hours to go there.[19] Coming back was somewhat easier.

Dec. 22: Nothing special. Mr. Terhorst busily practices the breviary and the missal.

Dec. 23: Sunday. Ordination to the priesthood of Rev. Gerhard Terhorst, who is intended for L'Anse.

Dec. 24: Examination day in our poor school, to my great sorrow! ——— God give me a capable teacher.

Dec. 25: ᴇChristmas.ᴇ First mass of Rev. Terhorst, who, thanks be to God, performed it very well, alone without assistance. May God grant that he become a good missionary.

Dec. 26: I have decided to dismiss the Poor Seymour right in the spring, since he is unqualified in every respect.

Dec. 27: Wood hauling day. I again visited sick Mr. O'Neil; I also wanted to visit Mrs. Dolman, but she had left her residence and I do not know where she went. Barbeau's account = $408 due me. // Notified Mrs. Sey-

---

[16]Archange Piquette (Pickette), 24, was the wife of Antoine Pickette, 30, a fisherman. Living with them were Mary Pickette, 58, John, 20, Charles, 18, and Angelique Bouduif, 90. Federal Census, 1860, Chippewa County, #211.

[17]On this day Baraga wrote to Fr. Murray: "As I was sorry when I heard that you bought Fr. Menet's black cow, so am I now glad to hear that you sold her again. I hope you have lost no money by the transaction. If I live fifty years more, I would never keep a cow." Baraga to Murray, Sault Ste. Marie, December 19, 1860. Orig. in BBC-A 355 E.

[18]At this time Michael Nolin, 69, and Mary, 54, had four children at home: Lesette, 23, Angelique, 21, Charlotte, 19, and Nicholas, 15. Federal Census, 1860, Chippewa County, #207. Michael Nolin was a local chief, also called Watab.

[19]This journey was made on showshoes.

mour that at the end of April or beginning of May they must leave because of ᴱSeymour's total incapacity.ᴱ

Dec. 28: The 2nd mail arrived, but brought me only 1 letter and some ᴱnewspapers.ᴱ Today I told the stupid Seymour that he must leave at the end of April or beginning of May.

Dec. 29: A windy, snowy, but not cold day. The ice decreases, instead of getting thicker. // Read ᴱnews-papersᴱ all day. // Saturday between feast days, but not a single confession!

Dec. 30: Sunday. Few people in church. Two sermons to empty pews. Only a few children came to catechism.

Dec. 31: The 30th anniversary of my arrival in America, namely Dec[ember] 31, 1830. // Mild, calm weather.[20]

## 1861

Jan. 1: New Year's Day, a day of sadness, very few people were at holy mass, but I preached in both languages. // The river is not yet frozen over; there was not one person from the other shore in church. // Not at all cold, but much snow.

Jan. 2: Today I went to visit the poor sick Archange Aiabens Piquette. She still doesn't have her right senses.

Jan. 3: Today this poor Archange was brought to Francis Gournou. // ᴱRiverᴱ frozen over hard, people can cross on it.

Jan. 4: I handed the statutes and faculties to Rev. Terhorst. May God grant that he will make good use of all the remaining time of his life.[21]

Jan. 5: Mrs. Lavigne invited me and Mr. Terhorst to a supper, and we went there, much against my wish and incli-

---

[20]Although he was collecting the pewrents from others, Barbeau had not paid his own. On this day Baraga ordered a barrel of flour for $7 but deducted $5 for the unpaid pewrent. Baraga to Barbeau, Sault Ste. Marie, December 31, 1860. Orig. in CLSSM; in BBC-A 343 E.

[21]Bishop Eis wrote: "Prayer heard; he has been a good missionary. 1901."

nation. In the evening I visited the sick Mr. O'Neil, and will hear his confession tomorrow, and the day after administer the last sacraments to him.

Jan. 6: <u>Sunday & Epiphany</u>. Preached twice; the church was rather full because many people came from the other side, since the ice is so good, but there is much snow on it.

Jan. 7: This morning I went to O'Neil, but he is better and so I will not yet administer the last sacraments to him. // Today the children are coming to give their names for first communion and confirmation. // The old ᴱGeorge Johnstonᴱ 22 is lost since yesterday morning. They are seeking him everywhere, on both sides of the river.

Jan. 8: Finally, this morning they found the poor old Johnston frozen, on the north side of the canal. While drunk, he did not know where he was going, became weak and froze to death — terrible! —

Jan. 9: At 11 o'clock I began the French catechism lessons for first communion, with <u>one</u> boy, Lacaille!

Jan. 10: Arranged a waiting room for the girls between the 2 schools, so that they remain separated from the boys as much as possible.

Jan. 11: Two ᴱmailsᴱ arrived, in which I received rather good news, but still no draft. // It is extremely cold. Received the Ordo but not yet the Almanac.

Jan. 12: I believe that ᴱlast nightᴱ was the coldest which we have had so far; and all day it was the coldest day. This morning it was ᴱ40 degrees below zero.ᴱ 23

Jan. 13: <u>Sunday</u>. Nothing special. Preached twice and announced that I will be away for 2 or 3 weeks.

Jan. 14: Day of Departure. The journey was good and pleasant. At 12:30 arrived at Bellanger's (Andre), and there

---

[22]George Johnston, 64, was a hotel keeper. Federal Census, 1860, Chippewa County, #160. Polly Cadotte Johnston grew up under George Johnston's roof.
[23]Bishop Eis noted: "An old timer."

we took our mid-day meal. At 4 arrived at Major Rains.[24] In the evening the old man was somewhat ᴱin liquor.ᴱ

Jan. 15: Offered mass at 6:30 at Major Rains, then set out, and at 1 o'clock arrived at Carlton's sawmill, where we ate with Samuel Thibault. At 4:30 arrived at Peter Gafney's. The day began nice, but turned stormy.

Jan. 16: Mass at 5:30, then I rode to Stanard's lighthouse. On the way I baptized the 2 Rice children in Detour and at Stanard's I baptized one. Then I returned to Peter Gafney's.

Jan. 17: Mass at 6 o'clock. In the morning I remained with Gafney and read; in the afternoon at 1 we rode away, and at 4 P.M. we arrived, with much fatigue because of the deep snow, at Carlton's sawmill. In the evening I heard confessions at Sam Thibault's.

Jan. 18: At 5:30 offered mass at Thibault's at which there were some communions. Then rode on; the morning was nice, but we were soon overtaken by a terrible storm, and I felt the cold very much. We rode to St. Joseph's Island, to William O'Neil's to warm ourselves. From there we rode to Richardson's where I was given a fresh horse, which brought me in a few hours to Sailor's Encampment.

Jan. 19: At 7 offered mass at Sailor's Encampment, and announced confessions for the evening.

Jan. 20: Sunday. At 7:30 said the first mass for communicants, among whom were 3 first communicants. At 10 o'clock I said the second mass, at which I preached in English, and then confirmed 20.

Jan. 21: Very cold night. At 7 offered mass at Major Rains. In the afternoon I rode to Andrew Bellanger, where I remained overnight. I had some confessions in the evening.

Jan. 22: At 5 A.M. I brought holy communion to 2 people. I

[24]Cf. January 21, 1858.

wished to leave very early, but Stafford[25] came late, and at 7 we rode away. It was very cold, otherwise a nice day. We went as far as John Johnston where we arrived at noon and ate. Then I rode with Stafford to Garden River, where at 4 P.M. we arrived at Payment's.

Jan. 23: At 7 said mass in Payment's chapel. Later I wanted to ride to Perrault. However, I decided to go there next week and then stay there over Sunday. // Gave instructions for confirmation.[26]

Jan. 24: Mass at 8 o'clock at Payment's, then gave instructions for confirmation and heard confessions all day.

Jan. 25: Mass at 7:30, then I had a baptism and a marriage.[27] Gave instructions for confirmation and heard many confessions the rest of the day.

Jan. 26: There were many communions at mass. Great confession day because of tomorrow's confirmation.

Jan. 27: ˪Septuagesima˪ Sunday. At 8 I offered the first mass in Payment's chapel, at which there were very many communions.

Jan. 28: After the holy mass I carried the Holy Eucharist to sick Larose. Later I went to Crochiere about the school and subscribed $30 for 6 months for the school.

Jan. 29: At 7:30 offered mass, then I wanted to go on to Perrault's, however, Michael Nolin came and said that his daughter has again vomited blood and is very sick; therefore I remained here today in order to bring her the Holy Eucharist tomorrow morning.

Jan. 30: Said mass earlier and then carried the Holy Eucharist to Watab's sick daughter. At 10 I left, and after a fa-

---

[25]Thomas Stafford was an English-born cabinetmaker, 45. His wife was Mary, 36. They had four children. Federal Census, 1860, Chippewa County, #75.

[26]Baraga instructed Barbeau to pay Stafford for his trouble in transporting him. Baraga to Barbeau, Garden River, January 23, 1861. Orig. in CLSSM; in BBC-A 350 E.

[27]Marriage Certificate, Paymentville, Sugar Island, January 24, 1861. Orig. in possession of Joseph and Theresa Haller of Sault Ste. Marie; in BBC-A 353 E. Cf. September 8, 1859.

tiguing and cold journey on Lake George, I arrive at 2 P.M. at Ed Perreault's where I was quite comfortable.

Jan. 31:  Offered mass at Perreault's at 7. Later Indians came in, among whom are still many pagans. We spoke about building a church, 30 by 20.[28] In the afternoon I went in all the houses, only not in the last ones. At the same time I inspected the location for the church. In the evening I gave instructions for confirmation and had some confessions.

Feb. 1:  Offered mass at 7:30, at which there were some communions; in the afternoon I gave instructions for confirmation; in the evening I had confessions.

Feb. 2:  Ed Perreault takes over the job of construction the church ᴱat $2 per day.ᴱ // Again instructions for confirmation and many confessions.

Feb. 3:  ᴸSexagesimaᴸ Sunday. Mass at 10 at which there were more people than I believed were here. // 4 first communions and 13 confirmations. // In the afternoon vespers and a sermon.

Feb. 4:  Again said mass at Perreault's and then rode away at 9. At Church's[29] I bought ᴱall the lumber for the

[28]The first church was called Holy Cross but it is dedicated under the title of St. Joseph. Baraga and the Indians signed an agreement: "Bishop Frederic Baraga and Shawanibinessi, and all the Indians who live here at Point of Peninsula, all of them are happy that a Catholic church was built here in their village, and that one acre of land was selected to have here a church. Of this land and the church, no one will be the only owner, all together will own it; the priest will own it, so that he may say Mass here, and that he may preach here, and do all that the priest thinks that he must do; but the Indians will own it, to worship there, and that they do all things as much as they think Catholic Christians must do. The priest will never be able to sell it; and the Indians who are living here now, and who will be praying here (those who will be Christians) will not be able to sell this piece of land and the church." Agreement of ownership, Minisheing Church, January 31, 1861. Orig. in Franciscan Archives, St. Louis; in BBC-A 562 E.

[29]Philetus Swift Church, born c. 1812, came to Sugar Island in May 1845. With his wife, E.D., age 34 (Federal Census, 1850, Chippewa County, #77), he settled at the north junction of Lake George and the St. Marys River which became known as Church's Landing. In time he built a residence, two docks, a sawmill, small shipyard, dry dock, and a tug. He regularly employed ten to thirty-five Indians in the processing, production, and shipping of wood for steamboat fuel, cedar posts, fence rails, berries, jam, vegetables, maple sugar, fish, meat, furs, coal, and hay. His markets extended from Bruce Mine to Eagle Harbor. Church

church[E] for $150. // At 11 we arrived at Payment's. Payment, [F]the shoemaker,[F] takes over the plastering of the church.

Feb. 5:     At 6 A.M. offered mass at Payment; 4 communions. Then we rode on and at half past 11 we arrived at the Sault where I found a large number of letters, mostly pleasing. Among others 4875 francs. I H S [F]to the account of 12000![F] [L]Thanks be to God!!![L]

Feb. 6:     A great <u>letter writing</u> day. Otherwise nothing special. Read in the afternoon. // I handed the draft for 4875 francs to Barbeau. // Bought snowshoes, $3. They are very strong, not at all expensive.

Feb. 7:     [E]Last night it was very cold. Very cold morning.[E] // Again wrote several letters and did some reading. // Have been to Barbeau; he should pay $150 immediately to Church for the lumber.[E] Stupid!

Feb. 8:     Barbeau came to me and said that I should not pay Church in advance;[30] and that he (Barbeau) wants to take over the contract for the church on Sugar Island. Therefore I made [E]plans, and carried them to him in the evening.[E]

Feb. 9:     Great and profitable <u>letter writing day</u>: Leopoldine Society, Ludwig Mission Society, Hemann,[31] Amalia.

Feb. 10:    Sunday. As usual, 2 sermons, etc. // In the evening I went to visit Archange Piquette. // The weather is very mild, it will rain.

Feb. 11:    It rains this morning. The poor travelers! However the rain is a blessing, and the people want it. // Closed

---

had two sons, J. Wells and Philetus Munson. P. S. Church died on July 22, 1883, at the age of 71. Bayliss, pp. 164–65.

[30]Church did not always work within the law. Bayliss, pp. 173, 255–56.

[31]Joseph Anton Hemann was born on December 23, 1816, in Oesede, Germany. He was educated in Osnabruck and Muenster. He migrated to Canton, Ohio, in 1837 and to Cincinnati in 1839. There he became the first teacher of German in an American public school. From 1850 to 1865 he published the *Wahrheitsfreund*, and from 1850 to 1863 the Ohio *Volks-Zeitung*. Hemann died on June 28, 1897. Hemann occasionally asked Baraga for official approbation of books that he was publishing (February 2, 1859, A 651 G; August 16, 1859, A 721 G.). Baraga employed Hemann to publish some of his writings. Tolzmann to BBC, University of Cincinnati, December 27, 1985; in BBC-Hemann File.

the contract with Barbeau for the building of the Sugar Island church, $572.65. // Is it really right and pleasing to Thee? ———

Feb. 12: I regret the <u>letter to Church</u>! I wish I could have it back. Otherwise I am satisfied with Barbeau's bargain. He will also make 14 ᴱbenches.ᴱ

Feb. 13: <u>Ash Wednesday</u>. Today I wrote to Perrault to return to me the letter to Church, if he still has it. May God grant that he still has it! I H S

Feb. 14: Today at 10:30 Joe Perrault[32] came and brought back to me the letter addressed to Church which I wished so very much to have back. I H S I then went directly to Barbeau and took back the plans. In the afternoon Church also came and assured me that he would give me good lumber. — ᴸThanks be to God!ᴸ

Feb. 15: Nothing special. Catechism for first communion and confirmation, in French and Indian. // Made packages for Mrs. Bellanger, Mrs. Rains and Mrs. Gafney.[33]

Feb. 16: Wood hauling day (lasted since Jan[uary] 12) Edward Perrault came and undertook the building of the Holy Cross Church on Indian's Reserve, Sugar Island, and I gave him $25 ᴱfor provisions.ᴱ

Feb. 17: <u>Sunday</u>. Fairly many people in the church, especially from the other side, ꟳin the rear of the church.ꟳ 2 sermons, and Stations of the Cross.

Feb. 18: A very nice morning; also all day was nice. Read Butler and taught catechism a little.

Feb. 19: Stormy and snow. Almost all day I worked on a somewhat larger plan for the church: ᴱIndian Reserve, Sugar Island. Church of the Holy Cross.ᴱ

Feb. 20: Terribly stormy all day. The plan of ᴱsaid church of the Holy Crossᴱ is completed. // In the evening read

---

[32]Joseph Perreault was the son of Edward Perreault. Cf. September 12, 1861.
[33]These were his hostesses on his previous journey. On the same day he wrote to Major Rains: "I never heard before of your scandalous concubine. // Put her away without delay." BLS.

and prayed,[34] only a very few people, because it was so stormy.

Feb. 21: Today I ordered 7[35] bells from M. C. Chadwick, 17 Spruce (st.) [New York] = F4 of F 300 pounds at $35 for <u>Bayfield</u>, <u>Indian Reserve</u>, <u>Superior</u>, <u>Beaver Harbor</u>, = $105 [$140]; E1 of E 200 pounds at $25 for <u>Payments</u>; F2 of F 460 pounds at $55 for <u>Hancock</u> and <u>Negaunee</u> = $110; E1 small one of E 80 pounds for <u>Bad River</u>. ETotalE $250. (Money to be sent from Cincinnati.) Very stormy, blizzard, Csnow storm,C Lall day.L

Feb. 22: Stormy and cold all day, yet there were more people at the evening prayer than the day before yesterday.

Feb. 23: Again stormed and snowed terribly all day. A very hard winter for the poor people. This morning the EmailE arrived.

Feb. 24: <u>Sunday</u>. Rather many people in church. Everything as usual. I must often speak in regard to the Epew-rent,E which is very distasteful to me.

Feb. 25: This morning I sent Fabian on pew-rent collection. He collected little, very little. Some were not at home; Barbeau would not pay anything.[36]

Feb. 26: A very nice day, a real spring day. // Worked on the plans for the Reserve church. /// In the evening I had some confessions. Very few confessions for this Lenten season.

Feb. 27: <u>Confession day</u>. (Today Lalonde came again and filled his sack with potatoes.) In the evening read and prayed.

Feb. 28: Last day of the month; a mild day. Feb[ruary] is making a mild exit. Catechism as usual.

---

[34]This day was Wednesday of the first week of Lent. During this Lent Baraga conducted Lenten devotions with a sermon and prayers each Wednesday and Friday.

[35]Eight bells are listed. Baraga originally wrote "3 of 400 pounds" but itemized 4 bells at 300 pounds. He did not change the totals.

[36]Barbeau may have been angry because Baraga withdrew the contract from him.

March 1:     Letter writing day. — Letters to Glajeux,[37] Bishop of Hamilton [Bourget], etc. // Today I asked for, and finally received my account from Trempe and Hatch. I owe him $330! // In the evening read and prayed.

March 2:     Wood hauling day. Very mild; it was sloppy all day. // Made the plan for the steeple of Holy Cross church.

March 3:     Sunday. Not many people in the church, although it was nice weather. — In the afternoon Stations of the Cross as usual. // Nothing special.

March 4:     A terrible wind and blizzard. A real March day, sunny, windy, cold. // Catechism at 11 o'clock. // Barbeau gave Trempe and Hatch a check for $323, Epayable on the first of May next.E [38]

March 5:     I went to old Burke, to remind him of the Easter confession. A week from today he will make his Easter confession. // A nice day, not very windy. CThe snow is hard. It was very good walking.C

March 6:     EMid-Lent.E All day stormy and very cold. // Wrote and read all day. // In the evening, Electure E and prayer.

March 7:     A nice, only slightly windy day. // Lalonde's children came to beg. They appear to be very poor. Perhaps it is his fault. (Yes, if I only knew! ———)

March 8:     Windy, blizzard, but not cold. In the evening lecture and prayer. Few and EunprofitableE listeners.

March 9:     Ed[ward] Perrault came again and I gave him the plan for the "steeple". // Rather many confessions which came along on the occasion of the first communion.

[37]Baraga thanked him for the 4875 francs and for the large allotment of 12,000 francs. He mentioned that he purchased eight bells for the missions. Baraga to PFAP, Sault Ste. Marie, March 1, 1861. Orig. in PFAP; in BBC-A 494 F.
[38]On the same day Baraga sent Jacker instructions for the upper flooring of the house at Portage Lake and to buy what was needed from Bendry's sawmill. Baraga to Jacker, Sault Ste. Marie, March 4, 1861. Orig. in NDUA; in BBC-A 294 E.

March 10:     Sunday. First holy communion for 15 children; and 17 confirmations, very few. // Announced that tomorrow Rev. Terhorst will again begin school.

March 11:     Today Rev. Terhorst began to keep school, ᴱvery reluctantly, indeed.ᴱ It would be much more pleasing to me if he did it gladly. Perhaps he will do so later with more joy. ꜰI gave the pictures to Eusebe Salvail for his chapel.ꜰ [39]

March 12:     Bought a pair of moccasins for Fr. Terhorst, $1.25. He does not grumble any more about the school. // Today I went to old Burke to hear his Easter confession.

March 13:     This morning I carried the Holy Eucharist to old Burke, for Easter. // A nice March day, sunny, cold, windy. // Mr. Payment was here and said that the people would like me to come to his place ᴱfor their Easter duty.ᴱ

March 14:     Today there was a ᴱsick-callᴱ on the other side, somewhat higher up than the fort of the Hudson Bay Co[mpany], to an Indian. Wood hauling day. This time it lasted only 12 days because it was cold and windy always.

March 15:     A nice mild day. // William Miron was here. I gave him $2.50 to drive me to Mackinac.[40] How it will go from there, I do not know. // In the evening lecture and prayer and a few confessions.

March 16:     Very windy and cold. // At 11 o'clock Thibault came from Paymentville to take me there, and at 12 noon we drove away in a strong and very cold wind. At 2 P.M. we arrived at Payment's. // In the evening I had some confessions.

March 17:     Sunday. At 8 first mass, at which there were only 6 Easter communions. // A violent wind and one of the coldest days, Payment said, the coldest this winter. // At 10 o'clock the chapel was full, despite the severe cold. // In the evening I had some confessions.

[39]At St. Martin's Bay.

[40]Baraga planned to leave on Easter Monday, April 1, for the Third Provincial Council of Cincinnati.

March 18:    A very nice day! What a difference between yesterday and today! // A very heavy confession day; I heard confessions for perhaps 10 hours.

March 19:    This morning there were 60 Easter communions. / Many of those who confessed yesterday were not admitted because of the dance parties.[41]

March 20:    Very cold ᴱlast night.ᴱ The day was not as cold, but a strong wind and blizzard all day. // A few isolated confessions. There probably will be few Easter communions here this year.

March 21:    Beginning of spring. A nice beginning of spring in enormous snow! // Heard the confession of old Vasseur. // Not exactly cold, but windy.

March 22:    Brought the Holy Eucharist to old Vasseur for Easter. // Read all day the most interesting "Appeal to the People of the North."[42] Few confessions.

March 23:    Windy, but not cold. // Mrs. Lavigne brought some edibles as a present. // Mrs. Bonneau sent us beautiful ꟳboughsꟳ as usual every year. // Some confessions, although few ˢfor Palm Saturday.ˢ

March 24:    Sunday. Last night it stormed terribly all night and then again all morning. There were very few people at mass; nevertheless I preached twice, briefly.

March 25:·   ᴸAnnunciation of the Blessed Virgin Mary.ᴸ A mild day. Very few people in church. Some are working today.[43]

March 26:    Rather many confessions, all day from time to time.

---

[41]Dancing was a long-standing problem of the era. In 1866 the American Bishops wrote: "We consider it to be our duty to warn our people against those amusements which may easily become to them an occasion of sin, and especially against those fashionable dances, which, as at present carried on, are revolting to every feeling of delicacy and propriety, and are fraught with the greatest danger to morals." *Concilii Plenarii Baltimorensis* II, p. CXXI. Baraga personally addressed the issue in at least two letters: Baraga to Lefevere, Sault Ste. Marie, August 24, 1854. Orig. in NDUA; in BBC-A 137 E. Also, Baraga to Dusault, BLS, January 2, 1855.

[42]Author unknown. On March 4, 1861, Abraham Lincoln was inaugurated president of the United States. Bishop Eis remarked: "Beginning of Civil War."

[43]The Feast of the Annunciation was a holyday of obligation.

|  |  |
|---|---|
|  | // I received some consoling letters; [E]James Sweeney is coming.[E] |
| March 27: | [E]Last night[E] it snowed heavily again; I fear very much my [E]trip[E] which lies ahead of me. // Terribly stormy! [C]Big snowstorm![C] There is much snow everywhere, especially between the houses in the [E]fort[E] and in our [E]yard.[E] |
| March 28: | <u>Holy Thursday</u>. Blessing of the holy oils. [F]Poorly,[F] without competent assistance. // A very nice day, sunny, still, not cold. |
| March 29: | [E]Last night[E] it again snowed heavily, and it still is. What's with all this snow! [C]Stop.[C] [L]The end will not be at once —.[L] [44] Few confessions; extremely few present. |
| March 30: | A very mild sunny day. // Few confessions until now, 2 P.M. In the evening there were very many (and very unpleasant) confessions, although only up to about 9 o'clock. |
| March 31: | <u>Easter Sunday</u>. Today there were very many communions, perhaps 100. // Pontifical mass and two sermons. // Preparation for the impending and perhaps very fatiguing journey. |
| April 1: | Day of departure,[45] at 10 A.M. Rode to [the house of] Sobrero; then walked approximately 12 miles, partly on snowshoes, partly without, and then made camp. A good, not very cold night. |

[44] Lk 21:9.

[45] About this journey Baraga wrote: "I have no subject or questions whatever for discussion; I never had any in my quiet, simple and remote diocese. In order to reach Cincinnati in time for the Council, I must commence my voyage <u>per pedes Apostolorum</u>: I must go from here to Mackinac on foot, about two days and a half. Our Council will open on the 28th of April. Navigation never or seldom, commences here at the Sault before the first of May. If I waited for the opening of navigation here, I would yet be in my own residence on the 28th of April, not in Cincinnati. But by starting hence on the first of April overland, I hope to reach Mackinac by the 3rd; and soon after I hope to find boats there, because Mackinac is an open place, where the winds have a great sway, and break and drive away the ice, sooner than it can melt in our quiet St. Mary's river. Such is the prospect of the old Bishop of Marianopolis. Fortunately he is an old Indian Missionary inured to such inconveniences." Baraga to Purcell, Sault Ste. Marie, March 15, 1861. Orig. in NDUA; in BBC-A 176 E. As later entries indicate it was much more difficult for Baraga to reach the council in time.

April 2:   Broke camp at 6 A.M., and marched all day up to near 5 P.M., with much fatigue and weariness, and then camped in Frichette's hunting lodge.

April 3:   Broke camp at 5:30 and with much weariness, without snowshoes (because they caused me pain),[46] marched ahead until 1 P.M. when we came on the ice at Pine River. At half way Bellanger came with his horse to meet me. I remained overnight with him.

April 4:   At 6 A.M. rode away from Bellanger's, and at 7:30 arrived at Mackinac, where I heard nothing else but complaints about Murray, which is very sad.[47] At 8 departed with Theod[ore] Wendell and by 12 o'clock arrived at Sheboygan[48] where we remained overnight with J. Allair, whose wife is a Burke.

April 6:   Rode[49] 14 miles from Sheboygan with Lavigne's horse, which on the way back fell in a ᴱcrack [in the ice]ᴱ and there perished. In the evening camped very ᴱcomfortable.ᴱ

April 7:   <u>Sunday</u>. Alas, we could not observe this Sunday, but marched many miles on good and bad roads until evening when we camped in a bad, abandoned shanty which smoked very much; and there I said the <u>entire</u> long office of White Sunday.[50]

April 8:   Again trudged ahead on good and bad, but predominantly muddy roads, until the evening when we camped rather well at Grand Lake.

April 9:   Broke camp early, in order, if possible, to get to Thunder Bay by evening. The roads were bad, and much water everywhere; but we arrived, with God's help, in Alpena towards 7 P.M.[51]

---

[46]Fr. Chebul explained how snowshoes became painful: "The strings with which my snow shoes were tied to my moccasins froze and became hard as iron and caused my cruel wounds." Chebul to Globocnik, La Pointe, December 2, 1861. Printed in ZD; in BBC-B 1288 S.

[47]Bishop Eis added: "Poor Bishop." A probable cause of the complaints was Murray's inability to learn French. Murray was, in both his ministry and personal living, one of Baraga's most exemplary priests.

[48]The modern village of Cheboygan, east of Mackinac City.

[49]The spring shipping season had not begun on Lake Huron as Baraga had hoped.

[50]Bishop Eis noted: "How zealous in saying his Breviary!!"

[51]It took Baraga four days to travel the eighty miles between Cheboygan and Al-

April 10:     For the past few days I had not felt well, because of constipation; but today I could no longer remain up and went to bed. I took only a light breakfast, but no ᴱdinnerᴱ or ᴱsupper.ᴱ In the evening Mr. Lockwood came to me and we talked about a site for the building of a church here in Alpena. He wants to give us a lot ᴸfreeᴸ and for the second I am to pay him $40.[52]

April 11:     Worse than yesterday. My constipation causes me pain. I took no ᴱdinnerᴱ and remained in bed all day.

April 12:[53]  This morning and until about 4 P.M. I suffered considerable pains, remaining always in bed, and took neither ᴱbreakfastᴱ or ᴱdinner.ᴱ Finally, about 4 o'clock, I had a very abundant stool which completely relieved me.

April 13:     Today I am, thanks be to God, well. I paid James K. Lockwood $40 for Lot 8, Block 28. // No boat yet; however, the ice has been driven out by the wind.

---

pena. Bishop Eis commented: "What a terrible trip for an old man! And such roads!"

[52]Baraga described this part of his journey: "I could not wait for the navigation here at the Sault, because it first begins at the beginning of May, and on April 27 I already had to be in Cincinnati at the Provincial Council. Therefore I set out on the journey immediately after Easter, and went on snowshoes from here to Mackinac, and from there, partly on foot, partly on a dog sled, a journey of five days more towards the south, to where a small beginning of a town has been made, named Alpena, and where navigation usually begins already on April 15. When I arrived there, after much exertion and hardships, I became sick, (which almost never happens to me,) and had to remain in bed a few days. I have never been in this location before, because it is a new settlement. I learned that there are already many Catholics here and that soon many more will be settled here. I therefore bought a building site in this new, growing little town, and made arrangements for a church to be erected on it, and now it is under construction. Although it has cost me much effort and exertion to come to this location, I, nevertheless, thank Providence which has led me to there.

"After I had waited there a few days, a steamboat arrived on which I sailed to Cincinnati, to the third Provincial Council, which lasted from April 28 until May 5. After the close of the Council I went home, and then soon began my usual mission visitation tours." Baraga to LS, Sault Ste. Marie, August 10, 1861. Printed in LSB, xxxii, pp. 37–39; in BBC-A 696 G.

[53]On April 12, 1861, the United States Civil War between the North and South began. The war ended on April 9, 1865.

April 14:    <u>Sunday</u>. I was asked to preach, and preached at 10 o'clock.[54] In the afternoon I inspected the building site for the church, and was at the <sup>E</sup>blacksmith<sup>E</sup> Ankers who invited me to stay with him when I come again. // <sup>E</sup>John Lynn is authorized to make a collection for the erection of the church.<sup>E</sup>

April 15:    Still no boat. Spent the entire day in a cold little room, in great boredom[55] waiting for the news that a boat is coming.

April 16:    Yesterday and today John Lynn took great pains to make a collection, and he also accomplished much — on paper. // Still no boat.

April 17:    Rather cold this morning. I sat all day in my cloak. // Until now have never known what boredom was, as I do here. // <sup>L</sup>"The morning and evening were the eighth day."[L 56]

April 18:    One of the saddest days of my life. God protect me from such days! — Also outside it is a dusky, stormy day; it snows and storms terribly.

April 19:    Today I boarded a "fishboat" at 11 on which I was given assured hope that we shall land at Saginaw to-morrow evening. But we scarcely came to Harrisville, 38 miles from Alpena, and remained overnight with the hope of sailing further in the morning.[57]

[54]On this occasion Baraga did not offer Mass, probably because he did not have Mass supplies with him.

[55]Jacker described Baraga during waiting time: "I tell you the good old man had not the patience of a saint at such occasions. It was the energy of his will always bent on the thing before him, that caused him agonies; you could see how he suffered when the right kind of work was wanting. His mind, at such times, must have been in the state of a healthy stomach to which food is denied: a terrible gnawing! Once, when windbound on an island for three or four days, he wrote in his journal 'These were the most unhappy days I ever passed in my life', or some-thing similar. His mind was not at all fertile. He was no contemplative." Jacker to Finotti, on the Steamer *Hurd*, June 16, 1876. EJP; in BBC-AR 13, p. 120.

[56]Gn 1.

[57]Bishop Eis wrote: "How different is travel now! R.R. [railroad] cars."

April 20:     This morning the wind was contrary, and all passengers, 15 in number, decided to walk to Sable River, 18 miles from here; and I alone, (I could not walk now even a distance of one mile), remained here in Harrisville.

April 21:     <u>Sunday</u>. It is said that a boat is expected any minute, but none comes. // I spent all day in useful reading.

April 22:     This morning I set out at 6 to find a "fish boat" two miles from here[58] which was to go to Sable River. However, I had hardly gone a half mile when I turned back because I noted a contrary wind was brewing which now rages stormily all day; and because I felt such a tightness and oppressiveness in my chest that I could scarcely make it back. — What is this![59] — Finally, at 3 P.M. the "City of Cleveland" came, and I took it.

April 23:     At 7 P.M. I arrived at Bishop Lefevere's in Detroit.

April 24:     This morning I have finally again said holy mass. Not celebrated since April 5. // Rode the railroad to Cincinnati, where I arrived at 9 P.M.

April 25:     Bought various articles, especially nice cassock material. (More likely for my successor than for me.)[60]

April 26:     Have been with Rev. Huhr,[61] regarding mass wine, but accomplished nothing because he demanded $1.50 per gallon — Bought many articles at Benziger's.[62]

---

[58]Present day Springport.

[59]The "oppressiveness" continued for some time. Cf. May 28, 1861.

[60]Bishop Eis noted: "Used it himself." Baraga's statement suggests that he realized that something serious had happened to him and that he was not a well man.

[61]Rev. G. H. Huhr was stationed at St. Philomena's Church in Cincinnati. CALM, 1861.

[62]Fr. Terhorst tended the parish at Sault Ste. Marie during Baraga's absence. He was preparing to become pastor at L'Anse. Baraga assured Terhorst that his articles had been purchased, and that what he could not find in Cincinnati he would order elsewhere. He also informed him that he could not interest either Fr. Van Paemel (returned from Belgium) or any other priest or seminarian to come to the diocese. Baraga to Terhorst, Cincinnati, April 26, 1861. In BBC-A 666 E.

April 27:     All the bishops of the province are now here.[63] This afternoon at 4 o'clock we had a ᴱpreparatory meeting.ᴱ

April 28:     Sunday. Beginning of the Council. A solemn pontifical mass celebrated by the archbishop [Purcell]. Bishop Spalding preached on peace.[64] // In the evening I went with Hemann, etc., to the Catholic Institute where Rev. Gstir[65] gave a lecture.

April 29:     Nothing special. Council from 9 to 12, and from 4 until 6 or 7.

April 30:     In the evening I visited Mrs. Springer. She is not able to walk, ᴱpalsy.ᴱ

May 1:        Beginning of the ᴱMonth of Mary.ᴱ In the evening, at the beginning of the service for the Month of Mary, I preached in the cathedral.

May 2:        ᴱToday was the commemoration of the deceased Prelate [Fenwick] and other clergymen.ᴱ At 9 o'clock was a requiem mass at which I preached. // At noon we dined in the seminary.

May 3:        I wrote, in the name of the Council, to the Central Directors of the Ludwig Mission Society in Bavaria.[66]

May 4:        This noon, the Council, ᴸas regards consultations,ᴸ was adjourned. // In the afternoon I accomplished some business in preparation for my departure the day after tomorrow.

[63]Sometime during the council, Baraga gave a memorandum to Archbishop Purcell to take to Rome. In it he requested that (1) Cardinal Barnabo should correctly list the diocese as Sault Sainte Marie; (2) Archbishop Purcell should bring a copy of the Diocesan Statutes from Rome, and (3) a copy of the "Notizie." Baraga to Purcell, Cincinnati, April 27. Orig. in PFAR; in BBC–A 297 P.

[64]The bishops did not take a position on either the Union or the slavery issues. In part of the province, especially Kentucky, there were supporters of each position. The bishops issued a pastoral letter in which they revealed their anxiety about the conflict and urged their people to pray for peace. Because of the uncertainties they did not set a date for the next council.

[65]Rev. Archangelus Gstir, O.S.F., was stationed at St. Francis Seraphicus Church in Cincinnati. CALM, 1861.

[66]This letter was a formal thank-you letter. Baraga to LMV, Cincinnati, May 3, 1861. Orig. in LMVA; in BBC–A 554 G.

May 5:    Sunday. Solemn closing of the Council in the cathe-
          dral. // This morning a collection was taken for me at
          St. Mary's Church which brought in $77. At 3 P.M. I
          preached in this church.

May 6:    At 6 A.M. left Cincinnati, and by 4 P.M. arrived in To-
          ledo where we had to remain overnight.

May 7:    Departed from Toledo at 4 A.M. and at 7 arrived in De-
          troit, where I remained overnight because Mr. Van
          Paemel had not yet arrived.

May 8:    At 7 A.M. Mr. Van Paemel arrived and at 4 in the after-
          noon we[67] sailed from Detroit on the "Iron City".

May 9:    ᴸAscension of Our Lord.ᴸ Spent the entire day on the
          ᴱsteamboatᴱ in reading.

May 10:   At 12 noon arrived at the Sault where I received terri-
          ble reports about Thiele's drinking, which induced me
          to depart immediately for Lake Superior, if only the
          slow "Illinois" would arrive.

May 11:   All day I waited for the slow "Illinois." // This morn-
          ing and yesterday evening I wrote many letters. // At
          7 P.M. I departed on the "Illinois."

May 12:   Sunday, which I spent reading on the boat. At noon
          we arrived in Marquette. Mr. Duroc had gone to Ne-
          gaunee. Nothing but complaints about him as often as
          I show myself in Marquette. // In the evening we ar-
          rived at Portage Entry, and remained there overnight.

May 13:   Early in the morning we sailed from Portage Entry to
          Eagle Harbor where I saw the unfortunate Thiele, and
          heard terrible things about him from Bernard. // In
          the evening arrived in Ontonagon, where I met Fr.
          Andolshek and remained overnight.

May 14:   This noon sailed to La Pointe. Fr. Chebul was in Supe-
          rior where he went 5 weeks ago, but is prevented by
          the ice from returning.

---

[67]Van Paemel changed his mind and returned with Baraga to Sault Ste. Marie. He
took care of the parish while Baraga made his summer visitations.

May 15:      Early in the morning we arrived again at Ontonagon and remained there all day, whiling away the time. Fr. Andolshek left for Minnesota Mine to prepare for his trip to Eagle Harbor.

May 16:      At 10 A.M. sailed from Ontonagon, via Eagle Harbor, Eagle River and Copper Harbor.

May 17:      After a successful, but rather unprofitable journey of 6 days I arrived at 6 P.M. back in the Sault, where I met James Sweeney, but no one else.

May 18:      Wrote letters all day.

May 19:      <u>Sunday</u>. This morning Thiele arrived. He made a sworn promise not to drink any more intoxicating liquors as long as he remains in America. // In the evening Fr. Van Paemel went to Garden River.

May 20:      This morning Thiele went back again. // Mr. James Sweeney began to keep school today until a new teacher arrives.

May 21:      Fr. Van Paemel returned from Garden River this afternoon. / ᴱFr. Terhorst is preparing for his departure to L'Anse.ᴱ

May 22:      Spent the day in preparing, because I must immediately go up[68] again on the next "Northstar."

May 23:      The new teacher, William Donovan, arrived here. — Perhaps I have made a mistake in letting him come here.

May 24:      Mr. James Sweeney went to Portage Lake, on the "Illinois." // I am waiting for a boat to go to Detroit for another teacher, for Garden Island. I H S

May 25:      Waited all day for a boat. Finally at 6 P.M. I boarded the "City of Cleveland" bound for Detroit, however, we remained lying at the dock the entire night.

May 26:      <u>Sunday</u>. At 4 A.M. the ship departed. I spent the entire

---

[68]Baraga changed his mind and "went down" to Detroit on May 25.

holy day in reading. On the whole, we had a good journey.

May 27:    At 11 A.M. I arrived in Detroit where I immediately asked for Agent Dewitt C. Leitch,[69] but I could not find him.

May 28:    Today I applied 2 chest plasters. At 10 I found Agent Leitch in his ᴱoffice,ᴱ and spoke about Denis Harrington, but I could get no definite answer.

May 29:    Today at last, Agent Leitch gave Denis Harrington his ᴱappointment as teacher for the school at Garden Island.ᴱ // Fitch gave me $10 for Heaphy.

May 30:    <u>Corpus Christi</u>. At 5:30 offered mass in the cathedral; at 11 preached in English.

May 31:    At 9 A.M. we set out from Detroit on the propeller "Marquette". // May, which was mostly cold and unfriendly, makes a warm and glorious exit.

June 1:    Spent all day on the slow boat, "Marquette", by reading in Butler.[70]

June 2:    <u>Sunday</u>. At 1 A.M. I arrived in Mackinac. The boat did not want to sail to Beaver Harbor. At 10 I sang the high mass and preached in French and English.

June 3:    All day waited for a boat. I boarded at Wendell's.

June 4:    Morning, 9 A.M. still no boat, at 9 in the evening the propeller "Chicago" arrived which brought me to Beaver Island.

June 5:    Arrived at Beaver Island at 2:30 A.M., at Cable's dock, from where the good people brought me then to Beaver Harbor. Inspected Fr. Murray's church that has been started. // In the evening I sailed with Mr. Harrington to Garden Island.

---

[69]D. C. Leach was the Indian Agent for Mackinac and vicinity from 1861 to 1865. MPHC, 6, p. 348.

[70]Bishop Eis noted: "(Butler's Life of the Saints.)."

June 6:        This morning I introduced the new teacher, Harrington, but the Indians would not accept him.[71] We returned to Beaver Harbor, immediately.

June 7:        With a yearning waited for a boat. If a boat going to Chicago would have arrived, I would have even gone on it, unhappily. // In the afternoon made a deal with Goudreau[72] to take me to Detour for $14, and at 4 P.M. we departed.

June 8:        We did not land to camp, but slept in the boat.[73] All day it was calm, and we did not get very far.

June 9:        <u>Sunday.</u> All day it was calm and hot; and since I did not urge them to row because of the Sunday, we therefore glided slowly ahead. // At 8 P.M. arrived in Detour. Goudreau returned and I stayed with John Stanard.

June 10:      Spent all day with Stanard, waiting for a boat.

June 11:      No boat yet — morning. Towards noon I rode in a barge to Detour, to young Mr. Church,[74] and stayed there in the nice large house.

June 12:      About 2 P.M. the "Northern Light" arrived, and by 5 I was again in the Sault, where I found a great number of letters, but none profitable.

June 13:      Wrote many letters. At 9 P.M. I boarded the "City of Cleveland".[75] Good quiet journey. During the night it rained heavily.

---

[71]Harrington blamed the chief's son-in-law, Lambert, who was selling whiskey to the Indians, for his rejection. Harrington to Leach, Chicago, June 17, 1861. Orig. in NA-OIA; in BBC-B 438 E.

[72]The name "Goudreau" is first found in BLS, February 23, 1856. In the Petosky Historical Museum, there is a note by a Miss Pailthorp who collected early local memorabilia: "Father [Judge C. J. Pailthorp] told a story of Louis Goudreau and the ice parting in the St. Mary's river when Fr. Baraga prayed. He was a Catholic and his wife was a Protestant. He laughed and said, 'No Protestant has ever done that!'"

[73]Bishop Eis inserted "small" before the word "boat."

[74]Bishop Eis added: "A Protestant storekeeper."

[75]Baraga described this trip: "I usually begin with the southern part of my extensive

June 14:      At 11 A.M. I arrived in Marquette. Passage $5. I was thinking of going further, but remained there. Met the good Honorius Bourion, and <u>only</u> him.

June 15:      Made a ᴱbargain with Dr. McKenzie for his house at the saw-mill[76] for $284.ᴱ

June 16:      <u>Sunday</u>. Said mass at 8, at which there were some communions. At 11 I preached in English, French and

---

but sparsely populated diocese, but this year circumstances [the difficulty with Thiele] induced me to begin with the northern part.

"The first mission station that I visited was Marquette and Nigani [Negaunee] where last summer we began to build a church which will be completed this year. This is the second church in this region. The first was built 7 years ago, and is on the shore of Lake Superior. A priest is stationed by it. The second, which will be completed this summer, is 12 English miles inland, in the location Nigani, where the richest iron mines are being worked. No priest has been placed at this church as yet, but the priest from Marquette comes here from time to time and performs the divine service. The people there wish very much to have their own priest soon, but now I have none that I could place there. In the meantime I have made all preparations for that place there. I bought a rather large house, (such as we have them, of wooden framework,) which stood a few miles from the location. It was taken apart, loaded on wagons, and again erected near the church. In this way it was much cheaper for me than if I had built an entirely new house.

"From there I went to Cliff Mine where there are very big and rich copper mines. Father Andrew Andolshek labors as a zealous missionary. He also has to take care of the church at Eagle Harbor and holds divine services alternately, one Sunday at Cliff Mine and the other at Eagle Harbor.

"At La Pointe, (where 26 years ago I founded the first mission on Lake Superior,) Father John Chebul is now extremely active. If God will only give him the grace that he does not wear himself out too soon. He has a very extensive and difficult mission. Last winter he was called to a sick man who lives 90 English miles away from La Pointe. There was no other means but to make the entire journey, there and back, on foot with snowshoes. He needed 6 days to get there, and every night had to sleep outside in the forest. And since he did not know that the journey would last so long, he took provisions with him for only 3 days. Therefore, he had to live very sparingly and suffer hunger besides the hardships of the journey. He remained there a few days, instructed the Indians and half-breeds, and baptized about 30 persons, mostly adults. He is now able to teach and preach in Indian very well. A gentleman, who sent an article to a German journal about this mission journey, says, among other things, the following: 'The Rev. Father Chebul belongs to the Diocese of Sault Ste. Marie and we can only congratulate the Right Reverend Bishop Baraga for obtaining such priests who offer up to God all their poverty, and all their efforts and burdens, with apostolic love for the salvation of their flocks.'

"I visited still other mission stations in which everything goes on in good order, and about which there is nothing special to report. A few days ago I came home again, where I am occupied with answering the many letters that arrived during my absence. Next week I shall again go on a mission visitation journey, to visit the southern part of this diocese." Baraga to LS, Sault Ste. Marie, August 10, 1861. Printed in LSB, XXXII, pp. 37–39; in BBC-A 696 G.

[76]Next to "saw-mill" the word "Negaunee" was erased.

German and confirmed 12 persons. In the evening I again had some unpleasantness with the priest [Duroc]. [L]Lord, what will You have me do? Speak, Lord, for your servant is listening.[L] [77] In I H S I beg You, give me a better one [priest]! —

June 17: Rode up to Negaunee. Thanks be to God, the church is good and nice, and located properly; [E]only the floor must be planed at some joints.[E]

June 18: Have had unpleasantness with Mr. Duroc. // I received the lot at Negaunee for the $25 which I paid last summer.

June 19: This morning I had many German confessions. Spent the day reading Butler. // Francis X. Nolin[78] was very rough with Mr. Duroc. *Quarrel*.[79]

June 20: I have decided not to pay any more attention to the complaints of the people against Mr. Duroc. // In the evening I gave him a written assurance that I will leave him in Marquette.

June 21: At 5 A.M. the "Northstar" arrived, but remained at the dock until noon. // At 7:30 we arrived at Portage Lake where I looked at Fr. Jacker's 2 churches.

June 22: At 10 A.M. I arrived at Eagle Harbor, at Mr. Andolshek's.

June 23: Sunday. At 8 o'clock offered mass in the Holy Redeemer church in Eagle Harbor, and at 11 preached in English, German and French, after the high mass confirmed 3 children.

June 24: The Canadians are usually lukewarm Christians. I had only one French confession.

June 25–26: Spent the day reading Butler, waiting for French confessions, but they did not come.

June 27: At 9 departed for the Cliff, where we arrived at 1 P.M.

---

[77]1 Sm 3:10.

[78]Francis Nolin was 38, a hunter and fisherman. He was married and possessed property of $50. Federal Census, 1860, Marquette County, #337.

[79]After this event there was a marked change in Baraga's attitude toward Duroc.

June 28:     Viewed the large and powerful machinery at Cliff Mine. Otherwise read Butler.

June 29:     <u>My 64th birthday</u>. Confession day. This morning many Frenchmen came to visit me. Misère! —

June 30:     <u>Sunday</u>. Several French confessions. Not many communions. Said mass at 8, and at 11 preached 3 times and confirmed 8 persons; all did not come here that were intended for confirmation.

July 1:     July begins cool. The morning was cool, the day was warm. // Wrote some letters.

July 2:     Left Cliff Mine at 9 A.M. and at noon came to Eagle Harbor. // In the afternoon I was called to a sick Canadian in Garden City, to whom I administered the last sacraments.

July 3:     Spent the entire day lonesomely reading. Wrote a letter to Fr. Van Paemel, and transmitted $7 to L[ouis] Trempe for 5 gallons of mass wine.

July 4:     <u>Day of general sinning and misfortune!</u> This year however, not as <u>general</u> as heretofore.[80] // All day waiting vainly for the "Northstar".

July 5:     Finally the "Northstar", which had celebrated its 4th of July in Marquette, came to Eagle Harbor, about 4 P.M., and I went ᴱon board.ᴱ

July 6:     At 6 A.M. we arrived in Bayfield, and at 8 at La Pointe. In the afternoon we rowed to Bayfield where we remained overnight.

July 7:     <u>Sunday</u>. At 7 said mass in Bayfield, at 10 preached in English, French and Indian. In the afternoon we returned to La Pointe for vespers.

July 8:     Rowed to Bad River where we spent the night with Haskins. Myriads of mosquitoes.

July 9:     At 7 o'clock said mass in Bad River and preached in Indian. At noon we departed and at 7 P.M. reached La

---

[80]Bishop Eis added: "July 4 Celebration, U.S."

Pointe. NB. On July 6 I agreed with Perinier that Rev. J[ohn] Chebul will have his board with him until July 6, 1862 ($72).

July 10: Nothing special. ᴱStatementᴱ about the $50 which the Agent Gen[eral] Webb[81] will reclaim for me.

July 11: Anthony Lamoroux[82] has repaired the doors for us which now swing quite well.

July 12: Went to Bayfield, where I bought ᴱlathsᴱ [shingles], 6000 for $14; and made an agreement with Perinier for vaulting, $10.

July 13: Nothing special. In the evening I had some confessions.

July 14: Sunday. Mass at 7:30, at 10 preached in English, French and Indian. In the afternoon, Stations of the Cross. // At 9 P.M. I sailed away on the "Planet".

July 15: At 4 A.M. I arrived in Ontonagon where I found Patrick O'Flanigan, who now speaks French fairly well. / At 8 we rode to Minnesota Mine. / Today I finally received the check from Paris for 5200 francs (nothing less than $977!! —)

July 16: In the afternoon we went to Maplegrove, where we stayed overnight with O'Flanigan.

July 17: At 8 o'clock said mass in the Maplegrove church. At noon we went for dinner to the good Mrs. McCabe.[83] In the afternoon we came back to Minnesota Mine.

---

[81]General Luther E. Webb (1827–1880) was the agent for the Chippewa Indians at Bayfield, 1861–1867. WHC, 9, p. 452.

[82]Antoine Lammeraux was a 31-year-old boat builder. He was married and had four children. LaPointe Census, 1860. Orig. in WHS; in BBC-LaPointe File.

[83]John McCabe, 36, was an Irish-born blacksmith. His wife, Catherine, 29, was born in England. They had five children. Federal Census, 1860, Ontonagon County, #396. Their oldest daughter, Mary, was a boarder at the Sault and at Chatham. She later became Mother Mary Augustine. Cf. D, October 4, 1858 n. 3. Sometime after the house in which Bishop Baraga died in Marquette had been sold and moved, John McCabe purchased the building. He and his family lived there until his death and that of his wife; in 1909 his heirs sold it to the Fleury family. Leo, Wilfred, and Clara Fleury, interview with Rev. N. Daniel Rupp, Summer 1977. Transcript in BBC. In September 1988, the Diocese of Marquette and the Bishop Baraga Association acquired the property.

July 18:    Wrote several letters, among others also the answer to the questions from the Sacred Congregation of the Propagation of the Faith.[84]

July 19:    This morning it is very foggy. In the afternoon very nice and ᴱwarm.ᴱ Again wrote letters.

July 20:    Wrote letters. In the evening I had some confessions. Fr. Fox had very many confessions.

July 21:    ᴸIX <u>Sunday</u> after Pentecost.ᴸ At 7:30 said mass in St. Mary's church at Minnesota Mine. At 10 I first consecrated the cemetery, and at the high mass I preached in 3 languages. After the mass there were about 20 confirmations. // In the afternoon we drove to Ontonagon Village where there were vespers at 5 at which I preached in English.[85]

July 22:    At half past 7 said mass in Ontonagon, and then waited all day for a boat.

July 23:    This morning at 5 A.M. the "City of Cleveland" arrived in Ontonagon; I sailed on it at 7:30 for $5 passage to Portage Lake. // Fr. Fox still owes me $300.

July 24:    At 5 A.M. we arrived in Portage Lake and at 7 had mass. // In the afternoon we went to Hancock — distressed.

July 25:    <u>St. James</u>. Very warm. At 2 P.M. the "Iron City" arrived and at 4 left again. Fr. Jacker brought me a check for $200.

July 26–27: Continually read in "Church Lexicon". // All day boats coming and going.

July 28:    ᴸX <u>Sunday</u> (after Pentecost).ᴸ Said mass at 8:30, then after mass I preached, to empty pews, in French and German. At 11 o'clock there were very many people; I preached in English. After the mass I had about 18 confirmations.

---

[84]Propaganda requested information about the organization, personnel, activity, and resources of the diocese. Baraga to PFAR, Minnesota Mine, July 18, 1861. Orig. in PFAR; in BBC-A 496 L.

[85]On this day Baraga accepted Frederic Eis as a student for the diocese. Cf. D, November 1, 1856 n.

July 29:   At 10 A.M. I departed from Portage Lake and at 7 P.M. arrived in L'Anse.

July 30:   In the afternoon we held a council, to evict the rascal J. B. Metakosige[86] from the mission, but he will not leave voluntarily.

July 31:   Since J. B. Metakosige would not go away willingly, I went to the ᴱJustice of the Peace,ᴱ Foot,[87] who issued a ᴱwarrantᴱ to have the rascal arrested.

Aug. 1:    As soon as the scoundrel John Metakosige got ᴱwindᴱ of his arrest, he cleared out this morning.

Aug. 2:    At 8 A.M. we sailed from L'Anse, and at 7 P.M., after a tedious ride,[88] we reached Portage Lake where I met Mr. Seif.[89] In the evening Fr. Fox arrived on <u>foot</u> with his 2 pupils. I took Mr. J. Sweeney with me for Mackinac.

Aug. 3:    Today I bought at Shelden's many ᴱcarpenter toolsᴱ for Fr. Terhorst, (ᴱas per account.ᴱ)

Aug. 4:    <u>Sunday</u>. From today on there will be 2 masses said every Sunday at Portage Lake, in <u>Houghton</u> as well as in <u>Hancock</u>. Today I pontificated in Hancock,[90] delivered 3 sermons, blessed the church under the protection of St. <u>Anne</u>, and confirmed 48.

Aug. 5:    At 2 P.M. I sailed with Mr. Sweeney on the "City of Cleveland" for Marquette, $3.50 ᴱeach at half price,ᴱ and we arrived in Marquette that night. // Aug. 6. In the morning I said holy mass, and we left only at 4 P.M.

---

[86]John Metakosige was about 70 years old, married, father of two children. He was a hunter. Federal Census, 1860, Houghton County, #1146.

[87]Oscar J. Foote was born in New York, c. 1822. He came to Houghton (later Baraga) County in 1856 and was a farmer there until his death in 1897. Among the many public offices he held was justice of the peace. Sawyer, vol. II, pp. 1014–15.

[88]Bishop Eis added: "small boat."

[89]Sebastian Seif, a priest of the Milwaukee Diocese, came to the Upper Peninsula in the summer of 1861. He was assisting Fr. Jacker when Baraga met him. On August 4, with Fathers Jacker and Fox, he assisted Baraga at the dedication of St. Anne's Church in Hancock, at the pontifical mass, and at the confirmation. Seif received a certificate of approval from Baraga (BLS, October 12, 1861) and returned to Wisconsin.

[90]Cf. Rezek, II, pp. 261–62.

Aug. 7:  At 6 A.M. we arrived in the Sault, and Mr. Sweeney remained on the same "City of Cleveland" for Mackinac.

Aug. 8:  I took $115 from L. P. Trempe, and sent it to La Pointe for Fr. Chebul in a box with various church articles. However, this box did not go ahead yesterday, but it will go with the next "Northstar", besides a barrel of flour for Ant. Lamoureux = for his $5.

Aug. 9–10:  Wrote many letters[91] and made preparations for the next journey. // Paid Church and Payment.

Aug. 11:  <u>Sunday</u>. Preached in English and French. Preparations for the journey to the missions of Lake Michigan.[92]

Aug. 12:  Waiting for the steamer "Michigan", but it did not come. Withdrew money from Trempe as it will be seen from his ᴱbill.ᴱ

Aug. 13:  At 6 A.M. the "Michigan" arrived. I went on board, but we did not leave Sault Sainte Marie until 9:30. We arrived at Mackinac at 9 P.M.

Aug. 14:  This noon I departed from Mackinac and at 8 P.M. arrived at Cross Village.[93]

[91]One of these letters was to Fr. Murray: "Don't be discouraged, but push forward with energy and confidence. The greater the trouble in a good work, the greater the merit before God. — If the work frightens you, think of the reward. Write to me soon again, dear Fr. Murray, and tell me how you are getting along, and how is your scattered congregation. God bless you. Your affectionate friend in Jesus." Baraga to Murray, Sault Ste. Marie, August 8, 1861. Orig. in BBC-A 304 E. Baraga also wrote to Fr. Terhorst, assuring him that his articles would be sent to him. "Write me soon how is everything at L'Anse." Baraga to Terhorst, Sault Ste. Marie, August 10, 1861. Orig. in NDUA; in BBC-A 395 E.

[92]Before he left, Baraga thanked the treasurer and members of the PFAP "for this new blessing [400 francs for Mass intentions] that I have received through your letter." Baraga to PFAP, Sault Ste. Marie, August 11, 1861. Orig. in PFAP; in BBC-A 483 F.

[93]Baraga wrote to Vienna: "It is now three months since I sent my last report to this Most Rev. Central Direction. Since then much has again occurred in the missions of this diocese, pleasing to a Christian heart.

"I visited the southern part of this diocese where are our most important Indian missions. The population of these missions is always increasing. The population of Cross Village especially had increased so much that its mission church is already much too small. We therefore decided, when I was there, to enlarge it considerably. I encouraged the Indians that they should work on it themselves so as not to be compelled to hire carpenters and pay dearly. The In-

Aug. 15:  ᴸAssumption of the Blessed Virgin Mary.ᴸ At 7 I offered mass and at 10 o'clock I preached in Indian. In the afternoon I preached again.

Aug. 16–17:  Nothing special. Read, wrote calendars and letters.

Aug. 18:  Sunday. Mass at 7, at 10 I preached in Indian and again after the Stations of the Cross. In the evening we talked about lengthening the church here in Cross Village by about 20 feet.

Aug. 19:  At 10 A.M. moved on to Middle Village, where we arrived at 2. In the evening visited a sick person and heard her confession.

Aug. 20:  At 7 A.M. said mass in Middle Village and preached. At 10 I rode to Little Traverse where I arrived at 3 P.M. // In the evening I told Fr. Sifferath that he probably will be transferred to Cross Village, and Fr. Zorn to Little Traverse.

Aug. 21:  Today Gijigobinessi came here with many Indians and spoke against the priest; however, I found out that he alone is against the priest, the others like him, therefore I will leave him here. ($15 for land. Gave $130 to Fr. Sifferath.)

Aug. 22:  At 10 A.M. departed for Sheboygan and arrived there at 7 P.M. Although all the Indians were not there, there were rather many.

Aug. 23:  At 6:30 said mass and preached, and confirmed 6. At 10 departed, and after a tedious ride arrived again at Little Traverse at 8:30.

Aug. 24:  Read most of the time. In the evening heard sick Wasson's confession.

---

dians of this mission, who have been converted already for such a long time, are able to work very well. They build their houses themselves and also make boats for themselves.

"In the neighboring mission, Middle Village, the pleasing and consoling necessity for enlarging the mission church has likewise already taken place, for which the Indians belonging to this mission have shown themselves willing. This winter they will make all the necessary preparations to enlarge their church next spring." Baraga to LS, Sault Ste. Marie, November 11, 1861. Orig. in LSA; in BBC-A 697 G.

Aug. 25:

Sunday. At 7 o'clock I said mass and at 11 I preached to a packed congregation and confirmed 26 persons. I preached again in the afternoon after vespers.

Aug. 26:

At 7 A.M. rode to Agaming to St. Francis Church where I said mass and preached and confirmed 10 persons. At 10 o'clock I was again in Little Traverse. It was a stormy ride (both ways). Today I am waiting for the Indians from Grand Traverse to come for me. // 4 P.M. Just now 5 Indians came here from Grand Traverse. They sailed from there at 10 A.M. and are here already, in 6 hours!!!

Aug. 27:

At 7 A.M. we departed from Little Traverse and after continuous rowing we came, by 6 P.M. just a little over half way, where we camped.

Aug. 28:

Went on at 6 A.M. and after an unpleasant journey, rowing continuously, I arrived at 7 P.M. sick in Eagletown.

Aug. 29–30:

Sick in bed.

Aug. 31:

At 9 A.M. I arose, but I still feel weak.

Sept. 1:

ᴸXV Sunday after Pentecost.ᴸ I still feel weak, but I said mass at 6:30 and preached at 10, and confirmed 6. // However in the afternoon I did not preach.

Sept. 2:

After mass I rode to Northport, and waited there for a propeller for Mackinac.

Sept. 3:

All day I waited in vain with the good James Nolan for a propeller, reading Butler.

Sept. 4:

At noon the propeller "Hunter" arrived from Chicago; I boarded it, and that night arrived at Mackinac.

Sept. 5:

Fr. Thiele is very dissatisfied here; he yearns to return to Cliff Mine, and that is just my wish also, thanks be to God! I H S

Sept. 6:

At noon came the "Seabird" and I sailed up to Church's. There we remained lying overnight.

Sept. 7:

At 5 A.M. departed from Church's and at 6:30 arrived at the Sault where I received 20 letters; some were very good, others rather good. Among them was one from Munich with $400. God be in I H S.

Sept. 8:

ᴸxvi Sunday after Pentecost.ᴸ Preached in English and French. // At noon Ed[ward] Perrault came up and I expressed my displeasure to him because he withdrew too much [money] from L[ouis] Trempe. // Wrote many letters in the afternoon.

Sept. 9:

This morning I sent Fabian [Landreville] and his brother to Indian Reserve[94] with bed, table, etc. // Wrote letters.[95]

[94]Baraga was planning an extensive visit and church construction: "To my great consolation and spiritual joy I have also founded a new mission and built a mission church on the so-called Sugar Island, on [the] Saint Mary's River, 20 English miles away from Saut Sainte Marie. Here is a small settlement of Indians, some of whom are already baptized. Others are still pagans. In order to provide them with a better opportunity to become converted, and to attain their eternal salvation, I had a small church built, which, on October 27, I blessed to God under the name of St. Joseph. The church was full of Christians and pagans, and all were pleased that in this desolate and remote Indian location, a church now stands in which the sublime sacrifice of the New Testament is offered and the holy sacraments are administered, and where they hear the redeeming truths of the Christian religion in their own native language.

"I remained with these Indians almost three weeks, said Mass every morning and instructed them morning, noon and night. I have the most firm hope that all the Indians of this location will be converted, and perhaps still others will settle here in order to live near a church. I promised them that I shall visit them every month and each time stay with them five or six days. I also recommended to them to assemble in the church every Sunday, morning and afternoon, to pray and to sing, even if I am not there. And this they now do precisely. When they assemble, they say the rosary and sing holy hymns in their own language. One of them leads along, and the others answer.

"This church, although small and built only of wood, (like all of our churches,) has, nevertheless, cost much money, because the wages of the carpenters are so high. I went into debt considerably.

"Next spring, when I again have some money, I intend to build another small church, in an Indian settlement of St. Martin's Island, in Lake Michigan, in order to make also these Indians accept Christianity. Some of them have already expressed the wish to be converted, if only a missionary would come to them. Now, this I want to do this winter, and next spring I shall build there a small church.

"These churches in Indian settlements have especially this advantage, that the Indians assemble in the church on Sundays also when no missionary is with them, and there pray and sing." Baraga to LS, Sault Ste. Marie, November 11, 1861. Orig. in LSA; in BBC-A 697 G.

[95]One of these letters was to Bishop Lefevere: "When I saw your Lordship at Detroit in the first part of May, you promised to contribute towards the support of our Indian Missionaries $200 annually; but at the same time you told me that you could not well furnish it for this year before 2 or 3 months. Four months are

Sept. 10:     Wrote very many letters.

Sept. 11:     Fabian has not returned. // Fabian came in the afternoon bringing the ᴱsashesᴱ [for the windows].

Sept. 12:     Fabian painted sashes all day, and is finished with everything. (Ed[ward] Perrault and son were paid ᴱin full.ᴱ)

Sept. 13:     This noon Fr. Thiele came with Mr. Sweeney, returning to his mission at Cliff Mine on the "Michigan".

Sept. 14:     Wrote and read. Nothing special.

Sept. 15:     ᴸxvii <u>Sunday</u> (after Pentecost).ᴸ Said mass at 8 and at 10 preached in English and French. // I became angry[96] because of a boy's unauthorized ringing of the bell.

Sept. 16:     Today I received a check for $200 from Bishop Lefevere as a contribution to the maintenance of our missionaries in Emmet county, etc.

Sept. 17:     Today Rev. Andolshek came down here from the Cliff. He wants to go to the Redemptorists. He will hardly be satisfied there.[97]

Sept. 18:     Nothing special.

Sept. 19:     Preparation for the mission at St. Joseph, Indian Reserve.

Sept. 20:     Departure for St. Joseph's Church, Indian Reserve. It rained all day and the portage of 3 miles was unusually bad, etc.

Sept. 21:     Today I went into all the houses of the small village and made inquiries everywhere whether the Indians

---

now gone by since that time, therefore I request your Lordship to send me a good draft for the above amount." Baraga to Lefevere, Sault Ste. Marie, September 9, 1861. Orig. in NDUA; in BBC-A 177 E.

[96]This seems to be correct, from the context. However, in the original German Baraga wrote *necht* instead of *mich*, which would change the phrase to read "I did not get angry." In wilderness areas the ringing of a bell at an unusual time signals a disaster, a special gathering, or some other major event. The ringing of the church bell could have caused a disturbance to the entire town.

[97]Bishop Eis added: "No, did not stay."

living there wanted to be converted, and I received gratifying answers. // Rather many confessions.

Sept. 22: ᴸXVIII <u>Sunday</u> (after Pentecost).ᴸ At 10 o'clock offered mass and preached. The little church was all filled, thanks be to God in IHS. In the afternoon vespers and sermon.

Sept. 23: Today the Indians cleaned up the place around the church, which is very stony.

Sept. 24: After the mass we rode away with Ed[ward] Perrinier, and at 1:30 arrived at the Sault. // I rode away immediately, and at 7 P.M, arrived at Payment where I propose to remain until Monday.

Sept. 25: After mass I carried the Most Holy Sacrament to Makotchid's[98] wife, who has been sick for a long time.

Sept. 26–27: Read all day. One single confession and one baptism. Ready for all services.[99]

Sept. 28: Read Butler all day. Some confessions.

Sept. 29: <u>Sunday</u>. Said mass at 7 for the communicants. At 10 sang a high mass and preached in French and Indian. In the afternoon Indian vespers. // P. S. Church promised us $25 ᴱtowards the expenses of the addition to the Payment Chapel.ᴱ

Sept. 30: Left after mass and at noon arrived at the Sault. // ᶠOne quart of ground corn for poor Bapt. Quebec.ᶠ [100]

Oct. 1: Wood hauling day. Nothing special. // Same as Oct[ober] 2.

Oct. 3: Today I made a tabernacle for St. Joseph, Indian Reserve.[101]

---

[98]Henry Makotchid, age 34, was a Michigan-born fisherman. He and his wife had one child. Federal Census, 1860, Houghton County, #1145.

[99]Baraga also sent a thank you to the PFAP for 100 francs for Mass intentions. Baraga to PFAP, Payment, September 27, 1861. Orig. in PFAP; in BBC-A 484 F. The original designates the location from which Baraga wrote as Sault Ste. Marie.

[100]Meaning unclear.

[101]St. Joseph Mission, Indian Reserve, is also known as Minisheing. It is located near the center of the eastern side of Sugar Island, across from Gem Island.

Oct. 4:        Still working on the tabernacle and started the steps.

Oct. 5:        Patrick O'Flanagan finally came down today, on his way to Milwaukee. // Finished the steps today.

Oct. 6:        ᴸxx Sunday after Pentecost.ᴸ Preached in English and French. // In the evening Mr. Seif came down and left immediately on the same boat. Patrick O'Flanagan left for Montreal.[102]

Oct. 7:        Made the altar cards for St. Joseph.

Oct. 8–9–10:   All these days worked for ᴱSt. Joseph's Church, Indian Reservation.ᴱ

Oct. 11–12:    Made a nice little baptismal chest for St. Joseph's.

Oct. 13:       ᴸxxi Sunday after Pentecost.ᴸ Preached in French and English.

Oct. 14:       Worked all day on the frames for the Stations of the Cross.

Oct. 15:       Finished the 14 frames for the Stations of the Cross. // Finally received my diocesan Statutes from Rome.

Oct. 16:       Worked all day for ᴱSt. Joseph's church.ᴱ

Oct. 17:       Worked again. Rev. Van Paemel, who has been sick for several days, declared today that he wants to return to Belgium, because he feels unfit for the care of souls.[103]

Oct. 18:       Worked all day, and now everything is completed for St. Joseph's Church.[104]

---

[102]Because of the Civil War, the U.S. government was conscripting young men from the Catholic seminaries. Some bishops closed their seminaries and sent their students to Canada.

[103]Baraga wrote to Archbishop Purcell to acknowledge receipt of the Statutes and the Annuario Pontificio. He concluded: "But now another very disagreeable thing. The Rev. Mr. Van Paemel, who is now with me here, is always sick, and wants to go back to his own country, Belgium. So I will be all alone again. Therefore I wish to have Mr. Bourion, my theologian, with me; perhaps I could ordain him in the course of the ensuing winter, to help me a little. I request Your Grace, as a particular favor, to pardon me, and secondly, to charge me only for the time Mr. Bourion was at the Seminary." Baraga to Purcell, Sault Ste. Marie, October 17, 1861. Orig. in NDUA; in BBC-A 178 E.

[104]Bishop Eis added: "Whenever, in his pastoral visits, Bishop Baraga found any carpenter repairing to be done, he did it on the church or priest's house. He carried

Oct. 19:     Made and arranged some details for the church and mission of St. Joseph.

Oct. 20:     ᴸxxᴵᴵ Sunday after Pentecost.ᴸ Mr. Van Paemel is still sick and weak and so today I had to perform everything alone, first mass, second mass, ᴸvesper(s) and all.ᴸ

Oct. 21:     Packing day for transporting the interior furnishings of St. Joseph's church. // Today I gave Mr. Van Paemel (not an Exeat which he did not want, but) the permission to go to Belgium for the restoration of his health.

Oct. 22:     Day of departure. The morning was nice, in the afternoon it rained before we reached Payment, yet thanks be to God, nothing has been damaged. // I stayed with Payment over night.

Oct. 23:     In the morning said mass at Payment, and then departed for St. Joseph's mission where we arrived at noon without mishap. In the afternoon we set up the altar, etc.

Oct. 24–25:  Continually working in the church of St. Joseph. // Put up the ᴱwoodshed.ᴱ

Oct. 26:     The people worked on the shed and carried the wood in. I should have gone in all the houses but went only to the chief, but he had not yet arrived. In the afternoon and evening I had rather many confessions.

Oct. 27:     ᴸxxᴵᴵᴵ Sunday after Pentecost.ᴸ Mass at 10 and sermon. Blessed the church. // In the afternoon Stations of the Cross and sermon. In the evening a long instruction.

Oct. 28:     Today after mass again instructions in the 5 prayers.[105] In the evening, instructions.

Oct. 29:     ᴱShedᴱ completed and all the wood brought in. The shed is just large enough for the 4 ᴱcords of wood.ᴱ //

---

a few tools with him. I saw him framing himself the 14 Stations for St. Peter's Cathedral at Marquette." Baraga made frames for a third set of Stations for Beaver Island. Cf. D, September 4–6, 1862.

[105] The Lord's Prayer, Hail Mary, Doxology, Creed, and Act of Contrition.

Fabian should have left this afternoon, but the wind was too strong.

Oct. 30: Today it rained. Fabian went to Perrault and will wait there for nice weather to sail. — No, he sailed <u>immediately</u>. // Today Mr. Bourion arrived at the Sault, as Caspar reported to me.

Oct. 31: Performed everything, as usual, and went to all the houses.

Nov. 1: ᴸ<u>Feast of All Saints</u>.ᴸ The 8th anniversary of my consecration. Misère!!!

Nov. 2: Everything as usual. Today I began to instruct for first holy communion. There are altogether 9 coming for instructions. // Many confessions in the evening.

Nov. 3: ᴸXXIV <u>Sunday</u> after Pentecost.ᴸ Many confessions in the morning. Mass at 10:15. // In the afternoon vespers and sermon. / In the evening many confessions.

Nov. 4: "The sky hangs just like on November days." — Performed everything as usual, instructions in the morning, noon, and evening.

Nov. 5: Again performed everything as usual. I wanted to go around to the houses, but tomorrow I shall make my farewell visitations, because the day after I intend to depart, ᶜprovided it is well to do so.ᶜ

Nov. 6: Today I went into the houses, but found few at home. Instructions for the first holy communion. In the evening I had many confessions.

Nov. 7: First communion for 6 persons. After the mass I rode away and after a good journey, reached the Sault at 3 P.M. // Rev. A. Van Paemel left this morning on the "Illinois", for ever. I H S

Nov. 8–9: Wrote some letters. Busily read English with Mr. Bourion.

Nov. 10: ᴸXXV <u>Sunday</u> after Pentecost.ᴸ First mass at 8, high mass at 10 and 2 sermons. Catechism and vespers.

Nov. 11: ᴸSt. Martin.ᴸ Wrote to the Leopoldine Society.

Nov. 12:  This morning I consecrated 4 altar stones.

Nov. 13:  Visited Mrs. Tessak. On the other side, buried Mrs. Marie Driver.

Nov. 14:  Nothing special. Reading English with Mr. Bourion.

Nov. 15:  Church stoves were set up. // It is said that the boats have stopped <u>coming up</u>. They are still going down. // Mr. Bourion received the <u>four minor orders</u>.

Nov. 16:  Said mass in the winter chapel for the first time this fall.

Nov. 17:  XXVI <u>Sunday</u>. Said mass twice, preached in English and French, taught catechism and sang vespers. // This morning Mr. Bourion received the subdiaconate.

Nov. 18:  An excellent day, like summer. For the past several days we have had splendid weather. I H S / Visited poor Mrs. Tessak.

Nov. 19:  Another great day. The last boat "Michigan" is expected up here today. // The afternoon and evening were stormy. // The "Michigan" has arrived and remains overnight. // The last boat up.

Nov. 20:  Very stormy, but not cold. In the afternoon the old "Michigan" went up.

Nov. 21:  Administered the last sacraments to sick Mrs. Tessak. Mild weather, but windy. Still no snowflakes, but one already can see the <u>snowbirds</u>[106] so snow cannot be far away.[107]

Nov. 22:  Still no snow this morning.

Nov. 23:  Our first snow; it is watery. <u>Wood hauling day</u>.

Nov. 24:  ᴸLast <u>Sunday</u> after Pentecost.ᴸ 2 masses, 2 sermons, (good) catechism, vespers. // Mr. Bourion's diaconate.

---

[106]Snow buntings are six-inch white birds, which summer and breed in the Arctic and migrate to the northern United States for the winter.

[107]On this day Baraga sent a duplicate copy of his will and testament to Archbishop Purcell. BLS.

| | |
|---|---|
| Nov. 25: | Nothing special. Several people came to [F]print money. Yes, print,[F] i.e. to take it [borrow] without bringing it back [F]I cannot[F] [refuse them]. |
| Nov. 26: | I again visited the poor, sick Tessak. She suffers much, and will perhaps suffer for a long time. |
| Nov. 27: | I was called to the other shore, to old Mrs. Cantin, to whom I administered the last sacraments. |
| Nov. 28: | This morning the old "Michigan" went down. It is said that the "General Taylor" is still above. |
| Nov. 29: | This morning the "General Taylor" went down, and this is the last boat for this year. The canal is not at all frozen yet. |
| Nov. 30: | St. Andrew. Saturday, but no confessions. // It is snowing rather hard. |
| Dec. 1: | [L]I Sunday of Advent.[L] Performed everything, as usual. // During the first mass Mr. Bourion received the holy priesthood. |
| Dec. 2–3: | Nothing special. Gave faculties to Mr. Bourion. Visited the sick Marie Tessak. |
| Dec. 4: | Rather cold and also rather much snow. // Today Mr. Bourion received one quarter beef, 130 pounds.[108] We shall see how long it will keep. He also has 2 geese. |
| Dec. 5: | I bought a coal lamp for Caspar, it gives the cheapest light in the world. // Mrs. Tessak died. |
| Dec. 6: | [L]St. Nicholas.[L] Read Butler all day. All the snow melted. |
| Dec. 7: | Very mild weather. // This morning Mr. Bourion sang his first mass; a requiem mass [L]for the deceased[L] Mrs. Tessak. |
| Dec. 8: | [L]II Sunday of Advent.[L] [F]At the same time the patron feast[109] of all the Disunited States of America, espe- |

[108]When Bourion first arrived at the Sault, he volunteered to eat the same meals that the bishop ate. Upon discovering the frugal, meatless fare of the bishop, Bourion quickly retreated from his promise. Rezek, I, p. 174.

[109]Baraga placed the diocese under the patronage of Mary and ordered that the Feast of the Immaculate Conception be celebrated with special fervor and splendor.

cially of this diocese.<sup>F</sup> // First solemn mass of Rev. Mr. Bourion. I preached only in French. / The <sup>E</sup>pews<sup>E</sup> went for only $306.[110] // Very mild weather.

Dec. 9:     It is raining. Very mild, gentle weather; no more snow.

Dec. 10:    A dark dreary day. The last speck of snow has melted during the night. The fresh meat is in great danger of spoiling.[111]

Dec. 11:    Preparation for the journey to St. Joseph's mission. Read Butler a little.

Dec. 12:    Departure at 7:30. A beautiful summer day. A good journey except there was a bit of water in the portage. At noon I arrived at St. Joseph's. In the afternoon I went to some of the houses, and then I made some improvements in the house and sacristy.

Dec. 13:    After mass I preached and especially recommended confession. / A very nice, mild day. / In the evening, prayers and instructions.

Dec. 14:    After mass I preached again; then I went into some houses. / In the evening I had many confessions.

Dec. 15:    <sup>L</sup>III <u>Sunday</u> of Advent.<sup>L</sup> At 10 o'clock a high mass. There were quite a few confessions. I preached on the 10 commandments of God, after the mass on the commandments of the Church. Very nice weather.

Dec. 16–17:  Again preached in the morning and evening and had some confessions. Still beautiful weather.

Dec. 18:    At the holy [mass] I had 3 first communions. After mass I rode away, and arrived at Payment at 3 P.M. on a nice day.

Dec. 19:    Said mass in the morning, then read and wrote some <sup>F</sup>calendars.<sup>F</sup> / Before noon the weather was nice and mild; in the afternoon it became cold and windy.

---

Statutes, 1856, #1, #2. At the Sixth Provincial Council of Baltimore, 1846, the bishops named the Blessed Virgin under the title of the Immaculate Conception as the Patroness of the United States.

[110]Persons chose their pews according to the amounts they bid for "pew rent."

[111]The weather remained mild for an additional nine days. Neither Bourion nor Baraga commented about the effect of the mild weather on the meat!

Dec. 20:   ᴱLast nightᴱ it was very cold and it snowed a bit. A strong, cold north wind. / In the afternoon I felt constipated, ᴱ(constipation), costive, (costiveness.)ᴱ In the evening, ᴱcalm and mild weather.ᴱ

Dec. 21:   Today I suffered much from constipation. At noon I did not eat anything at all. — Oh! Were I only home! —— finally at 4 o'clock I had ᶠrelief ᶠ and now am well. // All day I had confessions.[112]

Dec. 22:   ᴸIV <u>Sunday</u> of Advent.ᴸ Said mass today in the chapel at Paymentville and preached ᴱ3 sermons.ᴱ // In the afternoon ᴱvespers and Indian sermon.ᴱ

Dec. 23:   Departure. We could not sail away in a boat because of the ice. Chief John Sayer let me ride in his ᶠdog sledᶠ to the Sault where I arrived towards 3 P.M.

Dec. 24:   Preparation for ᶠChristmas.ᶠ There were many confessions, mostly in the evening. Mr. Bourion, especially, had many confessions, up to 11 o'clock in the evening.

Dec. 25:   ᶠChristmas.ᶠ Mr. Bourion sang the high mass, and I preached in English rather ᴱmiserable.ᴱ

Dec. 26–27: Read and wrote some letters. / The weather is alternating, ᴱmild and cold, also a strong wind.ᴱ

Dec. 28:   ᴱPretty cold.ᴱ At noon and in the afternoon rather mild.

Dec. 29:   <u>Sunday</u>. Preached in English and French. ᴱMild weather.ᴱ There is almost no ice ᴱon the river.ᴱ

Dec. 30:   ᴱSoft weather.ᴱ Read all day. <u>Wood hauling day</u>.

Dec. 31:   The last day of the year 1861. Very mild weather, no ice on the river. (31 years in America.)

## 1862

Jan. 1:    <u>New Year's Day</u>. A very stormy day, fine snow, cold, windy. Thanks be to God it is cold; would that it were very cold, so we can get some ice.

---

[112]Despite his pain and discomfort Baraga heard confessions all day.

Jan. 2:
ᴱLast nightᴱ it was rather cold, as also this morning; otherwise a very nice quiet day.

Jan. 3:
Again very cold all day. Thanks be to God; this makes good ice on the river. // Today I wrote 8 letters[113] to the missionaries, regarding the omission of the collect ᴸ"For the Pope."ᴸ

Jan. 4:
Cold night, cold morning. The river is now frozen over, however, I do not know whether one can now cross on it. // Edward Perrault came here on his way home.

Jan. 5:
ᴸSunday between Circumcision and Epiphany.ᴸ Strong ice, the people cross it ᶠas they must.ᶠ The Payments came on the ice from Garden River. Thanks be to God. — // ᶠCatechism for 1st communion was announced. // The weather has become milder! . . .ᶠ

Jan. 6:
ᴸEpiphany of the Lord.ᴸ At 10 preached in English and French. Few people in church, as usual on feast days. ᶠMild weather!!ᶠ The ice is breaking up. —

Jan. 7:
Read all day. The ice on the opposite shore, is indeed, bad, but below it is good. Sleds with two horses arrived from Sailor's Encampment.

Jan. 8:
Today I gave Eusebe Salvail the ᴱlumber-billᴱ for St. Martin's Bay chapel. I H S

Jan. 9:
Made plans for ᴱSt. Martin's Bay chapel of the Immaculate Conception of the Blessed Virgin Mary.ᴱ

Jan. 10:
Again drew plans all day for St. Martin's chapel.

Jan. 11:
ᴱLast nightᴱ it was rather cold. ᴱThe river is frozen over again.ᴱ // Drew plans all day and wrote many letters.

Jan. 12:
ᴸSunday within the Octave of Epiphany.ᴸ This Sunday

---

[113]Only the letter to Fr. Murray remains. The first part of the letter, in which Baraga instructed Murray to omit the Collect "For the Pope," is crossed out. The letter continues: "I wish you a happy year and good progress and success in it. You have yet much to do in your laborious Mission, before you can stop and lay down on your laurels. Take courage and persevere to the end; you are doing the work of God, and He will constantly help you. Your most affectionate friend in Jesus." Baraga to Murray, Sault Ste. Marie, January 3, 1862. Orig. in BBC-A 362 E.

I had nothing to do; Mr. Bourion preached and taught catechism. // Stormy.

Jan. 13: I received the 1862 Ordo. // Coldest day yet.

Jan. 14: Much colder today. This morning the thermometer registered −19°. / Drew plans, wrote letters, etc.[114]

Jan. 15: <u>Confession day</u>. Stormy all afternoon. // Preparation for tomorrow's departure.

Jan. 16: I wanted to leave today, but it was stormy in the morning and Fabian had no inclination to travel. Later it was very nice, and remained nice all day.

Jan. 17: Day of departure. A nice, still morning, but rather cold. // Good traveling; at 3 I was at Sailor's Encampment and I turned in to Tudey Rains.[115]

Jan. 18: This morning at 6 I rode away from Tudey's, but I did not go farther than Richardson's, when I returned to Tudey's because no one lives any longer at ᴱCarlton's sawmillᴱ and at P. Gafney's only he and she.

Jan. 19: ᴸII <u>Sunday</u> after Epiphany.ᴸ ᴱBy misinformationᴱ I preached only in <u>French</u>. I very urgently recommended confession to them, but I had only a few confessions in the evening.

Jan. 20: Said mass at 6:30 at which there were only 4 communions. Read all day and in vain waited for confessions. In the evening there were a few confessions.

Jan. 21: At 6 A.M. offered mass, then on to Gashkiwang, where we arrived at 3. The entire family of J. B. Rousseau came to confession.

Jan. 22: Early at 6 said mass at which there were some communions. After the mass I went further and on the way saw Sam[uel] Thibault and family. We wanted to come to Bellanger by evening, but we missed him, and at 11 P.M. arrived at Minisheing where we stayed over night with Perrault.

---

[114]E.g. "Wrote to the <u>owners of the Boats</u> about <u>half-price passage</u>." BLS. At least one owner honored this request. D, June 14, 1862.
[115]Tudor Rains was a son of Major Rains.

Jan. 23:    After a pleasant and short ride, we arrived at the Sault at 11 o'clock [A.M.].

Jan. 24:    Offered holy mass early, and then rode to Minisheing to remain there over Sunday. Windy and cold. At 8 A.M. I arrived at Shawan's, remained there some time and at 10 arrived at Minisheing.

Jan. 25:    At 7 A.M. offered mass and preached, and announced holy baptism next morning for those to be baptized.

Jan. 26:    ᴸIII <u>Sunday</u> after Epiphany.ᴸ Sang mass at 10 and preached. In the afternoon Stations of the Cross and baptisms. // In the evening I had rather many confessions.

Jan. 27:    At the holy mass at 7, rather many communions. In the evening a few confessions.

Jan. 28:    Mass as usual at 7; then the return journey during which I baptized a child at Michael Nolin's. // Very stormy.

Jan. 29:    Again stormy and fine snow. Otherwise nothing.

Jan. 30:    Again stormy and fine snow. // Still no mail, although hourly awaited for the last 5 days. Probably the ice at Mackinac has broken up.

Jan. 31:    Again very windy, otherwise nothing.

Feb. 1:    Perrault was here. A nice, but windy day. Still no ᴱmail.ᴱ Today already the second is ᴱdue.ᴱ // <u>Wood hauling day</u>.

Feb. 2:    <u>Sunday and Candlemas</u>. Preached in English. // In the evening I received a ᶠcheck for 2200 francs to the account ofᶠ 10,000 (francs) . . . . I H S

Feb. 3:    Nothing. The weather is nice and not very cold. I hope to have a nice trip.

Feb. 4:    Preparation for departure for St. Martin's Bay.[116]

---

[116]Before leaving Baraga thanked the PFAP for the 2200 francs which he had received and added: "I give thanks for them [the benefactors] to God and to all those who, for the love of Him, do good for this diocese and for its bishop who does not have one cent of revenue apart from that which he receives from the Old World. I live in the greatest frugality, contenting myself with that which is

Feb. 5:  Day of departure.[117] A mild, still day. // <In the beginning I was worried, that burning pressure in my chest appeared immediately, but I did not pay any attention to it and it disappeared, and disappeared forever; during the entire journey I did not feel anything of it. ᴸThanks be to God.ᴸ I H S>

Feb. 6:  Second day on the way. Very well and ᴱcomfortable.ᴱ

Feb. 7:  At 2 P.M. we arrived at the Indian location. I lodged in the house of three sisters which was very neat and orderly arranged. // I went to the old chief and talked to him about religion, but he answered that in no way did he want to become a Christian.

---

actually necessary; and ordinarily my table is poorer than that of the other inhabitants of the Sault. However, my annual expenses are great, because there are many very poor missions in this diocese that need the aid of the bishop.

"The past summer I have had a small church built on an Indian Reservation, where there are only Indians or savages. This mission gives me much consolation. I visit it every month, and each time I stay there five or six days in order to instruct the catechumens, the neophytes, and those who have already received baptism, but who do not yet know much about the Catholic religion. Every Sunday that I spend there, I have the consolation of seeing the church full; and they tell me that it is as full every Sunday even when I am not there. They ring the bell at ten o'clock and all enter. They say the morning prayer and the rosary and sing spiritual hymns. In the afternoon they ring again, and when all have gathered, they sing vespers in the Chippewa language, because we have the privilege, granted by one of our councils, of singing them ᴸin the vernacular.ᴸ

"I am about to depart for another Indian Mission, where as yet there is no church. Tomorrow morning I shall leave. I fear that this will be a difficult journey, a journey of three days, always on foot and on snowshoes, while camping every evening, under the 'North Star', on the snow. It is the only way to get there in the winter. I propose to have a little church constructed there also next summer; and if I succeed in that, as I hope, I shall have there again the same consolation of seeing the Indians come to church every Sunday.

"Although old, I am obliged to care for these missions myself, because the priest who is with me at the Sault does not speak Indian. But I do it with pleasure. May the good Lord give me the strength to do it yet for a long time, for His glory and for the salvation of souls." Baraga to PFAP, Sault Ste. Marie, February 4, 1862. Orig. in PFAP; in BBC-A 498 F.

[117]Baraga gave greater detail about this journey: "I have just now finished my mission visitation tour for this year, and now I hasten to make a brief report about it for the Central Direction. These bishop's visitation of mine have special hardships which the Rt. Rev. Bishops in more civilized countries, here and in Europe, do not have. This year especially an untold misery and a pressing want for the necessities of life are spread here everywhere because of the terrible Civil War which rages horribly in the interior of this country, previously so happy and peaceful. Thousands and hundreds of thousands of useful people, who were the bread-winners for their families, are torn away from their feeble parents, their helpless wives and children, whereby thousands of families come

Feb. 8: Today I spoke to the 3 daughters about religion, but these poor creatures said very positively that they do not want to accept the religion.

Feb. 9: ᴸv <u>Sunday</u> after Epiphany.ᴸ I called the chief and as many who wanted to come, to the house of the 3 daughters and talked to them about the necessity of the Christian religion, however, the chief said explicitly that neither he nor any of his people wanted to accept the religion. // After that I went on to Bellanger where there were many Canadians and ᴱhalf-breeds,ᴱ all of whom came to confession.

Feb. 10: This morning I rode from Bellanger to Pine River, then walked very well, without snowshoes, until 2 P.M.; then we camped.

---

into extreme poverty. Everywhere where one comes it is depressing to hear wailing and moaning. However, I must admit that in this diocese, so remote, there is less to see and hear in this regard than in the southern parts of this country, in the actual theater of this most deplorable war.

"In regard to my personal discomforts and inconveniences, they consist particularly in the lack of adequate means of communication in the winter time. In the winter before last I made journeys much too difficult on foot, the results of which I felt in my chest the entire last summer. If I walked only a short distance I felt discomfort in my chest. I believed that my journeys on foot would now be at an end. But at the beginning of last winter I felt an urgent desire to visit a band of Indians who live three days' journey from here, to convert them, if possible, to the Christian Catholic religion. As yet I have never been in that locality, because it is out of the way and the approach to it is difficult. I had little hope of being able to get there. However, I did not want to abandon all hope without having made an attempt. I therefore made ready my snowshoes, took a guide and set out on the journey.

"I scarcely had gone a mile when I already felt such heaviness and pressure in the chest that I thought I would have to fall. I recommended myself to God and walked on. I could not bear the thought of giving up this attempt for conversions. — Thanks be to God! — The pressure gradually decreased and finally disappeared entirely. Although for several successive days I went over very difficult roads, I, nevertheless, felt no difficulty any more. On the third day I came to the Indians. I rested a little, and then went to visit them. They were real savages who knew nothing about God and His Son, whom He had sent. At the beginning I had little hope for such people, but soon the power of the divine word showed itself. I might say it penetrated into their hearts against their will. Now several of this band are already converted and baptized, and at present there is hope that, with God's help, all of them will be converted. I am thinking of erecting a small chapel there when I go there again, so that I, or later, some other missionary when he comes, will say mass, preach and catechize in it. At present I am compelled to take care of this mission myself, because, although the priest who is with me in Sault Ste. Marie can preach well in English and French, he does not speak Indian." Baraga to LS, Sault Ste. Marie, August 30, 1862. Printed in LSB, xxxiii, pp. 1–6; in BBC-A 698 G.

Feb. 11:      Again marched all day, well and comfortable.

Feb. 12:      This morning ᴱ2 mails [mail carriers]ᴱ caught up to us, and then went on ahead to the Sault, making an excellent ᴱtrailᴱ so that I arrived here already at 4 P.M. I H S

Feb. 13:      Thanks be to God, I do not feel tired at all, and I feel very well. // Wrote letters.

Feb. 14:      Again wrote some letters.[118] // A very nice, but cold day.

Feb. 15:      Very cold. I went to Aiabens. Otherwise read.

Feb. 16:      Septuagesima <u>Sunday</u>. Very cold all day. Again to Aiabens. She feels somewhat better.

Feb. 17:      Milder weather. // Nothing special.

Feb. 18:      ditto

Feb. 19:      ditto // In the evening Jourdain came with 3 dogs.

Feb. 20:      Day of departure. Good traveling; at 6:45 left the Sault and at 1:45 I was at Goulais Bay, <u>7 hours</u>.[119]

Feb. 21:      I immediately called some girls, <u>four</u>, for the first com-

[118]One letter was to his niece, Marie Gressel, who wrote about the illness of his sister, Amalia: "I received your letter. . . . I am writing to you instead of Amalia this time as you say that she is oblivious to almost everything and spends most of the day sleeping. I am still healthy and able once again to take long trips as I was 40 years ago. I returned from a 6 day trip the day before yesterday without feeling any hardship or tightness along the way.

"God willing, next week, I will leave again for a 4 or 5 day trip to another area where the Indians also live." Baraga to Marie Gressel, Sault Ste. Marie, February 14, 1862. Printed in Jaklic, p. 605.

[119]Baraga gave more details about this visit: "Hardly had I returned from that mission when I prepared to go to another which already has been visited by the Jesuits as long as they were here. It is only a day's journey distant from here. On the appointed day I got up early in the morning and confidently set out on the journey. I again was afraid of my pressure on the chest, however,—thanks be to God!—I walked all day easily and rapidly over hill and valley. The Indians were surprised when they saw me coming, and were glad. I remained with them many days, said holy mass for them daily and instructed them. At this opportunity many of them also made their first holy communion. But they were especially glad when I promised them that in spring I would have a small church built for them, so that when I come here I will no longer say holy mass and announce the word of God in a poor hut, but instead, in a nicely decorated church." Baraga to LS, Sault Ste. Marie, August 30, 1862. Printed in LSB, xxxiii, pp. 1–6; in BBC-A 698 G.

munion, and instructed them every day in the morning and afternoon. In the evening, confessions.

Feb. 22: Rather many communions at mass, then instructions in the morning and afternoon. In the evening there were some confessions.

Feb. 23: Sexagesima <u>Sunday</u>. Offered mass at 10 at which the Indians sang. In the afternoon, vespers and a sermon. In the evening, rather many confessions.

Feb. 24: At the mass there were quite a few communions. Then instructions for 1st communion. I visited some of the houses.

Feb. 25: The last instructions for 1st communion, and confessions for 1st communion.

Feb. 26: At the mass there were 4 first communions. After the mass at about 8, I left and towards 2 P.M. arrived at the Hudson Bay Co[mpany]'s house, and at 2:45 came home.

Feb. 27: Very cold night. This is a stormy and very cold day. Thanks be to God I am here and not on the trail.

Feb. 28: An even colder night; all day it is very cold. Today I wrote 6 letters. Otherwise I read.

March 1: Milder weather. Read Butler all day.

March 2: Quinquagesima <u>Sunday</u>. 18 first communions, 20 confirmations. // Strong reprimand because of non-payment of ᴱpew-rents.ᴱ

March 3: Mild weather, snow. // [Read] the whole day and wrote Indian calendars.

March 4: Today the weather is mild and calm, ᶜsnow is soft and watery.ᶜ Poor ᴱtravelers.ᴱ / Again read and wrote calendars.

March 4–6:[120] Nothing special. Very soft weather. Read all day and wrote some letters.

[120]Baraga omitted mention that March 5 was Ash Wednesday.

March 7:     Day of departure for Garden River, with Alfred Payment. At 9 o'clock arrived at Garden River. In the evening I had some confessions.

March 8:     Mass at 7, then from time to time confessions all day long. In the evening, rosary.

March 9:     ᴸI <u>Sunday</u> of Lent.ᴸ At 7:30 I had the first and at 10 the second mass at which I preached in French and Indian. In the afternoon, ᶠStations of the Crossᶠ and sermon.

March 10–      Everyday I said mass at 7, then catechism before
14:          noon, and in the afternoon [instruction] for 1st communion and confirmation. In between times, confessions, especially in the evening, and every evening, ᶠrosary.ᶠ

March 15:    A heavy day for confessions for 1st communion and many others.

March 16:    ᴸII <u>Sunday</u> of Lent.ᴸ First mass at 7:30, second at 10, at which there were 17 first communions and 16 confirmations, besides the sermons in French and Indian. // In the afternoon Stations of the Cross and rosary.

March 17:    Mass at 7, then I carried the Holy Eucharist to 3 sick people on the Canadian side. In the evening, rosary.

March 18:    Mass at 5, then I left for the Sault where I arrived at 9 A.M. // Found some letters and newspapers waiting [for me].

March 19:    Read all day and wrote some letters. Caspar, the unsteady, gave me notice of quitting. I do not know whether I shall be able to talk him into remaining.

March 20:    Caspar today promised me very firmly to remain with me forever. // Mr. Bourion went with Mr. Alfred Payment to Garden River to persuade . . . Charles Makay to separate from Marianne.

March 21:    In the afternoon Mr. Bourion returned. C[harles] Makay left Marianne.

March 22:  Wrote to Cardinal Barnabo[121] about the premature ordination of Mr. Bourion.[122] Confession day. Otherwise read Gury's Theology,[123] which I should do every day.

March 23:  ᴸIII Sunday of Lent.ᴸ Said mass at 8, otherwise nothing special.

March 24:  Continually nice weather. // Read all day in Gury. // Preparation for ᶠenlarging the building.ᶠ

March 25:  ᴸAnnunciation of the Blessed Virgin Mary.ᴸ Said mass at 8, at 10 preached in English.

March 26:  Today we began preparations for the ᶠaddition to the building.ᶠ

March 27:  Resolved: that Tardif[124] is to move to another house, and then I will use the house in which she now lives, lengthened 12 feet, I will live in it.[125] // Very nice weather continues.

March 28:  Today I began to work for the St. Mary's Church, Goulais Bay. Made the tabernacle.

March 29:  Windy, unfriendly weather; in the afternoon very bright, but windy and cold.

March 30:  ᴸIV Sunday of Lent.ᴸ Today it is windy, and it snows, or rather hails. // There will be no addition made; the house will be only changed a little. — ᴱWhat next?ᴱ

March 31:  March makes an "exit" worthy of it: windy, somewhat cold, sunny.

---

[121]Alexander Cardinal Barnabo was born in Foligno, Italy, in 1801 and elevated to the cardinalate in 1856. He was the prefect of the Sacred Congregation of Propaganda.

[122]Bourion did not meet either the age or education requirements for ordination.

[123]*Compendium Theologiae Moralis*, Jean Pierre Gury, 1860. NCE, Vol. 6, p. 866.

[124]Christine Tardif, 24, was the organist and song leader for the church at Sault Ste. Marie. Her husband, Peter, was 25. They had a son, 3, and a daughter, 1. Federal Census, 1860, Chippewa County, #168. It is not known why Baraga would have a family move.

[125]Bourion demanded use of the rectory for himself, his mother, and his sisters. Kohler to Beckx, December 26, 1863. Orig. in ACSM; in BBC-Mss. 26.

April 1:    A very nice April 1. Very nice still weather. // Decided Mrs. Tardif will room with Miss Polly; at $1.50 per month.

April 2:    A dusky, rainy day. Read Butler all day.

April 3:    Early in the morning it snowed, then it was rather nice but windy.

April 4:    Very windy. // Read Butler all day. For several days Fabian does not come to work any more.

April 5:    This morning it snowed quite a bit. Very windy all day. Read.

April 6:    ᴸPassion <u>Sunday</u>.ᴸ Very stormy! There were very few people at holy mass. Almost no women.

April 7:    Nice day, mild weather. // Read Butler. // Election day — drinking day! Brawling day!

April 8:    Windy, otherwise nice. Christine Tardif moves out tomorrow.

April 9:    Windy, nice weather. Christine Tardif moved out.

April 10:   Fabian has been working for several days for St. Mary's Church, Goulais Bay.

April 11:   Fabian began to work on the alteration of the house. / Very nice, clear weather, but always very windy = Equinoctial storms, by way of observation.

April 12:   Very windy all day. // This afternoon towards 4, the 17 year old son of St. Cyr from Sugar Island drowned coming across weak ice.

April 13:   Palm <u>Sunday</u>. Nothing.

April 14:   This morning Thomas Prior began to work on the house with Fabian. Thomas Stafford makes the chimney.

April 15:   The work on the house goes ahead slowly. // Towards evening it rained. // Stafford.

April 16:   Last night it rained heavily. Very muddy, very windy. Equinoctial storms continue, as a footnote. This wind is good for drying the roads.

April 17: Holy Thursday. Blessing of oils. Poorly, with only one priest. The chimneys are finished.

April 18: Good Friday. A very windy, rainy day. Terribly dirty and muddy everywhere. (A splendid pen!)[126]

April 19: Holy Saturday. Very windy and rainy. Work on the house progresses slowly. Rather cold.

April 20: LEaster.L Mr. Bourion sang the high mass, and I preached in English. // A very nice day.

April 21: Rather nice, but somewhat windy. // Fabian works alone today. Made the Fstairway.F

April 22: An extremely stormy, dark day! Thomas Prior works with Fabian.

April 23: Again a most stormy, but otherwise nice day. Sunny, and rather cold. // Fabian works alone again.

April 24: Today we began to move. Misère!!

April 25: Nothing. Read. Back and forth from the renovated house.

April 26: An unusually nice spring day. // Fabian has still a half day's work in order to finish everything downstairs.

April 27: I LSundayL after Easter. It snows and rains. // At 5 P.M. the first boat came up, the "City of Cleveland"; and immediately after that the "Northern Light".

April 28–29–30: Nothing special. Work on the house. Disappointment, Echagrin, trouble,E moving.[127]

May 1: 2 steamers arrived, the "Planet" and "Seabird". Nice, but windy day.

May 2–3: FMoving,F Cmoving C . . . // "Iron City" came up. // Rainy and windy.

May 4: II Sunday after Easter. Nothing special. Weather nice but windy.

---

[126]Baraga was probably using a new pen.
[127]Bishop Eis added: "into his new house at the Sault."

| | |
|---|---|
| May 5–6: | Still very windy, otherwise nice. // This evening Mr. Bourion left for Marquette, on the "General Taylor."[128] |
| May 7: | Very nice weather, a little windy. Read Butler. |
| May 8–9: | Nothing. Very nice warm weather. Continuously reading Butler. The moving is suspended until Mr. Bourion returns. // Made a contract with Caspar = $1000 after my death! |
| May 10: | Read all day. // In the evening a man came who was sent by Agent Leatch [sic], and asked me how much I would ask for a building lot in L'Anse for a school building. (I intend to ask $25 for a lot, 50 by 100 feet.)[129] |
| May 11: | III Sunday after Easter. Said mass twice and preached in English. At 2 P.M. Mr. Bourion returned from Marquette and sang the vespers. |
| May 12: | Spent the entire gloomy, rainy day in reading. |
| May 13: | ᶠMoving back again.ᶠ Everything must be brought back from the small house. |
| May 14–15: | Nothing special. Read all day. Nice weather. |
| May 16: | Departed for St. Joseph's mission. Arrived there at 11 A.M. In the evening I preached and heard some confessions. A nice warm day. |
| May 17: | Dark day. Mass early in the morning and preached a little. At noon I called them for instructions but only 4 came. In the evening prayers and some confessions. // Rather cold. |
| May 18: | IV Sunday after Easter. A terribly stormy day; snowed rather heavily. // Mass at 10 o'clock and an Indian sermon. In the afternoon Indian vespers. // All day I suffered much from the cold. |

[128]Bourion became the first pastor at St. Paul's Parish, Negaunee, a few miles west of Marquette where his uncle, Fr. Duroc, was pastor.

[129]Baraga authorized Trempe to receive $25 for the lot on which the L'Anse schoolhouse was built. Baraga to Leach, Sault Ste. Marie, September 27, 1862. Orig. in NA-OIA; in BBC-A 632 E.

May 19: This morning the ground was covered with 1 inch of snow. On the way back from St. Joseph's mission, Mr. Zögel[130] came to meet me. But as I came home Mr. Bourion related his observations of him which made me decide to send him away. // Munich check for $400.

May 20: George Sayer delivers the building wood to Goulais Bay. Mr. Zögel is still here, waiting for a steamboat. // Nice weather.

May 21: A dusky day; I am afraid it will rain. — It rains all day. // No boat down yet.

May 22: At noon today the "Iron City" came down here, and Mr. Zögel sailed on it for Detroit. // George Sayer returned from Goulais Bay. // Fr. Kohler is here; and in Garden River.

May 23: It is considerably cold, so that I have to keep a fire in the stove all day. I saw some snowflakes fall.

May 24: Prepared some things for the trip to Goulais Bay. Otherwise read all day.

May 25: V Sunday after Easter. Prepared some things for the intended journey. In the evening I was called to old Bagage, but she was unconscious.

May 26: This morning I wanted to leave, but it rains. Now I am thinking of leaving only next week.

May 27: Today we carried the Indian books over to this house, and I handed the key to the other house to Mrs. Tardif.

May 28: Nothing special. Boats come and go, but none brings the Rev. Gaess.

May 29: ᴸAscension of Our Lord Jesus Christ.ᴸ Mass at 8, then high mass at 10, I preached in English and French.

May 30: Fr. Kohler was here, for a farewell. I gave him 136 Anamie-mas ᴸfree.ᴸ

---

[130]Baraga asked Bishops Lefevere, Farrell, Pinsonneault, Lynch, and McCloskey whether he should accept Rev. Joseph Zögel. BLS, May 20, 1862.

May 31:    Nice exit for May.

June 1:    ᴸSunday within the Octave of Ascension.ᴸ Mass at 8 and high mass at 10, preached in English and French.

June 2:    Departed for Goulais Bay. Strong contrary wind. We could not get far, and stayed overnight with old Mackay on Gros Cap.

June 3:    At 10 A.M. we arrived at Goulais Bay; and we immediately went to work. The Indians worked industriously; they brought over all the pieces for the foundation and also many boards.[131]

June 4:    At noon all the boards, shingles, etc., were on the spot, and Fabian Landreville and James Prior immediately began to work on building the church.

June 5:    This evening the ꟳframe of the churchꟳ was already set up, and also some of it already girdled.

June 6:    The ᴱraftersᴱ are also all cut, but they cannot be put in place today because it is too windy.

June 7:    Early this morning, at 5 A.M., I sailed from Goulais Bay, and with a favorable wind arrived at the Sault by 12 noon. Here I met Fr. Tellier and Br. Donovan who want to go to Fort William. They will wait here for an opportunity.

June 8:    Pentecost. Fr. Tellier said mass at 8 and I at 10, besides 2 sermons.

June 9–10:    Fr. Tellier is still here. // I am waiting for the "Traveler" to leave for the missions on Lake Superior.

---

[131]Baraga described this construction in greater detail: "Now this summer I have fulfilled this promise of mine, thanks be to God! I have bought a large amount of boards and other lumber, as well as shingles, had everything transported there by water, then hired two French carpenters who in a short time erected a nice little church. Then I bought some lime and had the entire interior of the building sheathed with laths and plastered with mortar, so that it appears as if it were of masonry. The whole had cost about 250 dollars. The Indians are pleased and are grateful that they have this church, and I also am satisfied that it is there. Because the Indians, even when no missionary is with them, assemble every Sunday and holyday, in the morning and in the afternoon, in the church where they have one, to pray the rosary and sing holy hymns at the usual hour for divine services." Baraga to LS, Sault Ste. Marie, August 30, 1862. Printed in LSB, xxxiii, p. 106; in BBC-A 698 G.

266

June 11:    Fr. Tellier is still here, waiting for Fr. Ferard[132] who should come here on Saturday.

June 12:    Departure on the steamer "Traveler", at 9 A.M. ᴱHalf priceᴱ $4.50 to Ontonagon.[133]

June 13:    About 8 A.M. we arrived at Portage Lake. There I saw Fr. Jacker and Sweeney, and again sailed away.

June 14:    At 4 A.M. we came to Ontonagon, and at 8 I rode up to Minnesota Mine. Fr. Fox had gone to Ontonagon Village before I arrived in Minnesota Mine.

June 15:    ᴸMost Holy Trinity <u>Sunday</u>.ᴸ I was alone in Minnesota

---

[132]Martin Ferard was born at Tours, France, on September 8, 1817. He entered the Society of Jesus in 1839 and was ordained in 1847 in New York. That same year he was sent to Montreal to assist typhus victims. In the fall he returned to New York (Fordham), where he taught French until 1855 when he was sent as missionary to Fort William. From 1860 to 1870 he was superior and pastor at Chatham, Ontario. He worked in various Ontario locations until 1890, interrupted by a term, 1873 to 1877, as pastor at Sault Ste. Marie, where in 1876 he began to keep the parish records in English. Ferard died in Montreal on January 10, 1891. Cadieux, p. 887.

[133]Baraga praised the priests who served the Lake Superior region: "In the summer I make my visitation journeys by water; to some places also by land, riding. In spring I visited the missionaries in the copper mines, all of whom are very active in the service of God for the salvation of the souls entrusted to them. There is a scarcity of priests in the mines on Lake Superior. These mines are constantly increasing, new churches are being built, and very often one and the same priest has two or three different churches and congregations to attend, which is often connected with many difficulties because of the distances of the churches from each other. So, for example, the Reverend Edward Jacker has two churches to attend, and the number of Catholics at both churches amounts to 4000. There a second priest would be much desired, so that a priest would be at each of these two churches. So also has the Rev. Henry L. Thiele two churches with large congregations to attend, situated far from each other. Again, another of my priests, the Rev. Martin Fox, has four churches and congregations to attend which are distant far from each other. But he makes all possible effort to provide his various congregations with divine service on Sundays and holydays. How I wish very much to give him an assistant, if I only had him. So also has Rev. John Chebul four churches and missions to attend which are several days journey distant from each other. He most zealously endeavors, as well as he can, to attend to them. But he is thereby ruining his health. It is my greatest wish to send another missionary to those regions, if I only could find one. However, it is difficult to find capable priests and missionaries for this diocese, because in every station in this diocese three or four languages are necessary, the English, French, German, and in some also the Indian. Priests who are able to speak so many languages well and fluently are rare. Several missionaries who could preach in different languages have been compelled to leave this diocese, because their state of health no longer permitted them to render such difficult mission services." Baraga to LS, Sault Ste. Marie, August 30, 1862. Printed in LSB, xxxIII, pp. 1–6; in BBC-A 698 G.

Mine; heard some confessions, said mass at 8, sang the 10 o'clock mass, preached in English, sang vespers in the afternoon, preached in German and English, gave benediction and administered one baptism.

June 16: We went to Maplegrove and stayed overnight with Mr. Flanagan.

June 17: At 8 A.M. said mass in Maplegrove, then returned to Minnesota Mine.

June 18: After the mass I went to visit the numerous, well organized school at Minnesota Mine, and then we left for Ontonagon Village where we arrived at 2 P.M. // To Fr. Chebul I sent $90 by Daniel Metakosige.

June 19: Corpus Christi. At 8 said mass in Ontonagon church, at 10 preached in English and confirmed 17 persons. // First communions.

June 20: At 12 noon left Ontonagon for Minnesota Mine.

June 21: I heard some confessions for tomorrow's confirmation, and others. Otherwise read.

June 22: ᴸII Sunday after Pentecost.ᴸ At 8 I celebrated in St. Mary's Church, Minnesota Mine, and at 10 preached in English. After the high mass I had 40 confirmations. // Children's first communion. // At 6:30 P.M. I preached in German and French at St. Patrick's Church, Ontonagon. // P. M. O'Flanagan arrived here today, on vacation. // At 8 I boarded the "Iron City".

June 23: At 3 A.M. I arrived in Eagle River, and then I went to Fr. Thiele, whom I found sick, in Clifton.

June 24: At 7 offered mass in Clifton, then I went to Eagle River, in the expectation that the "Traveler" would arrive from Ontonagon, but it did not come.

June 25: Stayed with Mr. Austrian[134] overnight, and all day. Fi-

---

[134]Julius Austrian was a trader and an employee of the American Fur Company and owner of a sawmill three miles south of present-day Bayfield in 1842. In 1852 he was government agent at La Pointe. Austrian, who was Jewish, and his wife, Hannah, were friends of Baraga and Van Paemel at La Pointe (and, after 1854, also at Bad River). The 1860 census at La Pointe includes his name but by 1862 he had moved to Eagle River. Here he was "the leading businessman around." Chaput, p. 88.

nally at 7 P.M. the "Traveler" came, on which I sailed from Eagle River.

June 26: At 5 A.M. I arrived in Hancock, and then said holy mass in St. Ann's Church at 7 o'clock.

June 27: The 10 anniversary of this diary. Read all day. // In the evening Rev. Michael McLaughlin came.[135]

June 28: This morning I accepted Rev. McLaughlin, because he also speaks French, and sent him right today to Sault Sainte Marie. ———

June 29: ᴸIII Sunday after Pentecost.ᴸ My 65th birthday. I H S // At 8:30 said mass and preached in German and French. Misère! — At 11 preached in English and confirmed 12 persons. // At 3 P.M. I gave Patrick M. O'Flanagan the tonsure and the 4 minor orders.

June 30: Until now there were some very warm days, but today it is cool again. Read Fr. Jacker's Church Lexicon all day.

July 1: At 8 A.M. Fr. Terhorst from L'Anse came here to Hancock, and took me with him to L'Anse where we arrived at 6 P.M.! — Misère — The house is good and comfortable, but it costs me about $500.

July 2: At 7 o'clock said mass at L'Anse and preached in Indian. At 2 P.M. the small steamer "Miner" arrived, on which I arrived again in Hancock at 6 P.M.

July 3: At 7 this morning I conferred the ᴸTonsure and 4 minor ordersᴸ on James Sweeney.[136] // In the afternoon left on the "Planet."

July 4: Day of general misfortune and sinning.[137] For me never so much as this time! — At 4 A.M. we arrived in

---

[135]Michael McLaughlin came from Chicago to Hancock. On June 27 Baraga received him because he spoke French and sent him to Sault Ste. Marie. Baraga dismissed him on November 28, 1862, because he had "too great a love for intoxicants." Rezek, I, pp. 175, 180. In 1866 he was in Omaha for a few months but was also dismissed from there.

[136]At least since April (BLS, April 27, 1862) Sweeney had been living with Fr. Jacker and learning Latin, theology, and Indian. BLS, November 28, 1861, and March 19, 1862. Jacker referred to conducting a seminary in Hancock from 1862 to 1865, eventually with four candidates. Jacker to Finotti, Mackinac, February 27, 1877, in BBC-AR 13, p. 161.

[137]Bishop Eis commented: "U.S. celebrates."

|          | Marquette, but I remained all day on the boat. Would that I had stayed with Duroc! — |
|----------|---|

July 5:    At noon I arrived at the Sault where I found many letters waiting, among others also the Paris check for $1428[138] and some odd cents. // Fr. Hanipaux[139] is here. // He has been at Garden River for a long time.

July 6:    ᴸIV Sunday after Pentecost.ᴸ Mass at 8, and at 10 preached in French. Rev. McLaughlin sang the high mass. He is a poor singer. Too bad! // Messrs. Trempe, Ryan,[140] and Gager are now trustees in charge.

July 7:    Fr. Hanipaux is still here. // Fabian and Jim Prior have finished the church at Goulais Bay in 17 days.

July 8:    Fr. Hanipaux is still here. // In the afternoon he left.

July 9:    Today we began to eat the 45 pounds of ᴱbarley soup.ᴱ // Read all day.[141]

July 10:   Read and wrote some letters. // Jim Prior went to Churchville and brought back in the evening ᴱ1800 feet lath boards.ᴱ // Also Condonnier came up here, but he went back immediately, and will come here again Sunday afternoon.

July 11:   ᴸCorrectedᴸ 50 A[namie] M[asinaigan], cut out ᴸthe things to be read to the people.ᴸ

July 12:   Nothing. Read all day; no! Also corrected 60 A[namie] M[asinaigan].

July 13:   V Sunday after Pentecost. For the first time, Rev. Mi-

---

[138]Baraga thanked the PFAP for the 7500 francs, payable through Fr. Lafond in New York. This was the first time that the check was payable in the United States rather than in Europe, and Baraga concluded: "I hope that this arrangement will remain for some time." Baraga to PFAP, Sault Ste. Marie, July 6, 1862. Orig. in PFAP; in BBC-A 468 F.

[139]Joseph-Urbain Hanipaux, born in France on May 3, 1805, was ordained in 1829. In 1837 he entered the Society of Jesus and arrived in Canada on May 31, 1842. From 1845 to 1870 he was at Manitoulin Island. Hanipaux died in Quebec on March 12, 1872. Cadieux, pp. 888–89.

[140]Thomas Ryan, 33, a merchant, and his wife, Ann, 25, were both born in Ireland. They had one son, James, 2. Federal Census, 1860, Chippewa County, #120.

[141]Bishop Eis added: "Read."

chael McLaughlin preached here in English, rather well; if he only preached like that also in French. He will regularly teach catechism.

July 14–15–16:    To Goulais Bay and back. ᴸThanks be to Godᴸ for everything there! God grant that a good use will always be made of it.

July 17–18:    Made plans for the Alpena church, 60 by 30. I intend to have it made by Jim Prior and Fabian Landreville.

July 19:    <u>Confession day</u>. Preparation for the journey to Arbre Croche.

July 20:    ᴸVI Sunday after Pentecost.ᴸ Said mass at 8 and at 10 preached in <u>French</u>. // "Seabird" ᴱexpected.ᴱ

July 21:    Waited all day for the "<u>Seabird</u>"; meanwhile read and wrote letters.

July 22:    Finally the "<u>Seabird</u>" came and at 10 A.M. I sailed for Mackinac, where I arrived in the evening, and then stayed in the ᴸpresbyteryᴸ overnight.

July 23:    At 7 A.M. said mass at Mackinac and at 9 sailed on Deslauriers' packet for Sheboygan (Duncan), where we arrived, with a favorable wind, (ᴸthanks be to God!ᴸ) already by noon. There I met (ᴸPraise Godᴸ) Fr. Murray who is preparing the children (ᴸPraise Godᴸ) of Duncan for confirmation.

July 24–25:    Quartered with Patrick McDonald. At 7 A.M. Mass, otherwise read all day. // Heard some confessions.

July 26:    All day, from time to time, heard confessions. Otherwise read Reeve's Church History.

July 27:    ᴸVII <u>Sunday</u> (after Pentecost).ᴸ Mass at 8 in Sheboygan, St. Mary. At 11 preached in English. After the sermon I had 33 confirmations.

July 28:    Read all day.

July 29:    Departure for Mackinac where I arrived at 5 P.M. Boarded with Wendell.

July 30:    Waited for a boat to the Sault, meanwhile read.

July 31:     Since no boat wanted to go to the Sault, I left for Detroit[142] at 10 A.M. on the propeller, "Rocket", ᴸfreeᴸ, Captain Gaylord.

Aug. 1:      At noon arrived in Port Huron, and from there to Thunder Bay. // I was looking for Fr. Kilroy,[143] but I could not find him; he was at a mission.

Aug. 2:      Since no boat goes from Port Huron to Alpena, I therefore went, at 8 A.M. on the "Forester" ($1.50) to Detroit where I arrived at 1 P.M., and ᴱfortunatelyᴱ met Bishop Lefevere who gave me $200 for 1862. However, neither here can I find a boat for Thunder Bay.

Aug. 3:      ᴸVIII <u>Sunday</u> after Pentecost,ᴸ 1st [Sunday] of Aug[ust]. Said mass at 7, and at 11 preached in the cathedral.

Aug. 4:      Bought wine and candles for our missionaries.[144]

Aug. 5:      "Planet" arrived at 8 A.M. and at 1:30 it goes to Mackinac, etc. (It only left Detroit at 3 o'clock.)

Aug. 6:      At 6 P.M. I arrived in Mackinac.

Aug. 7:      The Indians from Cross village should have left this morning, but the wind was unfavorable and ᶠbad weather seemed likely,ᶠ and so we did not leave.

Aug. 8:      We should have departed early, but it rained heavily. We sailed at 12 noon and reached Cross Village at 7 P.M. Scarcely had we arrived in the mission when a terrible thunderstorm broke. I H S

[142]Baraga had previously made arrangements to pick up building supplies for the proposed church in Alpena. BLS, July 21, 1862.

[143]Lawrence Kilroy was born in 1803 at Tisarn, Ireland. In 1834 he came to Detroit where, in 1839, he received minor orders from Bishop Rése and, on March 26, 1842, was the first priest ordained by Bishop Lefevere. He was pastor at Holy Trinity in Detroit, 1842–1847, and assistant to Fr. Viszosky in Grand Rapids until 1850. On January 14, 1850, the church and rectory burned; Kilroy's invalid mother and his sister who were visiting at the time both perished. After this tragedy Kilroy was sent to the St. Clair region where, in three years, he founded seven parishes. From 1857 until his retirement in 1881 he was pastor at St. Stephen's Church, Port Huron. He died on July 23, 1891, at Columbus, Michigan, where he is buried.

[144]While he was in Detroit, Baraga wrote to Murray informing him that if he wanted wine in the future he should send five dollars to him at the Sault and Baraga would send him five gallons. Baraga to Murray, Detroit, August 5, 1862. Orig. in BBC-A 359 E.

Aug. 9:      From time to time, visits from Indians; otherwise read.

Aug. 10:     ᴸIX <u>Sunday</u> (after Pentecost),ᴸ 2nd [Sunday] of Aug[ust]. Said mass early, at 6, at 10 preached in Indian ᶠat Cross [Village]ᶠ and confirmed 17.

Aug. 11:     Talked with Fr. Weikamp about his ᴱfarm.ᴱ

Aug. 12:     Read all day.

Aug. 13:     Departure for Middle Village at 9 o'clock.

Aug. 14:     In Middle Village read all day. Heard some confessions, French, etc.

Aug. 15:     ᴸ<u>Assumption</u> of the Blessed Virgin.ᴸ In Middle Village offered mass at 7, preached at 10 and confirmed 11 persons. After vespers preached again.

Aug. 16:     After the mass I left for Little Traverse, and arrived there at 1 P.M.

Aug. 17:     ᴸ<u>Sunday</u> (after Pentecost),ᴸ 3rd [Sunday] of Aug[ust]. Said mass at 7, at 10 preached in Indian and Fr. Sifferath said holy mass.

Aug. 18:     At 6 I said holy mass and then went to Bear River, where I preached in Indian and Fr. Sifferath said holy mass.

Aug. 19:     After the holy mass I departed from Little Traverse and came via Middle Village to Cross Village at 3. I thought of sailing for Mackinac only the next morning, but since the wind was favorable we therefore sailed at 5 P.M. from Cross Village and arrived at Mackinac at midnight. We needed 7 hours, because it was calm and the Indians had to row.

Aug. 20:     At 7 offered holy mass at Mackinac. // In the afternoon I rode with Louison Martin to Pointe St. Ignace to visit Fr. Piret.

Aug. 21:     At 7 offered mass at Pointe St. Ignace, then returned to Mackinac where I arrived at noon.

Aug. 22:     Yesterday I received a sad letter against Michael McLaughlin, and today I wrote <u>circulars</u> to the ᴱbishops against him.ᴱ

Aug. 23:      Heard some confessions, otherwise read. Again wrote circulars.

Aug. 24:      ᴸxɪ <u>Sunday</u> (after Pentecost),ᴸ 4th [Sunday] in Aug[ust]. At 10 I sang the high mass and then preached in English and French. In the afternoon vespers and benediction. // In the evening I had some confessions.

Aug. 25:      Again wrote some circulars, waiting for the "Backus."

Aug. 26–27–28:      Continually writing for the slow "Backus"; finally it came at 7 and left at midnight.

Aug. 29:      At 3 P.M. I arrived in the Sault and received many letters, some very pleasing. I H S Among them one from the Leopoldine Society with $437.50. // Thanks be to God a thousand times! With Fr. McLaughlin all goes well. I H S In the evening wrote many letters.

Aug. 30:      Wrote letters all day; among them also a rather detailed report to the Leopoldine Society.

Aug. 31:      ᴸxɪɪ <u>Sunday</u> (after Pentecost)ᴸ 1st [Sunday] in Sept[ember].¹⁴⁵ Said mass at 8. After that Fr. Gaess arrived. He had lost all his trunks on the "Planet". I appointed him to Mackinac.

Sept. 1:      Today the ꜰ4 Daughters of the Heart of Mary,ꜰ who for 14 days have waited here for the "Plowboy," left for Manitouline. They made us 4 nice altar bouquets.

Sept. 2–3:      Wrote letters almost all the time.

Sept. 4:      Prepared the Stations of the Cross pictures for Beaver Harbor, ᴱready to be placed in the frames.ᴱ ¹⁴⁶

Sept. 5:      Today Fr. Gaess went by "Seabird" to Mackinac. // The Stations of the Cross pictures are completed.

Sept. 6:      The Stations of the Cross were packed and sent to

---

[145] In September and October Baraga designated the Sundays of the month according to the weeks of these months.

[146] On this day Baraga learned that his sister, Amalia, had died on August 10, 1862. He wrote his niece, Marie Gressel: "I received your letter dated August 15 in which you inform me of the death of my beloved sister. As it was only with Amalia that I corresponded, my writing to Trebnje is now ended." Baraga to Marie Gressel, Sault Ste. Marie, September 4, 1862. Printed in Jaklic, p. 606.

Trempe, from where they will be sent to Beaver Harbor on the "Backus".[147]

Sept. 7:  [L]XIII <u>Sunday</u> (after Pentecost)[L] 2nd in Sept[ember]. Preached in English and French. (The "Backus" came and left with the [E]box.[E]) Expecting the Ursuline Sisters;[148] they haven't arrived yet. I hope they will come . . . <(On the 9th they left New York.)>

Sept. 8:  [L]<u>Nativity of the Blessed Virgin</u>.[L] Wrote letter and read.

Sept. 9:  Today the [Ursuline] Sisters of East Morrisania [New York] are leaving for Minnesota Mine (according to a report [L]dated Sept[ember] 3.[L]) Today [F]two workers[F] began to work on the "flat roof".

Sept. 10:  Worked on the roof. // Nothing special. Read all day. A very nice day, as well as yesterday.

Sept. 11–12:  Read. // Work is diligently being done on the "flat roof", [F]despite the rain.[F]

Sept. 13:  The flat roof is finished. // Today I expect the Ursulines; as well as Mr. Sweeney. He does not come for a long time.

---

[147]Baraga wrote to Murray: "I am glad to be able to transmit you so nice a set of Stations. I took great pains to pack it up so as not to be spoiled or injured. If they only don't let stand the box in the rain, all will be safe. The frames are not yet perfectly dry; you could get black paint, and very cautiously give a slight touch in places where there is dust, etc. The holes of the nails you could cover with black paint, and put some paint in, but take care not to let fall any of the paint on the beautiful pictures." Baraga to Murray, Sault Ste. Marie, September 6, 1862. Orig. in BBC-A 329 E.

[148]Mother Mary Magdalene de Pazzi Stehlin (September 21, 1802–1868) was prioress of the Ursuline Community in Odenburg, Hungary. In 1848 she, with two other sisters and two postulants, came to St. Louis to teach German girls. In 1855 she and eleven sisters founded the Ursuline Community at East Morrisania, New York. From this house she was instrumental in the establishment of several other Ursuline houses in the New York area. In 1862 several members of the East Morrisania community came to Ontonagon. In 1864 she went to Hungary seeking funds and recruits. Stehlin to LMV, Raab, Hungary, July 19, 1864. Orig. in LMVA; in BBC-B 958 G. Because of a decline in the population and financial support, the remaining Ursulines in Ontonagon moved, in 1867, to Canada, six sisters going to Quebec and two to Three Rivers. Mother Mary Magdalene died at Odenburg. Baraga described her: "an experienced, wise, enterprising woman who has established many beautiful religious foundations." Kummer, p. 238. This Ursuline community is completely separate from the Ursuline Sisters in Chatham, Ontario, who had been in Sault Ste. Marie, 1853–1860.

Sept. 14:      ᴸXIV <u>Sunday</u> (after Pentecost),ᴸ 3rd [Sunday] in Sept[ember]. Noteworthy day! The <u>Ursulines</u> arrived and continued on the "Illinois". Moreover, Mr. <u>Sweeney</u> came, and Mr. <u>O'Flanagan</u>, since the seminary in Milwaukee disbanded for fear of conscription.[149]

Sept. 15:      Mr. Patrick M. O'Flanagan received the holy order of sub-diaconate. // Scenes and unpleasantness because of the school.

Sept. 16:      This morning Mr. Patrick O'Flanagan received the diaconate.[150] At 1 P.M. he left on the "Mineral Rock".

Sept. 17:      This morning Mr. Sweeney received the sub-diaconate. A rainy day.

Sept. 18:      Mr. Sweeney diaconate. // Preparation for journey to Minisheing.

Sept. 19:      Mr. Sweeney's priesthood. // Departure for St. Joseph. Fr. Sweeney went on the "Northern Light" to Hancock.[151] Fr. Konen[152] came here on the "Northern Light".

[149]Because seminarians were adult, unmarried men, they were subject to the military draft for the Northern (Union) Army.

[150]Baraga explained: "Mr. O'Flanagan was in some hurry, but this does not hurt him. Where he is now he will learn German and complete his theology as well. It pleases me that Your Episcopal Grace's splendid seminary continues to flourish and to always increase. According to what Mr. O'Flanagan says, I believe that after a certain time it will be interrupted." Baraga to Henni, Sault Ste. Marie, September 30, 1862. Orig. in MADA; in BBC-A 681 E. There is a contradiction between this letter and the entry of September 14 about whether the Milwaukee seminary was still open.

[151]"On the 20th of September 1862 Rev. James Sweeney came to Father Jacker as assistant. His arrival sounded new signals among the young people. The strictures he placed — and sometimes made usefully felt — on dances and like gatherings are still remembered by the survivors. Enjoying the fullest confidence of his pastor Father Sweeney pitilessly enforced his principles, so that his name spelled terror to the merry-makers in the surrounding hills. Traversing the parish in his ministerial duties nothing escaped his keen observation. Among the young men he found one of college training, but, who for want of means had given up higher aspirations and was about to disappear among the every day men. Him he presented to Father Jacker with whose encouragement and help he resumed the given-up studies. To this one another one was added and Edmund Walsh and William Dwyer soon formed the nucleus of a college. Under the professorship of Father Jacker they were as rapidly advanced as their talents permitted. The life of the two priests and their students resembled much that of a community and in 1865 when the students, together with Rev. Peter Gallagher, were raised to the priesthood at the instance of their preceptor, serious thoughts were entertained as to laying the foundation to a religious community." Rezek, II, pp. 262–63.

[152]Nicholas Joseph Konen came from the diocese of Fort Wayne, arriving at Sault

Sept. 20: Some confessions in the church of ᴸSt. Joseph,ᴸ Minisheing.

Sept. 21: ᴸxv <u>Sunday</u> (after Pentecost),ᴸ 4th [Sunday] in Sept[ember]. Performed everything at St. Joseph. // Many confessions. // 39th anniversary of my priesthood.

Sept. 22: Rained all day. // I visited the houses, ᴱup and down.ᴱ

Sept. 23: Return. Heavy rain and strong contrary wind.

Sept. 24: Departure for Goulais Bay. A very nice day, ᴱcalmᴱ favorable wind in the afternoon.

Sept. 25–26–27: Worked busily on the church; set up all the pews, made the altar, (communion) rail, Stations of the Cross and everything. // In the evening I had some confessions.

Sept. 28: ᴸxvi <u>Sunday</u> (after Pentecost), 1st in Oct[ober]. Feast of the Seven Dolors of the Blessed Virgin.ᴸ // Today I said the first mass in the new church ᴸof the Blessed Virgin Mary,ᴸ and preached in Indian, in the morning and afternoon. Instead of vespers, we had the devotion of the Stations of the Cross.[153]

Sept. 29: Return to Sault Sainte Marie. A very nice day and favorable wind, thanks be to God! // Scarcely was I home when Jo[seph] Perrault came and took me to his sick wife Angelique. // Stayed overnight with Alfred Payment.

Sept. 30: This morning I said mass at Payment. // Joseph Payment plastered the ᶠbrother'sᶠ room.

Oct. 1: Wrote letters and read.

Oct. 2: At 1:30 P.M. my right ear plugged! I H S // In the evening Fr. Thiele came down, to obtain an Exeat for

---

Ste. Marie on September 19, 1862. Baraga sent him to replace Fr. Thiele at Clifton but dismissed him on November 8, 1862.

[153]In the church of St. Mary's in Goulais Bay there is still a small picture of Our Lady of Sorrows. On the reverse, in Baraga's writing, is the inscription: "On the feast day of the Seven Sorrows of the Blessed Virgin Mary, in the year of the Lord 1862, the first mass was celebrated in this church of the same Most Blessed Virgin Mary, conceived without sin. Goulais Bay." Baraga Inscription, Goulais Bay, September 28, 1862. Orig. in St. Mary's Church, Goulais Bay; in BBC-A 821 L.

himself; which I gave him. (During the night my ear opened up again. I H S)

Oct. 3:
Joseph Payment only now completed his small ᴱjob.ᴱ (No! tomorrow.) This morning Fr. Thiele left on the "City of Cleveland" for Clifton.

Oct. 4:
Today Payment completed his plastering job. $7. // A terrible stormy day!

Oct. 5:
ᴸXVII Sunday (after Pentecost),ᴸ 2nd [Sunday] in Oct[ober]. Fr. McLaughlin said the holy Stations of the Cross.

Oct. 6–7–8:
All these days terrible storms and pouring rain. // Wrote letters and read.

Oct. 9–10:
Worked on the tabernacle for Goulais Bay. // Rainy.

Oct. 11:
A nice morning. All day was nice. // Completed the tabernacle.

Oct. 12:
ᴸXVIII Sunday (after Pentecost),ᴸ 3rd [Sunday] in Oct[ober]. I had a sharp sermon against dancing parties. With what result? —

Oct. 13–14–15:
Always busy working for the Blessed Virgin Mary Church at Goulais Bay.

Oct. 16–17:
Still another Sister went to Ontonagon. I H S // The ᴱsteelbellᴱ for ᴸSt. Maryᴸ has arrived. The yoke[154] was broken.

Oct. 18:
ᴸSt. Luke.ᴸ A day of sad memories. ————[155]

Oct. 19:
ᴸXIX Sunday (after Pentecost),ᴸ 4th [Sunday] in Oct[ober]. Fr. McLaughlin gave a very good sermon on penance.

Oct. 20:
Made a large cross for St. Mary's, Goulais Bay. // Received and wrote letters.

Oct. 21:
This morning I conferred the ᴸtonsureᴸ on the good Caspar Schulte, and ordained him as ᴸdoorkeeperᴸ and ᴸacolyte,ᴸ in order to dedicate him for all his life to the service of the church, and to make him a member ᴸof the court of the church, among the lower clergy.ᴸ

---

[154]"Cross-beam."
[155]Cf. D, October 18, 1856 and 1860.

// This morning Fr. Thiele went down on the "Traveler".

Oct. 22–23–24: Nothing special. Caspar is in retreat. // Some snow in the evening.

Oct. 25: Today Caspar finished his retreat of 3 days, which he will now have to make annually about this time.

Oct. 26: ᴸxx <u>Sunday</u> (after Pentecost),ᴸ 5th [Sunday] in Oct[ober]. Today Fr. McLaughlin established the ᴱAltar Society.ᴱ God bless it. // Caspar Schulte made his consecration and permanent vows.[156] God bless him.

Oct. 27–28–29: Nothing special. Preparation, partly for Goulais Bay, partly for Minisheing. // Chapel and church stoves set up.

Oct. 30: Departure for Minisheing, where I arrived at 12 noon.

Oct. 31: Said mass at 7 and preached. Announced that I will instruct in the <u>evening</u>, especially the ᶜyoung people,ᶜ which I want to do there now always in the evening.

Nov. 1: ᴸ<u>Feast of All Saints</u>.ᴸ 9th anniversary of my consecration. Misère! — A gloomy day; ᶜit was hardly or scarcely day all day.ᶜ

Nov. 2: ᴸxxi <u>Sunday</u> (after Pentecost),ᴸ 1st [Sunday] in Nov[ember]. Mass at 10, etc., as also <u>yesterday</u>. In the evening several confessions.

Nov. 3: Mass at 7 at which there were several communions. Then departed, and at 2 arrived home where I received terrible reports and letters about the drinking of <u>McLaughlin</u> and <u>Konen</u>, which made me decide not to go to Goulais Bay but to Ontonagon.[157]

Nov. 4: At noon I departed from the Sault on the "Northern Light", but we did not come any further than Whitefish Point where we remained lying at anchor.

Nov. 5: All day at Whitefish Point, lying at anchor.

Nov. 6: At 4 A.M. after lying for 36 hours at Whitefish Point, we finally got under way, and at 4 P.M. we arrived in

[156]Schulte vowed perpetual celibacy.

[157]Deacon Patrick O'Flanagan was at Ontonagon. Baraga planned to ordain him so he could replace one of the two priests he would now dismiss for drinking.

Marquette where Mr. Duroc came to me on the boat. We remained there 8 hours.

Nov. 7:    At 3:30 P.M. we arrived in Hancock where I sent a letter to Ontonagon so as to have Mr. O'Flanagan come here; and I await him here in Hancock. Good reports about Mr. Sweeney.

Nov. 8:    I wrote many letters today against <u>McLaughlin</u> and <u>Konen</u>. // I am waiting for the "Iron City" and Mr. O'Flanagan.

Nov. 9:    ᴸXXII <u>Sunday</u> (after Pentecost),ᴸ 2nd [Sunday] of Nov[ember]. At 8 I offered holy mass at St. Ann's in Hancock, and at 10 preached in English and German. // In the afternoon Mr. Flanagan came down on the "Iron City". He wishes to be ordained in the Minnesota Mine church and I approved this reasonable request and shall also fulfill it.

Nov. 10:   Early this morning said mass in Hancock, and then set out on the way with Fr. Jacker[158] and Mr. O'Flanagan to Minnesota Mine. At 10 P.M. we reached the ᴱhalf-way-house,ᴱ and I was so tired and exhausted that I reached the house with great effort.[159]

Nov. 11:   At 6 A.M. we departed from the ᴱhalfway-houseᴱ and by 4:30 without special difficulty, reached Maple-grove, where I stayed overnight with O'Flanagan.

Nov. 12:   At 7 I said holy mass in the Maplegrove church, then went on slowly, and towards 11 reached Minnesota Mine. // In the afternoon we rode to Ontonagon where I lodged overnight with Mr. Schick.

Nov. 13–14:  Spent these two days with the good Sisters, in continuous reading.

Nov. 15:   In the afternoon I rode to Minnesota Mine, and stayed overnight with Fr. Fox.[160]

---

[158]"Jacker" inserted in pencil.

[159]Bishop Eis remembered this event well and wrote in the margin: "This memorable journey from Hancock to Minnesota Mine, now Rockland, is 40 miles. The Bishop was sick, the road bad and muddy and the weather cold and wet. The bishop was dragged along in the middle between the two companions, Rev. Jacker and P. M. O'Flanagan. They walked on foot all the way — 40 miles."

[160]Bishop Eis personally witnessed all these events and made a Diary notation: "<u>Saturday, P.M. 9 o'clock</u>. There was no meat nor bread in the house for next day's

Nov. 16: ᴸxxııı <u>Sunday</u> (after Pentecost),ᴸ 4th [Sunday] in Nov[ember] (3rd omitted)[161] Great festivity in the Minnesota church of St. Mary — pontifical mass and <u>ordination</u> of <u>Mr. P. M. O'Flanagan</u>. // In the evening I rode to Ontonagon Village and stayed overnight with the Sisters.

Nov. 17: Read all day, waiting for the "Mineral Rock".

Nov. 18: Finally this morning, at 7, the "Mineral Rock" arrived.

Nov. 19: In the afternoon I boarded the "Mineral Rock" where Capt[ain] McKay[162] received me very nicely and gave up his own room for me.[163]

---

big ordination dinner. So Rev. Fox had a calf about 4 months old, which he told a young Student, Frederick Eis, and another boy to kill that night. Next morning Rev. Fox went to a neighbor and begged bread — 2 loaves. Thus having plenty of meat and bread, some young ladies were called in after the Mass to cook, and there was a big feast. Bishop Baraga rose at three o'clock that Sunday morning, and with the assistance of student F. Eis, fixed a stool for the altar faldistorium to sit upon during the Ordination, and otherwise got things ready about the church. There were tacks but not a pin in the house. Only one bed which the bishop got. Rev. Jacker slept on the old lounge, Rev. Fox on the barn floor, leaning against the bedroom door. The Bishop opened the door from the inside and Rev. Fox rolled in upon him." A more detailed account is found in Rezek, ı, pp. 178–79.

[161] According to the *Ordo* of 1862, the "3rd Sunday of November" was omitted.

[162] John McKay was captain of the *Mineral Rock*. McKay was 40, his wife, Elisabeth, was 31. They had three children, George, 12, Elisabeth, 10 and John, 7. Federal Census, 1850, Chippewa County, #106. McKay befriended Fr. Chebul on his voyage from the Sault to Ontonagon in 1859 and also tended Baraga's needs: "When B. Baraga visited Bayfield and La Pointe for the last time he was very feeble, and his hands would tremble, being partly paralyzed. Father Chebul accompanied him on the boat on the return voyage to Marquette. McK. was captain of the boat. At dinner B. Baraga tried to eat a little soup, but his hand trembled so much that he spilt most of the soup before the spoon reached his mouth. Captain McK. saw this. 'Father Chebul,' says he, 'take my place at the head of the table!' Reluctantly F. Chebul obeyed, not knowing what the captain meant to do. Presently the captain went down to B. Baraga and, seating himself at his side, he fed the bishop with the spoon, holding the bishop's head with his other hand. This sight moved the passengers, especially the ladies, to tears, as the captain was otherwise a 'rough-spoken man.' They followed him out after dinner and thanked him in the name of humanity and Christianity for his kind act to Bishop Baraga." Verwyst, p. 314. His last command was the S. S. *Manistee*, which carried ore from Marquette to Duluth. The ship was lost between Marquette and Bayfield in November 1885. A note in a bottle found the following spring read: "Aboard the S.S. Manistee: A terrible storm. I think we are lost. Regards to all in this world." It was signed "John McKay, captain." Dr. Julian Wolff, Jr., of Duluth, called him the "dean of the Great Lakes skippers." Kitzman, p. 3.

[163] Bishop Eis observed: "This was the last boat of the season that year, to call at Ontonagon, and fortunately took the bishop to his home — the Sault."

Nov. 20:    Only this evening the "Mineral Rock" left Ontonagon and with great effort crossed the bar.[164]

Nov. 21:    At 7 A.M. we arrived in Eagle Harbor and remained lying there for 9 hours. In the evening we sailed and reached Copper Harbor during the night.

Nov. 22:    We remained lying all day in Copper Harbor because it was very stormy.

Nov. 23:    ᴸXXIV <u>Sunday</u> (after Pentecost),ᴸ 5th [Sunday] in Nov[ember]. At 8 A.M. we left Copper Harbor and at 4 P.M. arrived at Portage Lake. At 9 in the evening we left Portage Lake.

Nov. 24:    At 10 A.M. we arrived in Marquette and remained there all day, loading ᴱiron ore and pig iron.ᴱ In the evening we wanted to go on, but a storm arose and we remained in the bay at anchor.

Nov. 25:    All day laid at anchor, and the ship rolled very much which made me very sea sick.

Nov. 26:    We sailed early at 6 o'clock and in the night we came to Weshking Bay where we waited at anchor for the morning.

Nov. 27:    At 9 A.M. arrived at Sault where the saddest reports awaited me. <u>Gaess</u> has gone away to Minnesota, <u>Konen</u> has not yet come down from Lake Superior. Sault Sainte Marie remains all winter long without a priest.[165] // In the evening the "Traveler" came down, the <u>last boat</u>.

Nov. 28:    Early today the "Traveler" went down, the last boat. // Wrote various and many letters.[166]

---

[164]The combination of river flow and lake current regularly causes large sand bars to form rapidly at the mouth of the Ontonagon River.

[165]Bishop Eis added: "Then the Bishop had to do all the pastoral duties himself."

[166]Baraga caused great dissatisfaction among the parishioners at the Sault because Fr. McLaughlin seemed to be doing so well. Since McLaughlin came from Detroit, Baraga wrote to Lefevere: "You told me, when I saw you at Detroit last summer, that a certain Irish priest, by the name of Michael McLaughlin, was a hard drinker, and that you were obliged to send him away from Detroit on account of his drunkenness.

"I had the misfortune to receive that priest into my diocese, ~~by of his~~ and he behaved well for two or three months, but of late we perceived that he was drinking whisky again, secretly. As soon as I knew it, I dismissed him, not to let

Nov. 29:    Again wrote many letters which will go with the first over ᴱlandmailᴱ on Dec[ember] 1.¹⁶⁷

Nov. 30:    ᴸI Sunday in Advent.ᴸ First mass at 8, high mass at 10, at which I preached in English and French. // In the afternoon catechism and vespers.

Dec. 1:    It snows, but otherwise ᴱcalmᴱ and not very cold. Preparation for the trip tomorrow to St. Mary, Goulais Bay, ᶠif it is nice.ᶠ

Dec. 2:    At 6 A.M. we departed for Goulais Bay, ᶜhowever,ᶜ but as we came opposite Weshking Bay we found so much ice that we gave up the trip. I then went to visit old Okanishage, to induce him to accept holy baptism. He promised to come to the Sault for New Year to let himself be baptized. ᴵWe shall see.ᴵ

Dec. 3:    It snows quite a bit; otherwise calm and not so cold. // Regular wood hauling day. //

Dec. 4:    Read all day. // Caspar is very much dissatisfied, he

---

it come to a greater scandal. But some persons wondered, why I sent him away, and were even dissatisfied with me, not knowing that he was in a habit of getting intoxicated.

"I therefore request Your Lordship, to give me a written statement about that priest, that I may show it to whom it may concern." Baraga to Lefevere, Sault Ste. Marie, November 28, 1862. Orig. in NDUA; in BBC-A 179 E.

¹⁶⁷One letter was to Fr. Murray: "Your esteemed note of the 8th ult[imate] came to hand only the day before yesterday. I am glad to hear that you have been to Sheboygan; you are a very active priest indeed; but I am not glad to hear that you found things so in disorder. Well, dear Father Murray, it is not your fault; you certainly do what you can for Sheboygan; and you must promise me to continue to do so, because Mackinac is again without a priest, unfortunately, M̷r̷/C̷a̷s̷s̷ left Mackinac without my permission, which is a great sin for a priest. I sent immediately the sentence of Interdict after him, which no other can canonically s̷o̷l̷v̷ solve but I. He is gone to M̷i̷n̷n̷e̷s̷o̷t̷a̷/and I wrote to the Bishop o̷f̷ S̷t̷/ P̷a̷u̷l̷/that he cannot receive him, unless he despises the Holy Canons of the church of God, which that Bishop will never do.

"I don't tell you to go to Sheboygan this winter, it would be too laborious for you, but next spring I hope you will go. According to promise, I will furnish you means to finish that church inside.

"I am quite astonished to hear that you are making such improvements in your o̷w̷n̷ own church, with so limited mean! Building 32 pews! Ceiling the inside up to the windows! And all that without the help of your poor Bishop, who is now poor & infortunate indeed. — I am now all alone at the Saut; I was obliged to send away my priest, M̷i̷c̷h̷a̷e̷l̷ M̷c̷L̷a̷u̷g̷h̷l̷i̷n̷/for drinking whisky.

"God bless you, dear Father Murray, and conserve your health & courage." Baraga to Murray, Sault Ste. Marie, November 29, 1862. Orig. in BBC-A 367 E.

threatens to go away which I fear very much. // It is snowing; <sup>E</sup>calm.<sup>E</sup>

Dec. 5:  It snowed very much. // <sup>E</sup>Ryan[168] came in and told me things which fully satisfy me that I did right in dismissing McLaughlin.<sup>E</sup>

Dec. 6:  Read all day. Saturday; no confessions!

Dec. 7:  <sup>L</sup>II <u>Sunday</u> in Advent.<sup>L</sup> Performed everything. After the Stations of the Cross was a <sup>E</sup>meeting of the Altar Society.<sup>E</sup>

Dec. 8:  Immaculate Conception. Visited Mrs. Ryan on her sickbed. Otherwise read.

Dec. 9:  Toothache and swollen. Read all day. Mild.

Dec. 10:  Toothache and swollen, more than yesterday.

Dec. 11:  Toothache and swollen, from time to time considerably painful toothache. // Very mild weather, <sup>C</sup>slush.<sup>C</sup> <sup>F</sup>The edges of the rivers have disappeared.<sup>F</sup> Poor travelers, <sup>E</sup>mail carriers.<sup>E</sup>

Dec. 12:  A very nice day. Read. Joseph [Cadron] from Goulais Bay came here; I engaged him for the 29th of Dec[ember], to go with him on the 30th to Goulais Bay. Misère.

Dec. 13:  <sup>E</sup>Last night<sup>E</sup> it snowed heavily. No! It had rained, and it still rains. Very mild weather. The poor <sup>E</sup>mail-carriers!<sup>E</sup> // Saturday before III Sunday of Advent and not even one confession! // In 1856 there were 100 confessions, and on the following morning 70 communions.[169]

Dec. 14:  <sup>L</sup>III <u>Sunday</u> of Advent.<sup>L</sup> The pews were auctioned; very <sup>E</sup>low!<sup>E</sup> $272. Everything decreases in the Sault! // Rainy weather. // Only one <sup>E</sup>Indian<sup>E</sup> confession!

Dec. 15:  Very mild weather; the snow has almost entirely melted. // Bought a <u>barrel of apples</u> for $3.

---

[168]A parish trustee.
[169]This entry is evidence that Baraga occasionally re-read parts of his diary.

Dec. 16:     Wood hauling day, by convenience, because there was still much of the previous wood. // Rather cold. // Instructed old Mrs. Lacaille for first communion.

Dec. 17:     <sup>E</sup>Last night it was very cold.<sup>E</sup> // Nice weather, but cold.

Dec. 18:     <sup>E</sup>Carpet taken up and cleaned.<sup>E</sup> Fresh straw [placed] under the <sup>E</sup>carpet.<sup>E</sup>

Dec. 19:     <sup>E</sup>Last night very cold, and all day cold.<sup>E</sup>

Dec. 20:     Some few confessions. // In the evening the first <sup>E</sup>mail.<sup>E</sup>

Dec. 21:     <sup>L</sup>IV Sunday of Advent.<sup>L</sup> Auctioned the pews on the gallery.

Dec. 22–23:  Nothing special. Few confessions and few Christmas candles. Very nice weather and not at all cold. It does not want to snow, although we wish for snow.

Dec. 24:     <sup>L</sup>Vigil.<sup>L</sup> Many confessions all day long, but in the evening only up to 6 P.M. After supper 3 more came. // Very mild weather.

Dec. 25:     <sup>F</sup>Christmas.<sup>F</sup> Very many communions at the 6 o'clock mass, also rather many at the 8 o'clock mass, but none at the 10. // Very mild weather. All is thawing.

Dec. 26:     Very mild weather and no snow, <sup>E</sup>no sleighing yet.<sup>E</sup>

Dec. 27:     Still no second mail. // Very few confessions.

Dec. 28:     Sunday. Continuously mild weather and no snow. Joseph [Cadron] went to Garden River to Fr. Kohler.

Dec. 29:     Today it snows a little. // In the afternoon Fr. Kohler came up here to go tomorrow to Goulais Bay.[170]

Dec. 30:     We have very little snow, too little for good sleighing. // This morning Fr. Kohler left for Goulais Bay. // Mild weather, wind still.

Dec. 31:     Beautiful weather! The old 1862 makes a nice exit.

---

[170]Baraga gave no reason why Fr. Kohler went to Goulais Bay in his place.

The 32 anniversary of my arrival in America. — Misère! ——— Not even one single confession.

## 1863

Jan. 1:  New Year's Day. There were, contrary to all expectations, very many people in the church. // Still very mild and windstill weather.

Jan. 2:  For the last 3 or 4 nights my ear plugs so that I heard nothing, but in the morning it disappeared again; last night it came again, but it did not go away this morning. We shall see how long it will last. I H S

Jan. 3:  Extremely mild weather. The snow has all melted. No ice on the river.

Jan. 4:  Sunday. It rains heavily!! ᴱPoor travelers!ᴱ Thanks be to God I was not obliged to go to Goulais Bay. // My deafness continues.

Jan. 5:  Spent the entire day sadly in my deafness.

Jan. 6:  ᴸEpiphany of Our Lord. J[esus] C[hrist].ᴸ Snowstorms and rather cold, therefore few people in the church. // In the evening I heard well.

Jan. 7:  This morning I was deaf again. // It is rather cold. // Wood hauling day (23 days.)

Jan. 8:  Still deaf. I fear it will remain. ᴸMay your Will be done.ᴸ I H S

Jan. 9:  Last night the octave of my deafness ended. It did not last over 8 days. I now hear as well as before. Thanks be to God. I H S // Fr. Kohler returned from Goulais Bay. He baptized only 3 children, the others caused difficulties.

Jan. 10:  It snows considerably, but the snow is watery, because it is not at all cold. // Resisted boredom all day long by reading.

Jan. 11:  ᴸI Sunday after Epiphany.ᴸ Preached in English and French. // A beautiful day, somewhat cold. The river is not yet frozen.

Jan. 12:    It snows a little. Not very cold.

Jan. 13–14:    Stormy, windy, cold.

Jan. 15:    This morning it is very cold, but the river is not yet entirely frozen over. A very nice winter day.

Jan. 16:    Very cold. Now, finally St. Mary's River is frozen. However, I do not know if one can cross on it.

Jan. 17:    The coldest night St. Mary's River froze over solid so that one can drive over it with a horse.

Jan. 18:    ᴸII Sunday, after Epiphany.ᴸ Preached in English and French. // Nice weather, not very cold.

Jan. 19:    Mild weather; it snows a little, but much too little for our desires. // Preparation continues for the trip to St. Joseph.

Jan. 20:    Departure for St. Joseph Mission, Minisheing. Very mild weather.

Jan. 21–22–23:    In the small mission of St. Joseph I read mass every day at 7:30 and preached, and at 5:30 again said prayers and preached. // Heard confessions every morning.

Jan. 24:    Left at 9:30 and at 9 arrived in the Sault.

Jan. 25:    ᴸIII Sunday after Epiphany.ᴸ Preached in English and French. // Announced instructions for the first communion.

Jan. 26:    Continually mild weather; little snow; St. Mary's River is wide open in the middle. // Began ᶠcatechism for first communion.ᶠ

Jan. 27–28:    Caspar is sick. // Weather mild and calm.

Jan. 29:    Caspar is somewhat better. He got up. // At 10 A.M. I was called to sick Jane Teople[171] at Weshking Bay, I administered to her the 3 last sacraments, and remained there overnight.

[171]Jane Teople was 35, wife of the lighthouse keeper, Simon, who was 41. They had eight children. Federal Census, 1860, Chippewa County, #51.

Jan. 30:     This morning I again felt my deafness for a short time. I was too warm all night. At 1 P.M. I came home again.

Jan. 31:     This morning I was deaf. // Very stormy; blizzard with the little snow which is here. // Caspar is well again, thanks be to God.

Feb. 1:      Septuagesima <u>Sunday</u>. Preached in English and French; both good. I H S // Very cold and stormy.

Feb. 2:      I was deaf again this morning, but not for long, thanks be to God! Very stormy. It snows heavily, thanks be to God. // The river is again frozen over, although weak.

Feb. 3:      ᴱLast night was the coldest night of this winter. Cold all day.ᴱ

Feb. 4:      ᴱLast night was colder yet. Colder all day.ᴱ

Feb. 5:      Rather mild weather. // For several nights I am deaf each night, but in the morning towards 6 o'clock I hear again. <u>Wood hauling day</u>. // The ice is now very firm.

Feb. 6:      Mild weather; some snow. This morning I was not deaf. I H S

Feb. 7:      Milder than yesterday. Today we expect ᴱmail.ᴱ

Feb. 8:      <u>Sexagesima</u> Sunday. As usual. This morning the mail arrived. I received a letter from Paris, but still no check. (9000 francs)[172]

---

[172]Baraga received the check on the next day and immediately acknowledged this allotment: "Today I have had the honor to receive your esteemed letter of the last day of the past year through which I learn that the central councils have allotted to this Diocese of Ste. Marie the considerable sum of nine thousand francs for the year 1862.

"I thank the good Lord for it, (Who is kind to us through our benefactors, for it is He who inspires them to be kind to us,) and I thank the superiors and all the members of the Propagation of the Faith for this.

"Mr. Treasurer of the Propagation of the Faith tells me in his letter that if I have need of a small check he will have it sent immediately. But I prefer to wait and to receive together all that they should send me for 1862. While waiting I shall obtain credit with our merchants.

"The holy zeal of my benefactors for the propagating and the consolidating of the true faith in distant, even barbarous lands, gives me special consolation which I need very much this winter, because I am sometimes in distress. I am alone here at the Sault. I had an Irish priest with me, but he began to show an inclination for strong drink: and in order to avoid the scandal which could

| | |
|---|---|
| Feb. 9: | Caspar is sick again. Mr. Donovan performs the sacristan duties and often visits sick Caspar. |
| Feb. 10: | ditto |
| Feb. 11: | Very mild weather. Much snow. // Caspar is very sick. Wilson gave him a certain medicine which made him worse. |
| Feb. 12: | Today after mass I administered to Caspar the last sacraments, including Extreme Unction. |
| Feb. 13–14: | Caspar is still very sick. |
| Feb. 15: | Quinquagesima <u>Sunday</u>. Terribly windy, but otherwise not very cold. // Mr. Donovan often visits the sick. |
| Feb. 16: | For a long time last night Caspar hallucinated, 4 hours. // Mild weather. |
| Feb. 17–18–19: | Caspar is still sick and very weak. // Very mild weather. ᶜSlushy.ᶜ[173] |
| Feb. 20–21: | Caspar still sick. |
| Feb. 22: | ᴸI <u>Sunday</u> in Lent.ᴸ Very cold, otherwise clear weather. |
| Feb. 23: | Very cold morning. The day is nice and clear. |
| Feb. 24: | ˢSt. Matthew breaks the ice; if he does not find it, then he makes it . . . ˢ |

---

have occurred, I have dismissed him in the month of November last, several days before the end of navigation; and when there is no more navigation, then there is no more communication in this country. I have not been able to have another priest immediately; thus I find myself alone for all the functions of the holy ministry; I am reduced to the occupations of a simple priest for the entire winter. Aside from the inconvenience, this causes me a little misery at my age. The other day I was called to a sick person seven leagues from here, across the ice and snow, in a piercing cold.

"My congregation is mixed; I am obliged to preach every Sunday in English and in French; and in the afternoon I sing the vespers in Latin. In short, in my old age, I am no longer a bishop. I am a simple missionary once again. And the saddest thing is that I do not know when that will end for I do not know where I will find a priest for this place. I pray every day to the 'Master of the Vineyard' that he deign to send me a good laborer." Baraga to PFAP, Sault Ste. Marie, February 9, 1863. Orig. in PFAP; in BBC-A 482 F.

[173] Although no immediate results followed, Baraga began to solicit sisters for hospital ministry: "We wish very much to have some of your good Sisters of Charity for a large hospital at Portage Lake. The hospital is large indeed, but the patients are not very numerous, so that 3 or 4 Sisters would do for the present. Can we hope for some this spring? Please answer immediately." Baraga to Lefevere, Sault Ste. Marie, February 19, 1863. Orig. in NDUA; in BBC-A 181 E.

Feb. 25–26–27:     Caspar convalesces very slowly.

Feb. 28:     Caspar is now well. I H S Thanks be to God. // Mild weather.[174]

March 1:     ᴸɪɪ Sunday in Lent.ᴸ All as usual.

March 2:     Nice weather. Wood hauling day.

March 3–4–5:     Cold. By night, very cold.

March 6–7:     ditto. Very stormy. Caspar is well again, ᴸhoweverᴸ but weak.

March 8:     ᴸɪɪɪ Sunday in Lent.ᴸ 9 First communions. Misère! 13 confirmations.

March 9:     Very stormy and cold. A real March day — cold, windy, sunny.

March 10–11:     Stormy, blizzard. A real March day etc.

March 12–13–14:     Nothing special. The weather has become somewhat milder.

March 15:     ᴸɪᴠ Sunday in Lent.ᴸ As usual.

March 16–17–18:     Mild weather. The people are moving to the sugarbush.[175]

March 19–20–21:     Mild weather, sugar time. Few confessions. I am afraid that this year more than half will not make their Easter confessions.

---

[174]In a letter on this day Baraga explained some economic consequences of the Civil War: "You know, without doubt, that because of our unfortunate Civil War, the finances of the United States have come into a deplorable state. Our banknotes, without exception, have lost so much in value that a dollar is worth only 50 cents instead of 100; but a gold dollar is worth 100 cents. I believe that you now have an agent in New York, through whom you are sending us our respective allotments. If this agent pays our allotments in banknotes, we shall lose half; but I believe that he ought to pay in gold, because the checks that you send from Paris are valued in gold. I beg you to instruct me on the disagreeable matter; and to instruct also, if it is necessary, your agent at New York." Baraga to PFAP, Sault Ste. Marie, February 28, 1863. Orig. in PFAP; in BBC-A 472 F.

[175]The sugarbush or sugar camp was the location where maple syrup was gathered and processed into sugar, an essential part of Chippewa diet. Entire families went into the sugarbush.

| | |
|---|---|
| March 22: | ᴸPassion Sunday.ᴸ All as usual. Many people have already moved to the sugar huts. |
| March 23–24: | Nothing special. March has little that is special. |
| March 25: | ᴸAnnunciation of the Blessed Virgin Mary.ᴸ There were but few people in the church. I preached only in French. |
| March 26–27: | Again nothing special. Weather unpleasant; not very cold. |
| March 28: | Very stormy, blizzard, cold. |
| March 29: | ᴸPalm Sunday.ᴸ Blessing of palms, otherwise as usual. Only 3 holy communions the entire day! Last night was the coldest night of the winter, in my opinion. |
| March 30: | A nice day, mild weather. Wood hauling day. |
| March 31: | This morning it is very cold. March is making a cold exit. Afternoon, sunny, windy, cold — March. |
| April 1: | A very mild day; it snows all day long. // Rather many confessions. |
| April 2: | ᴱLast nightᴱ we had the strongest wind of this entire winter = the March moon is still with us, that is it. // Holy Thursday. I had to do the blessing of holy oils entirely by myself.[176] |
| April 3–4: | Performed all the ceremonies. Heard some confessions. How few Easter confessions and communions this year! |
| April 5: | Easter Sunday. The church was full; I delivered to them a generally useful sermon, but will it do any good? // A nice, mild, windstill day. |
| April 6: | Today I began to say week-day mass in the church. |
| April 7: | Fr. Kohler came up and stayed with us overnight. // Nice, clear, still weather. |
| April 8–9: | Wrote letters, made rosaries, read. // Nice weather, not very windy. |

---

[176]Bishop Eis commented: "Sad."

| | |
|---|---|
| April 10: | Today it rains; poor pedestrians! // Nice weather in the afternoon. |
| April 11: | Mild, still weather. On Easter Sunday there was little wind, and therefore, until Ascension day, there will not be much wind. |
| April 12: | ᴸLow Sunday.ᴸ Noteworthy! Sadly noteworthy! Low Sunday and not a single communion! This has certainly not occurred today in any other place in this diocese (or in other dioceses) where a priest resides. |
| April 13–14: | Nice and quiet weather. // Made small boxes for sending the holy oils to the missionaries. |
| April 15: | A splendid, still, warm day. — In the evening; thanks be to God, another day of boredom passed. |
| April 16–17: | Prepared the holy oils for shipment, and wrote letters to the priests that I will not come. // The weather is unusually nice. // The 2 stoves were taken out of the church. |
| April 18: | The weather is still unusually nice. // Some children's confessions. |
| April 19: | ᴸII Sunday after Easter.ᴸ As usual. There were very few people in the church. // The weather is uncommonly nice. |
| April 20: | Gloomy all day. / Now boredom also through the 20th. |
| April 21–22: | Continually nice weather. A splendid spring! Ice and snow all gone. The boats could have come a few days ago if they had known what we now know. (ᶜSlushyᶜ Muddy Lake.)[177] |
| April 23–24: | Caspar is making me a new cassock. NB. A few weeks ago he made me a new coat and two pants. (NB. From the cassock material enough is left for two more cassocks.) |
| April 25: | An uncommonly nice, mild, quiet day. |

[177]There were probably pools of water everywhere.

April 26: Lɪɪɪ Sunday after Easter.L There were very few people in the church, although the weather was very nice.

April 27: Warm, as in summer. I do not know why no boat comes.

April 28: Finally, today at 8 A.M. the "Mineral Rock" arrived; Capt[ain] McKay. And soon after that the small "Backus". The two holy oil boxes for Rev. Duroc and Jacker, etc., I gave to the Catholic Capt[ain] McKay. // At 4 P.M. also the "Cleveland", and at 5 the "Planet" arrived.

April 29–30: Splendid weather! A thoroughly nice April has a nice end, which is rare.

May 1–2: Fine weather! May is making a nice beginning. // Mrs. Lavigne keeps the Month of May.

May 3: Lɪv Sunday after Easter.L All as usual. // Cool weather. In the evening it snowed a little.

May 4–5: Cloudy weather, especially in the morning = April was nicer. / Received 100 portraits.

May 6–7: Today the "Backus" went down. I should make a note of the boats going and coming.

May 8: This morning the "Iron City" went up. // Splendid weather. "Northern Light" came up this morning.

May 9: The old "Michigan" came down today, and the "City of Cleveland". William Donovan went down on the "Michigan". // "Plowboy" came up here for the first time.

May 10: Lv Sunday after Easter.L As usual. There were very few people in the church because there was a little prospect of rain.

May 11: Small preparation for departure to Goulais Bay.

May 12: Departure for Goulais Bay, at 7 A.M. At first, no wind, and later a contrary wind. We arrived there only at 6 P.M.

May 13: All day arranged the altar. — In the evening there were many confessions.

May 14:      ᴸAscension of Our Lord Jesus Christ.ᴸ Many communions at the holy mass. There were no men in the church, all are out hunting.

May 15:      Return trip from 8 A.M. to 5 P.M.

May 16:      Rain and a strong wind. Thank God I am home. Wrote letters all day. // Rather many confessions.

May 17:      ᴸVI Sunday after Easter.ᴸ Preached in French and English, as usual.

May 18:      Small preparations for St. Joseph, Sugar Island.

May 19:      Departure for the small mission of St. Joseph, where I arrive at 1 P.M.

May 20:      Gave morning and evening instructions. At 2 P.M. Fr. Jacker came to me, to my great satisfaction.[178]

May 21:      Today Fr. Jacker returned to the Sault, and at noon went home on the "Seabird".

May 22:      At 1 P.M. I came home again and found Caspar sick.

May 23:      Caspar very sick, especially after he had taken a mercury medicine.

May 24:      Pentecost Sunday. Sad Pentecost! Caspar sick, and the boys who serve in the church clumsy.

May 25–26:   Caspar is still sick. Very unpleasant. Jim Prior covers the roof of the refectory, etc.

May 27:      Caspar is very sick. He again threatened to leave, even to desert.

May 28–
29–30:       Caspar is somewhat better, but very weak; he does nothing as of yet. Otherwise the old Trallalla.[179]

---

[178]About this visit Fr. Jacker wrote: "I had to seek him at the little church of Jesus the Friend of Children, he had built for the Indians on Sugar Island, 12 miles from the 'Soo.' He was giving them a week's mission, and I found him alone in the little sacristy. 'You must be hungry.' So indeed I was and sat down; but I was afraid to 'pitch in' at my stomach's (the Canadians say so for 'heart', even Fr. Lacombe in his Cree Dictionary) desire, for all that was left to him for two or three more days' provisions, were 1 loaf of bread, about ¾ pounds of cheese and a half bowl of sugar, with which he made — without any other ingredients — his morning's coffee, his dinner broth and his evening tea, i. e. when on mission. I did not stay long." Jacker to Finotti, Sault Ste. Marie, June 28, 1875. EJP; in BBC-AR 13, p. 89. Jacker was mistaken about the name of the mission.
[179]I.e., humdrum.

May 31: <u>L Holy Trinity Sunday</u>.L As usual. // Rev. Fr. O'Flanagan arrived at 6 A.M., said the first mass, and in the afternoon returned again to Eagle Harbor.

June 1: I am waiting for a boat to Detroit, to Agent Leach. // It is raining a little, thanks be to God! Otherwise cool. // Bought 13 pounds of cheese.

June 2: I am still waiting for a boat. // Nice weather, but very windy and cool.

June 3: Finally the "Traveler" came down here, but it is too late; tomorrow is a great feast day.

June 4: <u>Corpus Christi</u>. Very few people were in church, as usual for feast days. // After the meal, I carried the holy Eucharist to old Bagage. // After vespers I wanted to leave for Detroit but I missed the boat.

June 5–6: Cool weather, so that I must always keep up the fire. // Undecided whether I should go to Detroit or not. — Yes, if I would only know.

June 7: <u>L II Sunday after Pentecost</u>.L Today there were many people in the church. Preached in English and French. // Caspar feels weak and tired. If he only would not get sick again.

June 8: Caspar is better. // I keep waiting for a boat for Detroit. // A very nice calm day.

June 9: Still no boat for Detroit. The "Planet" is E over-due.E [180]

June 10: Finally the "Planet" came, at 8 P.M. and I embarked for Detroit.

June 11: Arrived in Detroit at 6 P.M. The agent was not there.[181]

---

[180]Baraga was also planning to visit some of the missions. On this date he informed Fr. Terhorst that he would be delayed a week in coming to L'Anse. Baraga to Terhorst, Sault Ste. Marie, June 9, 1863. Orig. in NDUA; in BBC-A 182 E.

[181]Before he left Detroit Baraga prepared a message for Agent Leach: "I came down yesterday on purpose to see you, but you were not in town, and I intend again to return again to the Saut tomorrow — I therefore write these few lines, to tell you what I came for. I wish to make a change with two of our schoolteachers. Mr. Montferrand who is now at L'anse, Lake Superior, wishes very much to come to the Saut as teacher because he is a Frenchman, and most of the inhabitants of the Saut are French or half French, they wish to have him for their school. And Mr. Donovan, who is our teacher at the Saut, is willing to take the Anse school. So all parties will be satisfied. But I would do nothing without telling you.

June 12–13:   The "Planet" was announced for today, but it did not leave, thank God!

June 14:   ᴸIII Sunday after Pentecost.ᴸ Said mass at 6:30 at the Sacred Heart.[182]

June 15:   Noteworthy day! = received permission from the agent for Donovan. From the Rector of the Redemptorists received $30 for masses. Accepted Mr. Michael Heuss.[183] Received hope for Mr. Andre,[184] and Rev. August Durst![185] ——— at midnight sailed from Detroit.

June 16:   Spent the entire day on the boat reading. // Quiet weather.

June 17:   At 2 P.M. arrived at the Sault.

June 18:   Read all day. // 2 unnecessary ᴱsick-callsᴱ = three year old girl of Grinneau, and Mrs. Lalonde.

June 19:   At 11 A.M. Mr. Peter Andrè arrived. He seems to be a serious and zealous man. I H S

June 20:   Rather a cool morning. A bit rainy.

June 21:   ᴸIV Sunday after Pentecost.ᴸ Preached twice, etc., as usual. // Cool, or rather cold.

June 22:   Waiting for a boat to sail to Portage Lake. / Cold and gloomy weather. // ᴱParis checkᴱ of 8385 francs.[186]

---

"I hope, Mr. Leach, you will have no objection against that change. Mr. Donovan is a very good man; Mr. Smith knows him well. He also solemnly promised to me, never to vote against the republican party. Mr. Montferrand will tender his resignation at the end of the second quarter and on the first of July Mr. Donovan will commence keeping school at L'Anse." Baraga to Leach, Detroit, June 12, 1863. Orig. in NA-OIA; In BBC-A 634 E.

[182]The Academy of the Sacred Heart for young ladies was then located between Beaubien and St. Antoine Streets on Jefferson Avenue, Detroit.

[183]Michael Heuss came to the diocese for a short time.

[184]Peter Andrè began his priestly career at St. Joseph (German) Parish in Detroit. He was in the Marquette diocese from June 15, 1863, to April 21, 1864. BLS. Andrè returned to Detroit where he served until his death on May 19, 1902.

[185]August Durst went to the Milwaukee diocese. His last known assignment was at St. Naziancz, Wisconsin, in 1909.

[186]In his acknowledgement Baraga wrote: "I still work alone; I have no priest with me here at the Sault. I hope, however, to have one in the month of September, if the good Lord wills it." Baraga to PFAP, Sault Ste. Marie, June 30, 1863. Orig. in PFAP; in BBC-A 506 F.

| | |
|---|---|
| June 23: | At 3 P.M. sailed on the slow "Illinois". |
| June 24: | At 6 A.M. arrived in Marquette. |
| June 25: | At 8 P.M. arrived in Hancock. I returned to the boat for the night. |
| June 26: | Said mass at L'Anse, and engaged Montferrand for the Sault . . . Misère! . . . |
| June 27: | Said mass at Hancock, and then on the "Illinois" again. |
| June 28: | ᴸV Sunday after Pentecost.ᴸ Arrived at the Sault at 5 P.M. |
| June 29: | My 66th birthday . . . . . I H S . . . It is raining a little, thanks be to God.[187] |
| June 30: | Fr. Sweeney came down here on his way to Canada. // It rains somewhat but too little. |
| July 1: | Received a letter from Fr. Durst, that on next Saturday, July 4, he will come for a visit. |
| July 2: | The school teacher Donovan goes today to the L'Anse. Gloomy, rainy day, rather cool. |
| July 3: | All this somewhat rainy day arranged and put in order the priest's room. |
| July 4: | Day of general sinning and misfortune for these un-United States. |
| July 5: | ᴸVI Sunday after Pentecost.ᴸ As usual. Stations of the Cross. Meeting of the Altar Society. Mr. Michael Heuss taught catechism. |
| July 6: | Nothing special. Very warm; no rain which we wish for very much. |

[187]Baraga wrote a supportive letter to Fr. Murray: "I am glad to hear that you have become a 'Justice of the Peace', and I hope you will do good again in that station, as you do everywhere. I am sorry for the ill treatment you met with at Detroit. Such an advocate of temperance as you are, to be called a 'toper' and 'drunkard'. That is a most glaring injustice. I wrote a sharp letter on that to Rev. Peters." Baraga to Murray, Sault Ste. Marie, June 29, 1863. Orig. in BBC-A 365 E.

July 7:     Montferrand has finally arrived. Donovan reached L'Anse before Montferrand left.

July 8:     Montferrand adjusts himself, and tomorrow he begins, I fear, his poor school.

July 9:     The school is very pitiful. I do not know how it will be in the coming weeks.

July 10:    Bought a whole cheese, 59 pounds. I will see how long it will last. // Fr. Fox stopped in with Mother Mary Magdalen <u>Stehlin</u> on his way to Canada.

July 11:    Gloomy weather. // Told Montferrand that he should divide the pupils into classes.

July 12:    ᴸVII <u>Sunday</u> (after Pentecost).ᴸ Preached twice, as usual. // In the morning it was so cold that I had to make a fire. In the afternoon warm, in the evening, very warm.

July 13:    Montferrand came with the very unpleasant report that because of his headache he can no longer keep school. Misère! Mr. Heuss keeps school meanwhile. / Fr. Kohler came.

July 14:    Waiting for the "Michigan". <u>Fr. Kohler</u> was here again. Cool, almost cold.

July 15:    "Michigan" not yet here this morning. // Cold! ᴱTo the shame of July I made a fire in my stove this morning.ᴱ // ᶠDispute between Lavigne and Mrs. Tardif.ᶠ

July 16:    ᴸWaiting for a steamboat.ᴸ // Very cool, yes, cold. This morning I made a fire in the stove, ᴱin spite of July.ᴱ

## Addendum

At the end of the third volume of the Diary, written upside down on the rear flyleaf, was the following expense account:

| 1863. | | |
|---|---|---|
| March 2 | Cassock - - - - | 9,00. |
| Apr. 1 | ᴱfour shirtsᴱ - | 5,00. |
| " 18 | ᴱVestcoatᴱ - - - | 2,50. |
| " 25 | ᴱbootsᴱ - - - | 6,50. |
| June 18 | ᴱshoesᴱ - - - | 1,25. |
| | Hat brush - - - | 50. |
| July 6 | Cloth and lining for pants | 4,00. |
| Aug. 27 | 2 pants - - | 13,00. |
| | Washing, 1 year - | 12,00. |
| | Books - - - - - - | 7,47. |
| 27 Aug. | Journey to Ont. | 10,00. |
| | do.    do. | 10,25. |
| | Cinc. Razor - - | 1,25. |
| 6 Nov. | 2 silk handkerchiefs | 1,00. |
| 23 Nov. | sent to Detr. | 13,00. |
| do. | 1 ᴱshirtᴱ - - - | 1,00. |
| Dec. 5 | ᴱPilot-clothᴱ - - - | 11,00. |
| Dec. | Mrs. Edwards, etc. . . | 3,00. |
| | #Sickness# | |
| do. | Cassock buttons | 1,35. |
| Dec. 22 | John Peck - - - | 5,00. |
| 1864, Jan. | ᴱSickness. Mrs. Edw.ᴱ | 4,00. |
| Jan. 22 | ᴱPantsᴱ - - - - - | 9,00. |
| March 30 | New boots       $6,50 | 7,50. |
| | Old repaired | 1,00. |
| Apr. 12 | Cassock repaired - | 2,00. |
| " 28 | ½ yrd, velvet for a vestcoat | 2,00. |

# APPENDIX A
## GUIDE TO PLACE NAMES

Many of the places that are significant in the life of Bishop Frederic Baraga or that he named in the Diary have had two or more names. The following list cites the current place name, with the earliest to the most contemporary name for it listed below. Occasionally a listing is given because that is the way Baraga spelled the name in the Diary.

*LOWER MICHIGAN*

*Burt Lake* (West shore)
Chaboigan
Shaboigan
Sheboigan
Sheboygan

*Cheboygan*
Duncan
Sheboygan

*Cross Village*
La Croix

*Good Hart*
Abitawaiing
Middle Village

*UPPER MICHIGAN*

*Assinins*
L'Anse

*Clifton*
Cliff Mine

*Escanaba*
Bay des Noques
Bay de Noc

*Houghton*
Portage Lake

*Rockland*
Minnesota Mine

LOWER MICHIGAN (Cont.)

*Harbor Springs*
L'Arbre Croche
Little Traverse

*Peshabestown*
Grand Traverse
Pishabetown
Eagletown

*Petosky*
Agaming
Bear River

UPPER MICHIGAN (Cont.)

*Sugar Island*
St. Joseph Mission
Minisheing
Indian Reserve

# APPENDIX B
## BARAGA'S TRAVELS DURING THE DIARY YEARS

| 1852 | Lake Superior | Journeys | Lower Michigan |
|---|---|---|---|
| June 27 | L'Anse | | |
| July 10–11 | Keweenaw Area Quincy Mine | | |
| July 12 | L'Anse | | |
| September 7–22 | Ontonagon Area | | |
| September 23 | L'Anse | | |
| October 6–22 | Keweenaw Area | | |
| October 20 | Eagle Harbor | | |
| October 23 | L'Anse | | |
| **1853** | | | |
| January 7–26 | Ontonagon Area | | |
| January 11 | Ontonagon Village | | |
| January 27 | En route | | |
| January 28–February 16 | Keeweenaw Area | | |
| February 17–March 2 | L'Anse | | |
| March 2 | En route | | |
| March 6 | | Bay des Noques | |
| March 9 | | Near Green Bay | |
| March 11–16 | | Milwaukee | |

303

| 1853 | *Lake Superior* | *Journeys* | *Lower Michigan* |
|---|---|---|---|
| March 17–28 | | Detroit | |
| March 28 | | Sandusky, Ohio | |
| March 29–July 26 | | Cincinnati | |
| July 27–August 2 | | Detroit | |
| August 2–4 | En route | | |
| August 4 | | Sault Ste. Marie | |
| August 5–7 | En route | | |
| August 7–9 | Eagle Harbor | | |
| August 9–11 | L'Anse | | |
| August 12– | | | |
| September 26 | Keweenaw Area | | |
| | Ontonagon Area | | |
| September 29– | | | |
| October 3 | L'Anse | | |
| October 3–9 | En route | | |
| October 6 | Probably in Eagle Harbor | | |
| October 9–12 | Sault Ste. Marie | | |
| October 12–13 | En route | | |
| October 13–25 | | Detroit | |
| October 26– | | | |
| November 14 | | Cincinnati | |
| November 10 | | Stonelick, Ohio | |
| November 14–21 | | En route | |
| November 21–26 | | New York | |

### Journey to Europe

| November 26– | | | |
|---|---|---|---|
| December 7 | | En route | |
| December 7 | | Liverpool | |
| December 8–20 | | Dublin | |
| December 22– | | | |
| January 3 | | Paris | |

### 1854

| January 3 | | Via Brussels to Malines | |
|---|---|---|---|
| January 3–5 | | Malines | |
| January 5 | | Via Louvain & Aachen to Cologne | |
| January 6 | | Via Dusseldorf to Cassel | |

| *1854* | *Lake Superior* | *Journeys* | *Lower Michigan* |
|---|---|---|---|
| January 7–8 | | Cassel | |
| January 8–10 | | Via Darmstadt, Bruchsal, Stuttgart, Ulm & Augsburg to Munich | |
| January 10–16 | | Munich | |
| January 17 | | Alt-Otting, Bavaria | |
| January 18 | | Linz | |
| January 19 | | Munich | |
| January 20–27 | | En route | |
| January 27–29 | | Ljubljana | |
| January 30–31 | | Trebnje | |
| February 1 | | Dobernic | |
| February 2 | | Trebnje | |
| February 5 | | Metlika | |
| February 12 | | Smartno | |
| February 14 | | Via Trieste to Ancona, Italy | |
| February 17 | | Loretto, Italy | |
| February 21–March 8 | | Rome | |
| March 8 | | Via Bologna, Florence, Padua & Venice to Trieste | |
| March 16 | | Ljubljana | |
| March 19 | | Loka | |
| March 25–28 | | Ljubljana | |
| March 28 | | Celje | |
| March 31–April 3 | | Graz | |
| April 4–27 | | Vienna | |

### Return to Sault Ste. Marie

| | | | |
|---|---|---|---|
| April 28 | | Linz | |
| April 29–May 3 | | Munich | |
| May 3 | | Augsburg | |
| May 5–20 | | Paris | |
| May 20–21 | | Via Brussels & Malines to Antwerp | |
| May 21–24 | | Antwerp | |

| 1854 | Lake Superior | Journeys | Lower Michigan |
|---|---|---|---|
| May 24 | | Via London to Liverpool | |
| May 24–27 | | Liverpool | |
| May 27–June 6 | | Via Liverpool to Halifax | |
| June 6 | | Halifax | |
| June 6–9 | | Via Boston to New York | |
| June 9–12 | | New York | |
| June 12–14 | | Washington, D.C. (Georgetown) | |
| June 14–July 31 | | New York | |
| August 2–10 | | Detroit | |
| August 11 | | | Mackinac |
| August 14–15 | | | Cross Village |
| August 16–17 | | | Little Traverse |
| August 18–19 | | | Chaboigan |
| August 20 | | | Mackinac |
| August 21–25 | Sault Ste. Marie | | |

### Episcopal Visitations to the Missions

| | | | |
|---|---|---|---|
| August 25–27 | En route | | |
| August 27– September 3 | La Pointe | | |
| September 4–18 | Ontonagon | | |
| September 18–22 | Sault Ste. Marie | | |
| September 22–25 | En route | | |
| September 25– October 6 | L'Anse | | |
| October 7– November 17 | Sault Ste. Marie | | |
| November 18– December 13 | | | Mackinac |
| December 13 | | | St. Ignace |
| December 14– February 10 | | | Mackinac |

### 1855

| | | | |
|---|---|---|---|
| February 10–11 | | | St. Ignace |
| February 12– March 10 | | | Mackinac |
| March 10–11 | | | St. Ignace |

| 1855 | Lake Superior | Journeys | Lower Michigan |
|---|---|---|---|
| March 12–<br>April 30 | (March 18 Bois<br>Blanc Island) | | Mackinac |
| April 30–May 2 | | En route | |
| May 2 | | Detroit | |
| May 4–June 20 | | Cincinnati | |
| June 20–23 | | Via Sandusky &<br>Detroit to Sault | |
| June 24–26 | Sault Ste. Marie | | |
| June 26 | | | Mackinac |
| June 28 | | | Cross Village |
| June 29–July 2 | | | Little Traverse |
| July 3–4 | | | Chaboigan |
| July 5 | | | Little Traverse |
| July 6–8 | | | Middle Village |
| July 9 | | | Cross Village |
| July 10–14 | | | Beaver Island |
| July 15 | | | Cross Village |
| July 16 | | | Mackinac |
| July 18 | | | Northport |
| July 19–23 | | | Pishabetown |
| July 24–29 | | | Mackinac |
| July 30–August 9 | Sault Ste. Marie | | |
| August 9–11 | Via Marquette &<br>Eagle River to<br>Eagle Harbor | | |
| August 12 | Eagle Harbor | | |
| August 14–16 | L'Anse | | |
| August 17 | Eagle River | | |
| August 18 | En route | | |
| August 19–<br>September 4 | La Pointe | | |
| September 4 | Ontonagon | | |
| September 5 | Eagle River | | |
| September 6–10 | L'Anse | | |
| September 11–16 | Eagle Harbor | | |
| September 17–<br>October 12 | Sault Ste. Marie | | |
| October 12–15 | Marquette | | |
| October 15–<br>November 9 | Sault Ste. Marie | | |
| November 10–14 | | | Mackinac |
| November 14–26 | | | St. Ignace |

| 1855 | Lake Superior | Journeys | Lower Michigan |
|---|---|---|---|
| November 26–27 | | | St. Helens Island |
| November 28–<br>December 31 | | | Little Traverse |
| **1856** | | | |
| January 1–7 | | | Chaboigan |
| January 8–21 | | | Little Traverse |
| January 21–27 | | | Cross Village |
| January 28–29 | | | St. Ignace |
| January 30–31 | En route | | |
| February 1–May 9 | Sault Ste. Marie | | |
| May 10–13 | | Detroit | |
| May 14–24 | | Cincinnati | |
| May 25–26 | | Detroit | |
| May 27–June 11 | | Cincinnati | |
| June 12 | | Detroit | |
| June 13 | En route | | |
| June 14–26 | Sault Ste. Marie | | |
| June 27–July 6 | Ontonagon | | |
| July 8 | La Pointe | | |
| July 9 | Superior | | |
| July 10 | Grand Portage | | |
| July 11–14 | Fort William | | |
| July 15–21 | Grand Portage | | |
| July 21–24 | En route (by canoe) | | |
| July 24–28 | Superior | | |
| July 29–August 7 | La Pointe | | |
| August 7–12 | Ontonagon | | |
| August 13–19 | Minnesota Mine | | |
| August 20–24 | Norwich Mine | | |
| August 25–28 | Ontonagon | | |
| August 29–<br>September 4 | Sault Ste. Marie | | |
| September 5–8 | Eagle Harbor | | |
| September 8 | Fulton Mine | | |
| September 10–15 | L'Anse | | |
| September 16–22 | Cliff Mine | | |
| September 22–24 | Eagle Harbor | | |
| September 25–<br>January 12 | Sault Ste. Marie | | |

| 1857 | Lake Superior | Journeys | Lower Michigan |
|---|---|---|---|
| January 12–15 | En route | | |
| January 15–19 | | | Mackinac |
| January 19 | | | St. Ignace |
| January 19–23 | En route | | |
| January 23–<br>February 2 | Sault Ste. Marie | | |
| February 2 | Garden River | | |
| February 3–4 | Payment's (Sugar<br>Island)/Garden<br>River | | |
| February 4–<br>May 26 | Sault Ste. Marie | | |
| May 26–28 | | | Mackinac |
| May 28–31 | | | St. Ignace |
| June 1–4 | | | Cross Village |
| June 4–8 | | | Garden Island |
| June 8–12 | | | Cross Village |
| June 12–14 | | | Middle Village |
| June 15–16 | | | Little Traverse |
| June 17–21 | | | Grand Traverse |
| June 22 | | | Little Traverse |
| June 23–25 | | | Chaboigan |
| June 26–29 | | | Little Traverse |
| June 29–July 1 | | | Middle Village/<br>Cross Village |
| July 2 | | | Mackinac |
| July 4–14 | | Detroit | |
| July 15–20 | Sault Ste. Marie | | |
| July 21 | Marquette | | |
| July 22 | Superior | | |
| July 23–27 | La Pointe | | |
| July 28–August 3 | Ontonagon | | |
| August 4–8 | Eagle Harbor | | |
| August 8–12 | Marquette | | |
| August 13–<br>February 12 | Sault Ste. Marie | | |

**1858**

| | | | |
|---|---|---|---|
| February 12 | | Bruce Mine | |
| February 13–14 | | Missisagi | |

| 1858 | Lake Superior | Journeys | Lower Michigan |
|---|---|---|---|
| February 15 | | La Cloche | |
| February 16 | | Jibaonaning | |
| February 17 | | French River | |
| February 18–19 | | En route | |
| February 20–22 | | Pinatangishing | |
| February 22 | | Barrie | |
| February 23 | | Via Toronto to Niagara Falls | |
| February 24 | | Buffalo | |
| February 25– April 19 | | Cincinnati | |
| April 20–25 | | Covington | |
| April 26–May 15 | | Cincinnati | |
| May 16–18 | | Gallipolis and Pomeroy, Ohio | |
| May 19–25 | | Cincinnati | |
| May 26–28 | | Detroit | |
| May 29–June 7 | Sault Ste. Marie | | |
| June 7 | | | Mackinac |
| June 8–13 | | | Cross Village |
| June 14–17 | | | Garden Island |
| June 18–21 | | | Middle Village |
| June 21–22 | | | Little Traverse |
| June 22–25 | | | Sheboygan |
| June 25–27 | | | Little Traverse |
| June 28 | | | Agaming |
| June 29 | | En route | |
| June 30–July 5 | | | Eagletown |
| July 5–11 | | | Northport |
| July 11 | | | Cat-head |
| July 12–14 | | | Mackinac and St. Ignace |
| July 14–18 | | | Mackinac |
| July 19–29 | Sault Ste. Marie | | |
| July 29–August 1 | Ontonagon | | |
| August 3–13 | La Pointe | | |
| August 13–24 | Superior | | |
| August 26– September 1 | Sault Ste. Marie | | |
| September 1–3 | L'Anse | | |
| September 3–6 | Portage Lake | | |
| September 6–13 | L'Anse | | |
| September 14–19 | Ontonagon | | |
| September 20–28 | Minnesota Mine | | |

| *1858* | *Lake Superior* | *Journeys* | *Lower Michigan* |
|---|---|---|---|
| September 28– | | | |
| October 3 | Maple Grove | | |
| October 4 | Ontonagon | | |
| October 5–15 | Eagle Harbor | | |
| October 15–18 | Eagle River/Cliff Mine | | |
| October 18 | Eagle Harbor | | |
| October 19 | Ontonagon | | |
| October 20 | Marquette | | |
| October 21– | | | |
| May 15 | Sault Ste. Marie | | |
| | | | |
| *1859* | | | |
| | | | |
| May 15 | | | Mackinac |
| May 17 | | | St. Ignace |
| May 19 | | | Cross Village |
| May 20–26 | | | Garden Island |
| May 26–31 | | | Cross Village |
| May 31–June 3 | | | Middle Village |
| June 3–6 | | | Little Traverse |
| June 6 | | | Sheboygan |
| June 7 | | | Little Traverse |
| June 8–9 | | | Bear River |
| June 9–13 | | | Grand Traverse |
| June 13 | | | Green River |
| June 14–15 | | | Cross Village |
| June 15 | | | Mackinac |
| June 16 | En route | | |
| June 17–29 | Sault Ste. Marie | | |
| June 29 | En route | | |
| June 30–July 1 | Portage Entry | | |
| July 2–4 | L'Anse | | |
| July 5 | Eagle Harbor | | |
| July 6 | Copper Harbor | | |
| July 7–9 | Eagle Harbor | | |
| July 9–11 | Cliff Mine | | |
| July 11–18 | Eagle Harbor | | |
| July 18–20 | Ontonagon | | |
| July 21–29 | Marquette/ Negaunee | | |
| July 29–August 3 | Portage Lake | | |
| August 4–9 | Sault Ste. Marie | | |
| August 9–13 | | | Mackinac |

| *1859* | *Lake Superior* | *Journeys* | *Lower Michigan* |
|---|---|---|---|
| August 14–19 | Sault Ste. Marie | | |
| August 20–22 | Marquette | | |
| August 23–30 | La Pointe | | |
| August 30 | Ontonagon | | |
| August 31–<br>   September 5 | Minnesota Mine | | |
| September 5–6 | Ontonagon | | |
| September 8–23 | Sault Ste. Marie | | |
| September 23–24 | En route | | |
| September 24 | Portage Entry | | |
| September 24–<br>   October 1 | Unknown | | |
| October 2–6 | Clifton | | |
| October 6–<br>   February 6 | Sault Ste. Marie | | |

| *1860* | | | |
|---|---|---|---|
| February 6–8 | En route | | |
| February 8–15 | | | St. Ignace |
| February 15–21 | | | Mackinac |
| February 21–23 | | | St. Ignace |
| February 23–25 | En route | | |
| February 25–<br>   May 1 | Sault Ste. Marie | | |
| May 1–2 | En route | | |
| May 3 | L'Anse | | |
| May 4–10 | Portage Lake | | |
| May 11–12 | Portage Entry | | |
| May 13–23 | Sault Ste. Marie | | |
| May 24 | En route | | |
| May 25 | La Pointe/<br>   Bayfield/<br>   Superior | | |
| May 25–<br>   June 3 | Superior | | |
| June 4 | La Pointe | | |
| June 5–8 | Bad River | | |
| June 8 | La Pointe/<br>   Bayfield | | |
| June 9–15 | La Pointe | | |
| June 14 | Bayfield | | |
| June 16–20 | Ontonagon | | |
| June 20 | Maple Grove | | |
| June 20–25 | Minnesota Mine | | |

| *1860* | *Lake Superior* | *Journeys* | *Lower Michigan* |
|---|---|---|---|
| June 25–27 | Ontonagon | | |
| June 28 | La Pointe/ Bayfield | | |
| June 29 | Bad River/ La Pointe | | |
| June 30 | Ontonagon | | |
| July 1–6 | Sault Ste. Marie | | |
| July 6 | Detour | | |
| July 7–9 | | | Mackinac |
| July 10–12 | | | Cross Village |
| July 12–14 | | | Garden Island |
| July 14–16 | | | Beaver Island |
| July 16–18 | | | Cross Village |
| July 18–20 | | | Middle Village |
| July 20–22 | | | Little Traverse |
| July 23 | | | Agaming |
| July 24–26 | | | Sheboigan |
| July 26–27 | | | Little Traverse |
| July 27–30 | | | Eagletown |
| July 30 | | | Northport |
| July 30– August 1 | | | Mackinac |
| August 2 | Sault Ste. Marie | | |
| August 3 | Marquette/ Portage Entry/ Copper Harbor | | |
| August 4 | Via Eagle Harbor, Eagle River & Ontonagon to La Pointe | | |
| August 5 | La Pointe | | |
| August 6 | La Pointe/ Bayfield | | |
| August 7 | La Pointe/ Bayfield | | |
| August 8–9 | La Pointe | | |
| August 10–11 | Bad River | | |
| August 11–12 | La Pointe | | |
| August 13 | Portage Entry | | |
| August 14–17 | L'Anse | | |
| August 17–21 | Houghton | | |
| August 20 | Hancock | | |
| August 22–30 | Eagle Harbor | | |
| August 30 | Eagle River | | |
| August 30– September 3 | Cliff Mine | | |

| 1860 | Lake Superior | Journeys | Lower Michigan |
|---|---|---|---|
| September 4–14 | Marquette | | |
| September 7, 10 | Negaunee | | |
| September 15–<br>January 14 | Sault Ste. Marie | | |

| 1861 | | | |
|---|---|---|---|
| January 14 | Rain's (Neebish Island) | | |
| January 15 | Gafney's (1 mile north of Detour) | | |
| January 16 | Detour/Gafney's | | |
| January 17–18 | St. Joseph's Island | | |
| January 18–21 | Sailors Encampment (Neebish Island) | | |
| January 22 | Johnston's (Sugar Island)/Garden River | | |
| January 22–30 | Payment's | | |
| January 30–<br>February 4 | Perrault's (south of Payment's) | | |
| February 4–5 | Payment's | | |
| February 5–<br>March 16 | Sault Ste. Marie | | |
| March 16–<br>20(?) | Payment's | | |
| March 20(?)–<br>31 | Sault Ste. Marie | | |
| April 1–4 | En route | | |
| April 4 | | | Mackinac |
| April 4–6 | | | Sheboygan |
| April 6-8 | | En route | |
| April 8 | | | Grand Lake |
| April 9–19 | | | Alpena |
| April 19–22 | | | Harrisville |
| April 23 | | | Detroit |
| April 24–<br>May 6 | | Cincinnati | |
| May 6 | | Toledo | |
| May 7–8 | | Detroit | |
| May 9 | En route | | |

| *1861* | *Lake Superior* | *Journeys* | *Lower Michigan* |
|---|---|---|---|
| May 10–11 | Sault Ste. Marie | | |
| May 12 | Via Marquette to Portage Entry | | |
| May 13 | Eagle Harbor/ Ontonagon | | |
| May 14 | La Pointe | | |
| May 15 | Ontonagon | | |
| May 16 | Via Eagle Harbor, Eagle River & Copper Harbor to Sault Ste. Marie | | |
| May 17–26 | Sault Ste. Marie | | |
| May 27–31 | | Detroit | |
| June 1 | En route | | |
| June 2–4 | | | Mackinac |
| June 4–5 | | | Beaver Island |
| June 5–6 | | | Garden Island |
| June 6–7 | | | Beaver Island |
| June 7–9 | En route | | |
| June 9-11 | Detour | | |
| June 12–13 | Sault Ste. Marie | | |
| June 14–21 | Marquette | | |
| June 16 | Negaunee | | |
| June 21 | Portage Lake | | |
| June 22–27 | Eagle Harbor | | |
| June 27– July 2 | Cliff Mine | | |
| July 2–5 | Eagle Harbor | | |
| July 6 | Bayfield/ La Pointe/ Bayfield | | |
| July 7 | Bayfield/ La Pointe | | |
| July 8–9 | Bad River | | |
| July 9–14 | La Pointe | | |
| July 12 | Bayfield | | |
| July 15 | Ontonagon/ Minnesota Mine | | |
| July 16–17 | Maple Grove | | |
| July 17–21 | Minnesota Mine | | |
| July 21–23 | Ontonagon | | |
| July 24 | Portage Lake/ Hancock | | |

*Appendix B*

| 1861 | Lake Superior | Journeys | Lower Michigan |
|------|---------------|----------|----------------|
| July 24–29 | Portage Lake | | |
| July 29–August 2 | L'Anse | | |
| August 2–3 | Portage Lake | | |
| August 4 | Hancock | | |
| August 5–6 | Marquette | | |
| August 7–13 | Sault Ste. Marie | | |
| August 13 | | | Mackinac |
| August 14–19 | | | Cross Village |
| August 19–22 | | | Middle Village |
| August 22–23 | | | Sheboygan |
| August 23–26 | | | Little Traverse |
| August 26 | | | Agaming/Little Traverse |
| August 27 | | | En route |
| August 28– September 2 | | | Eagletown |
| September 2–4 | | | Northport |
| September 4–6 | | | Mackinac |
| September 6 | Church's (2 miles SE of Payment's) | | |
| September 7–20 | Sault Ste. Marie | | |
| September 20–24 | St. Joseph Mission | | |
| September 24 | Sault Ste. Marie | | |
| September 24–30 | Payment's | | |
| September 30– October 22 | Sault Ste. Marie | | |
| October 22 | Payment's | | |
| October 22– November 7 | St. Joseph Mission | | |
| November 7– December 12 | Sault Ste. Marie | | |
| December 12–18 | St. Joseph Mission | | |
| December 18–23 | Payment's | | |
| December 23– January 17 | Sault Ste. Marie | | |

| 1862 | | | |
|------|---------------|----------|----------------|
| January 17–21 | Sailors Encampment | | |
| January 21 | Gashkiwang | | |
| January 22 | Minisheing | | |
| January 23 | Sault Ste. Marie | | |

| 1862 | Lake Superior | Journeys | Lower Michigan |
|------|---------------|----------|----------------|
| January 24–28 | Minisheing | | |
| January 28– | | | |
| February 5 | Sault Ste. Marie | | |
| February 5–7 | En route | | |
| February 7–10 | St. Martin's Bay | | |
| February 10–12 | En route | | |
| February 12–20 | Sault Ste. Marie | | |
| February 20–26 | Goulais Bay | | |
| February 26– | | | |
| March 7 | Sault Ste. Marie | | |
| March 7–18 | Garden River | | |
| March 18–May 16 | Sault Ste. Marie | | |
| May 16–19 | St. Joseph Mission | | |
| May 19–June 2 | Sault Ste. Marie | | |
| June 2 | Gros Cap | | |
| June 3–7 | Goulais Bay | | |
| June 7–12 | Sault Ste. Marie | | |
| June 13 | Portage Lake | | |
| June 14 | Ontonagon | | |
| June 14–15 | Minnesota Mine | | |
| June 16–17 | Maplegrove | | |
| June 17–18 | Minnesota Mine | | |
| June 18–20 | Ontonagon | | |
| June 20–22 | Minnesota Mine | | |
| June 23 | Eagle River | | |
| June 23–24 | Clifton | | |
| June 24–25 | Eagle River | | |
| June 26–July 1 | Hancock | | |
| July 2 | L'Anse | | |
| July 2–3 | Hancock | | |
| July 4 | Marquette | | |
| July 5–13 | Sault Ste. Marie | | |
| July 14–16 | Goulais Bay | | |
| July 17–22 | Sault Ste. Marie | | |
| July 23 | | | Mackinac |
| July 23–30 | | | Sheboygan (Duncan) |
| July 31 | | En route | |
| August 1 | | Port Huron | |
| August 2–5 | | Detroit | |
| August 6–8 | | | Mackinac |
| August 8–13 | | | Cross Village |
| August 14–16 | | | Middle Village |
| August 16–18 | | | Little Traverse |

| 1862 | Lake Superior | Journeys | Lower Michigan |
|---|---|---|---|
| August 18 | | | Bear River |
| August 19 | | | Via Little Traverse, Middle Village & Cross Village to Mackinac |
| August 20 | | | Mackinac |
| August 20–21 | | | St. Ignace |
| August 21–28 | | | Mackinac |
| August 29– September 19 | Sault Ste. Marie | | |
| September 20–24 | St. Joseph Mission | | |
| September 25–29 | Goulais Bay | | |
| September 29 | Sault Ste. Marie | | |
| September 29–30 | Payment's | | |
| September 30– October 29 | Sault Ste. Marie | | |
| October 29–30 | Payment's | | |
| October 30– November 3 | Minisheing | | |
| November 4–6 | Off Whitefish Point | | |
| November 6 | Marquette | | |
| November 7–10 | Hancock | | |
| November 11–12 | Maplegrove | | |
| November 12 | Minnesota Mine | | |
| November 12–14 | Ontonagon | | |
| November 15–16 | Minnesota Mine | | |
| November 16–20 | Ontonagon | | |
| November 21 | Eagle Harbor | | |
| November 21–23 | Copper Harbor | | |
| November 23 | Portage Lake | | |
| November 24–26 | Marquette | | |
| November 26 | Weshking Bay | | |
| November 27– January 19 | Sault Ste. Marie | | |

### 1863

| | | | |
|---|---|---|---|
| January 20–24 | St. Joseph Mission | | |
| January 24–29 | Sault Ste. Marie | | |
| January 30 | Weshking Bay | | |
| January 30– May 11 | Sault Ste. Marie | | |

| 1863 | *Lake Superior* | *Journeys* | *Lower Michigan* |
|------|-----------------|------------|------------------|
| May 12–14 | Goulais Bay | | |
| May 15–19 | Sault Ste. Marie | | |
| May 19–22 | St. Joseph Mission | | |
| May 22–June 10 | Sault Ste. Marie | | |
| June 11–15 | Detroit | | |
| June 16 | | En route | |
| June 17–23 | Sault Ste. Marie | | |
| June 24 | Marquette | | |
| June 25 | Hancock | | |
| June 26 | L'Anse | | |
| June 27 | Hancock | | |
| June 28–July 16 | Sault Ste. Marie | | |
| July 16 | End of Diary | | |

# APPENDIX C

## SHIP NAMES

*Note:* For the convenience of historians of the Great Lakes, this index lists the ships to which Baraga referred in his Diary and the dates of those references.

*Adriatic.*  1857, July 3

*Backus.*  1862, Aug. 25, 26, 27, 28, Sept. 6, 7; 1863, Apr. 28, May 6–7

*Baltimore.*  1852, Oct. 30; 1854, Oct. 6

*Bay City.*  1853, Mar. 28

*Burlington.*  1860, Dec. 4

*Chicago.*  1861, June 4

*City of Cleveland.*  1858, July 29; 1861, Apr. 22, May 25, June 13, July 23, Aug. 5, 7; 1862, Apr. 27, Oct. 3; 1863, May 9

*City of Superior.*  1857, Nov. 12

*Cleveland.*  1860, Oct. 19, 20, 25, Nov. 22, 24, 25, 29; 1863, Apr. 28

*Collingwood.*  1857, Aug. 24

*Forrester (Forester).*  1859, Nov. 27; 1862, Aug. 2

*Fountain City.*  1860, May 18

*Gazelle.*  1860, Sept. 14

*General Taylor.*  1856, Sept. 15, Nov. 10, 11, 12, 26, 28, Dec. 3; 1857, May 23, Aug. 4; 1861, Nov. 28, 29; 1862, May 5–6

*Globe.*  1860, Nov. 26, 27, Dec. 4

*Hunter.*  1861, Sept. 4

*Illinois.*  1855, July 29, Aug. 9; 1856, Nov. 5; 1857, May 8, 22, July 20; 1858, July 17; 1859, May 3, June 17, July 18, Aug. 3, 11, Sept. 23; 1860, July 31, Aug. 1, Sept. 14, Oct. 13, 19; 1861, May 10, 11, 24, Nov. 7; 1862, Sept. 14; 1863, June 23, 27

*Iron City.* 1857, Nov. 17; 1858, Aug. 1; 1858, Oct. 15; 1859, May 3, July 29, Aug. 19, Oct. 6; 1860, Sept. 28; 1861, May 8, July 25; 1862, May 2–3, 22, June 22, Nov. 8, 9; 1863, May 8

*Lady Elgin.* 1856, Nov. 3, 17, 25; 1857, May 9, Aug. 13, Nov. 17; 1859, May 3, 15, June 17, 26, Aug. 9, 30, Oct. 26, 30, Nov. 4, 27, 28; 1860, Apr. 29, 30, May 1, 10, July 2, Aug. 11, 12, Sept. 3–4, 12

*Manhattan.* 1855, Sept. 16; 1856, May 4, July 6, 28, Sept. 24, Oct. 22, Nov. 6; 1857, May 8

*Marquette.* 1861, May 31, June 1

*Michigan.* 1855, Apr. 27; 1857, Nov. 12; 1861, Aug. 12, 13, Sept. 13, Nov. 19, 20, 28; 1863, May 9, July 14, 15

*Miner.* 1862, July 2

*Mineral Rock.* 1856, Nov. 3, 11, 13, 14, 27, 28; 1857, Nov. 19, 21, 30; 1859, July 4, Oct. 14; 1860, May 12; 1862, Sept. 16, Nov. 17, 18, 19, 20; 1863, Apr. 28

*Montgomery.* 1859, June 29

*Niagara.* 1854, May 27

*Nile.* 1855, Apr. 30

*Northerner.* 1855, Aug. 18

*Northern Light.* 1858, July 24, Oct. 4, 19; 1859, May 3; 1860, Nov. 12; 1861, June 12; 1862, Apr. 27, Sept. 19, Nov. 4; 1863, May 8

*Northstar.* 1855, Sept. 4, 24; 1856, May 4, June 13, Nov. 9, 15; 1857, May 8, July 14, 27, Aug. 8; 1858, Apr. 18, May 28, Aug. 13, 24, Sept. 1, 13, Nov. 1; 1859, May 3, July 20, Aug. 3, 22, Sept. 6; 1860, May 21, 22, 23, 24, June 3, 15, 29, Aug. 2, Sept. 22, Oct. 23, 31, Nov. 5, 13; 1861, May 22, June 21, July 4, 5, Aug. 8

*Ogans.* 1856, Nov. 23, 24; 1860, June 15, 27

*Ontonagon.* 1860, Apr. 25, Nov. 13

*Pacific* (U.S.M.S.). 1853, Nov. 26

*Planet.* 1858, July 18; 1860, Oct. 30, Nov. 10, 22, 24, 25, 26, 29; 1862, May 1, July 3, Aug. 5, 31; 1863, Apr. 28, June 9, 10, 12–13

*Plowboy.* 1862, Sept. 1; 1863, May 9

*Princess.* 1859, July 4

*Rocket.* 1862, July 31

*Samuel Ward.* 1854, Aug. 25

*Seabird.* 1860, Apr. 27, Oct. 19, Nov. 9; 1861, Sept. 6; 1862, May 1, July 20, 21, 22, Sept. 5; 1863, May 21

*Stockman.* 1855, July 17

*Superior.* 1856, Apr. 29, Aug. 7, Oct. 30, Nov. 9, 10

*Traveler.* 1862, June 9–10, 12, 25, Oct. 21, Nov. 27, 28; 1863, June 3

*Troy.* 1858, July 11

*Webb.* 1856, Nov. 3, 9, 12

# BIBLIOGRAPHY

## Writings of Bishop Frederic Baraga

CHIPPEWA

*Abinodjiiag omasinaiganiwan* (Children's Reading-book). Buffalo, 1837; Detroit, 1845.

*Anamie Masinaigan* (Prayerbook). Paris, 1837.

*Gete Dibadjimowin, Gaie Dach Nitam Mekate-okwana ieg O Gagikewiniwan* (Old History, and also the first Instructions of the Missionary). Ljubljana, 1843.

*Jesus obimadisiwin oma aking, gwaiakossing anamiewin ejitwadjig, mi sa Catholique-anamiadjig gewabandanging* (The Life of Jesus Here on Earth, Prayerbook for those who confess the true Faith, that is who pray in a Catholic manner). Paris, 1837.

*Kagige Debwewinan, Kaging Ge-Takwendang Katolik Enamiad* (Eternal Truths to be Remembered by a Catholic Christian). Cincinnati, 1855.

*Katolik Enamiad O Nanagatawendamowinan* (Catholic Christian Meditations). Detroit, 1850.

*Katolik Gagikwe-Masinaigan* (Book of Catholic Religious Instruction). Detroit, 1846, 1858.

*Masinaigan gewabadamowad kakina anishinabeg enamiadjig* (Pastoral Letter: Little Book Addressed to all Indian Christians). Cincinnati, 1853.

CHIPPEWA / ENGLISH

*A Dictionary of the Otchipwe Language, Explained in English.* Cincinnati, 1853.

*Theoretical and Practical Grammar of the Otchipwe Language.* Detroit, 1850.

## Bibliography

ENGLISH

*Pastoral Letter to the English-Speaking Clergy and People of Upper Michigan.* Cincinnati, 1853.

FRENCH

*Arbege de l'Histoire des Indiens de l'Amérique Septentrionale* (A Short History of the North American Indians). Translation of *Geschicte, Character, Sitten und Gebräuche der Nordamerikanischen Indier.* Paris, 1837.

GERMAN

*Geschicte, Character, Sitten und Gebräuche der Nordamerikanischen Indier* (History, Character, Customs and Manners of the North American Indians). Ljubljana, 1837.

*Tagebuch* (Diary). 3 vols. 1852–1863. Published as *The Diary of Bishop Frederic Baraga, First Bishop of Marquette, Michigan.* Detroit, 1990.

*Vorlesung über die Gebräuche und Lebensweige der Indianer* (Lecture on the Customs and Manners of the Indians). Presented at St. Martin's Church, Cincinnati, August 23, 1863.

LATIN

*Statuta Dioecesa Sanctae Mariae* (Statutes). Cincinnati, 1856; Detroit, 1863.

OTTAWA

*Jesus obimadisiwin ajonda aking, gwaiakossing anamiewin ejitwadjig, mi sa Catholicque-anamiadjig gevabandanging* (The Life of Jesus Here on Earth, Prayerbook for those who confess the true Faith, that is who pray in a Catholic manner). Paris, 1837.

*Ottawa Anamie-Misinaigan* (Prayerbook). Detroit, 1832; Paris, 1837; Detroit, 1842, 1846; Cincinnati, 1855, 1858.

SLOVENE

*Dushna Pasha sa Kristjane Kteri Shele V'Duhu in V Resnizi Boga Moliti* (Spiritual Food for Christians Who Wish to Pray to God in Spirit and in Truth). Ljubljana, 1830, 1831, 1835, 1845, 1856, 1869, 1905.

*Nebeske Roshe* (Heavenly Flowers). Ljubljana, 1846.

*Obiskovanje Jesusa Kristusa V'Presvet Reshnijim Telesu, in Posdravjenje Marije Preshistic Devize* (Visitation of Jesus Christ in the Most Holy Sacrament and Salutation of the Immaculate Virgin Mary). Ljubljana, 1832 (2 printings), 1837.

*Od Pozheshevanja in Posnemaja Matere Boshje* (Veneration and Imitation of the Mother of God). Ljubljana, 1830.

# Bibliography

*Opominvanje eniga duhavniga Pastirja na svoje dushize v' sredu svetiga leta 1826* (Admonition of a Spiritual Pastor to His Sheep, in the Middle of the Holy Year 1826). Ljubljana, 1826.

*Popis Navad in Sadershanja Indijanov Polnozhne Amerike* (Description of Customs and Manners of Indians in Midnight America). Ljubljana, 1837.

*Premishljevanje Shtirih Poslednjih Rezhi* (Meditations on the Four Last Truths). Ljubljana, 1837.

*Slate Jabelke* (Golden Apples). Ljubljana, 1844, 1879.

## Secondary Sources

Armstrong, Benjamin. "Early Life among the Indians: Reminiscences from the Life of Benjamin Armstrong." *Wisconsin Magazine of History* 55 (Spring, Summer 1972): 175–96, 287–309; 56 (Autumn 1972, Winter 1972–73): 37–58, 140–61.

Bayliss, Joseph E., and Estelle L. Bayliss, *River of Destiny: The Saint Marys*. Detroit: Wayne State University Press, 1955.

Cadieux, Lorenzo, S.J., ed. *Lettres des Nouvelles Missions du Canada 1843–1852*. Montreal: Les Editions Bellarmin, 1973.

Chaput, Donald. *The Cliff: America's First Great Copper Mine*. Kalamazoo, MI: Sequoia Press, 1981.

Cicognani, Amleto Giovanni. *Sanctity in America*. Paterson, NJ: St. Anthony Guild Press, 1940.

Code, Joseph B. *Dictionary of the American Hierarchy (1789–1964)*. New York: Joseph F. Wagner, 1964.

*Concilii Plenarii Baltimorensis II*. Baltimore: John Murphy, 1868.

*Diocesan Process for the Canonization of Bishop Baraga*. 14 vols. Marquette, MI: Bishop Baraga Collection, 1972.

Dompier, James. *Captain James Bendry, Baraga's First Supervisor*. Baraga County Historical Pageant Souvenir Booklet. Baraga, MI 1969.

Gregorich, Joseph. *Life of Bishop Baraga*. Unpublished manuscript, Marquette, MI: Bishop Baraga Collection, 1970.

Heyl, Erik. *Early American Steamers*. Vol. 3. Buffalo: private publication, 1964.

*History of the Catholic Church in Wisconsin*. Milwaukee: T. J. Sullivan, 1895–1898.

*History of Northern Wisconsin Illustrated*. Chicago: Western Historical Co. 1881.

*History of the Upper Peninsula of Michigan*. Chicago: Western Historical Co., 1883.

Howard-Filler, Saralee. "USS Michigan." *Michigan History* 70 (July–Aug. 1986): 44–48.

Jaklic, Rev. Francis. *Misijonski Skof Irenej Frederic Baraga*. Unpublished manuscript. Marquette, MI: Bishop Baraga Collection, 1951.

Jamieson, James K. *By Cross and Anchor: The Story of Frederic Baraga on Lake Superior*. Calumet, MI: Roy W. Drier, 1965.

Jezernik, Maksimilijan. *Frederick Baraga*. New York: Studia Slovenica, 1968.

———. *Friderik Baraga: Acta Ecclesiastica Sloveniae*. Ljubljana, 1980.

Kitzman, Betty Lou. "Superior shipwrecks catalogued by Marquette speaker." *Marquette Mining Journal*, May 21, 1976.

Kohl, John George. *Kitchi-Gami: Wanderings round Lake Superior.* London: Chapman and Hall, 1860.

Kotnik, Rev. Bernard, O.F.M. "Baraga's Use of Butler's *Lives of the Saints.*" *Ave Maria Koledar* (Lemont, IL), 1974.

Kummer, Gertrude. *Die Leopoldinen-Stiftung (1829–1914).* Vienna: Dom-Verlag, 1966.

Kvasnicka, Robert M., and Herman J. Viola, eds. *The Commissioners of Indian Affairs, 1824–1977.* Lincoln: University of Nebraska Press, 1979.

Lambert, Bernard. *Shepherd of the Wilderness.* L'Anse, MI: Bernard J. Lambert, 1967.

Lamott, John. *History of the Archdiocese of Cincinnati, 1821–1921.* Cincinnati: F. Pustet Co., 1921.

Morse, Richard. *The Chippewa of Lake Superior.* Wisconsin Historical Collections, vol. 3, 1857.

Nute, Grace Lee. *Lake Superior.* Indianapolis: Bobbs-Merrill, 1944.

Parker, Capt. John G. *Autobiography of Captain John G. Parker.* Michigan Pioneer Historical Collections, vol. 30, 1905.

Patton, Constance Saltonstall. "Reminiscences of Life at Mackinac." *Michigan History* 20 (1920): 492–513.

Pilling, James Constantine. *Bibliography of the Algonquin Language.* Washington, DC, 1891.

Pisani, Camille Ferri. *Prince Napoleon in America, 1861.* London: Galley Press, 1959.

Praus, Alexis A. "Father Piret Lands in New York, 1846 — Document." *Mid-America* 37, 1955.

Quaife, Milo. *The Kingdom of St. James.* New Haven: Yale University Press, 1930.

————. *Lake Michigan.* Indianapolis: Bobbs-Merrill, 1944.

Rezek, Rev. Antoine. *History of the Diocese of Sault Ste. Marie and Marquette.* 2 vols. Houghton, MI, 1906.

Rupp, N. Daniel. "Bishop Baraga, Missionary to the Indians." In *Catholics in America, 1776–1976,* edited by Robert Trisco. Washington, DC: NCCB, 1976.

St. Paul, Mother M., O.S.U. *From Desenzano to "The Pines."* Toronto: Macmillan Co., 1941.

Sawyer, Alvah L. *A History of the Northern Peninsula of Michigan.* 3 vols. Chicago: Lewis Publishing Co., 1911.

Schenck, Theresa. "The Cadots: The First Family of Sault Ste. Marie." *Michigan History* 72, no. 2 (March/April 1988): 36–43.

Skolla, Rev. Otto. "Report." *Acta et Dicta* 7, 2 (October 1936): 217–68.

U.S. Bureau of the Census. *Federal Census,* 1850, Chippewa County, MI.

————. *Federal Census,* 1860, Chippewa County, MI.

————. *Federal Census,* 1850, Houghton County, MI.

————. *Federal Census,* 1860, Houghton County, MI.

————. *Federal Census,* 1850, Mackinac County, MI.

————. *Federal Census,* 1860, Ontonagon County, MI.

Verwyst, Rev. Chrysostom, O.F.M. *Life and Labors of Rt. Rev. Frederic Baraga.* Milwaukee: M. H. Wiltzius, 1900.

Vogt, Rev. Casimir, O.F.M. "Northern Wisconsin Pioneer-Memoirs of Casimir Vogt." In *Lesser Brothers* 3, 1969.

Walling, H. F., ed. *Atlas of the State of Michigan.* Detroit: R. M. & S. T. Tackabury, 1873.

Walling, Regis. *The Dates of Death of Baraga's Parents.* Unpublished manuscript. Marquette, MI: Bishop Baraga Collection, 1987.

# INDEX

Printed in the USA
CPSIA information can be obtained
at www.ICGtesting.com
JSHW011950201024
71961JS00037B/635